Critical Voices in Teacher Education

# EXPLORATIONS OF EDUCATIONAL PURPOSE

## Volume 22

---

*Series Scope*

---

In today's dominant modes of pedagogy, questions about issues of race, class, gender, sexuality, colonialism, religion, and other social dynamics are rarely asked. Questions about the social spaces where pedagogy takes place – in schools, media, and corporate think tanks – are not raised. And they need to be.

The *Explorations of Educational Purpose* book series can help establish a renewed interest in such questions and their centrality in the larger study of education and the preparation of teachers and other educational professionals. The editors of this series feel that education matters and that the world is in need of a rethinking of education and educational purpose.

Coming from a critical pedagogical orientation, *Explorations of Educational Purpose* aims to have the study of education transcend the trivialization that often degrades it. Rather than be content with the frivolous, scholarly lax forms of teacher education and weak teaching prevailing in the world today, we should work towards education that truly takes the unattained potential of human beings as its starting point. The series will present studies of all dimensions of education and offer alternatives. The ultimate aim of the series is to create new possibilities for people around the world who suffer under the current design of socio-political and educational institutions.

For further volumes:
http://www.springer.com/series/7472

Barry Down • John Smyth
Editors

# Critical Voices in Teacher Education

## Teaching for Social Justice in Conservative Times

 Springer

*Editors*
Barry Down
School of Education
Murdoch University
Dixon Road
Rockingham, WA
Australia

John Smyth
School of Education
University of Ballarat
University Drive
Mount Helen, VIC
Australia

ISBN 978-94-007-3973-4      ISBN 978-94-007-3974-1 (eBook)
DOI 10.1007/978-94-007-3974-1
Springer Dordrecht Heidelberg New York London

Library of Congress Control Number: 2012935859

Printed on acid-free paper

Springer is part of Springer Science+Business Media (www.springer.com)

# Foreword

## It Ain't Easy: Social Justice in Unjust Societies

It was over a decade ago, in New York City, when university faculty members were addressed by Mark Green, mayoral candidate for New York City. Green was advising those in higher education how to negotiate a growing conservative trend in education by those engaged in municipal teaching and research. He pointed out possible grants for us to apply for, reminding us that securing research money required certain nuance. As he discussed the importance of national, local and corporate sponsorship, he emphasized that the language we used was often more important than the actual grant application information forms. He paused, then advised us: *'Pay attention to the words you use as you apply for monies. Never use the word democracy, nor the phrase social justice. If you do, you won't get funded'*.

How do we educate for social justice in a world that is neither just, nor social? How do we avoid becoming just more voices with sound bites, lesson plans and speech/book titles, which include social justice, but never discuss the underpinning notions surrounding social *injustice* in education? In short, how do we authentically create a conversation and space to recognize that an educated and democratic citizenry cannot exist without pedagogical engagement (or intervention?) in existing curricular and formal school settings?

And, of course, there are no answers for these questions, only more questions. Indeed, Paulo Freire taught us that within our questions, we can begin to shape our answers . . . and then ask more questions. The Buddha reminds us that within humanity, we will continue to struggle, and that struggle is a part of being human. And so we begin a never-ending mission, a vision of a socially just teacher education, which must continually change to meet the needs of societies which continually change . . . we have some challenges here.

A critical pedagogy is a political pedagogy. Freire introduced us to the realization that teaching is a political act, and as educators, we are in subjective, anti-neutral worlds, which are orbited by curricular and administrative verbosity proclaiming objective neutrality. We enter into our pedagogical galaxies knowing that embracing subjectivity and dialogue is necessary ... but it ain't easy. In fact, it is damn hard. The authors and editors of *Critical Voices in Teacher Education: Teaching for Social Justice in Conservative Times* have created a volume which begins the conversation and actions needed to reconceptualize education as a social theoretical and political act, an act which is required to emerge, grow, morph and emerge again with societal changes. The volume has gathered teachers/scholars who have dedicated their lives to asking that question, *how do we educate for social justice in a world that is neither just, nor social?*

A pedagogy of social justice is inherently critical in its orientation. In the critical theoretical lens, we view societal conditions through the glasses of power. We ask: *What are the underlying forces of power influencing society? How does this power work? Who controls those who are in power? What finances control those who control those in power?* We begin with an etymological journey in tracing historical sources and current sources of power and the support of the power bloc(s). Along with the historical knowledge of power we investigate the historiographical narratives of power ... asking: *How does power perpetuate itself? How does society support this perpetuation? How do schools act as the backdrop to hegemonic curricula, which supports power? How are we, [even] as critical scholars often part of the power bloc?* And we ask questions of oppression: *Who are oppressed by power blocs at the local level, the pedagogical level, the societal level? How do we identify our own oppression as teachers (employees) of the power blocs? How does economy create oppression and curricular fascism in our schools?*

And, *how do we avoid sounding like whining, archaic Marxist theorists, who are disconnected with schools, teachers and children?* Part of a smart, socially grounded theory of critical pedagogy for social justice demands that we check our political egos at the door and join the audience as participants/mentors who do not view ideology through thin Prada lenses. Rather, we share our knowledges of society and theories of power with humility and leadership. We do exactly what Barry and John have encouraged the authors in this volume to do ... we recreate society as a dialogical and healthy entity, truly determined to find this elusive phrase, this dangerous phrase, *social justice*.

And, it ain't easy. It is hard work, important, no, essential work. Freire reminded us that we are cultural/societal workers, that we are part of the world we inhabit and that we are a privileged few who are able to facilitate learning and empowerment. However, he was ever mindful that facilitation and leadership be strong, be informed and also democratic ... there is no place for ego in this struggle. We have had decades of liberal ego in society, in politics and in the academy, it is time we join the dialogues shared in this volume and begin to ask questions which will create more questions from our pre-service teachers, our colleagues, our administrators and, most importantly, our students. When our students start asking the questions, we are on the way.

University of Calgary                                                              Shirley R. Steinberg

# Acknowledgements

We can trace the genesis of this edited collection back to 1995 when I (Barry) invited John to present a keynote address to a gathering of classroom teachers in Bunbury, Western Australia. Following John's insightful presentation on the changing nature of teachers' work, one member of the audience, a senior administrator in the Faculty of Education, asked pointedly 'How come you're still doing all that Marxist rubbish, John?' Today, we often reflect back on this exchange to remind ourselves not only of the obstacles and barriers to doing critical scholarship but the possibilities of creating truly transformative experiences for student teachers in universities and schools. That's what this book is about.

In pursuing this project, we invited a number of our Australian colleagues to share their understanding and experience of teaching for social justice in conservative times. We are appreciative of their time, energy and scholarly expertise. We also thank them for their courage in speaking back to a range of prevailing orthodoxies and misconceptions about what it means to teach. Drawing on their own unique career trajectories, passions and perspectives, the contributing authors demonstrate the importance of thinking and acting in ways that are ethically, morally and politically informed.

To our overseas contributors, we say a special thank you. To Marilyn Frankenstein, for signing up with a group of Aussies on the other side of the globe, we appreciate your insights into student activism and popular culture as sites of critical education. To Wayne Martino, who now resides in Ontario, we appreciate your ongoing connection back home and the way in which you articulate matters of gender identity and social justice for us.

We are especially grateful to our long-time collaborators who continue to inspire and work alongside us. To Peter McInerney, who shows a remarkable capacity to capture narrative stories and link them to issues of social justice, and Sol Smyth, who continues to nourish and support our individual and collective work in so many ways, we owe a special debt of gratitude.

To Brad Gobby, for his proficient and tireless manner in compiling and editing the chapters for submission, we thank you for getting us to the finish line.

To Springer Author Services staff, in particular Bernadette Ohmer, Annemarie Keur, Naomi Portnoy, Sandra Vermeij and Sunil Padman, we are grateful for your guidance in pulling the project together and making sure the production process ran smoothly.

To Shirley Steinberg and Ken Tobin, series editors, who backed the publication of this collection of essays, we thank you for your ongoing intellectual leadership and support in getting important ideas to press. We appreciate your willingness to contribute so thoughtfully to the Foreword and Afterword, respectively. We also express our gratitude to the late Joe Kincheloe who once again provided us with the impetus to create conversations around critical teacher development and social justice.

Finally, we express our collective gratitude to our families for their ongoing tolerance of our time-consuming labour of love.

## Illustrations

We wish to acknowledge the contributions of the artists who have generously granted permission to share their work in Marilyn Frankenstein's chapter *Studying culture jamming to inspire student activism.*

Avram Finkelstein and the Gran Fury, an artist collective of ACT UP activists, have produced some of the most memorable visual work of the movement, which can be viewed at:

http://digitalgallery.nypl.org/nypldigital/dgkeysearchresult.cfm?num=0&word= gran%20fury&s=1&notword=&d=&c=&f=&k=0&lWord=&lField=&sScope=& sLevel=&sLabel=&imgs=20&pNum

*The Santa Cruz Comic News*, http://www.thecomicnews.com/ is published by Thom Zajac and John Govsky. Established in 1984, *Comic News* has inspired the creation of over 100 'comic newspapers'. The print edition is a monthly journal of progressive editorial cartoons. The online edition features weekly updates, and the website also has an archive of thousands of progressive editorial cartoons going back to 2005.

John Sims, http://www.johnsimsprojects.com/, is a conceptual artist, mathematician and educator. He is currently teaching in the Department of Art and Public Policy at the New York University and curating a series of nine exhibitions and performances focusing on the visual language of mathematical ideas and process as a way to explore a spectrum of themes from geometric landscapes to the socio-political for the Bowery Poetry Club, http://www.bowerypoetry.com/.

## Permissions

Frankenstein, M. *Studying culture jamming to inspire student activism* from *Radical Teacher,* 89 (Winter 2010), pp. 30–46. Copyright 2010 by the Board of Trustees of the University of Illinois. Used with permission of the University of Illinois Press. Revised version.

Barry Down
Murdoch University
Rockingham
Western Australia

John Smyth
University of Ballarat
Mount Helen
Victoria

# Contents

# Chapter 1
# Introduction: From Critique to New Scripts and Possibilities in Teacher Education

Barry Down and John Smyth

## What Is This Book About?

This book is about the stories of teacher educators committed to pursuing social justice in teacher education. It draws on the struggles of those who have taught about issues of social justice within universities, their accumulated knowledge and their practices in classrooms. The purpose of the book is to provide a space where teacher educators can deconstruct their own pedagogies, empower individuals to develop critical consciousness, and inspire a future generation of teachers to engage in social justice activism. To this end, the book provides some insights into the daily realities of critical teaching in conservative times (Brookfield, 2005; Kincheloe, Slattery, & Steinberg, 2000; Shor, 1992).

The starting point of this book is Bartolome's (2007) call for greater political and ideological clarity in teacher education. By 'political clarity', Bartolome refers to 'the process by which individuals achieve ever-deepening consciousness of the sociopolitical and economic realities that shape their lives and their capacity to transform such material and symbolic conditions' (p. 264). In the case of 'ideological clarity', she refers to 'the process by which individuals struggle to identify and compare their own explanations for the existing socioeconomic and political hierarchy with the dominant society's' (p. 264). As Brookfield (2005) explains it, this kind of ideology critique in teacher education 'focuses on helping people come to an awareness of how capitalism shapes social relations and imposes— often without our knowledge—belief systems and assumptions (i.e. ideologies)

B. Down (✉)
School of Education, Murdoch University, Perth, Australia
e-mail: b.down@murdoch.edu.au

J. Smyth
School of Education, University of Ballarat, Mt Helen, VIC, Australia
e-mail: j.smyth@ballarat.edu.au

B. Down and J. Smyth (eds.), *Critical Voices in Teacher Education*, Explorations of Educational Purpose 22, DOI 10.1007/978-94-007-3974-1_1,
© Springer Science+Business Media Dordrecht 2012

that justify and maintain economic and political inequity' (p. 13). The contributing authors to this book share a common interest in exposing how these seemingly innocent ideologies operate through everyday behaviours, beliefs, routines and habits in schools and universities. Drawing on Brookfield again, this critical intellectual work involves seven key learning tasks: 'learning to challenge ideology, contest hegemony, unmask power, overcome alienation, pursue liberation, reclaim reason, and practice democracy' (p. 65). That is what this book attempts to do.

Each of the authors in this collection, through their own unique biographies, experiences and career trajectories, attempts to explain what it means for them both personally and intellectually to engage in teaching for social justice (Ayers, 2004; Bell, Washington, Weinstein, & Love, 2003; Shor & Freire, 2003). By sharing their stories, these teacher educators contribute to the generation of new knowledge about how teacher education can be 'deliberately designed and carried out to expose prospective teachers to a variety of ideological postures', thus enabling student teachers to 'critically examine the damaging biases they may personally hold, and the inequalities and injustices present in schools and in the society as a whole' (Bartolome, 2007, p. 281).

This book is not written as another 'text of despair' (Fine & Weiss, 1998); rather, it draws on Freire's (2004) advice that in 'speaking about reality as it is and *denouncing* it, also *announces* a better world' (p. 105). In pursuing this broader critical democratic project, the contributing authors attempt to create what Maxine Greene describes as a new 'social imagination' (1995) grounded in a spirit of hope, optimism and human agency (Freire, 1998). In the words of Giroux (2004), what is urgently required in these dangerous and conservative times is an alternative vision of 'democratic [teacher] education with its emphasis on social justice, respect for others, critical inquiry, equality, freedom, civic courage, and concern for the collective good' (Giroux, 2004, p. 102).

In pursuing these broader social and political goals, the authors set out in their own ways to address the following kinds of questions:

1. What does it mean to teach in socially critical ways?
2. What traditions and ideas inform this work?
3. How do these ideas challenge dominant ideologies?
4. What does it look and feel like in classrooms?
5. How do students understand, experience and respond to critical teaching?
6. What conditions both enable and constrain this kind of teaching?
7. What contradictions, dilemmas and conflicts do critical educators face?
8. What pedagogical approaches work best for them? How? Why?
9. What are the possibilities for social change?
10. What advice do they have for others?

## Why Is It Important at This Time?

One of the tasks of this book is to counter the damaging effects (Nicolas & Berliner, 2007) of the 'conservative assault' and 'new authoritarianism' on education (Giroux, 2004), with a particular focus on teacher education (Compton & Weiner, 2008; McLaren & Baltodano, 2005; Porfilio & Yu, 2006). There can be no doubt that we are living in a social, economic and political climate dominated by neoconservative and neoliberal efforts to realign education to serve the interests of global capitalism (McLaren & Farahmandpur, 2005). As a consequence, education is under siege on a number of fronts, including a 're-emergent scientism' (Denzin, Lincoln, & Giardina, 2006), 'business-minded prescriptions' (Cuban, 2004, p. 60), 'education *for* enforcement' (Saltman & Gabbard, 2003) and a 'pedagogy of the absurd' (Goodman, 2004). The harsh reality is that neoliberal prescriptions have resulted in reduced funding for public education, the introduction of high-stakes testing, the adoption of managerialist practices and marketised approaches to education.

Of major concern to the contributing authors of this book is the manner in which these policies have damaged the profession of teaching by reducing teacher autonomy, deskilling teachers' work, standardising curricula and introducing prefab lessons and scripted curricula (Saltman, 2000, p. 102). There is now mounting pressure from governments to push teacher education towards a 'back-to-basics' version of teacher training (Hinchey, 2006, p. 128). As Hinchey (2006) explains, this instrumentalist approach involves 'preparing teachers to simply accept and implement the goals and agendas of corporate America, becoming robotic technicians who unquestioningly follow the instructions of others and who lack the temerity to ask how well those instructions serve their students' (p. 128). The drive to deprofessionalising and deskilling teachers' work fits closely with the broader conservative political agenda to privatise education and deregulate teacher education institutions (Hoffman & Sailors, 2004). The argument is that university-based teacher education is overly theoretical and divorced from the real world of 'what works'. Bullough and Gitlin (1991) warn us about the dangers of teacher training orientations that encourage

> … a constricted view of teacher intellect through emphasis on teaching as technique, an extreme form of individualism, teacher dependence on experts, acceptance of hierarchy, a consumer or 'banking' view of teaching and learning (teacher is 'banker'; learning is consuming), a limited commitment to the betterment of the educational community and a conservative survivalist mentality among novice teachers. (p. 38)

The question is, therefore, what kinds of teachers do we need under these circumstances? In this book, the unequivocal answer is critically reflective practitioners (Brookfield, 1995; Kincheloe, 1993; Smyth, 1989, 1995) committed to teaching for social justice (Ayers, Hunt, & Quinn, 1998). Ayers (2004) describes these teachers as 'passionate, fervent people who are advocates for and allies of children and therefore somehow more naturally socially responsive, political, and even activist' (p. 111). The challenge ahead is to reclaim teacher education programmes as sites for social transformation (McLaren & Baltodano, 2005).

## What Is the Orientation of the Book?

Each of the contributing authors to this book demonstrates a preparedness to interrupt existing patterns and processes of teacher education with a view to transforming them in more socially just ways. They are committed to developing empowering pedagogies that are in the words of Bigelow (2006) 'grounded in the lives of our students; critical; multicultural; anti-racist, pro-justice; participatory, experiential; hopeful, visionary; activist; academically rigorous; and culturally and linguistically sensitive' (p. 7). To this end, the focus of their teaching is on producing teachers who are concerned with the moral question of 'why things are the way they are, how they got that way, and what set of conditions are supporting the processes that maintain them' (Simon, 1988, p. 2). In other words, the emphasis for them is on producing 'knowledge workers', as opposed to technicians/civil servants, who 'research, interpret, expose embedded values and political interest, and produce their own knowledge' (Kincheloe, 2001, p. 241). Being 'critical' in this sense, according to Kemmis and McTaggart (2005), occurs when

> We can ask whether their [teachers] understandings of their situations are less irrational (or ideologically skewed) than before, whether their action is less unproductive and unsatisfying for those involved, or whether the social relations between people in the situation are less inequitable or unjust than before. The product ... is not just knowledge but also different histories than might have existed if participants had not intervened to transform their practices, understandings, and situations and, thus, transformed the histories that otherwise seemed likely to come into being. (p. 597)

For many student teachers, the question often asked is why should we be bothered with critical reflection, I just want to teach? The domination of teacher education by this kind of 'how-to-ism' (Brosio, 1994, p. 323) should hardly be surprising given that most students have had limited opportunities to question school knowledge or life experience. As Shor (1987) points out, there are significant 'interferences to critical thought' including traditional pedagogies which serve to 'control, instruct, monitor, reward and punish students as they acquire appropriate content' (Riveria & Poplin, 1995, p. 225). In response to these shortcomings, the authors in this book believe critically reflective practice is an important political and educational act because, according to Brookfield (1995),

1. It helps us take informed actions.
2. It helps us develop a rationale for practice.
3. It helps us avoid self-laceration.
4. It grounds us emotionally.
5. It enlivens our classrooms.
6. It increases democratic trust (pp. 22–26).

Moving towards a critical pedagogy of teacher education, this edited collection endeavours to address a series of questions posed by Ginsburg and Lindsay (1995):

1. What messages about education and society do students encounter in the formal and hidden curriculum of teacher education programs?
2. Do these messages encourage an acceptance or a critique of existing social relations in communities, nations and the world system?
3. Do these messages convey an image of teachers as active or passive, change-orientated or conservative political actors or are teachers represented as apolitical?
4. How do students in these programs interpret and anticipate acting in relation to these messages?
5. What features of their current and future contexts serve to enable or constrain certain forms of political activity? (p. 14)

In an era of 'commodification of higher education' (Giroux, 2001, 2007), these kinds of questions provide an opportunity to pause and think anew about the possibilities of reclaiming the moral and ethical purpose of teaching. In pursuing this critical democratic agenda, each of the authors share Giroux's (2001) vision of creating 'a sense of critical public citizenship ... [and] notions of educated hope that keep alive forms of political agency capable of realizing a life outside of the dictates of the marketplace—and which are crucial to a substantive democracy' (p. 2). Giroux goes on to develop his argument further:

> Higher education should be defended as both a public good and an autonomous sphere for the development of a critical and productive citizenry. Rather than instrumentalize reason and commodify knowledge, higher education is defined through its attempts to develop capacities, skills, and knowledge for students to create the conditions necessary 'to govern democratically everyday life, the economy, civil society, and the state' (Panitch & Gindin, 1999, 22). (p. 2)

In working towards this goal, Goodman (1991) reminds us that, 'our work must be comprehensive .... In order to have a more meaningful impact upon future teachers, this orientation needs to be the focus of seminars, supervision, foundation courses, field experiences, and methods courses' (p. 74). He warns that without a coordinated effort, our effectiveness will be severely limited. It is our hope that this book will go some way towards making a difference in this ongoing critical democratic project.

## How Is This Book Organised?

There are three parts in this book. Part I provides an overview of the politics of teacher education at the beginning of the twenty-first century. The purpose is to scope the impact of neoliberalism on teachers' work in changing times and to identify some key pedagogical cornerstones of a socially critical teacher education. Part II focuses on the teaching of class, race, gender and social activism from the point of view of practitioners. Through their stories, we hope to gain a deeper understanding of the limitations and possibilities of critical teaching.

Part III examines the pedagogical thinking and practices of a group of teacher educators committed to reconceptualising the knowledge base and orientation of specific curriculum fields in teacher education.

Part I sets the scene with an analysis of the politics of teachers' work and the implications for critical teacher education. In Chap. 2, John Smyth examines what is happening to teachers' work with particular regard to casualisation and the loss of professional autonomy among teachers. In response, John urges us to reclaim the 'relational' dimensions of teaching as a means of creating some radically new 'story lines' around the ways we treat teachers. In Chap. 3, Peter McInerney considers how the broader neoliberal policy landscape is reshaping educational discourses. In this context, Peter advocates the centrality of social justice and the art of making hope practical in teacher education. In Chap. 4, Lawrence Angus pursues the idea of creating a critical ethnographic disposition and socially democratic imaginary as a counter to the neoliberal technical managerial prescriptions of what it means to teach. In Chap. 5, Barry Down delves further into the problems associated with technical instrumentalist approaches to teacher standards. He goes on to suggest how these standards might be reconceptualised in more socially critical ways. As a bookend to this section, John Smyth in Chap. 6 revisits the classed nature of teaching and the implications for constructing alternative social practices around relationships, knowledge and curriculum.

Part II investigates what it means to teach for social justice, focusing on class, race, gender and social activism. Jane Pearce begins Chap. 7 with a personal reflection on her own upbringing and teaching around questions of social class. Excavating the personal, Jane describes the consequences of deficit thinking on children and teachers and how the process of unsettling class biases can open new possibilities of engagement and critical consciousness. In Chap. 8, Nado Aveling confronts the complex and challenging pedagogical issues involved in anti-racist teaching among pre-service teachers. Drawing on years of classroom experience, she describes the issues and dilemmas of teaching against the grain on matters of whiteness and racism in teacher education. Turning to the challenge of disrupting hegemonic masculinity, Wayne Martino in Chap. 9 grapples with the question of what counts as a legitimate gendered personhood and the implications for the construction of a trans-imaginary politics of gender justice in schools. In Chap. 10, Lisa Cary describes a critical classroom incident or 'refusal' to explain how teachers are socially constructed and portrayed. Against this backdrop, Lisa suggests moving away from oppositional pedagogical approaches to strategic confrontation in the classroom. Marilyn Frankenstein closes this section with Chap. 11, which argues the pedagogical significance of studying culture jamming as a form of resistance and student activism. Marilyn draws on her work with the Yes Men to show the power of popular culture and art in confronting corporate greed.

Part III describes the challenges confronting teacher educators who want to interrupt dominant conceptions of the curriculum and create new visions and possibilities. In Chap. 12, Libby Lee-Hammond elaborates on the ways in which neoliberal policies and practices have infiltrated the domain of early childhood education with damaging effects. She argues that the introduction of testing regimes and back-to-basics reading and writing programmes and the erosion of social pedagogies have undermined the deeply held pedagogical values and practices of early childhood educators. In Chap. 13, Cal Durrant demystifies the persistent media crises around falling literacy standards in education. Taking a historical perspective, Cal argues that the literacy wars are hardly new and largely mirror the tensions around changing social and economic conditions and emerging technologies rather than any fundamental decline in standards. Wendy Cummin-Potvin expands on the literacy debates in Chap. 14, with a carefully crafted analysis of the links between social justice, critical pedagogy and literacy research conducted by pre-service teachers in primary school classrooms. Drawing on the work of the New London Group and a pedagogy of multiliteracies, Wendy articulates the power of framing such debates around the historical, cultural and ideological contexts of learning. In Chap. 15, Peter Wright turns our attention to the potential of 'performing hope' as a cultural process of personal, social and political transformation. Drawing on the experiences of a group of pre-service teachers, Peter describes what happens when students are exposed to processes of inquiry, engagement and reflection on lived experiences. In Chap. 16, Richard Tinning reflects on the conservative historical and social constructions of physical education in teaching. He describes the philosophical and pedagogical obstacles and barriers to thinking critically and how a more 'modest sociology' may offer some hope in (re)constructing a socially critical approach to health and physical education in schools. In Chap. 17, Robbie Johnson describes how the 'quiet violence' within the society and environment curriculum serves to sanitise and domesticate the political dimensions of teaching. She proceeds to explain how her own teaching in the remote state of Tasmania endeavours to engage pre-service teachers in ideological contestation through narrative pedagogy, making the personal political. In the final chapter, Sandra Wooltorton provides a critique of international and national sustainability policies and practices grounded in her own experiences on a small regional campus in the South West corner of Western Australia. Sandra's chapter highlights the numerous contradictions, tensions and ambiguities confronting teacher educators and community activists engaged in the politics of eco-justice pedagogy.

By way of conclusion, each of the authors in this collection starts from the premise that teaching is neither neutral nor innocent. Instead, they take the position that all teaching involves questions of social justice, equality and power. To this end, there is a shared view that teacher education is a major site of ideological struggle over the nature, purpose and processes of education. Moving beyond the constraints of neoliberal discourses and conservative tendencies in teacher education, these authors both individually and collectively advocate a different kind of politics of teacher education based on the principles and values of critical democratic education and the creation of a fairer and more socially just world.

# References

Ayers, W. (2004). *Teaching the personal and the political: Essays on hope and justice*. New York: Teachers College Press.

Ayers, W., Hunt, J., & Quinn, T. (1998). *Teaching for social justice*. New York: Teachers College Press.

Bartolome, L. (2007). Critical pedagogy and teacher education: Radicalizing prospective teachers. In P. McLaren & J. Kincheloe (Eds.), *Critical pedagogy: Where are we now?* (pp. 263–286). New York: Peter Lang.

Bell, L., Washington, S., Weinstein, G., & Love, B. (2003). Knowing ourselves as instructors. In A. Darder, M. Baltodano, & R. Torres (Eds.), *The critical pedagogy reader* (pp. 464–478). New York: RoutledgeFalmer.

Bigelow, B. (2006). Getting to the heart of quality teaching. *Rethinking Schools, 20*(2), 6–8.

Brookfield, S. (1995). *Becoming a critically reflective teacher*. San Francisco: Jossey-Bass.

Brookfield, S. (2005). *The power of critical theory for adult learning and teaching*. Berkshire, NY: Open University Press.

Brosio, R. (1994). *A radical democratic critique of capitalist education*. New York: Peter Lang.

Bullough, R., & Gitlin, A. (1991). *Becoming a student of teaching: Linking knowledge production and practice*. New York: RoutledgeFalmer.

Compton, M., & Weiner, L. (Eds.). (2008). *The global assault on teaching, teachers, and their unions: Stories for resistance*. New York: Palgrave MacMillian.

Cuban, L. (2004). *The blackboard and the bottom line: Why schools can't be businesses*. Cambridge, MA: Harvard University Press.

Denzin, N., Lincoln, Y., & Giardina, M. (2006). Disciplining qualitative research. *International Journal of Qualitative Studies in Education, 19*(6), 769–782.

Fine, M., & Weiss, L. (1998). Writing the 'wrongs' of fieldwork: Confronting our own research/writing dilemmas in urban ethnographies. In G. Shacklock & J. Smyth (Eds.), *Being reflexive in critical educational and social research* (pp. 13–35). London: Falmer Press.

Freire, P. (1998). *Pedagogy of freedom: Ethics, democracy and civic courage*. Lanham, MD: Rowman & Littleford.

Freire, P. (2004). *Pedagogy of indignation*. Boulder, CO: Paradigm Publishers.

Ginsburg, M., & Lindsay, B. (1995). Conceptualizing the political dimension in teacher education. In M. Ginsburg & B. Lindsay (Eds.), *The political dimension in teacher education: Comparative perspectives on policy formation, socialization and society* (pp. 3–19). London: RoutledgeFalmer.

Giroux, H. (2001). Critical education or training: Beyond the commodification of higher education. In H. Giroux & K. Myrsiades (Eds.), *Beyond the corporate university: Culture and pedagogy in the new millennium* (pp. 1–12). New York: Rowman & Littlefield.

Giroux, H. (2004). *The terror of neoliberalism: Authoritarianism and the eclipse of democracy*. Boulder, CO: Paradigm Publishers.

Giroux, H. (2007). *The university in chains: Confronting the military-industrial-academic complex*. Boulder, CO: Paradigm Publishers.

Goodman, J. (1991). Using a methods course to promote reflection and inquiry among preservice teachers. In B. Tabachnick & K. Zeichner (Eds.), *Issues and practices in inquiry-orientated teacher education* (pp. 56–76). New York: Falmer Press.

Goodman, K. (2004). NCLB's pedagogy of the absurd. In K. Goodman, P. Shannon, Y. Goodman, & R. Rapoport (Eds.), *Saving our schools: The case for public education, saying no to "No Child Left Behind"*. Berkeley, CA: RDR Books.

Greene, M. (1995). *Releasing the imagination: Essays on education, the arts, and social change*. San Francisco: Jossey-Bass.

Hinchey, P. (2006). *Becoming a critical educator: Defining a classroom identity, designing a critical pedagogy*. New York: Peter Lang.

Hoffman, J., & Sailors, M. (2004). Those who can't teach, can: Assessing the impact of No Child Left Behind on teacher education. In K. Goodman, P. Shannon, Y. Goodman, & R. Rapoport (Eds.), *Saving our schools: The case for public education, saying no to "No Child Left Behind"* (pp. 137–150). Berkeley, CA: RDR Books.

Kemmis, S., & McTaggart, R. (2005). Participatory action research: Communicative action and the public sphere. In N. Denzin & Y. Lincoln (Eds.), *The Sage handbook of qualitative research* (3rd ed., pp. 559–603). Thousand Oaks, CA: Sage.

Kincheloe, J. (1993). *Toward a critical politics of teacher thinking*. London: Bergin & Garvey.

Kincheloe, J. (2001). *Getting beyond the facts: Teaching social studies/social sciences in the twenty-first century*. New York: Peter Lang.

Kincheloe, J., Slattery, P., & Steinberg, S. (2000). *Contextualizing teaching: Introduction to education and educational foundations*. New York: Longman.

McLaren, P., & Baltodano, M. (2005). The future of teacher education and the politics of resistance. In P. McLaren & Companeras Y. Comaneros (Eds.), *Red seminars: Radical excursions into educational theory, cultural politics, and pedagogy* (pp. 131–146). Cresskill, NJ: Hampton Press.

McLaren, P., & Farahmandpur, R. (2005). *Teaching against global capitalism and the new imperialism: A critical pedagogy*. New York: Rowman & Littlefield.

Nicholas, S., & Berliner, D. (2007). *Collateral damage: How high-stakes testing corrupts America's schools*. Cambridge, CA: Harvard University Press.

Porfilio, B., & Yu, T. (2006). "Student as consumer": A critical narrative of the commercialization of teacher education. *Journal for Critical Education Policy Studies*. Retrieved April 20, 2006, from http://www.jceps.com/?pageID=articleID=56

Rivera, J., & Poplin, M. (1995). Multicultural, critical, feminine, and constructive pedagogies seen through the eyes of youth: A call for revisioning of these and beyond: Towards a pedagogy for the next century. In C. Sleeter & P. McLaren (Eds.), *Multicultural education: Critical pedagogy and the politics of difference* (pp. 221–244). New York: University of New York Press.

Saltman, K. (2000). *Collateral damage: Corporatizing public schools—A threat to democracy*. New York: Roman & Littlefield.

Saltman, K., & Gabbard, D. (Eds.). (2003). *Education as enforcement: The militarization of schools*. New York: Routledge.

Shor, I. (1987). *Critical teaching & everyday life*. Chicago: The University of Chicago Press.

Shor, I. (1992). *Empowering education: Critical teaching for social change*. Chicago: The University of Chicago Press.

Shor, I., & Freire, P. (2003). What are the fears and risks of transformation? In A. Darder, M. Baltodano, & R. Torres (Eds.), *The critical pedagogy reader* (pp. 479–496). New York: RoutledgeFalmer.

Simon, R. (1988). For a pedagogy of possibility. *Critical Pedagogy Networker, 1*(1), 1–4.

Smyth, J. (1989). Developing and sustaining critical reflection in teacher education. *Journal of Teacher Education, 40*(2), 2–9.

Smyth, J. (Ed.). (1995). *Critical discourses on teacher development*. London: Cassell.

# Part I
# Towards a Critical Politics of Teacher Education

# Chapter 2
# Problematising Teachers' Work
# in Dangerous Times

John Smyth

There are so many points at which teachers' work is being debased, demeaned, derided, denigrated, disparaged, distorted, deformed and compromised (to break the run of d's) that it is difficult to know quite where to start. In a sense, it does not matter much where I start, because we end up in the same place. Western democracies that have so enthusiastically embraced policies of neoliberalism have rendered teaching to the category of largely unvalued menial work—except for the indirect but arguable contribution it supposedly makes to the competitiveness of the national skills base of respective national economies. In short, the work of a once-valued proud profession has been interfered with to the point where the profession has been brought to its knees. The pertinent questions for this chapter are: How has this been allowed to happen? What form has it taken? More importantly, what is to be done about it? (But more about that in Chap. 6 and from other contributors to this book).

Over the past half-century or so, without over-romanticising it or suggesting that we have somehow experienced the loss of a 'golden age' of teaching (which never actually existed), around the world, the work of teaching is virtually unrecognisable from previous incarnations of what it meant to be a teacher or to engage in the work of teaching. How the work of teaching is conceptualised, experienced and thought about has undergone radical and profound change—and not always for the better.

For the purposes of this chapter, I want to take the contemporary issue of the casualisation and contractualisation of teachers' work within public (state) schools that is attracting considerable media and public attention in Victoria, Australia—from where I am writing this piece—and to use this as a kind of prism through which to examine the broader implications of what is being 'done to' teachers' work. At first glance, this might seem to be a fairly pedestrian industrial issue—and one that has more to do with teachers' personal self-interest than it has to do

J. Smyth (✉)
School of Education, University of Ballarat, Mt Helen, VIC, Australia
e-mail: j.smyth@ballarat.edu.au

B. Down and J. Smyth (eds.), *Critical Voices in Teacher Education*, Explorations of Educational Purpose 22, DOI 10.1007/978-94-007-3974-1_2,
© Springer Science+Business Media Dordrecht 2012

with the substance or core of the work of teaching. I would argue that in actuality, it goes much deeper than that to the very essence of how public policy regards teaching and, in turn, how teachers' think about their work and the impact it has on their professional identity. As the headline of a newspaper recently put it, 'Teachers adrift in failed system' (Watkins, 2011), with nearly 20% (one in five) of the state's teachers on insecure employment contracts, the majority of these being teachers in the early years of their careers.

It is not hard to make the argument that the increasing casualisation of the teaching force is the canary in the mine for a much deeper malaise that has come to settle upon the teaching work forces of most western countries. It is indicative of a panoply of insulting public policy measures that have been visited upon teachers, like standards, benchmarking, performance appraisal/management systems, accountability and high-stakes testing regimes and various forms of marketisation and market-sensitive mechanisms like 'school choice' and other image and impression management 'makeovers', all of which are designed to unremittingly push teaching and the work of schools in the direction of being more like 'businesses'.

If we put the casualisation of teaching into context in its sharpest and most direct form, then there can be no greater insult to crucial relational and capacity-building work like teaching—for that in essence is what teaching is—than to render it down to a form of meaningless piecework. A harsher reading might be that contract teaching amounts to a form of 'outsourcing' (Thrift, 2006) or privatisation within an increasingly greedy form of capitalism.

## How Casualisation Works: On Teachers and Teaching!

At the most proximal level, contractualisation fragments teaching in ways that detach it from having a history, a past or a future of any consequence—it becomes mired in the immediacy of the present, having only the limited horizon of what can be done with young people in short spans 6 or 9 months, with no regard to any discernible extended futures or identities these young people might be trying to forge for themselves. How often have we heard at awards nights and graduations about the impact a teacher might have had on the life of a young person, often decades later? Invariably, the reference is to teachers who have had the chance of being around young people for periods of years—not just short passing casual episodes of relief teaching.

What is happening with the 'revolving door' approach to provisioning a teaching force is a tearing away at the relational basis—or relational work—of teaching. Students are denied the opportunity of forming a continuing relationship with their teachers, but rather encounter them as disembodied and readily replaceable insecure pieceworkers, who are afraid to offend or challenge 'the system' for fear of contractual retribution. It is an interesting question as to what kind of subliminal message is being conveyed here to students and future citizens through a public policy approach that cowers teachers into being submissive operatives—afraid to question the system or to engage their students with radical ideas for fear of the consequences. As Connell (1993) put it, if teaching was meant to be thus, all it would require would be 'a computer with a cattle prod' (p. 63).

The argument most often put for the necessity of having insecure tenure of teaching is that it is necessary to 'keep teachers on their toes', thus purging schools of 'incompetents'. We are also told it is all being done in the interests of so-called management flexibility so that decisions can be taken so as to preserve the school's fiscal bottom line. If only it were so simple, on either count—but it is not. Schools are complex relational organisations which Connell (1993) attests to when he summarised it in these terms:

> Being a teacher is not just a matter of having a body of knowledge and a capacity to control a classroom... Just as important, being a teacher means being able to establish human relations with the people being taught. Learning is a full-blooded, human social process, and so is teaching. Teaching involves emotions as much as it involves pure reasoning. The emotional dimension of teaching has not been much researched, but ... it is extremely important. Teachers establish relations with students through their emotions, through sympathy, interest, surprise, boredom, sense of humour, sometimes anger and annoyance. School teaching, indeed, is one of the most emotionally demanding jobs. (p. 63)

As I have argued elsewhere (Smyth, Down, & McInerney, 2010, pp. 47–48), organising and operating public schools in ways that metaphorically amount to 'imprisoning minds' (Macrine, 2003) of teachers as well as students, around a flawed rhetoric of accountability and threats of fiscal punishment and privatisation, is a disciplinary reform logic that will not work in the long run. Schools are not places that flourish under external threats or attempts to use boot-camp tactics of control, command and scripting of what goes on, no matter how good the intent. The evidence on this is so incontrovertible and hardly warrants rehearsal here, yet school reformers continue to remain policy deaf to this message. They simply do not get it! Schools are places that require substantial risk-taking, innovation and experimentation by teachers and students if learning is to occur, and this means high levels of trust, care and respect. Teaching is fundamentally emotional work that involves getting up close to students and drawing heavily on social, emotional resources and energy necessary for continual improvisation. Connell (1996) put this succinctly when he said that 'Good teaching ... involves a gift relation ... It is founded on a public rather than a private interest' (p. 6).

## It Is a Highly Pertinent Question, Therefore, as to Where Casualisation and Contractualisation Are Coming From

Behind the move to increasing forms of contractualisation in teaching and a range of welfare service provisions is a quite dramatic shift in the notion of 'trust'. Scholars in the field of the 'new public management' or the 'new public administration' (Clarke, Cochrane, & McLaughlin, 1994; Clarke, Gewirtz, & McLaughlin, 2000;

Gunter, 2011; Hood, 2000; Newman, 2001; Newman & Clarke, 2009; Pollitt, 1996) have argued for some time that there has been an erosion underway over the past 30 years of old forms of 'collegial' and 'professional' trust that relied on the possession of high levels of knowledge and commitment to the values of public service and providing for 'users' and 'clients'. For example, Newman identifies three different forms of trust:

- *Knowledge-based trust* is formed over time and through experience of, and information about, the other party. It is based on a longer-term stake in the relationship which leads to 'give and take' and elements of reciprocity . . . .
- *Identity-based trust* is formed through common patterns of identification and the principles of mutuality and loyalty . . . .
- *Calculus-based trust* derives from rational calculation and relationships of exchange. It invokes instrumental behaviour . . . and is linked to the operation of incentives and threats of sanctions (p. 100).

The 'calculus-based' approach to trust that is in the ascendancy at the moment relies on economically rational motives and 'stick and carrot' methods in which 'all of the tasks, goods, and services are described, calculated, and settled' (Knijn & Selten, 2006, p. 26). The assumption here is that providers are primarily animated by economic rewards (or fear of their withdrawal) rather than altruism, internal codes of ethics, pride in doing a good job or regarding it as socially worthwhile work. We can see this in the press towards making schools and teachers deliver on targeted outcomes and measurable results that can be published in consumer-oriented league tables. What lies behind this view is what has been labelled 'organised distrust' (Knijn & Selten, 2006, p. 26) and the attendant notion that professionals, such as teachers, can no longer be trusted in the professional sense. What is at stake is the way schools have become implicated into national economic competitiveness. This is considered to be far too important to be left to the whim, idiosyncrasies and ethical mores of individuals—it is something, despite the customer-driven rhetoric that accompanies it, that must be orchestrated and controlled by governments.

I do not want to unnecessarily trawl over the uniformly depressing ground already covered by others in terms of the demise of teaching, so much as I want to puncture that pessimistic account by pointing to the way in which we might begin a more optimistic reclamation.

## Using the 'Relational' to Reclaim Teachers' Work

I have argued extensively elsewhere (Smyth, 2010) that the effect of the 'audit explosion' that accompanies the casualisation of teaching and that is crucial to giving the process of schooling its continuing legitimacy is *prima facie* a 'technology of mistrust' (Armstrong, 1991). As I put it then, and the situation worsens by the day, the 'insidious way in which auditing does it ugly work [is through] producing fear, loathing, hatred, and feelings of having ones' work diminished, at the same time as feeling dirty, implicated and complicit' (Smyth, 2010, p. 172). When professionals like teachers are brought within this inspectorial orbit to the extent that they have, then as Power (1996) says, it is a signal that 'society has lost confidence in itself', to the point that:

> ...a society tries to tell reaffirming stories, [to] make explicit what was implicit [thus] creat[ing] more and more formal accounts that can be checked. An anxious society invests heavily in evaluative practices of self-affirmation and new industries of checkers are created. It is not so much a loss of trust that has occurred but a desperate need to create it through the management of formal appearance.

The perversity is that:

> ... all this checking makes a certain style of management possible, one that is now firmly established. The problem is not evaluation and assessment as such, but the belief that with ever more of it, real excellence can be conjured into existence. The opposite is almost certainly the case; increasing evaluation and auditing are symptoms of mediocrity rather than its cure. (p. 18)

As recent Australian higher education trends indicate, the even more ridiculous scenario is 'Coming up, a body to rank rankers' (Hare, 2011).

The argument has been put in the social sciences, more generally, of the pressing need for a 'spatial turn' (Gulson, 2005, 2008; Gulson & Symes, 2007a, 2007b; Soja, 2000) to replace current impoverished context-free linear explanations (Saul, 2010) of the way the world operates. The claim is that we need a much more nuanced paradigm with which to understand the relational complexity of our lives, and that 'cause' and 'effect' approaches are demonstrably not up to the task. In a similar vein, I am proposing a re-conceptualisation of teaching that exemplifies a 'relational turn'.

## What, Then, Might Constitute the Basis of Such a 'Relational Turn' in Teaching?

The kind of questions that would need to underpin a reinvention of schools and teaching around what I am envisaging as 'relational spaces' (Smyth, 2010, pp. 173–174) would be ones that would embrace:

- How is teaching connecting to the life experiences, aspirations and expectations of students?
- In what ways is learning a happy, enjoyable, enlivening and fulfilling experience for students?
- How is teaching enlarging or expanding the cultural map for the most excluded or marginalised students?
- How is the school creating a context for students to bond that produces a sense of belongingness and attachment to the school?

- How are students being encouraged and made to feel comfortable and safe in speaking out in challenging the status quo? Indeed, how are students being educated to regard the status quo?
- How are parents being brought into meaningful partnerships in the education of their children?
- How is successful learning being acknowledged, recognised and celebrated?
- How does the school work at creating itself as part of a wider vibrant public sphere?
- How is leadership distributed as part of a democratic set of practices that acknowledges multiple sources of expertise?
- How are decisions made in the school in an informed way, rather than as a consequence of knee-jerk reactions to sectional vested interests?
- How are students being given significant ownership of their learning?
- How is the wider debate about the crucial importance of a culture of teaching being sustained and maintained in the school?
- How are students' imaginations about big ideas being fired and kept alive?
- What is it that makes teaching for some teachers such a creative, satisfying and rewarding activity? (Smyth, 2007, p. 225)

Both appreciating and 'mapping the relational spaces' (Fry & Hovelynck, 2010, p. 141) implicit in this constellation of self-and-collective reflective probes will not come without significant challenges and costs—because all of these are questions that strike at the very heart of the neoliberal policy regime that dominates education, and the answers to them are the obverse of the neoliberal project. The task is effectively one of totally dislodging, dismantling, demolishing and extirpating the current deeply entrenched infatuation with the 'managerial school' (Gewirtz, 2002).

'High' stakes relationships' (Smyth, 2007, p. 232) of the kind I am advocating coalesce around placing the interests and life chances of young people at the centre of all aspects of teaching and schooling—rather than those of 'the system', government, the economy or 'big business'. In other words, it is an ideology in which young people are invested with 'relational power' (Warren, 2005) and accorded 'relational trust' (Bryk & Schneider, 2002) in the pursuit of an ensemble of underpinning principles and ideas that include:

- Teaching has to actively acknowledge and respect the aspirations, experiences, cultures and family backgrounds of students.
- Teaching has to be an active and identity-affirming process for students, rather than a passive transmission delivery process that produces oppositional identities among students.
- Teaching has to start from the position that students have something worthwhile to say about what they would like to learn, how they would like to learn it and with whom.
- Teaching has to take seriously the views of students about what kind of knowledge they see as being relevant to the kind of futures they want to construct.
- Teaching needs to provide the crucial scaffolding for student learning, but in ways that allow students spaces for their ideas and interests.

- Teaching needs to provide students with ways of owning their behaviour and learning about the consequences of their actions on their learning.
- Teaching needs to occur in ways in which teachers get to know and respect their students and students get to know and respect their teachers.
- Teaching has to endorse authentic forms of assessment that describe student growth and development, not synthetic modes of assessment that traumatise and rank and rate students in competitive ways to be used as commodities and pawns in some insidious and destructive game of international economic competitiveness.
- Teaching needs to be rigorous and challenging in engaging young minds with important ideas and issues (Smyth, 2007, p. 232).

## Creating Relational Spaces in Teaching

The notion of 'relational spaces' I am envisaging is already well underway in feminist identity narratives (Picchietti, 2002), in post-structural geography (Murdoch, 2006), in human geography (Hubbard, Kitichin, & Valentine, 2008) and in parts of management (Fry & Hovelynck, 2010; Steyaert & Van Looy, 2010). It is not difficult to posit the claim that schools are quintessentially relational places. While students learn 'stuff' that will allegedly equip them for later in life, even more importantly, they are learning and acquiring dispositions and understandings about how to relate to people, how to experience and inhabit institutions (like schooling), how to relate to their environment, communities, neighbourhoods, regions and the nation, globally, as well as to 'big ideas'—long after the content they learn in classrooms is obsolete. Part of the 'bigger idea' I am parlaying with here is captured in human geographer Nigel Thrift's (2008) notion of 'non-representational theory', summarised thus by Steyaert and Van Looy (2010, p. 1) as:

> ... not extracting a representation of the world from the world, but 'because we are slap bang in the middle of it', we are coconstructing it with numerous human and nonhuman others. (Thrift, 1999, p. 297)

The reason so much is being made these days about notions like the 'self-managing school' (Caldwell & Hayward, 1998; Caldwell & Spinks, 1988, 1992, 1998; cf. Smyth, 1993, 2008, 2011) and 'distributed leadership' (Leithwood, Mascall, & Strauss, 2009) within education is that such utterances, repeated often enough and implemented in a fake fashion, are necessary because, as Sheldon Wolin (2000) noted, we live in a kind of 'inverted totalitarianism' in which 'democracy is embalmed in a public rhetoric precisely to memorialise its loss of substance' (p. 20).

We desperately need a reinvention of 'everyday relational practice' (Steyaert & Van Looy, 2010, p. 4) so as to acknowledge and remind us of the core social realities of what kind of places schools are and, in particular, the kind of social and emotional work that schools do. Invoking Habermas (1989), Fry and Hovelynck (2010) talk about the imperative of developing 'a healthy relational sphere' in which people 'have respect for one another and see each other as working equals' (p. 141). Summarising Habermas' well-known thesis, they say:

> Every person in the interaction is seen as having a perspective of value. Within these ideal conversational moments, the players experience a temporary suspension of status differential, they discuss any topic related to a locus for action, and they operate under an assumption of inclusivity. (p. 141)

The kind of reinvention we have spoken about elsewhere (Smyth et al., 2010) has been organised around three interacting themes—relationships, power and pedagogy—within a notion we refer to as the 'relational school' (Smyth, Angus, Down, & McInerney, 2008, 2009; Smyth & Fasoli, 2007). This working ensemble might be a useful way of drawing this chapter together, while providing a practical window on some of the theoretical arguments we have been pursuing.

The way we see it, when schools take it as their inalienable primary mission, to engage the minds and lives of young people, then they are really tacitly acknowledging the salience of five major issues:

- People-intensive nature of schools
- Need to place relationships at the centre
- Knowing intimately who their students are
- Foregrounding student voice as being crucial to learning
- Preparedness to invest in relational power (Smyth et al., 2010, p. 39)

We think the following quote from a teacher neatly encapsulates what is highly problematic about how power is frequently exercised in schools—to the significant detriment of students:

> Kids, this is the game we are playing: if you fail, it is because there is something wrong with you, not the game itself. (Smith, 2006, p. 122)

What this conveys are the hallmarks of a perspective that run counter to the kind of relational spaces that I have been arguing for in this chapter and that underpin long-term educative relationships:

- It unfairly apportions blame.
- It is non-negotiable as to multiple contributing factors—many that possibly reside some distance from the classroom.
- It is hierarchical and condescending.
- It is non-pedagogical in the way it excludes students from learning about and from failure.
- It smacks of an arrogant form of managerialism.

One thing we have learnt from social theorists and sociologists is that power is never unidirectional—even in the seemingly most oppressive/repressive situations. There are always cracks, crevices and interstices within which resistance can be and is exerted. Schools are classic illustrations of this. A counterview to the one put by the teacher in Smith (2006) above, and that acknowledges the political reality of schools as socially constructed entities, is that when students do not learn, it can be in large part because they are making an active choice regarding their preparedness to subject themselves to the authority of the school and what it is offering them. In other words, when students 'fail to learn', they are refusing to put their trust in the school or to acknowledge the legitimacy of the institution of schooling in their lives. In this sense, whether learning occurs or not in school is highly provisional on whether the students are prepared to make the social and emotional investment in it in order to develop the social connections necessary to learn.

When teachers are treated in ways in which they become the public mouthpieces of an agenda decided at a distance from classrooms—and when teachers become cyphers and conduits of government policy—then the relational spaces necessary for working with young people in spontaneous and improvised ways are severely eroded at the level of the interpersonal.

When educational policies have as their primary focus controlling teachers and distancing them from students—their background, histories, families, lives and cultures and aspirations—then students are likely to resist this kind of disembodied curriculum and label it as irrelevant.

When what constitutes learning is arbitrarily determined by externally set national curriculum, standards, targets and outcomes and is enforced by testing regimes—then it will not be surprising if students reject this as not constituting 'a curriculum for life' (Portelli & Vibert, 2001) and therefore not worth investing in.

When what is considered 'best' for students is presented as worthwhile, satisfying and rewarding life pathways for those students whose lives and backgrounds outside of school are consistent with the mores and classed agenda of the school, while those who are considered 'deviant' are relegated to diminished vocational pathways—then such forms of tracking are likely to be treated with scepticism by some students.

The importance of relationships in schooling and the work of teaching is not something that can be left to chance, whim, discretion or the willingness of individual teachers to pursue—it is far too significant for that. The importance of creating a viable and sustainable relational environment for all young people in schools ought to be a consistent message that is thoroughly infused at all policy levels—not just as an optional add-on to be done if time permits and if teachers feel so disposed. How a school fosters relationships that connect to young people, their lives and aspirations ought to be the defining raison d'etre of the school and the work of teaching. If this means relegating the managerial, marketisation, monitoring and other peripheral agenda to the subservient positions they deserve to occupy in schools in support of the 'relational', then that would be a highly desirable paradigmatic shift.

The consequences of not getting this 'right' are already well on display in many schools:

- Students who are increasingly alienated and 'disengaged'—the official euphemism for students who are responding to uninspiring curriculum, pedagogy and forms of assessment—by physically and emotionally withdrawing from learning and eventually rejecting it partially (truanting) and then completely, by 'dropping out' and giving up on school

- Increasingly muscular behaviour management policies that are being invoked and posited instead of an engaging curriculum and teaching that should be inspiring young people to learn and to aspire to become 'an educated person' (Levinson, Foley, & Holland, 1996)
- 'Tuned out', 'switched off', 'burnt out', demoralised and disheartened teachers who have become cogs in a system that is making them increasingly cynical through its incessant reforms, and that has replaced consistent support of the work by handing everything over to the market to sort out, rectify and regulate by mechanisms like 'school choice' and 'league tables'

If we return now to the rationale that animated the discussion at the beginning of this chapter around the need to avoid casualised and contractual approaches to teaching, then it is possible to summarise the case for the 'turn to relation' as requiring the bringing into existence of a number of conducive conditions. These are conditions that represent a significant but crucial culture shift, requiring at minimum some quite radically new 'storylines' around the way we treat teachers involving:

- *The de-institutionalisation of relationships* (Osterman, 2000)—which is to say, removing the distant and impersonal way schools insulate themselves from the way they relate to students and community through rules, policies and bureaucratic procedures
- *Emphasising the creation of capabilities*—which, as Sen (1992, 1999, 2002) argues, is about assisting people to (1) identify the kind of lives they want to lead, (2) providing them with the skills and knowledge to do that and (3) helping them understand and confront how their political, social and economic conditions will allow or impede them
- *Building relational trust* (Bryk & Schneider, 2002)—in the form of social exchanges that bring with them 'respect', 'personal regard for others', 'competence' and 'integrity' and the set of mutually interrelated dependencies that come with these and that constitute a valuable organisational and institutional resource
- *Divesting ownership of decision making over learning* to learners who have a meaningful stake in what and how they learn and how that learning is assessed and reported upon
- *Humanising relationships* (Bartolome, 1994; Noguera, 1995)—so that fear, threats and retribution are removed as the basis for learning and, as a consequence, a climate is created in which it is safe to take risks
- *Eliminating the stress that comes with inequality* by deconstructing hierarchy (Spring, 2007, p. 50) and banishing harmful competition—so that energy, emotion and learning time are not dissipated in dealing with the extraneous and unhealthy effects of competition
- *Having an improvisational view of teaching* (Smyth, 2005)—that goes beyond the arbitrary imposition of standards and that instead licences and legitimates courageous, exploratory and experimental approaches (Smyth et al., 2008, p. 159)

None of these are qualities or attributes that are by and large celebrated in the work of teaching by those outside if it, nor can they be fostered or achieved by insecure piece-rate workers. In this respect, it is hard to find a more apt note on which to end this chapter with than the prescient title of Bingham and Sidorkin's (2004) book—*No Education Without Relation.*

# References

Armstrong, P. (1991). Contradiction and social dynamics in the capitalist agency relationship. *Accounting, Organisations and Society, 16*(1), 1–25.

Bartolome, L. (1994). Beyond the methods fetish: Toward a humanizing pedagogy. *Harvard Educational Review, 64*(2), 173–194.

Bingham, C., & Sidorkin, M. (Eds.). (2004). *No education without relation.* New York: Peter Lang Publishing.

Bryk, A., & Schneider, B. (2002). *Trust in schools: A core resource for Improvement.* New York: Russell Sage.

Caldwell, B., & Hayward, R. (1998). *The future of schools: Lessons from the reform of public education.* London: Falmer Press.

Caldwell, B., & Spinks, J. (1988). *The self-managing school.* Lewes, UK: Falmer Press.

Caldwell, B., & Spinks, J. (1992). *Leading the self-managing school.* Lewes, UK: Falmer Press.

Caldwell, B., & Spinks, J. (1998). *Beyond the self-managing school.* London/Philadelphia: Falmer Press.

Clarke, J., Cochrane, A., & McLaughlin, E. (Eds.). (1994). *Managing social policy.* London/Thousand Oaks, CA: SAGE Publications.

Clarke, J., Gewirtz, S., & McLaughlin, E. (Eds.). (2000). *New managerialism new welfare?* London/Thousand Oaks, CA: SAGE Publications.

Connell, B. (1993). *Schools and social justice.* Toronto, ON: Our Schools/Our Selves Education Foundation.

Connell, R. (1996). *Prepare for interesting times: Education in a fractured world* (Inaugural professorial address). Sydney, Australia: University of Sydney.

Fry, R., & Hovelynck, J. (2010). Developing space for diversity: An appreciative stance. In C. Steyaert & B. Van Looy (Eds.), *Relational practices: Participative organizing* (pp. 139–154). Bradford, UK: Emerald.

Gewirtz, S. (2002). *The managerial school: Post-welfarism and social justice in education.* London/New York: Routledge.

Gulson, K. (2005). Renovating educational identities: Policy, space and urban renewal. *Journal of Education Policy, 20*(2), 141–158.

Gulson, K. (2008). Urban accommodations: Policy, education and a politics of place. *Journal of Education Policy, 23*(2), 153–163.

Gulson, K., & Symes, C. (Eds.). (2007a). *Spatial theories of education: Policy and geography matters.* New York: Routledge.

Gulson, K., & Symes, C. (2007b). Knowing one's place: Space, theory, education. *Critical Studies in Education, 48*(1), 97–110.

Gunter, H. (2011). *The state and education policy.* London: Continuum.

Habermas, J. (1989). *Structural transformations of the public sphere.* Cambridge, MA: MIT Press.

Hare, J. (2011, 12 January). Coming up, body to rank rankers. *The Australian (Higher Education),* pp. 19 & 20.

Hood, C. (2000). *The art of the state: Culture, rhetoric and public management.* London: Oxford University Press.

Hubbard, P., Kitichin, R., & Valentine, G. (Eds.). (2008). *Key texts in human geography*. London: Sage.

Knijn, T., & Selten, P. (2006). The rise of contractualisation in public services. In J. Duyvendak, T. Knijn, & M. Kremer (Eds.), *Policy, people and the new professional: De-professionalisation and re-professionalisation in care and welfare*. Amsterdam: Amsterdam University Press.

Leithwood, K., Mascall, B., & Strauss, T. (Eds.). (2009). *Distributed leadership according to the evidence*. New York: Routledge.

Levinson, B., Foley, D., & Holland, D. (Eds.). (1996). *The cultural production of the educated person: Critical ethnographies of schooling and local practice*. Albany, NY: State University of New York Press.

Macrine, S. (2003). Imprisoning minds: The violence of neoliberal education or "I am not for sale". In K. Saltman & D. Gabbard (Eds.), *Education as enforcement: The militarization and corporatization of schools* (pp. 203–211). London/New York: Routledge Falmer.

Murdoch, J. (2006). *Post-structuralist geography: A guide to relational space*. London/Thousand Oaks, CA: SAGE.

Newman, J. (2001). *Modernising governance – New labour, policy and society*. London: Sage.

Newman, J., & Clarke, J. (2009). *Public, politics and power: Remaking the public in public services*. London: Sage.

Noguera, P. (1995). Preventing and producing violence: A critical analysis of responses to school violence. *Harvard Educational Review, 65*(2), 189–213.

Osterman, K. (2000). Students' need for belonging in the school community. *Review of Educational Research, 70*(3), 323–367.

Picchietti, V. (2002). *Relational spaces: Daughterhood, motherhood, and sisterhood in Davia Maraini's writings and films*. Cranbury, NJ: Associated University Presses.

Pollitt, C. (1996). *Managerialism and the public services: Cuts or cultural changes in the 1990's?* (2nd ed.). Oxford, UK: Blackwell.

Portelli, J., & Vibert, A. (2001). Beyond common standards: Toward a curriculum for life. In J. Portelli & P. Solomon (Eds.), *The erosion of democracy in education: From critique to possibilities* (pp. 63–82). Calgary, AB: Detselig Enterprises.

Power, M. (1996, October 18). I audit, therefore I am. *Times Higher Education Supplement*, p. 18.

Saul, J. (2010, June 8). *Freedom and globalisation*. Paper presented at the Melbourne Writers' Festival, RMIT Capitol Theatre, Melbourne.

Sen, A. (1992). *Inequality re-examined*. Cambridge, MA: Harvard University Press.

Sen, A. (1999). *Development as freedom*. Oxford, UK: Oxford University Press.

Sen, A. (2002). *Rationality and freedom*. Cambridge, MA: Harvard University Press.

Smith, D. (2006). Not rocket science: On the limits of conservative pedagogy. In K. Cooper & R. White (Eds.), *The practical critical educator: Critical inquiry and educational practice* (pp. 121–131). Dordrecht, The Netherlands: Springer.

Smyth, J. (Ed.). (1993). *A socially critical view of the self-managing school*. London: Falmer Press.

Smyth, J. (2005). Policy research and "damaged teachers": Toward an epistemologically respectful paradigm. In F. Bodone (Ed.), *What difference does research make and for whom?* (pp. 141–159). New York: Peter Lang Publishing.

Smyth, J. (2007). Teacher development against the policy reform grain: An argument for recapturing relationships in teaching and learning. *Teacher Development: An International Journal of Teachers' Professional Development, 11*(2), 221–236.

Smyth, J. (2008). Australia's great disengagement with public education and social justice in educational leadership. *Journal of Educational Administration and History, 40*(3), 221–233.

Smyth, J. (2010). The politics of derision, distrust and deficit—The damaging consequences for youth and communities put at a disadvantage. In E. Samier & M. Schmidt (Eds.), *Trust and betrayal in educational administration and leadership* (pp. 169–183). London/New York: Routledge.

Smyth, J. (2011). The *disaster* that has been the 'self-managing school'—Its genesis, trajectory, undisclosed agenda, and effects. *Journal of Educational Administration and History, 43*(2), 95–117.

Smyth, J., Angus, L., Down, B., & McInerney, P. (2008). *Critically engaged learning: Connecting to young lives*. New York: Peter Lang Publishing.

Smyth, J., Angus, L., Down, B., & McInerney, P. (2009). *Activist and socially critical school and community renewal: Social justice in exploitative times*. Rotterdam, The Netherlands: Sense Publishers.

Smyth, J., Down, B., & McInerney, P. (2010). *'Hanging in with kids' in tough times: Engagement in contexts of educational disadvantage in the relational school*. New York: Peter Lang Publishing.

Smyth, J., & Fasoli, L. (2007). Climbing over the rocks in the road to student engagement and learning in a challenging high school in Australia. *Educational Research, 49*(3), 273–295.

Soja, E. (2000). *Postmetropolis: Critical studies of cities and regions*. Cambridge, MA: Blackwell.

Spring, J. (2007). *A new paradigm for global school systems: Education for a long and happy life*. Mahwah, NJ: Lawrence Erlbaum & Associates.

Steyaert, C., & Van Looy, B. (2010). *Relational practices: Participative organizing*. Bradford, UK: Emerald Publishing.

Thrift, N. (1999). Steps to an ecology of place. In D. Massey, J. Allen, & P. Sarre (Eds.), *Human geography today*. Cambridge, UK: Polity Press.

Thrift, N. (2006). Re-inventing invention: New tendencies in capitalist commodification. *Economy and Society, 35*(2), 279–306.

Thrift, N. (2008). *Non-representational theory: Space/politics/affect*. London: Routledge.

Warren, M. (2005). Communities and schools: A new view of urban school reform. *Harvard Educational Review, 75*(2), 133–173.

Watkins, S. (2011, January 7). Teachers adrift in a failed system. *The Age*, p. 9.

Wolin, S. (2000). Political theory: From vocation to invocation. In J. Frank & J. Tamborino (Eds.), *Vocations of political theory* (pp. 3–22). Minneapolis, MN: University of Minnesota Press.

# Chapter 3
# Rediscovering Discourses of Social Justice: Making Hope Practical

Peter McInerney

## Introduction

A belief that we live in an egalitarian society is deeply ingrained in the Australian psyche, yet, from time to time, there are sharp reminders that this idea is a fantasy sustained by popular myths and misconceptions. In March 2011, the Australian Council of Social Services (ACOSS), the peak body of the community services and welfare sector and national voice for the needs of people affected by poverty and inequality, expressed alarm at the growing demands for welfare services—a demand so great charities have had to turn many needy people away from their doors. In the midst of a resource boom that has generated billions of dollars in company profits, it is estimated that 2.2 million people (or 11% of Australians) are in poverty compared with 7.6% in 1994. Most distressingly, approximately 12% of Australian children live in poverty (Australian Council of Social Services [ACOSS], 2011). A widening gap between the rich and poor, surging unemployment, and a million people living in housing stress, are tangible signs that Australia is becoming a more unequal and polarized society under the ascendancy of neoliberal governance. Nowhere is this gap more apparent than in the greatly reduced life expectancy, educational achievement and employment opportunities of the vast majority of Aboriginal and Torres Strait Islander people. There is a cultural dimension to injustice as well. As a nation, we project an image of a tolerant, multicultural society, but the pall of racism rooted in the legacy of a 'White Australia' policy still lingers in the darker recesses of communities, social institutions and parliaments. Government policies, including the wars against Iraq and Afghanistan, anti-terrorism laws and harsh immigration detention policies have helped to demonize asylum seekers,

P. McInerney (✉)
University of Ballarat, Mt Helen, VIC, Australia
e-mail: p.mcinerney@ballarat.edu.au

B. Down and J. Smyth (eds.), *Critical Voices in Teacher Education*, Explorations of Educational Purpose 22, DOI 10.1007/978-94-007-3974-1_3,
© Springer Science+Business Media Dordrecht 2012

create a climate of fear and legitimize racism against Arab and Muslim Australians. Aided and abetted by right-wing newspaper columnists and radio shock jocks, Islamophobia has penetrated Australia's suburbs and rural communities.

As social institutions, schools are not quarantined from what happens in society at large. Injustices arising from the poverty, deprivation, homelessness, racism and other forms of oppression, visit classrooms on a daily basis, often with disastrous consequences for the education of young people. Furthermore, schools that maintain a hegemonic curriculum and engage in sorting and streaming, and assessment practices that discriminate against students are complicit in the reproduction of injustices (Connell, 1993). In spite of sporadic efforts on the part of governments to tackle these issues, the persistence of educational disadvantage remains a great blight on Australia's social landscape. Education is crucial to young people's chances for a better life, but school retention rates, academic achievement and participation levels reveal that students from low-income families (particularly indigenous children and those living in remote locations) are more likely to drop out of school before competing formal schooling, thereby shutting down employment and further education options (Smyth, Down, & McInerney, 2010). However, in the neoliberal state, the problems of illiteracy, disengagement and poor school retention are typically attributed to the failings and weaknesses of individuals, rather than faults within the institution of schooling and the political system. The net effect of this pathologizing discourse is to shift responsibility for the problem of youth failure away from governments to families and their communities. Teachers and schools too are caught up in this blaming game because they are deemed to be a major part of the problem and hence are expected to provide the solutions.

In this chapter, I want to reaffirm the critical importance of teaching for social justice at a time when many of the hard-won reforms of the 1970s and 1980s are under threat from conservative and neoliberal policymakers. Whilst it might be tempting to revisit the past to recapture the social democratic spirit of the Disadvantaged Schools Programme, it is crucial that schools, teachers and teacher educators rediscover and refashion discourses of social justice that are more responsive to the economic, social and cultural conditions of contemporary society. In particular, 'we do need to rethink the complex ways that class, race, gender, ethnicity, disability and so on intersect with each other to create new identities in the contemporary globalised world' (Lingard, Mills, & Hayes, 2000, p. 112). Given the extent of structural inequalities, the task of working for a more just society cannot be accomplished solely within schools. However, as Connell (1993) points out, teachers can be vital agents for change since:

> [t]hey more than any other group of adults concerned with the education of children know where the shoe pinches—where things are not working well. Teachers have, among them, an enormous fund of experience and ideas, which if tapped represents a tremendous asset for progressive reform. (p. 58)

In spite of the pressures to conform to externally imposed curricula, narrowly based testing regimes and functionalist approaches to teaching and learning, I believe that a 'politics of possibility' (Giroux, 1985) can be brought to bear in working for more socially just schooling. Teachers have agency and can still exercise a degree of collective autonomy in the context of their own schools. I emphasize 'collective' because far-reaching and sustainable change cannot be achieved through the heroic efforts of individuals—the task requires a whole school reform and system-wide approach. For this to occur, educators have to actively resist efforts to reduce their status to that of high level technicians and affirm the intellectual, political and moral dimensions of their work.

A courageous vision of how schools can work for the most disadvantaged is a crucial element to this goal, but it has to be anchored in practice if it is to become an authentic resource for progressive social change (Freire, 2004). 'Making hope practical' (McInerney, 2004, 2007) demands some insight into the pedagogical strategies and resources in schools and communities that transform unjust schooling arrangements. The chapter begins with an overview of the major influences on education policymaking and orientations to social justice in contemporary times. Informed by the writings of Nancy Fraser (1997, 2005), I present a framework for understanding the economic, cultural and political dimensions of justice around the notions of redistribution, recognition and representation. With reference to this framework, I then describe the ways in which teachers and schools, in cooperation with local communities, can (and do) develop more socially just structures, curriculum and pedagogies at the grassroots level. Finally, I suggest how teacher education programs that have a major focus on social justice and education might support and enhance the work of teachers in schools.

## Rethinking Social Justice in a Global Age

Although the idea (or ideal) of social justice does not have a single or universally accepted meaning, the distinctly Australian expression of 'giving everyone a fair go' seems to have popular currency. Griffiths (1998) captures some of this sentiment in her view of social justice as an appropriate term to describe the unifying factors underlying a general movement towards a fairer and less oppressive society. She goes on to explain:

> This is a movement towards opening up from the few to the many the rewards and prizes and enjoyments of living in society—including schooling. This movement focused on social class in the first half of this century but now includes 'race', gender, sexuality and disability. (p. 301)

These words convey some sense of the dynamic nature of discourses on social justice and point to the ways in which new agendas are being incorporated into movements for social change as a consequence of globalization, the ascendancy of neoliberal governance, the emergence of new social movements around identity politics, and growing economic inequalities in society. What follows is a brief explanation of these factors, their influence on education and relevance to the issue of educational disadvantage.

## *Globalization*

Whether we talk in economic, cultural or political terms, it is impossible to ignore the grip of globalization on people's imaginations, its impact on daily lives and education policy. The phenomenon is also changing the way we debate about the notion of justice. According to Fraser (2005), in the heyday of social democracy, disputes about social justice were framed around a 'Keynesian-Westphalian frame' (p. 1) based on respect for territorial sovereignty. In this situation:

> ... arguments about justice were assumed to concern relations among fellow citizens, to be subject to debate within national publics, and to contemplate redress by national states. (p. 1)

However, many of the problems confronting humanity—ecological crises, global warming, the spread of AIDS, terrorism, poverty and the threat of nuclear war, to name but a few—transcend national boundaries and can only be tackled through international cooperation and agreements between nations. Local economies are now more vulnerable to the forces of global capitalism following the removal of tariff barriers and the adoption of international monetary policies. Restructuring of global capitalism has led to regional unemployment, 'rust belt economies' and the penetration of multinational economies into Australian communities, as exemplified in the 'McDonaldization' of Australia. A globalization discourse has found its way into education policy with schools being exhorted to skill up young people so that Australia can compete effectively in the global economy. Schools are also caught up in testing regimes which attempt to make international comparisons of school outcomes and performances, especially in subjects such as mathematics (Carnoy, 1998).

## *Neoliberalism*

Closely allied to globalization, adoption of neoliberal policies and market-driven model governments in OECD countries threaten to undermine the safety net principles of the welfare state. In a new twist of rhetoric, neoliberal apologists tend to stress the concept of recipient obligation rather than entitlements when it comes to welfare benefits. As economic rationalist thinking has taken hold, state and federal governments have largely abandoned principles of social justice in favour of a market-driven approach to the delivery of human services. Education is often viewed as a cost rather than an investment (Bradley, 2006), and a language of efficiency, choice and parental responsibility has come to dominate the policy landscape. In this new business climate, schools are expected to embrace a culture of managerialism, operate more like private businesses and focus on the so-called basics of literacy and numeracy.

## New Social Movements

Discourses on social justice and schooling are also being influenced by social movements centring on the demands for cultural recognition and human rights of groups previously excluded from the mainstream debates on social policy. Beginning with feminism, we now have the emergence of political movements intent on securing rights and recognition for a diversity of groups including gay and lesbian people, the disabled, indigenous people, ethnic communities, victims of crime, refugees, prisoners of conscience, religious minorities, to name but a few. In the new climate, a 'politics of recognition' (Fraser, 1997) has triggered new debates about the nature and causes of oppression and the courses of action to be pursued in alleviating social injustice. This has impacted on schools. Traditionally ameliorative measures revolved around the logic of compensatory education programs aimed at reducing the impact of poverty on children, but increasingly schools are expected to enact curriculum which is responsive to the multiple forms of social and cultural oppression embedded in the community at large. The expansion of multicultural education and the introduction of womens studies, anti-racism programs and Aboriginal studies in schools testify to this shift in direction. However, in what might be regarded as an extreme right backlash to political correctness and progressive social legislation, we are now witnessing the growth of organizations espousing nationalist, racist, sexist and religious fundamentalist ideologies.

## Poverty and Economic Inequality

Rising levels of economic inequality and poverty in Australia, as documented by Greig, Lewins, and White (2003), Vinson (2007), and Schraeder (2004) and ACOSS (2011), have reinforced long-standing patterns of disadvantage experienced by low socioeconomic groups. From a schooling perspective, these realities underscore the necessity of keeping social justice on the agenda and increasing (rather than diminishing) resources for programs to tackle educational disadvantages arising. In times when there has been a shift towards cultural explanations of oppression and injustices, they also confirm the need to hold fast to those analyzes grounded in the political economy and social class.

How should we conceptualize social justice today? In the past, social injustices were largely viewed through an economic lens with greatest emphasis attached to poverty and deprivation as measured by household income, employment, access to housing and other factors. The political solution to these problems was seen to reside in the application of redistributive justice, a notion closely associated with the work of John Rawls (1973) and brought to some degree of fruition in welfare state policies. However, as Young (1990) explains, merely redistributing material goods and services without confronting and transforming oppressive structures will not provide lasting solutions to inequalities and educational disadvantage. As I have alluded to above, the nature and causes of injustice have cultural, social and political dimensions that demand new responses from governments, policymakers and education institutions.

A growing awareness of the multifaceted nature of injustice has generated considerable discussion amongst philosophers and sociologists about the new discourses and relative importance that should be attached to economic and cultural factors. [See, in particular, the debates between feminist writers Iris Young (1990, 1997) and Nancy Fraser (1995, 1997).] According to Fraser, 'the most general meaning of justice is parity of participation' (p. 5) in spheres of economic, cultural and political life—a radical democratic interpretation of the principle of equal moral worth 'that requires social arrangements that permit all to participate as peers in social life' (p. 5). Fraser's (2005) reframing of justice around notions of distribution, recognition and representation is especially helpful in understanding the nature of injustices that permeate schools. She claims that people can suffer from (a) mal-distribution stemming from economic inequalities and the class structure of society, (b) status inequality or misrecognition arising from institutionalized hierarchies and cultural dimensions of injustice and (c) misrepresentation in the political life and decision-making processes of communities. What does this mean for schooling? According to Bates (2006), educational policy based around principles of social justice requires:

> the redress of maldistribution of educational access and resources through the redistribution of public resources to areas of greatest need; the redress of misrecognition through the implementation of policies of inclusion and the withdrawal of public support from institutionalised forms of exclusion ... and the redress of misrepresentation through the democratisation of educational leadership and the development of those capabilities that will facilitate the participation of all in the learning society and the creative enjoyment of its complex technical and cultural diversity. (p. 282)

Clearly, the magnitude of these injustices requires concerted action across the broad spectrum of society. Schools alone cannot transform the structural factors that lead to the maldistribution of wealth nor can they eliminate racism, sexism and other forms of social exclusion and cultural oppression. However, teachers in tandem with parents, teacher unions and community groups, can play an active role in contesting inequitable education policies and practises, advocating for a fairer funding system for disadvantaged schools, developing more socially just curriculum and fostering a sense of optimism, belongingness and trust amongst students.

## Teaching for Social Justice

A powerful case can be made for teaching for social justice but what does it mean in practise? Burns-Thomas (2007) suggests that it involves working simultane-ously on the immediate context—'the critical educational practices in schools and communities' (p. 3)—and the larger picture as it relates to oppressive social and economic structures. With regard to the former, Nieto (2000) explains that a concern for social justice means 'looking critically at why and how our schools are unjust for some students' (p. 183), a practise that involves:

> analyzing school policies and practices—the curriculum, textbooks and materials, instructional strategies, tracking, recruitment and hiring of staff, and parent involvement strategies—that devalue the identities of some students while overvaluing others. (p. 183)

Aside from focusing on the individual lives of children in school, teaching for social justice can also be said to involve the development of curricula and pedagogies that promote an understanding of the causes of human oppression; educate children about human rights, global poverty and the environment; model democratic practices and encourage action in support of oppressed groups. From this perspective, being concerned about social injustices involves seeing schooling as a preparation for active citizenship, not just a place for individuals to compete for credentials that will further their vocational aspirations. Cochran-Smith et al. (2009) argue that teaching for social justice 'reflects a central and essential purpose of teaching in a democratic society, wherein the teacher is an advocate for students whose work supports larger efforts for social change' (p. 349). Importantly, teaching for social justice should not proceed from some abstract position removed from the lives of students and the classroom, rather, as Kohl (1998, p. 286) reminds us, 'we have to root our struggles for social justice in the work we do on an everyday level in a particular community with a particular group of students'. Ayers et al. (1998) sums up the challenge as follows:

> Teaching for social justice demands a dialectical stance: one eye fixed firmly on the students—Who are they? What are their hopes, dreams, and aspirations? Their passions and commitments? What skills, abilities and capacities does each bring to the classroom—and the other eye fixed firmly at the concentric circles of context—historical flow, cultural surround, economic reality ... the fundamental message of the teacher for social justice is: You can change the world. (Ayers, Hunt, & Quinn, 1998, p. xvii)

This does not mean abandoning standards or engaging in laissez-faire pedagogies. On the contrary, as Rose points out 'those of us concerned with social justice need to take back the discussion of "standards", "rigor" and "academics" from conservative spokespeople and reframe it in a way consonant with a social justice agenda' (Ayers et al., 1998, p. 52). In a very real sense, socially just outcomes for children can only be realized when teachers implement a rigorous and engaging curriculum, work to improve literacy and numeracy standards, create a climate of trust and care for students and practise democracy in their own classrooms.

Having identified the broad parameters of teaching for social justice, I now focus on school structures, curricula and pedagogies that address issues of distributive, recognitive and representative justice discussed previously.

## *Distributive Justice*

Anyon (2005) points out that an unjust economy and the policies through which it is attained create enormous barriers to educational success for many young people. Children from poor families are generally the least successful in schooling and the hardest to teach by traditional methods. According to Connell (1994), they are 'the least powerful of the school's clients ... [and] the most dependent on schools for their educational resources' (p. 125). Arguably, distributive justice in education has been something of a driving force in government initiatives to create a more accessible education system, firstly in elementary schooling and latterly in secondary and tertiary education (Connell, 1993). The compensatory education programs of the 1970s and 1980s sought to ameliorate educational inequality through a greater allocation of resources to schools serving low socioeconomic communities. Although a step in the right direction, the Disadvantaged Schools Program even at its height was a small scale project reaching a minority of students. Indices of disadvantage continue to play a role in differential funding arrangements for schools, but a great divide in education is sustained through Commonwealth funding arrangements which have seen a massive shift of monies to elite, well-endowed private schools. To the nation's shame, the socioeconomic status of students still remains a major factor in accounting for the great discrepancies in educational achievement amongst students.

Clearly, there are limits to what schools can achieve in reducing economic inequalities. Far-lasting change can only be achieved by reforming public policy to generate sustainable employment opportunities, guarantee fair wage conditions and improve the physical and social infrastructure of urban communities. Distributive justice demands that a much greater share of public resources be directed to schools and communities in greatest need. For their part, schools and teachers have a responsibility to ensure that the funds available to them are utilized in ways that cater for the most marginalized students rather than sustaining privilege through programs focused exclusively on the academically elite and talented.

Whilst a good deal of emphasis in distributive justice is attached to the fairer al-location of material goods, Connell (1993) suggests that non-material goods need to be factored in to the equation. Importantly, the curriculum itself should be regarded a key element in distributive justice. Although the notion of a curriculum entitle-ment underpins education policy, there is a tendency on the part of middle-class educators to harbor low expectations of students from working-class backgrounds. Assuming that they do not have the aptitude to engage in intellectually challenging work, they are often consigned to non-academic or vocationally oriented courses. A 'pedagogy of poverty' (Haberman, 1991) perpetuates educational disadvantage by limiting post-school employment and tertiary education options for young people in low socioeconomic communities. According to Connell, an inclusive common curriculum 'must be provided to all students as a matter of social justice' (p. 46). In the light of these concerns, teachers might ask: How does poverty impact on the lives and opportunities of our students? Are all students able to access educational programs and resources that meet their individual and collective needs? What policies and practises are in place to support students who do not have access to resources, such as computers, newspapers and texts, in their homes?

Directing funds to support the needs of the most disadvantaged is a crucial element in teaching for social justice, but as Connell (1993, p. 18) reminds us education is a social process in which the question of 'how much' cannot be separated from the 'what'. Simply redistributing resources without confronting the fundamental issues of class, patriarchy and racism within the curriculum will not ensure social justice in schooling.

## *Recognitive Justice*

According to Gale and Densmore (2000), recognitive justice advocates three necessary conditions for social justice: the fostering of respect for different social groups through their self-identification, opportunities for self-development and self-expression and the participation of groups in decision-making through group representation, historically, the interests and aspirations of minority groups have not always been well served by schools. A competitive, academic curriculum has tended to privilege the knowledge and values of white, middle-class males from dominant groups in society whilst excluding girls, working-class students and those from a minority culture. Rich literacy practises of ethnic groups, working-class communities and indigenous Australians have often been ignored or devalued. However, there are promising signs of change. Schools are creating a climate of support for reconciliation with Aboriginal people, and many have shown a greater willingness to confront issues to do with gender, disability, multiculturalism and the environment.

Teachers and schools can do much to promote the ideals of recognitive justice in education through curricula and pedagogies that build relationships based on mutual trust, respect and care (Smyth, Angus, Down, & McInerney, 2008), and by fostering an understanding and appreciation of cultural diversity. Acknowledging the importance of students' family and cultural backgrounds, socially committed teachers value and utilize local funds of knowledge to enhance student learning. A connectionist pedagogy (Goodman & Kuzmic, 1997; Prosser, Lucas, & Reid, 2010) allows them to link classroom learning to the diverse lives, backgrounds and aspirations of their students. Place-based education (McInerney, Smyth, & Down, 2011; Smith, 2002) can play an important part in supporting the principles of recognitive justice by 'authorising locally produced knowledge' (Mills & Gale, 2001, p. 10) and engaging students in forms of learning that promote community development, civic responsibility and a commitment to the welfare of others (Melanville, Berg, & Blank, 2006). However, as Gruenewald (2003) points out, place-based learning needs to incorporate a critical dimension that encourages educators and young people 'to reflect on the relationship between the kind of education they pursue and the kind of places we inhabit and leave behind for future generations' (p. 3). Rather than endorsing the status quo, a critical pedagogy of place seeks to raise young people's awareness of inequitable structures and oppressive relationships within communities. Just as importantly, it invites young people to contemplate social action in support of the most oppressed and to work for a more just society.

Pursuing a critical pedagogy is not an easy path for teachers, but there are resources for nurturing the critical capacities of students and promoting social activism. In *Rethinking Globalization*, Bigelow and Peterson (2002) claim that teachers can assist students to gain an understanding of social justice by getting them to connect their everyday habits to global concerns, such as climate change, water scarcity, poverty and trade. However, beyond explaining injustices, they also suggest that teachers can encourage students to think about what action they can take to make a difference within their own communities. For this to happen, they must be actively involved in decision-making forums and processes within schools and communities.

## *Representative Justice*

The dimension of representative justice encompasses the political realms of governance structures, decision-making processes and the ways in which individuals and groups participate in civic life. In the context of schools, it applies to the ways in which students, parents, teachers and community members are actively engaged in developing a shared educational vision and socially just education programs for young people. According to Giroux, youth have increasingly been left out of discussions about democracy, rights, justice and compassion. 'We need to create spaces for youth to speak, represent themselves, and organize,' he says (Ayers et al., 1998, p. 290). Delpit states that one of the most revolutionary tasks of socially committed educators is to teach young people the skills and perspectives needed for real participation in a democratic society (Ayers et al., 1998, p. 51). Giving students a say in what they learn and how they learn is surely one of the most fundamental aspects of representative justice. Schools that are committed to democratic ideals take seriously what students have to say about the content of the curriculum, the conditions that affect their learning, the approaches to teaching and the fairness or otherwise of assessment and reporting practises. Goodman (1992) argues that teachers can play a pivotal role by creating 'islands of democracy' in their own classrooms and by designing learning experiences that promote democratic sensibilities amongst young people.

Research into the factors that enhance school retention and student engagement (Smyth & McInerney, 2007; Smyth et al., 2008, 2010) confirms the critical importance of student voice and democratic practises in connecting students to school. When students are routinely involved in negotiating curriculum with their peers and teachers, they not only develop a greater sense of ownership of their learning but also learn something of the politics of compromise and decision-making.

Shor (1996) captures a sense what is involved in representative justice through his notion of the dialogic school where decisions are made on the basis of dialogue, debate, research and informed discussion within the community. This provides an authentic example to young people of what it means to live in a democratic community.

In summary, teaching for social justice is a political, pedagogical and moral commitment that engages teachers in working for redistributive, recognitive and representative justice in their own schools and communities. Perhaps the idea of 'teaching for social justice' does not fully capture what is involved. Writing about his philosophy as a school principal, George Wood comments:

> I do not believe you can teach for social justice—you must live for social justice. To learn about social justice is to experience it ... For educators, the only response to this is to make our schools places where social justice is practised. (Ayers et al., 1998, p. 248)

Wood makes it clear that we have to look beyond social justice as a curriculum package. It is only when schools are communities where social justice is practiced that can we claim to be teaching that justice.

Up to this point, the focus has been on school-based practises that support the idea of socially just curriculum. What are the implications for teacher educators? How might they support novice teachers to undertake this challenging work? I now want to consider some of the dilemmas and possibilities confronting teacher educators engaged in this task.

## Teacher Education for Social Justice

Advocacy for a social justice agenda in teacher education features prominently in the writings of Cochran-Smith (2000, 2004), Darling-Hammond (2005), Delpit (1995), Kohl (2003), Giroux (2006), Nieto (2005, 2009), Ayers (2004), Connell (1993), Griffiths (1998), Gale and Densmore (2000), and Smyth (2006) and the work of education networks for social justice in the United States and elsewhere. Challenging traditional approaches, Cochran-Smith claims that the most important goals of teacher education should encompass social responsibility, social change and social justice. In a similar vein, Nieto (2000) contends that equity needs to be placed at the forefront and centre of teacher education, rather than being confined to the margins. She argues:

> If teachers and prospective teachers learn to challenge societal inequities that place some students at a disadvantage over others, if they learn to question unjust institutional policies and practices, if they learn about and use the talents of students and their families in the curriculum, if they undergo a process of personal transformation based on their own identities and experiences, and, ... if they are prepared to engage with colleagues in a collaborative and imaginative encounter to transform their own practices to achieve equal and high-quality education for all students, then the outcome is certain to be a more positive one than is currently the case. (p. 186)

Teacher education programs in Australian universities typically have components which focus on the social context of teaching and attempt to develop an awareness of the influence of gender, social class, ethnicity, disability, racism and other factors on the education of students. However, there are impediments to implementing social justice agendas in teacher education. Delpit (1995) claims that prospective teachers are often exposed to descriptions of failure rather than models of success, especially with regard to students from single-parent households, culturally diverse backgrounds and low socioeconomic circumstances. A deficit discourse is perpetuated in policy and practise through the use of labels such as 'at risk', 'learning disabled' and 'the underclass' (p. 178). Aspiring teachers come to believe that 'culturally different' children are mismatched to the school setting and cannot be expected to achieve as much as white middle-class students. Negative indoctrination of this kind can lead to lowered academic expectation and a tendency to focus on the basics of numeracy and literacy to the exclusion of rigorous and engaging curriculum.

A second issue arises from the move towards a privatized, market-based model of teacher training based on so-called scientific evidence supporting the introduction of short courses for graduates to enter the teaching profession. It could well be the case that many newly appointed teachers will enter the profession with scant knowledge of, or exposure to, the social and cultural foundations of education, or to the pedagogy, learning theories and complete clinical internship under the guidance of experienced teachers (Abbate-Vaughn, 2005; Cochran-Smith, 2004). An interrelated problem concerns the highly technicist approaches to teaching and learning that underpin a good deal of education reform in the neoliberal state. Teacher educators have always had to confront the 'method fetish'—the belief that techniques and methodologies are all that are needed to teach effectively—but now, more than ever, teachers' work is being construed in highly instrumental ways with the pressure on teachers to teach to the test, concentrate on the basics of literacy and numeracy and deliver a vocationally oriented curriculum (Abbate-Vaughn,2005; Whitehead, 2007). According to Giroux (2005), a 'conservative assault' and 'new authoritarianism' have worked their way into teacher training institutions with calls for more practise-based training and an emphasis on skills and competencies rather than critical literacies and social activism. Indeed, there has been a deliberate attempt to discredit the social justice agendas of schools and teacher education programs, especially those promoting critical literacies and social activism which are seen to be politically and ideologically motivated.

A further problem stems from the apparent disjuncture between theory and practise (Borrero, 2009)—between what prospective teachers learn about social justice in their university courses and the difficulties of putting this knowledge into practise in schools. Lacking in-school support, feeling isolated, threatened and disillusioned, they have a tendency to give up on their pre-service ideals and revert to 'safe' methods of teaching (Chubbuck, 2008). In the circumstances, they are inclined to blame teacher educators for their inadequate preparation for the difficulties encountered in classroom teaching.

In summary, there are at least three pressing challenges to sustaining a commitment to the vision of socially just teaching proposed by Nieto (2000) and Cochran-Smith (2004):

- How to affirm the relevance of teaching for social justice—to view it as an outcome in education not just an add-on
- How to reconceptualize teaching as intellectual, transformative work and encourage the development of critically reflective practises amongst teachers
- How to support teachers to keep the vision of social justice alive when they embark on their teaching careers.

## Social Justice as an Outcome

All too often, social justice is seen as an add-on rather than constituting the core of teaching and learning in schools and teacher education programs. What counts in schooling outcomes is often restricted to the functional aspects of literacy and numeracy as measured by blunt instruments, such as the NAPLAN tests, administered through centralized education systems. However, whether students succeed or not in formal education largely depends on the relational, cultural and social aspects of schooling (Smyth et al., 2008). Cochran-Smith (2004) calls for teacher educators to 'demonstrate to others that social justice itself is a valid outcome and an essential purpose of teacher preparation' (p. 168), as opposed to letting others define effective teacher education in the narrower terms of student achievement in standardized tests. Cochran-Smith et al. (2009) make the argument that school success for the most disadvantaged students is highly dependent on socially just teaching practises. Accordingly, teacher education for social justice 'is an agenda that not only does not shortchange attention to students' learning but in fact makes enhancing students' learning and their life chances its core commitment' (p. 349). Shields and Mohan (2008) reinforce this view:

- Teaching in socially just ways is not only a prerequisite for students' intellectual growth and improved outcomes, but for educating citizens who will become agents of change for themselves and others in the quest for a more just society. (p. 289).

## Teaching as Intellectual and Transformative Work

To suggest that teachers should work in transformative ways by speaking out against unjust schooling practises and working collectively to affect school reform runs counter to popular conceptions of their roles as implementers rather than innovators, or doers, rather than thinkers. Nieto (2005) argues that there needs to be a fundamental shift in the culture of teacher preparation to include issues other than 'curriculum and pedagogy. In her view, it means 'encouraging teachers to view teaching as intellectual work, to learn about their students' identities and lives, and to be intellectually curious and questioning' (p. 40). Rather than conceiving of the problem of teacher education as a purely technical', it needs to be regarded as 'an intellectual and political question related to issues of equity and social justice' (p. 40). The development of critically reflective practises amongst teachers (and teacher educators) is a crucial element in this shift. According to Nieto (2005), unless prospective teachers have access to texts that challenge conventional knowledge and unless they engage in deep reflection about their own knowledge and the curriculum they will teach, they are unlikely to develop the practise of questioning mainstream knowledge (p. 34).

## Connecting Theory and Practice

How can new teachers combine effective classroom practise with a vision for social justice? According to Borrero (2009), new teachers need to be able to have access to this combination 'not only through curriculum in their teacher education program, but through a community of other new teachers dedicated to social justice' (p. 222). Borrero claims most dedicated new teachers will become skilful at their craft within a few years of their teaching but 'what will keep them active, passionate, and driven to stay in the classroom … is a vision for success that goes beyond classroom practice' (p. 226). Support teams and mentoring arrangements involving school practitioners and teacher educators can play a role in furthering this goal. Borrero describes how the Teacher Education for the Advancement of a Multicultural Society (TEAMS) Program at the University of San Francisco supports newly appointed teachers through professional development activities that focus on community engagement.

Putting a theory of socially just teaching into practise is problematic in the current political context. Kohl (2003) acknowledges that any radical teacher education program 'has to consider the tension between developing critical, perceptive, skilled and motivated new activist teachers, and the grim realities and struggles they will be likely to face while working in poor urban public schools' (p. 142). For Kohl, this involved developing anti-racist curriculum and helping teachers to develop skills that would enable them to teach to high standards 'while they developed material that respected the knowledge of the students and the school's community' (p. 143). Importantly, it implied preparing them as much as possible to work against the grain and be willing to see themselves as change agents. In the program he developed in San Francisco, Kohl sought to expose students to experienced people whose work in education and social justice had been effective.

## Concluding Comments

In this chapter, I have sought to show how teachers and teacher educators can work in socially just ways to confront the systemic barriers to education experienced by many young people. This is a complex and demanding task in the current political climate where neoliberal and neoconservative reforms have damaged the profession of teaching and undermined the notion of education as a public good. In spite of the impediments, many teachers are fired with a passion for social justice and demonstrate on a daily basis a willingness to go the extra yards for students who are doing it tough. However, social justice in schooling cannot be achieved solely by the efforts of individuals. It is crucially important that those engaged in this work, teachers reword, build alliances with colleagues, administrators and citizens committed to practises of freedom, justice and equality (Anyon, 2005). Because the task of reforming education cannot be separated from the larger goal of building a more equitable society, critical educators need to become community activists who link educational issues to community concerns, such as employment, wage justice, housing, public transport and welfare. As Shields and Mohan (2008) point out, teachers are not social workers or politicians, and they cannot be expected to effect change in the immediate material and social conditions of their students' lives. However, 'they can and should develop pedagogical understandings and strategies that make the classroom more inclusive, more equitable, and that make it a training ground for democratic citizenship' (p. 297).

Certainly the challenges are daunting, but there are resources of hope in schools and communities that can promote the ideals of socially just schooling.

## References

Abbate-Vaughn, J. (2005). Book review of walking the road: Race, diversity, and social justice in teacher education. *Educational Studies, 38*(3), 298–302.

Anyon, J. (2005). *Radical possibilities: Public policy, urban education and a new social movement.* New York: Routledge.

Australian Council of Social Services. (2011). *ACOSS Indicators of inequality fact sheet.* Redfern, Australia: ACOSS.

Ayers, W. (2004). *Teaching the personal and the political: Essays on hope and justice.* New York: Teachers College Press.

Ayers, W., Hunt, J., & Quinn, T. (Eds.). (1998). *Teaching for social justice.* New York: Teachers College Press.

Bates, R. (2006). Public education, social justice and teacher education. *Asia-Pacific Journal of Teacher Education, 34*(3), 275–286.

Bigelow, B., & Petersen, B. (2002). *Rethinking globalization: Teaching for justice in an unjust world.* Milwaukee, WI: Rethinking Schools Press.

Borrero, N. (2009). Preparing new teachers for urban teaching: Creating a community dedicated to social justice. *Multicultural Perspectives, 11*(4), 221–226.

Bradley, D. (2006, Friday June 23). Quality of education a class struggle. *Adelaide Advertiser,* p. 18.

Burns-Thomas, A. (2007). Supporting new visions for social justice teaching: The potential for professional development networks. *Penn GSE Perspectives on Urban Education, 5*(1), 1–18.

Carnoy, M. (1998). Globalisation and educational restructuring. *Melbourne Studies in Education, 39*(2), 21–40.

Chubbuck, S. (2008). A novice teacher's beliefs about socially just teaching: Dialogues of many voices. *The New Educator, 4*, 309–329.

Cochran-Smith, M. (2000). Editorial: Teacher education at the turn of the century. *Journal of Teacher Education, 51*(3), 163–165.

Cochran-Smith, M. (2004). *Walking the road: Race, diversity and social justice in teacher education.* New York: Teachers College Press.

Cochran-Smith, M., Barnatt, J., Lahann, R., Shakman, K., & Terrell, D. (2009). Teacher education for social justice: Critiquing the critiques. In W. Ayers, T. Quinn, & D. Stovall (Eds.), *The handbook of social justice in education* (pp. 625–639). London: Taylor & Francis.

Cochran-Smith, M., Shakman, K., Jong, C., Terrell, D., Barnatt, J., & McQuillan, P. (2009). Good and just teaching: The case for social justice in teacher education. *American Journal of Education, 115*, 347–377.

Connell, R. (1993). *Schools and social Justice.* Leichardt, Australia: Pluto Press.

Connell, R. (1994). Poverty and education. *Harvard Educational Review, 64*(2), 125–149.

Darling-Hammond, L. (2005). Educating the new educator: Teacher education and the future of democracy. *The New Educator, 1*(1), 1–18.

Delpit, L. (1995). *Other people's children: Cultural conflicts in the classroom.* New York: The New Press.

Fraser, N. (1995). Debate: Recognition or redistribution? A critical reading of Young's 'justice and the politics of difference. *The Journal of Political Philosophy, 3*(3), 166–180.

Fraser, N. (1997). *Justice interruptus: Critical reflections on the "postsocialist" condition.* New York: Routledge.

Fraser, N. (2005). Reframing justice in a globalizing world. *New Left Review, 36*(1–19).

Freire, P. (2004). *Pedagogy of hope: Reliving pedagogy of the oppressed.* Boulder, Colorado: Westview Press.

Gale, T., & Densmore, K. (2000). *Just schooling: Explorations in the cultural politics of teaching.* Buckingham, PA: Open University Press.

Giroux, H. (1985). Theories of reproduction and resistance in the new sociology of education: A critical analysis. *Harvard Educational Review, 53*(5), 257–293.

Giroux, H. (2005). The conservative assault on America: Cultural politics, education and the new authoritarianism. *Cultural Politics, 1*(2), 139–164.

Giroux, H. (2006). *The Giroux reader.* Boulder, CO: Paradigm Publishers.

Goodman, J. (1992). *Elementary schooling for critical democracy.* New York: State University of New York Press.

Goodman, J., & Kuzmic, J. (1997). Bringing a progressive pedagogy to conventional schools: Theoretical and practical implications from Harmony. *Theory into Practice, 36*(2), 79–86.

Greig, A., Lewins, F., & White, K. (2003). *Inequality in Australia.* Port Melbourne, Australia: Cambridge University Press.

Griffiths, M. (1998). The discourses of social justice in schools. *British Educational Research Journal, 24*(3), 301–316.

Gruenewald, D. (2003). The best of both worlds: A critical pedagogy of place. *Educational Researcher, 32*(4), 3–12.

Haberman, M. (1991). The pedagogy of poverty versus good teaching. *Phi Delta Kappan, 23*(4), 290–294.

Kohl, H. (1998). Some reflections on teaching for social justice. In W. Ayers, J. Hunt, & T. Quinn (Eds.), *Teaching for social justice* (pp. 285–287). New York: New York Press.

Kohl, H. (2003). *Stupidity and tears: Teaching and learning in troubled times.* New York: New Press.

Lingard, B., Mills, M., & Hayes, D. (2000). Teachers, school reform and social justice: Challenging research and practice. *Australian Educational Researcher, 27*(3), 99–115.

McInerney, P. (2004). *Making hope practical: School reform for social justice*. Flaxton, Australia: Post Pressed.

McInerney, P. (2007). From naive optimism to robust hope: Sustaining a commitment to social justice and teacher education in neoliberal times. *Asia-Pacific Journal of Teacher Education, 35*(3), 257–272.

McInerney, P., Smyth, J., & Down, B. (2011). 'Coming to a place near you?' the politics and possibilities of a critical pedagogy of place-based education. *Asia-Pacific Journal of Teacher Education, 39*(1), 3–16.

Melanville, A., Berg, A., & Blank, M. (2006). *Community based learning: Engaging for success and citizenship*. Washington, DC: Coalition for Community Schools.

Mills, C., & Gale, T. (2001). *The 'ideal': What does this mean for schools and their communities?* Paper presented at the Australian Association for Research in Education, Fremantle.

Nieto, S. (2000). Placing equity front and centre: Some thoughts on transforming teacher education for the new century. *Journal of Teacher Education, 51*(3), 180–187.

Nieto, S. (2005). Social justice in hard times: Celebrating the vision of Dr. Martin Luther King, Jr. *Multicultural Perspectives, 7*(1), 3–7.

Nieto, S. (2009). *Social justice in education: Preparing teachers for diversity*. Chicago: National-Louis University.

Prosser, B., Lucas, B., & Reid, A. (Eds.). (2010). *Connecting lives and learning: Renewing pedagogy in the middle years*. Kent Town, SA: Wakefield Press.

Rawls, J. (1973). *A theory of justice*. Oxford, UK: Oxford University Press.

Schraeder, T. (2004). Poverty and health in Australia. *New Doctor, 80*, 17–19.

Shields, C., & Mohan, E. (2008). High quality education for all students: Putting social justice at its heart. *Teacher Development, 12*(4), 289–300.

Shor, I. (1996). Education is politics: Paulo Freire's critical pedagogy. In P. McLaren & P. Leonard (Eds.), *Paulo Freire: A critical encounter* (pp. 25–35). London: Routledge.

Smith, G. (2002). Place-based education: Learning to be where we are. *Phi Delta Kappan, 83*(8), 584–594.

Smyth, J. (2006). The politics of reform of teachers' work and the consequences for schools: Some implications for teacher education. *Asia-Pacific Journal of Teacher Education, 34*(3), 301–319.

Smyth, J., Angus, L., Down, B., & McInerney, P. (2008). *Critically engaged learning: Connecting to young lives*. New York: Peter Lang.

Smyth, J., Down, B., & McInerney, P. (2010). *Hanging in with kids in tough times: Engagement in contexts of educational disadvantage in the relational school*. New York: Peter Lang.

Smyth, J., & McInerney, P. (2007). *Teachers in the middle: Reclaiming the wasteland of the adolescent years of schooling*. New York: Peter Lang.

Vinson, T. (2007). *Dropping off the edge: The distribution of disadvantage in Australia*. Richmond, Australia: Jesuit Social Services and Catholic Social Services Australia.

Whitehead, K. (2007). Addressing social difference with prospective teachers who want "to make a difference". *Asia-Pacific Journal of Teacher Education, 35*(4), 367–385.

Williams, R. (1989). *Resources of hope*. London: Verso.

Young, I. (1990). *Justice and the politics of difference*. Princeton, NJ: Princeton University Press.

Young, N. (1997). Unruly categories: A critique of Nancy Fraser's dual system's theory. *New Left Review, 222*, 147–160.

# Chapter 4
# Preparing Teachers as Informed Professionals: Working with a Critical Ethnographic Disposition and a Socially Democratic Imaginary

Lawrence Angus

There can be little doubt that we currently live in interesting educational times. During the past 20–30 years, there have been major changes in government and public thinking about education. This has occurred in Australia and in most Western countries (Alexander, 2009; Lingard, 2010) and also in many developing nations (Nordtveit, 2010). There has been what Ball (2006, p. 10) and many others regard as 'a major *transformation* in the organising principles of social provision right across the public sector'. Although Ball's main concern is with education, his point is that the nature of western society as a whole, including its underlying values and organising norms, has substantially changed in less than a generation. In this chapter, I describe changes in values and policy directions that have occurred in Australia and elsewhere and explain the impact of such changes on the teaching profession. I will argue that the changes, by and large, have had a deleterious effect on teaching and have, in fact, contributed to a substantial deprofessionalisation of teachers to the point that serious debate is needed on what kind of schooling is desirable for the twenty-first century and what kind of teachers universities should be endeavouring to educate.

## Teaching Within an Entrenched, Neoliberal Policy Regime

In western societies, like Australia, governments seem to have become enchanted by a narrow kind of economic rationality (Pusey, 1991) that embraces managerialism, competition, standards, markets and measurement, all of which have become characteristic of institutional life in the twenty-first century. When it comes to education as a social institution, Anderson (2009) maintains that, compared with

L. Angus (✉)
School of Education and Arts, University of Ballarat, Mt Helen, VIC, Australia
e-mail: l.angus@ballarat.edu.au

B. Down and J. Smyth (eds.), *Critical Voices in Teacher Education*, Explorations
of Educational Purpose 22, DOI 10.1007/978-94-007-3974-1_4,
© Springer Science+Business Media Dordrecht 2012

the humanistic goals that had largely characterised education a generation ago, 'economic goals have undeniably become front and center in the wake of the ascendancy of neoliberalism with its emphasis on the individual's human capital and its promotion of a competition state that has intensified competition among individuals' (p. 51). The discourse of neoliberalism has had a profound effect on the nature of education and the education profession. It is in this relatively newly established status quo that teacher graduates will have to try to restore an 'educational rationality' rather than the current, particularly narrow, 'economic rationality' (Pusey) to the institution of education.

In order to drive national economic competitiveness, there has been an emphasis on so-called failing schools and teachers and on regulating schools and teaching in order to ensure that 'standards' are raised. This thinking has resulted in policies of narrow accountability, market competition among schools and the use of 'league tables' to rank 'successful' and 'failing' schools against each other. The logic assumes that individual teachers and students are to blame for 'poor performance'. This way of framing education is extremely dangerous and damaging to educational values as it decreases the professional autonomy of educators (Anderson, 2009; Ball, 2006, 2003). The 'standards agenda' displays a managerial approach to policymaking that results in teaching and learning being regarded as technical processes that occur within the 'black box' of the school.

My colleagues and I have argued elsewhere (Smyth, Angus, Down, & McInerney, 2009) that the type of teacher professionalism that is assumed to be appropriate within the neoliberal policy perspective might be described as 'technical/managerial'. We have elaborated on this constrained conception of teacher professionalism (pp. 96–101) in a way that is summarised in Table 4.1, and we have distinguished this restricted view from an engaged, relational type we have described as 'participative/professional'. As previously (Smyth et al., 2009, p. 96), I need to acknowledge that the terms 'technical', 'managerial', 'participative' and 'professional' have no universal or unproblematic meanings. I use them below not in an attempt to construct any actual binary but simply to distinguish between different ways of conceptualising teacher behaviour. Nonetheless, the 'participative/professional' way of conceptualising teaching, I would argue, describes the kind of courageous, socially responsible and politically informed teacher graduates that are needed to grapple with the threats and possibilities of the future.

If we accept that the role of teacher education institutions is to prepare teachers who are well informed and who think about, and are active in debates about, education and the nature of the education profession, then we might anticipate that teacher graduates should be steeped in the characteristics listed in the right-hand column of the figure. We would expect them to be engaged, critically reflective practitioners who regard themselves as 'players' in educational politics and policy. At stake in the politics of education are different values, principles and approaches to 'doing' education. But educational ideas and values seem to be largely missing from the current education policy agenda, which is strongly aligned with the needs of the economy (Apple, 2001; Pusey, 1991). This linkage has profound implications for ways in which the purposes of education are regarded.

**Table 4.1** 'Technical/managerial' and 'participative/professional' ways of seeing professional educational practice (Adapted from Smyth et al., 2009, p. 97)

| Technical/managerial | Participative/professional |
|---|---|
| *Characterised by* | |
| *Implementation* mentality associated with top-down, external control and educational conformity to specified rules and ends | *Reformulation* mentality associated with internal expertise and processes and openness to educational alternatives |
| *Bureaucratic/hierarchical roles* specified by managerialist rationality | *Social actors* in a specific context in which roles are open, at least in part, to negotiation and change |
| People at the school level are largely *objects* of organisational management/policy, which is *done* to them | People at the school level are largely *subjects* who participate in the creation/utilisation/adaptation of organisational policy and practices |
| *Technical rationality* prevails with an emphasis on delivery of mandated requirements and top-down accountability for performance | *Social/educational* concerns and issues prevail with an emphasis on being answerable to community needs and to professional, educational values |
| School-level participants *take* problems as defined by policy/hierarchy: problems and solutions are identified in school effectiveness and/or managerial discourses to which 'best practice' and the incorporation of school effectiveness factors should apply | School-level participants *make* problems as identified through the 'good practice' of local participants: issues are identified in relation to the local context and within a broad understanding of the relationship between educational and social responsibilities |
| Emphasis is on *efficiency and effectiveness*: achieving pre-specified results and targets | Emphasis is on *worthwhileness*: achieving educational and social gains that are empowering to local participants |
| *Performativity*: students as 'clients' and emphasis on narrowly defined student and teacher performance as specified in a top-down manner | *Engagement*: students as 'members' and co-learners with teachers and others who strive to be relevant to and respectful of local contexts |
| *Results in* | |
| Linear outcomes/predicted results/deprofessionalisation | Uncertain effects/diverse consequences/professional responsibility |

An important distinction can be made between the two broad conceptualisations of teacher professionalism outlined in Table 4.1 in terms of their relationship to social context. In technical/managerial approaches, context is largely a backdrop or a source of inputs to which the school must respond by appropriate managerial action. Close monitoring and accountability measures ensure that schools use their limited autonomy to 'do the right thing' in terms of imposed policies and mandates which are implemented largely unquestioningly. That is, the approach allows for very little, if any, real discretion at the local level. The emphasis is on the end product—the achievement of performance indicators and the implementation of mandated policies such that prescribed results are achieved and targets are met. In participative/professional approaches, however, the definition of problems and solutions within a school is a very complex matter. They are likely to be seen as related to the interaction between education and society and as matters that need to be addressed by schools as a whole rather than by managerial, technical means. In this conceptualisation, the school is likely to be regarded as a site of social, political and cultural interaction and negotiation. Educational processes and education policy are not seen as neutral, and participants are regarded as social and political actors rather than occupants of organisational roles. In other words, the participative/professional orientation requires an activist, socially critical perspective.

## What Do You Mean, Critical?

The literature on critical engagement in education is enormous (e.g. Anderson, 2009; Kinchloe, 2004; Mingers, 2000). This is partly because the term 'critical' has a number of possible interpretations. Mingers suggests four aspects of 'being critical', all of which involve some kind of reflective engagement and critique:

- Critical thinking—the *critique of rhetoric* (i.e. challenging people's arguments and propositions; suspending belief about particular statements; thinking outside the square about alternatives)
- Questioning conventional wisdom—the *critique of tradition* (i.e. not taking things for granted; challenging the status quo; questioning fundamental assumptions and established patterns of power and authority)
- Challenging the one dominant view—the *critique of authority* (i.e. refusing to accept that there is a single 'correct' answer to anything or 'one best way' of doing thing; recognising that there is a multiplicity of perspectives and questioning dominant view in order to try to see the world through the eyes of others)
- Being sceptical of information and knowledge—the *critique of objectivity* (i.e. recognising that knowledge and information are never value-free or objective; accepting that information and knowledge always reflect and/or are shaped by structures of power and interest)

(Adapted from Mingers, 2000, pp. 225–227)

A critical, *ethnographic* disposition would incorporate all of these aspects of being critical and, according to Lather (1986, p. 64), would be capable of pursuing 'transformative agendas' that 'challenge the *status quo* and [would] contribute to a more egalitarian social order'. Such critical thinking presents a direct contrast to positivist, technical-rational policy science, which fails to question the social circumstances out of which data and policy directives arise because they tend to assume the existence of a natural, 'real' social order which has a neutral, underlying value consensus. By treating conventional social and educational arrangements and social circumstances as if they occur naturally, this approach reifies existing social and political conditions, which are therefore treated as if they are immutable things that must necessarily be the way they are. The presumed neutrality and objectivity of such a disposition implicitly endorses the status quo and is consistent with current technical-rational approaches to education. These assume neutrality and common sense within a management paradigm of accountability. The neoliberal framework, market arrangements and heavy compliance regimes under which schools have increasingly had to operate have pushed and shoved teachers towards an impersonal attitude towards students and communities. According to Thomson, Hall, and Jones (2010, p. 652), this has resulted in an educational narrowing that inhibits more humane, richer, relevant, authentic and socially responsible forms of teaching while simultaneously eroding educational creativity and imagination through the

> ... equation of organizations, teachers and pupils into categories and numbers, where schooling is seen as infinitely calculable and available for calibration and permanently available for forensic dissection through apparently objective, scientific and transparent computational practices.

In such ways, students have become subject to a 'pedagogy of under-attainment' (p. 651) as they are translated into 'good data'. However, these authors remind us that

> ... good data [is] not the same as good education if that is taken to mean students being productively engaged in learning which is worthwhile and gives access to powerful concepts which have explanatory power in the world. (p. 653)

In contrast, critical approaches to understanding schools, teachers, students and learning attempt to deal with schools and communities as social sites in which wider social relations are played out and mediated through the everyday lived experiences and perceptions of the human agents involved. This is what Willis (2000) had in mind when he famously wrote about the 'ethnographic imagination' in a deliberate reference to the 'sociological imagination', which, as Mills (1959) explained, enables us to think beyond our 'personal troubles' by translating them into 'public issues' that require political action. This strategy helps us perceive the connections between our personal, micro-political lives and the larger macro forces that bear down upon and influence our society and our work. Particularly since the publication of by Willis (1977) of *Learning to Labor* in 1977, critical versions of ethnography, informed largely by theories of class, feminism and post-structuralism, have been important in illuminating the shortcomings of education in contributing to a more just and equitable society. A critical ethnographic perspective is particularly important for people who are intent on becoming teachers because, as McInerney (2009, p. 33) pointedly asks, 'if teachers don't critically reflect on their professional lives, how can we foster critical reflection amongst students?'

The kind of 'critical ethnographic disposition' referred to in the title of this chapter, then, is one that aims towards emancipatory and democratic goals, or, as Thomas (1993, p. 4) puts it, 'Critical ethnography is conventional ethnography with a political purpose'. Therefore, critical, socially relevant ethnography, which incorporates a spirit of professional enquiry and curiosity, interrogates how things came to be the way they are, what social forces sustain and maintain the situation and how people accommodate, resist and interrupt prevailing discourses. My point is not that all pre-service teachers need to become critical ethnographic researchers, but that, by adopting a spirit of enquiry, critique and interrogation in their everyday observations and practice, they will become better able to reflect on their work and to question, analyse and understand their own educational locales and the state of education more broadly. An immediate priority for such interrogation is the current economic framing of education, in which the education policy framework has become narrow and instrumental, and principals, teachers and, most importantly, students, in keeping with a technical/managerial perspective, are treated as objects of policy.

## Asserting and Contesting Subject Positions in Education

McGraw (2011, p. 105) explains that, instead of schools acknowledging their skills and competence and opening up for them new and empowering 'possibilities of being and knowing', many young people experience the 'worst' aspects of schooling. She states:

> At its worst, [school] narrows opportunities and creates formidable whirlpools of anxiety, fear and distrust. Schools 'sort' and 'shove' young people in ways that are both physical and imagined. They 'track, separate, segregate, apply the kind of "sorting machine" that favours the privileged and treats the others as mere objects, mere "things"' (Greene, 2008). This institutional preference for dividing and selecting, for noting and disregarding, leads to poor attendance at school, resistance, disengagement and early school leaving. (McGraw, 2011, p. 105)

Such schools are obviously not the best environments for enthusiastic teacher graduates who want to make a positive difference to the lives of their students, but many schools are like this within the current education policy regime. Moreover, it is not only students but also teachers who are terribly constrained within the current climate. As McGraw points out:

> Teachers too are struggling to maintain their own professional and personal identities in a profession that is increasingly moving beyond their control ... Teachers, like young people are shoved forcefully to the side and pressured to conform to the political, social and economic agendas of the day. They too are left feeling disoriented, disarmed and disengaged. Amidst such pressure, opportunities for open dialogue are minimised and relationships suffer. (2011, p. 110)

This last point is critical. The extraordinary emphasis on simplistic accountability through an overwhelming reliance on children's comparative performances on standardised, high-stakes testing cannot but have had a narrowing effect on educational practice. The thinking behind policies of narrow accountability, competition and the use of 'league tables' to rank schools against each other is more concerned about the culpability of individual students, schools and, particularly, teachers than with any form of progressive education or redressing educational injustice and inequality. Pushed into the background are the issues and problems of everyday life that must be dealt with inside and outside classrooms as part of the education of young people. The accountability regime defines what is 'officially' important educationally, but the multiple forms of educational disadvantage, and the many causes of disadvantage that exist in and around schools, have become largely irrelevant to considerations of educational reform. Local knowledge, locally generated, relevant curriculum and shared good teaching and learning practice tend to be disregarded. Hence, the need for the kind of teacher education programmes advocated by Darling-Hammond (2000, p. 170), which would 'engage prospective teachers in studying research and conducting their own enquiries through cases, action research, and the development of structured portfolios about practice', and would regard 'the job of teacher education as developing the capacity to enquire sensitively and systematically into the nature of learning and the effects of teaching'. Darling-Hammond (2000, p. 170) maintains that the benefits of teaching pre-service teachers about forms of enquiry are significant:

> Training in enquiry helps teachers learn how to look at the world from multiple perspectives, including those of students whose experiences are quite different from their own, and to use this knowledge in developing pedagogy so they can reach diverse learners.

Most importantly, Darling-Hammond (2000, p. 170) maintains:

> Developing the ability to see beyond one's own perspective, to put oneself in the shoes of the learner and to understand the meaning of that experience in terms of learning, is perhaps the most important role of universities in the preparation of teachers.

In order to exercise their critical ethnographic dispositions and to see beyond their own perspectives, pre-service teachers need to be helped to confront any deficit orientation of their own towards working-class children and their communities and, where necessary, transform their view into an assets-based orientation which would acknowledge, respect and value the alternative knowledge base and curriculum resources that can be drawn upon from within working-class communities and cultures (Cummins, 2001; Moll, Amanti, Neff, & Gonzalez, 1992; Smyth et al., 2009). By incorporating such assets into their teaching, teachers would be engaging in advocacy education while learning and teaching collaboratively with their students. Such collaborative power creation, according to Cummins (2001, p. 653), would 'start by acknowledging the cultural, linguistic, imaginative and intellectual resources poor children bring to school'. The kind of socially informed, qualitative understanding of the social context of schools and the lives and experiences of students that such a collaborative approach to pedagogy requires is vastly different from the managerial and measurement orientation of the neoliberal framework. It obviously offers a much richer notion of what being a teacher entails. As Cochran-Smith and Lytle (2004) explain:

> Teaching goes far beyond what teachers do when they stand in front of students, just as student learning is not limited to the classroom... It is about how teachers and their students construct the curriculum, commingling their experiences, their cultural and linguistic resources, and their interpretive frameworks. Teaching also entails how teachers' actions are infused with complex and multilayered understandings of learners, culture, class, gender, literacies, social issues, institutions, 'herstories' and histories, communities, materials, texts, and curricula.

This kind of socially critical and culturally relevant teaching takes account of the 'historically accumulated and culturally developed bodies of knowledge and skills essential for household or individual functioning and well-being' (Moll et al., 1992, p. 132). Moll and his colleagues are notable for their work in working-class communities 'to develop innovations in teaching that draw upon the knowledge and skills found in local households' (p. 132). Drawing on the concept of 'funds of knowledge', they argue that, 'by capitalizing on household and other community resources, we can organize classroom instruction that far exceeds in quality the rote-like instructions these children commonly encounter in schools' (p. 132). Instead, the teacher

> ... will know the child as a 'whole person', not merely as a 'student', taking into account or having knowledge about the multiple tiers of activity within which the child is enmeshed. In comparison, the typical teacher-student relationship seems 'thin' and 'single-stranded', as the teacher 'knows' the students only from their performance within rather limited classroom contexts. (Moll et al., 1992, pp. 133–134)

The important task for teacher educators is to develop the radical potential of this concept of 'funds of knowledge' among pre-service teachers so they can ensure that their classrooms will not be sealed off from the 'social worlds and resources of the community' (Moll et al., 1992, p. 134), which are alive and flourishing beyond the walls of the school. It is important for pre-service teachers to understand that, within their communities, children are already active and knowledgeable participants, not the 'passive bystanders' (p. 134) they are typically assumed to be in conventional classrooms and 'at risk' discourses. The critical ethnographic disposition of future teachers would come to the fore in investigating their students' worlds and attempting to make the school environment less strange and more familiar to them. According to Moll and colleagues, the pedagogical situation could then become one in which 'learning is motivated by the children's interests and questions; in contrast to [conventional] classrooms, knowledge is obtained by the children, not imposed by the adults' (p. 134). The school community would be viewed as a source of 'cultural and cognitive resources with great, potential utility for classroom instruction' (p. 134). This view, the authors point out:

> ... contrasts sharply with prevailing and accepted perceptions of working-class families as somehow disorganized socially and deficient intellectually; perceptions that are well accepted and rarely challenged in the field of education and elsewhere. (Moll et al., 1992, p. 134)

A critical ethnographic disposition would be cultivated in pre-service teachers by helping to make them alert to the rich social contexts of schools, the worth of local knowledge, the professional importance of locally generated and shared good teaching and learning practice and the power of curriculum and methods that are relevant to local circumstances. Such a disposition would seek out, and take into account, the knowledge, norms, cultures, assets and resources that young people bring with them to school. Pre-service teachers and teachers, as ethnographers within their communities, would attempt to uncover the different ways of seeing and knowing practised by students and their families.

In such ways, pre-service teachers would come to celebrate the essential human agency, creativity and obduracy of educators, community members, students and policy players at all levels, who work within the constraints of social structures, embedded power relations and professional cultures in order to create a 'space for challenge' of the obstacles to achieving social justice in education. Pre-service teachers, from a critical ethnographic perspective, would realise there is no avoiding the conclusion that education is a political and ideological arena in which they will be important players. Most importantly, it is critical that future teachers become alert to both micro- and macro-political influences on the nature of their work. As Bartolomé (2007) points out, they need to be able to critically examine dominant ideologies and taken-for-granted assumptions and practices that can thwart democratic education. She advises:

> This [approach] could include exposing students to (and encouraging them to provide insight given their own experiences) alternative explanations for the academic under-achievement of minorities, to the myth of meritocracy and how such a theory works to explain and justify the existing social (dis)order, and how assimilationist models reinforce antagonistic social relations and fundamentally undemocratic practices. What I am suggesting is that the teacher education curriculum (coursework and practicum experiences) be deliberately designed and carried out to expose prospective teachers to a variety of ideological postures so that they can begin to perceive their own ideologies in relation to others' and critically examine the damaging biases they may personally hold, and the inequalities and injustices in schools and in the society as a whole. (Bartolomé, 2007, p. 281)

Pre-service teachers must learn to become participative/professional teacher activists who will have sufficient confidence to assert their professionalism despite the climate of top-down managerial control and the powerful effects on the public consciousness of the neoliberal discourse of markets, testing, accountability, standards and the like.

## Addressing the Declining Professional Autonomy of Educators

The decline in the professional autonomy of teachers over the past three decades must be reversed. According to Ball (2003), the concept of 'performativity' has become associated with strategies of surveillance (such as publishing test scores and ranking schools) that consolidate a culture of compliance within the education profession. Teachers have become caught up in the 'politics of blame' as 'high-stakes' testing has imposed a powerful constraint on their work. The effect is that conceptions of what constitutes a 'good' teacher get distorted as do long-held and previously accepted beliefs about the purposes of schooling. The situation, as described by Fitzgerald (2008, p. 126), has reached the point where teachers have been 'removed from public debate and are now required to deliver organizational objectives; objectives that are linked with the demands of the global marketplace and economic capital'. Carr and Hartnett (1996, p. 195) regard this situation as a direct attack on teacher professionalism:

[T]he professionalism of teachers is based on the recognition of their right to make autonomous judgments about how, in particular institutional and classroom contexts, to develop their students' capacity for democratic deliberation, critical judgment and rational understanding. Without this kind of professional company, teachers have no protection against external coercion and pressure, and they quickly become neutral operatives implementing the 'directives' of their political masters and mistresses.

Within such a climate of mistrust, teacher subject positions have been challenged. Being a member of a profession implies the ability to assert what Bourdieu might call its professional culture or, more precisely in his terms, to define the professional field of teaching in terms of its distinctive cultural and symbolic capital. Members of the teaching professional field, then, should be able to define, assert and defend a body of norms and knowledge that, although never entirely stable, gives the profession grounds for claiming internal and external legitimacy. Thus, although contested, members are likely to keep asserting the status of their broad professional body of knowledge and, if they cannot, the nature and status of the profession will become more problematic as 'the cultural capital of the [professional] field is lost' (Oakes, Townley, & Cooper, 1998, p. 263).

Like Fitzgerald and the others quoted above, I would argue that the teacher professional field has been attacked and shaped in subtle and not-so-subtle technical/managerial ways for almost a generation. The importance of market competition, for example, has become universally recognised as a pragmatic imperative for schools. This is a strong illustration of the material effects of the performativity emphasis that Ball (2003) has emphasised. The cultural capital of the professional field has been problematised, and the characteristics of what might once have been widely associated with 'good teaching' (e.g. curriculum expertise, teaching and learning innovation, a social justice orientation, making the curriculum relevant in local contexts) would seem to have been devalued. In Bourdieu's terms, previously asserted versions of professional capital have been contested and reconstructed. As Oakes and colleagues (1998, p. 273) put it:

... redefining the [professional] field's dominant capital may not directly affect actors' intrinsic properties [e.g. a teacher's knowledge about and commitment to inclusive curriculum] but it does affect their relational properties (their position), because it affects their overall capital, and therefore their standing in the field. This, in turn, will have implications for an individual's sense of positional identity.

Mechanisms of market, managerialism and accountability, therefore, can be seen as transformative technologies in the implementation of change as much as being outcomes of change in themselves. They act as 'relay devices' that link 'government "mentalities" and policies with everyday organisational realities' (Ball, 1997, p. 327). Such 'realities' affect one's subject position and freedom of action. The discourses that link managerialism and standards, for instance, to the extent that they become regularised into organisational thinking and practices in schools, have a profound effect on understandings of the nature of education and of the education profession. The overall effect is that not only do conceptions of what constitutes a 'good' teacher get distorted in this process, but so do long established beliefs and understandings about the purposes of schooling:

Schooling has therefore mutated from a way of preparing young people for broader purposes (such as participation in democratic society) to a mechanism of selection and preparation for the local and global labour market. In other words, the unquestioned purpose and responsibility of schools is [now] to provide the workforce necessary to compete in the global economy. (Fitzgerald, 2008, p. 124)

The upshot is that technical/managerial, market-oriented, economically rational norms and assumptions have seemingly been imposed within a supposedly value-neutral education policy discourse. The professionalism of teachers has been restricted, and the technical/managerial orientation has promoted a conservative and backward-looking conception of the appropriate relationships between schools and communities. An alternative educational future will require a form of teacher professionalism that, in both conceptual and practical terms, is far more relational and participative than that which currently prevails. Within the dominant top-down educational discourse, accountability has taken on the status of a political ideology and has become a shorthand, or 'relay device', for a suite of policies that build into a relatively solid neoliberal framework of management, surveillance and control. The ideology of accountability has grown increasingly powerful. However, alternative 'educational' values, such as relevance, responsiveness, critique, student-centred learning and concern with the social context of schooling, could become more dominant within a policy discourse that was education-led or 'pedagogy-led'.

The focus on instruction and test taking ignores the point that the major influences on the school performance of children exist outside rather than inside the school. Therefore, in thinking about preparing future teachers, we need to think about how education, as a social institution, systematically advantages and/or disadvantages certain types of people in certain types of communities. I would claim that all students deserve to be treated in a more dignified, engaged and respectful manner than seems to be the case within the current ideology of top-down managerialism. However, the plight of those who have been 'othered' (Ball, 2008; Delpit, 1995) and put at an increased disadvantage must particularly be brought to the attention of the next generation of teachers, who, if the ideas I have been putting forward in this chapter are to be realised, will have to be informed, critical educational reformers. As activist teachers, they will need to convince policymakers and fellow educators that schools must reach out to all young people, particularly disadvantaged young people, and move to meet them rather than expect them to adjust to entrenched school and teacher paradigms that reflect the norms of unacknowledged privilege. Schools may then have some success in engaging all students in relevant and interesting school experiences.

## Are Student Teachers Willing to Be Critical, Reflective and Resistant?

The taken-for-granted norms and assumptions embedded in the neoliberal policy framework are important not only because of their anti-educational effects on education but also because they displace and marginalise alternative, more humanistic conceptions of education that are associated with the participative/professional approach to teaching. For pre-service teachers to become critical, reflective and activist practitioners, therefore, they will have to overcome the hegemonic effects of the neoliberal regime and understand that what it means to be a teacher has been continuously reconstructed through the reshaping of educational norms and values. Educators are operating in environments in which the emphasis is on outcomes and policy compliance is the order of the day. The 'increased account-ability pressure [has] created conditions where participants became additional agents of the external accountability system, not self-governing agents of their own expectations' (Webb, 2005, p. 2,004). To the extent that Webb is correct, teachers have lost their professional/participative disposition and have succumbed to technical/managerialism. It is therefore no surprise that student teachers, as they become more familiar with schools, are likely to take on board the pragmatic requirements of compliance with policy mandates and will be wary of rocking the boat. Yet, for progressive, socially critical teacher educators located in universities, as Holloway and Gouthro (2011, p. 29) remind us, 'the main goal … should be to prepare critically reflective educators who can engage with learning in a wide range of contexts'. The benefits of such critical reflection have been established in the teacher education literature and include developing the capacities to continually improve one's teaching practice, to make connections between theory and practice in useful ways and to develop collegial work relationships through shared reflection on good practice. Generally, critical reflection is still associated with virtually all forms of professional growth.

Given such apparent benefits, it is little wonder that pre-service teachers usually respond positively to the concept of reflective practice. They tend to remain positive when their lecturers talk about linking critical reflective practice to improving their level of engagement with students and making their pedagogical practice more explicit and relevant. However, things can become more difficult when critical reflective practice is linked to the social outcomes of education like promoting democratic opportunities for learning and developing a social justice orientation that requires inclusive teaching and learning. Some students start to become uncomfortable when encouraged to consider the dynamics of gender, race and class in relation to educational outcomes. Discussions about power and privilege and the implications of formal schooling in processes of advantaging and disadvantaging children can be regarded by some student teachers as 'political' and not 'educa-tional', so it is a big leap for them to advocate for social justice and democratic change. As Holloway and Gouthro (2011, p. 30) point out, there is a substantial literature on student resistance to becoming 'radical' and advocating resistance and change in relation to racial issues, feminist issues or critical theory. Fundamental to developing a sense of democratic, emancipatory possibilities within the teaching profession is the realisation amongst teacher educators that, if they are to address important issues of power, pre-service teachers

> … require critical literary skills to question, investigate, reflect, and act upon these concerns within their own teaching contexts. They must develop a more sophisticated understanding of racial, religious, political, and economic structures that impact upon their learning situations. (Holloway & Gouthro, 2011, p. 32)

But the bottom line for all educators, including pre-service teachers, is that we must examine ways in which schools, like other social institutions, contribute to the construction and legitimation of advantage and disadvantage and to the broader cultural production and legitimation of societal norms. Student teachers would be encouraged to develop a relational perspective on education in order to see schools as important sites in which social processes and education politics are played out. The legitimation of the values implicit in neoliberal discourse has made it difficult for alternative discourses to be 'heard', but, as Bowe, Ball, and Gold (1992) emphasise, any discourse is open to continuous amendment and reinterpretation, especially at the school level. More recently, Braun, Maguire, and Ball (2010, p. 549) have maintained that:

> [An] analytical and conceptual approach towards what happens in schools in relation to policy work foregrounds teachers and other education workers as key actors, rather than merely as subjects in the policy process. Policy enactment involves creative processes of interpretation and recontextualisation – that is, the translation through reading, writing and talking of text into action and the abstraction of policy ideas into contextualised practices.

From a teacher's perspective on educational policy, then, there is always some capacity for school-level reinterpretation and adaptation as alternative professional judgments and educational practices are asserted by professional/participative teachers. Pre-service teachers, as much as any other educators, must become active participants in such debates and overcome the institutional expectation that, in a hierarchical system, teachers should act according to what senior officials have mandated and expect to see. The kind of democratic social responsibility and commitment to social justice that that might be expected from critically reflective, professionally informed, beginning teachers, then, would be reflected in attempts to make schools inclusive of all learners, even the most problematic ones. It ought to be possible for all schools to be inclusive and for them to pursue educative, socially responsible, democratic goals. Indeed, throughout the history of most western societies over the past 150 years, it was generally assumed that education would provide a mechanism for enhancing social democracy and eliminating injustice and economic marginalisation. So, what's stopping us from doing that?

## Conclusion: Working with a Socially Democratic Imaginary

The fact that education is a social institution that has not managed to achieve its historic democratic and egalitarian objectives does not mean we should give up trying. But if schools are to be successful in their democratic mission, teachers must be encouraged to experiment with various definitions of desirable future selves working in the best interests of all young people, their families and the future society they envisage.

To explain the concept of a 'socially democratic imaginary', I need first to explain what Taylor calls a '*social imaginary*'. Taylor (2007, p. 119) states:

What I am trying to get at with this term is something much broader and deeper than
the intellectual schemes people may entertain when they think about social reality in a
disengaged mode. I am thinking rather of the ways in which they imagine their social
existence—how they fit together with others and how things go on between them and their
fellows, the expectations that are normally met and the deeper normative notions and images
that underlie these expectations.

Taylor explains that a social imaginary has several important elements. It relates
to the way 'ordinary people imagine their social surroundings', not in a theoretical
sense but in terms of an imagined, future reality which is understood for the present
as depicted in images, dreams and stories; it is shared by large groups of people and
it provides a set of common understandings that are tightly 'interwoven with an idea
of how [things] ought to go' (p. 120) and which therefore confirm certain ideas and
practices as legitimate. A social imaginary, therefore, is socially constructed, widely
shared and has a tremendous pedagogical effect on populations in legitimating what
is regarded as normal, natural and appropriate. It influences how people think about
the nature and scope of government and social institutions like education.

The most powerful and dominant social imaginary in the current historical
period, according to Rizvi and Lingard (2010), is 'the neo-liberal imaginary', the
dominance of which in education policy is the subject of their book. These authors
explain the emergence in education of the various elements of neo-liberalism into
a relatively coherent set of discourses and practice in which large numbers of the
general public 'imagine their social existence' (p. 19). The task for activist, critically
informed education professionals is therefore to problematise and 'reimagine'
the neo-liberal imaginary and replace it with a more desirable and educationally
appropriate alternative. I am suggesting a 'socially democratic imaginary' as an
appropriate, educative and socially just alternative. Within such an imagined state
of democratic schooling, professional/participative teachers, like the 'street-level
bureaucrats' celebrated in the work of Lipsky (1980), would exercise autonomy and
discretion in critically appraising and reinterpreting mandated policy in the social
and democratic interests of their students, communities and the common good.
As Bottery (1999) explains, there are particular goals of democracy and social
responsibility that educational institutions, if their teachers are thinking clearly
and critically in terms of a socially democratic imaginary, would be obliged to
pursue in a democratic society. For Bottery (1999, p. 301), the basic democratic
responsibilities of schools and teachers would include:

- Facilitating in participants a constructive and critical voice for its own sake, for
  this is a skill they will require if democracy is to exist in more than name
- Empowering a level of participation greater than that required purely for the best
  results, as it also is a skill which those within a democracy need to practise
- Helping the next adult generation to vocalise and search for ways of creating the
  good society, for in a democracy, this is a product of many voices, not just the few
- Recognising that public institutions have commitments beyond that of the profit
  and loss ledger and that this involves concerns with issues of equity and justice,
  as well as economy and efficiency

- Ensuring that those who work in such organisations are good role models for this younger generation, for if they are not allowed, or do not show an interest in these matters themselves, how can a new generation be expected to understand the need or the practice?

In keeping with such a socially democratic imaginary, and consistent with participative/professional notions of teaching, beginning teachers would be expected to contribute to education debates and to work with fellow teachers and school communities towards provisionally agreed positions on educational issues. Teachers, students, administrators and school communities would develop the practice of critical scrutiny in the knowledge that decisions about education involve negotiated cultural and political choices, conflicts and contested questions of value rather than simply questions of efficiency and effectiveness. Such an approach would be consistent with teachers seeing their role as not merely conveying knowledge for consumption but 'helping students to become creative, critical thinkers and active social participants, and to become capable of redefining the nature of their own lives in the society in which they live' (Gordon, 1985). To be educative in this sense, teachers will need to embody principles of professional judgement, reflective practice and critical scrutiny.

The beginning of the twenty-first century has been beset a series of enormous threats and enormous future possibilities. The threats include the danger of intolerance, terrorism, war, further global economic crises and the difficulty of sustaining the planet at a time of massive pollution and global warming. The possibilities include greater global collaboration in dealing with these threats, living more harmoniously with each other and with the environment and ensuring that the next generation can be sufficiently ingenious, flexible and adaptable to solve problems and create a more cooperative, democratic and equitable world. I have not specifically addressed these threats and possibilities in this chapter, but I want to conclude on the point that they are fundamental in any imagination of a future world in which today's and tomorrow's teachers will strive to make a difference. As Hursh and Henderson (2011, p. 182) point out, there is much work to do because, at present:

> Schools are more often places where teachers and students learn what will be on the test rather than seeking answers to questions that cry out for answers, such as how to develop a healthy, sustainable environment or communities where people are actually valued for who they are rather than what they contribute to the economy.

The aim of this chapter has been to critically consider what teacher education institutions need to do to prepare teachers who are sufficiently courageous, socially responsible and politically informed to make the right kind of difference. To do this, they must be willing to critically reflect on themselves and what is going on around them, including the nature of their courses, their practices and those of their lecturers and other teachers, their experiences in classrooms and schools and the current education system and imagined alternatives. They must realise that all of this is value-laden and inherently political. The socially democratic imaginary that I have proposed should be regarded as much more than a simple, pleasant ideal.

It is a way of conceptualising the kind of teachers and schools we need for the kind of future we want. Pre-service teachers can be assisted to imagine themselves into the reality of becoming active, informed agents who have a social responsibility to reconnect the nexus between schooling and democratic engagement and to shape themselves and their schools into the kind of educators and educational institutions that will enable all young people and their communities to contribute as citizens, workers and participating members in their preferred future.

# References

Alexander, R. (Ed.). (2009). *Children, their world, their education: Final report and recommendations of the Cambridge Primary review*. London: Routledge.

Anderson, G. (2009). *Advocacy leadership: Toward a post-reform agenda in education*. New York: Routledge.

Apple, M. (2001). *Educating the 'right' way*. New York: Routledge/Falmer.

Ball, S. (1997). Good schools/bad schools: Paradox and fabrication. *British Journal of Sociology of Education, 18*(3), 317–336.

Ball, S. (2003). The teacher's soul and the terrors of performativity. *Journal of Education Policy, 18*(2), 215–228.

Ball, S. (2006). *Education policy and social class*. London: Routledge.

Ball, S. (2008). *The education debate*. Bristol, UK: The Policy Press.

Bartolomé, L. (2007). Critical pedagogy and teacher education: Radicalizing prospective teachers. In P. McLaren & J. Kinchloe (Eds.), *Critical pedagogy: Where are we now?* (pp. 263–286). New York: Peter Lang.

Bottery, M. (1999). Global forces, national mediations and the management of educational institutions. *Educational Management Administration & Leadership, 27*(3), 299–312.

Bowe, R., Ball, S., & Gold, A. (1992). *Reforming education and changing schools*. London: Falmer Press.

Braun, A., Maguire, M., & Ball, S. (2010). Policy enactments in the UK secondary school: Examining policy, practice and school positioning. *Journal of Education Policy, 25*(4), 547–560.

Carr, W., & Hartnett, A. (1996). *Education and the struggle for democracy*. Buckingham, UK: Open University Press.

Cochran-Smith, M., & Lytle, S. (2004). Practitioner inquiry, knowledge, and university culture. In J. Loughran, M. L. Hamilton, V. LaBoskey, & T. Russell (Eds.), *International handbook of research of self-study of teaching and teacher education practices* (pp. 602–649). Dordrecht, The Netherlands: Kluwer.

Cummins, J. (2001). Empowering minority students: A framework for introduction (classic reprint). *Harvard Education Review, 71*(4), 649–675.

Darling-Hammond, L. (2000). How teacher education matters. *Journal of Teacher Education, 51*(3), 166–173.

Delpit, L. (1995). *Other people's children: Cultural conflict in the classroom*. New York: The New Press.

Fitzgerald, T. (2008). The continuing politics of mistrust: Performance management and the erosion of professional work. *Journal of Educational Administration and History, 40*(2), 113–128.

Gordon, L. (1985). Towards emancipation in citizenship education: The case of Afro-American cultural knowledge. *Theory and Research in Social Education, 12*(4), 1–23.

Greene, M. (2008). Response to Chapter 3. In J. Cammarota & M. Fine (Eds.), *Revolutionizing education* (pp. 45–48). New York: Routledge.

Holloway, S., & Gouthro, P. (2011). Teaching resistant novice educators to be critically reflective. *Discourse: Studies in the Cultural Politics of Education, 32*(1), 29–41.

Hursh, D., & Henderson, J. (2011). Contesting global neo-liberalism and creating alternative futures. *Discourse: Studies in the Cultural Politics of Education, 32*(2), 172–185.

Kinchloe, J. (2004). *Critical pedagogy*. New York: Peter Lang.

Lather, P. (1986). Research as praxis. *Harvard Educational Review, 56*(3), 257–277.

Lingard, B. (2010). Policy borrowing, policy learning: Testing times in Australian schooling. *Critical Studies in Education, 51*(2), 129–147.

Lipsky, M. (1980). *Street-level bureaucracy: Dilemmas of the individual in public services*. New York: Russell Sage.

McGraw, A. (2011). Shoving our way into young people's lives. *Teacher Development, 15*(1), 105–116.

McInerney, P. (2009). Towards a critical pedagogy of engagement for alienated youth: Insights from Freire and school-based research. *Critical Studies in Education, 50*(1), 23–35.

Mills, C. (1959). *The sociological imagination*. London: Oxford University Press.

Mingers, J. (2000). What is it to be critical? Teaching a critical approach to management undergraduates. *Management Learning, 31*(2), 219–237.

Moll, L., Amanti, C., Neff, D., & Gonzalez, N. (1992). Funds of knowledge for teaching: Using a qualitative approach to connect schools and classrooms. *Theory into Practice, 31*(2), 132–141.

Nordtveit, B. (2010). Towards post-globalisation? On the hegemony of western education and development discourses. *Globalisation, Societies and Education, 8*(3), 321–337.

Oakes, L., Townley, B., & Cooper, D. J. (1998). Business planning as pedagogy: Language and control in a changing educational field. *Administrative Science Quarterly, 48*(2), 257–292.

Pusey, M. (1991). *Economic rationalism in Canberra: A nation-building state changes its mind*. Cambridge, UK: Cambridge University Press.

Rizvi, F., & Lingard, B. (2010). *Globalizing education policy*. New York: Routledge.

Smyth, J., Angus, L., Down, B., & McInerney, P. (2009). *Activist and socially critical school and community renewal: Social justice in exploitative times*. Rotterdam, The Netherlands: Sense Publishers.

Taylor, C. (2007). Cultures of democracy and citizen efficacy. *Public Culture, 19*(1), 117–150.

Thomas, J. (1993). *Doing critical ethnography*. London: Sage.

Thomson, P., Hall, C., & Jones, K. (2010). Maggie's day: A small-scale analysis of English education policy. *Journal of Education Policy, 25*(5), 639–656.

Webb, P. (2005). The anatomy of accountability. *Journal of Education Policy, 20*(2), 189–208.

Willis, P. (1977). *Learning to labor: How working class kids get working class jobs*. Westmead, UK: Gower.

Willis, P. (2000). *The ethnographic imagination*. Cambridge, UK: Polity Press.

# Chapter 5
# Reconceptualising Teacher Standards: Authentic, Critical and Creative

Barry Down

## Introduction

In the context of a 'conservative restoration' (Apple, 2000) and neoliberal reforms which have not only eroded the democratic and egalitarian purposes of public education (Giroux, 2004) but lead to a deskilling of teachers' work (Smyth, 2001), this chapter seeks to provide a more troubling (Jenesick, 2001) perspective on the recently announced National Professional Standards for Teachers (NPST) (2011). On 9 February 2011, Australian Education Ministers and the Australian Institute for Teaching and School Leadership (AITSL) (2011), hailed the new standards 'as a crucial milestone in the national education reforms of Australia'. It was claimed that the standards would 'promote excellence in teaching and provide a nationally consistent basis for recognizing quality teaching'. This would be achieved by making 'explicit what teachers should know, be able to do and what is expected of effective teachers across their career'. The Federal Minister for School Education, Peter Garrett, said 'it is an historic move toward making every school a great school' (9 February 2011). According to the official documents, the intent is to:

- Provide consistent benchmarks to help teachers assess performance
- Provide a means of identifying and recognising teachers who excel against national standards
- Increase public confidence in the professionalism of teachers
- Make a statement of what constitutes teacher quality
- Provide a framework that offers a direction and structure to guide the preparation, support and development of teachers
- Raise the status of teaching

B. Down (✉)
School of Education, Murdoch University, Perth, Australia
e-mail: b.down@murdoch.edu.au

B. Down and J. Smyth (eds.), *Critical Voices in Teacher Education*, Explorations of Educational Purpose 22, DOI 10.1007/978-94-007-3974-1_5,
© Springer Science+Business Media Dordrecht 2012

Specifically, the standards framework will be used as the basis for:

- Accrediting initial service teacher education programmes
- Reliable, fair and nationally consistent registration
- Recognising and certifying exemplary teacher practice

Putting aside the political spin for a moment, it is hard to disagree with the prevailing view that standards are not important. We would all like better standards for our teachers and students alike. After all, who would oppose rigorous teaching standards? My argument is, therefore, not about whether standards are desirable or not but with the problematic nature of the top-down, technical, decontextualised and depoliticised versions currently doing the rounds. Given the worldwide infatuation with standards at all levels of education over the past three decades (Ravitch, 1995), it seems timely to pause and critically reflect on the implications of standards-based approaches to teacher education. In examining the new standards framework as it relates to graduate teachers, I want to pursue four main questions. First, how is it that standards have become part of a commonsense and largely uncontested discourse? Second, what hidden assumptions and cultural messages about the 'good teacher' are conveyed? Third, what kinds of teacher subjectivities and identities are valued or devalued? Finally, how might we reconceptualise teacher standards in ways that are more authentic, critical and creative?

In pursuing this line of enquiry, I argue that despite the best intentions the NPST produces a largely conservative and instrumentalist conception of what it means to teach. Other than acknowledging the significant role of teachers 'in preparing young people to lead successful and productive lives', there is scant regard given to the more complex and challenging task of elaborating on the philosophical, ethical, contextual and political dimensions of teaching (Kincheloe, Slattery, & Steinberg, 2000). Thus, the NPST reduces teaching to a mere practical matter concerned only with content, planning, assessment, management and reporting. Whilst each of these may be important and necessary attributes for graduate teachers to have, they are by themselves insufficient and ultimately perpetuate technicist and back-to-basics approaches to teacher education (Hinchey, 2006, p. 128). As a consequence, teachers are tacitly instructed 'to undervalue the domain of theory while avoiding questions of the ideological, psychological, and pedagogical assumptions underlying their practice' (Kincheloe, 2011, p. 89). Against this backdrop, I want to do two things in this chapter: first, to provide a general critique of the Australian teacher standards; and second, to suggest some alternative ways of reconceptualising the NPST based on an understanding of and commitment to a socially just, democratic vision of teaching.

## What's Wrong with Teacher Standards?

On the surface, standards appear to be relatively innocuous and innocent. There is a consensus among a broad alliance of neoliberals, conservatives, economic modernisers and social progressives about the benefits of improving educational standards for all (Apple, 2001). Whilst the motives may vary, the goal is essentially the same. Australia's future prosperity, economic productivity and national competitiveness is dependent on raising educational standards, and this can only be achieved by aligning education more closely to the needs of the economy (Down, 2009). As the blame shifts 'onto schools', there is a prevailing view that if 'teachers and curricula were more tightly controlled, more closely linked to the needs of business and industry, more technically oriented, with more stress on traditional values and workplace norms and dispositions, then the problems of achievement, of unemployment, of international economic competitiveness and so on, would supposedly largely disappear' (Apple, 2000, p. 114).

In response, the Rudd and Gillard Labor governments have rolled out a suite of policy measures, euphemistically described as an Education Revolution, among them: the Australian Curriculum, the National Assessment Programme in Literacy and Numeracy (NAPLAN), My School website, the National Professional Standards for Teachers (NPST) and Rewards for Great Teachers. The assumption behind these policy prescriptions is that standards will only improve when teachers are held accountable for teaching certain standards of knowledge and skills (Australian Curriculum), student achievement is measured by standardised paper and pencil tests (NAPLAN), schools are subjected to greater public scrutiny and transparency (My School website), teachers are prepared to 'world-class' standards (National Professional Standards for Teachers) and 'great teachers' are given performance pay bonuses (Rewards for Great Teachers). This kind of policy triage has considerable political appeal because it not only provides governments with a 'can do' list of targets, performances and outcomes (Fielding, 1999) but the politics of blame ensures that principals, teachers, students, families and their communities are held personally responsible when things go wrong, not social systems. In this context, I want to consider three interrelated problems with current conceptions of teacher standards—technical instrumentalism, the complexity of teaching and student engagement—and why they are unlikely to raise teacher standards.

## Technical Instrumentalism: Controlling Teachers' Work

Whilst the NPST certainly contain many elements of good teaching which should be encouraged, the emphasis is primarily on the preparation and certification of teachers who can readily assimilate into the dynamics of contemporary policy settings and priorities (Smyth & Shacklock, 1998). For instance, the NPST insists that graduate teachers must be able to demonstrate an understanding of their subjects, curriculum content and teaching strategies; design lessons that meet the requirements of curriculum, assessment and reporting; interpret student assessment data; create rapport and manage student behaviour; demonstrate knowledge of legislative requirements; and provide clear directions to students. The domination of teacher standards by this kind of 'how-to-ism' (Brosio, 1994, p. 323), or 'means-end thinking' (Phelan, 2009, p. 106), should hardly be surprising in a climate where teachers' work is being 'overdetermined and over-regulated' via the imposition of a national curriculum, national testing and interventions into pedagogical decision-making (Ball, 1993, p. 106). Underlying these coercive policy manoeuvres is a view of teachers as mere 'deliverers', 'testers' and 'technicians' (p. 107) of a predetermined curriculum and instructional procedures devised by external experts. As Hinchey (2006) explains it, teachers are required to be 'robotic technicians who unquestioningly follow the instructions of others and lack the temerity to ask how well those instructions serve their students' (Hinchey, 2006, p. 128). In other words, there is an increasing separation of conception from execution, or what Braverman (1998) calls a 'degradation labour', as instrumental ideologies gain authority and influence over teacher preparation and classroom pedagogy (Giroux, 1988, p. 123).

In terms of the argument being mounted here, standards are a mechanism of ideological control. Teachers are preoccupied with learning 'what works' or with mastering the best way to set goals, plan lessons, organise classroom activities, manage behaviour and evaluate student learning (NPST, 2011, pp. 12–13). The problem with the NPST is that it strips away the intellectual nature of teaching, leaving only:

> ... a constricted view of teacher intellect through emphasis on teaching as technique, an extreme form of individualism, teacher dependence on experts, acceptance of hierarchy, a consumer or 'banking' view of teaching and learning (teacher is 'banker'; learning is consuming), a limited commitment to the betterment of the educational community and a conservative survivalist mentality among novice teachers (Bullough & Gitlin, 1991, p. 38).

Weil (2001) adds to this concern, by arguing that 'standards serve as a straight-jacket' because 'they impose teaching as an act of functional, instrumental control—of technological device—not an act of compassion, caring, and love'. For him, standards are 'a means of covertly managing people and knowledge for private ends' (p. 519). Weil goes on to explain how standards 'surreptitiously beguile students, teachers, and community into believing that there is no political agenda, no advocacy of cultural norms, no prevalence of hierarchical classifying and sorting, that standards are a neutral, generic conception and operation applicable equally and fairly in the interest of everyone' (p. 518). Phelan (2009) captures the essence of the problem of technical instrumentalism when she writes:

> There is no deliberation about educational purposes, no consideration of authority in teaching, no apparent concern for the manner in which schools shape and are shaped by social inequities, no reference to the complex responsibility of the teacher and teacher educator towards the life of children and for the continuance of the world (Phelan & Sumison, 2008). When did (teacher) education become so small (Smits, 2008)? (p. 107).

Thus, standards operate in 'insidious ways' to perpetuate 'commonsensical ideas' about teaching and learning that privileges certain pedagogical knowledge (e.g. psychology, measurement and management) whilst removing issues of oppression and social justice from the agenda (Kumashiro, 2004, p. 6). In short, 'pragmatism and technologies of control replace ideological dispute' (Ball, 1989, p. 143).

## *The Complexity of Teaching: Teaching Is More Than Method*

In the context of top-down, technical standards, the complexity of teachers' work is largely erased as teaching is reduced to simplistic checklists of what content, practical strategies and evaluation techniques teachers should master. The underlying rationale of the NPST (and the Australian Curriculum and NAPLAN) is that 'knowledge can be broken down into discrete parts, standardized for easier management and delivery and measured through predefined forms of assessment' (Giroux, 1988 p. 124). Giroux describes curricula approaches of this sort as 'management pedagogies' because they assume that 'the behavior of teachers needs to be controlled and made consistent and predicable across different schools and student populations' (p. 124). Underlying this 'administrative rationality' (Ball, 1989, p. 143) is the assumption that 'no thought is necessary; it's just common sense to assume that, if one wants to teach somebody something, you simply break down the information into separate pieces, go over the pieces until the learner has mastered them, then test him or her to make sure the pieces have been "learned" (Goodman, 1986)' (Kincheloe, 2001a, pp. 101–102). The problem with reductionist views of teaching of this kind is that the primary emphasis is on following the 'correct' method or procedure whilst 'blocking out' consideration of the complexity of both the contextual environment (Kincheloe, 2001b, p. 39) and the daily realities of teachers' work (Connell, 1989).

In the case of contextual complexity, Kincheloe (2001b) points out that one of the major limitations of reductionist standards is that it allows teachers, educational leaders and curriculum developers to 'run away from complexity and hide in a shelter of mediocrity'. This leads to 'low-level thinking' because 'knowledge production is no longer an act of insight, contextual analysis, intuition, and creative brilliance, as much as it is procedure' (p. 27). The upshot is that teachers are not encouraged to develop 'the analytical, research, and interpretative skills or scholarly dispositions to move their practice to a higher cognitive level' (p. 51). Kincheloe argues that this 'is not the result of a lack of general ability' rather teachers 'are victims of a system not configured to produce scholars' (p. 51). For this reason, Kincheloe (1993) advocates the importance of creating new forms of critical teacher thinking capable of helping teachers to understand 'the construction of their consciousness and the ways that social and institutional forces work to undermine their autonomy as professionals' (p. 26). In the tradition of Paulo Freire (2000), teacher scholars show a preparedness to problematise knowledge by asking more penetrating questions about 'what is' and by exploring 'what might be' (Simon, 1992, pp. 3–4). In this perspective, teachers and teacher educators become 'knowledge workers' (as opposed to technicians/civil servants) who 'research, interpret, expose embedded values and political interest, and produce their own knowledge' (Kincheloe, 2001a, p. 241). These teacher scholars, Kincheloe writes:

- Take into account the democratic, moral, ethical and cognitive context
- Push students to understand where content came from, the means by which it was produced and how it was validated as knowledge worthy of inclusion in the curriculum

- Induce students to use these contextual understandings to reflect, research and evaluate information presented to them
- Cultivate skills that can be used after the confrontation with content to enable them to learn new content in novel situations
- Prepare students to produce new content in relation to the context in which they are operating (p. 22)

Turning to the complexity of teachers' daily work, the NPST is again largely silent. Advocates of the NPST are most comfortable when reducing teaching to a list of standards which are easily identifiable, calculable and transparent. For experienced and novice teachers alike, however, the realities of classroom life are underscored by 'endemic uncertainties' (Lortie, 2002). Lortie's classic sociological study of teachers' work provides a timely reminder of the 'fragility and complexities' of teaching and why standards are notoriously difficult to specify (p. x). Lortie's observations are worth repeating at length:

> Compared with other crafts, the work processes in teaching, and the products sought by teachers, are difficult to measure by several assessment criteria. We speak of teaching goals as 'intangible' and thus underline their insubstantial qualities. Persons who make tangible products may use a fixed and reliable model as a guide for comparing intermediate outcomes with the goal; craftsmen in tangible fields use working models, blueprints, plans, and detailed specifications. Teachers process no physical standards of this kind; they may find the very idea inconsistent with respect for the individuality of children and young people. ... The teacher's craft, then, is marked by the absence of concrete models for emulation, unclear lines of influence, multiple and controversial criteria, ambiguity about assessment timing, and instability in the product (pp. 135–136).

What Lortie is saying here is that teaching cannot be reduced to tangible lists of products, processes and outcomes because the work is far too nuanced and unpredictable for that. Teaching involves 'people work', and this occurs under a set of unique circumstances: 'the low degree of voluntarism in the teacher-student relationship, the problem of extracting work from immature workers, and the grouped context of teacher endeavors' (p. 137). Connell (1989) makes a similar point when she argues that 'teaching is a labour process without an object. At best, it has an object so intangible—the minds of the kids, or their capacity to learn—that it cannot be specified in any but vague and metaphorical ways' (pp. 123–124). Despite Connell's best attempt to list 'all the bits' (and it is a very long list) that make up teachers' work, there appears to be 'no logical limit to the expansion of an individual teachers' work' (p. 125).

## *Student Engagement: There Is No Teaching Without Learning*

Perhaps the most troubling aspect of the NPST is the extent to which students are treated as passive objects in a process over which they have little or no say. Where students are mentioned, it is in the context of what teachers need to know about students 'physical, social and intellectual development', especially those students from 'diverse linguistic, cultural, religious and socioeconomic backgrounds' in order to more effectively organise, manage, evaluate and report on the essential knowledge to be learned (NPST, 2011, p. 8). There is no question that teachers need to know their students well, but the underlying version of teaching being put forward here is a 'banking pedagogy' that treats students as 'depositories' or 'receptacles to be filled' with officially sanctioned knowledge. Missing is any notion of students and teachers as active participants capable of producing knowledge, generating meaning and taking social action (Freire, 2000, p. 72; Shor, 1992). Because the NPST fails to develop a coherent and integrated vision of teaching, in particular the value of democratic schooling and the grounding of curriculum in students' experiences, passions and interests, the end result is a fairly emaciated version of teaching (Smyth, Angus, Down, & McInerney, 2008).

On this point, Giroux (2005) reminds us that 'knowledge is not merely produced in the heads of experts, curriculum specialists and teachers' (p. 159) rather it is intensely relational work requiring teachers and students to negotiate the curriculum (Smyth, Down, & McInerney, 2010). Putting it another way, Freire (1998) states 'That there is, in fact, no teaching without learning' (p. 31). In a similar vein, Ohanian (1999) reveals that 'kids don't necessarily learn what teachers teach' (p. 146). Whilst this point appears to be self-evident, politicians and policymakers continue to act as though it does not really matter. As Ohanian says, the 'Standardisto documents littering the land are irrelevant to the lives of children' (p. 8). Kohl (1994) adds to this concern by arguing that students 'not-learning', or their 'willed refusal of schooling for political or cultural reasons' (p. 28), is a result of a mismatch between what the authorities, teachers and administrators want them to learn and what students themselves want to learn (p. 28). Despite some sage advice from Dewey (1997) on the importance of students participating in the construction of their own learning, the 'scope and sequence chart mentality' (Ohanian, 1999, p. 15) persists unabated. In this context, Dewey captures the central dilemma facing teachers today:

> There is, I think, no point in the philosophy of progressive education which is sounder than its emphasis upon the importance of the participation of the learner in the formation of the purposes which direct his activities in the learning process, just as there is no defect in traditional education greater than its failure to secure the active co-operation of the pupil in construction of the purposes involved in his [sic] studying (p. 67).

What Dewey is alluding to here is the fundamental importance of taking into account students' experience, knowledge and interests in the learning process. Progressive educators like Maxine Greene (1995) argue that so long as schooling is preoccupied with standardisation, high-stakes testing, target setting, accountability and transparency measures, it will continue to 'screen out the faces and gestures of individuals, of actual living human beings' (p. 11). In a surprisingly self-reflexive turn, Diane Ravitch (2010), one of the leading proponents of the neoliberal reform agenda in America, confesses to having had a change of mind based on the evidence. It is worth recounting at some length how she began to reassess the damaging impact of the standards and accountability movement on education:

As I flipped through the yellowing pages in my scrapbooks, I started to understand the recent redirection of my thinking, my growing doubt regarding popular proposals for choice and accountability. Once again, I realized, I was turning skeptical in response to panaceas and miracle cures. The only difference was that in this case, I too had fallen for the latest panaceas and miracle cures; I too had drunk deeply of the elixir that promised a quick fix to intractable problems. I too had jumped aboard the bandwagon, one festooned with banners celebrating the power of accountability, incentives, and markets. I too was captivated by these ideas. They promised to end bureaucracy, to ensure that poor children were not neglected, to empower poor parents, to enable poor children to escape failing schools, and to close the achievement gap between rich and poor, black and white . . . . All of this seemed to make sense, but there was little empirical evidence, just promise and hope. I wanted to share the promise and hope. I wanted to believe that choice and accountability would produce great results. But over time I was persuaded by accumulating evidence that the latest reforms were not likely to live up to their promise. The more I saw, the more I lost the faith (pp. 3–4).

For those of us (including the authors in this book) who are deeply sceptical and increasingly outraged by market-driven prescriptions to fix education, these are indeed remarkable words of contrition. Ravitch's musings remind me of the lyrics in Leonard Cohen's song Anthem—'Ring the bells that still can ring, Forget your perfect offering, There is a crack in everything, That's how the light gets in'. Let us hope he is right. Our children deserve much better than what is currently being served up in the name of education. If we are serious about creating a truly democratic and engaging pedagogy (Smyth et al., 2008) as envisaged by Dewey and other democratic educators, then there is an urgent need to shift the conversations around teacher standards in a socially critical direction. Shor (1992) provides some useful advice to get us started:

To be democratic implies orientating subject matter to student culture—their interests, needs, speech, and perceptions—while creating a negotiable openness in class where the students' input jointly creates the learning process. To be critical in such a democratic curriculum means to examine all subjects and the learning process with systematic depth; to connect student individuality to larger historical and social issues; to encourage students to examine how their experience relates to academic knowledge, to power, and to inequality in society; and to approach received wisdom and the status quo with questions (p. 16).

Drawing on Shor's conception of an empowering education for teachers and students, I want to conclude this chapter by considering how we might begin to reconceptualise each of the standards in the NPST.

## Reconceptualising Teacher Standards

As a way into this discussion, I want to draw on three qualities of the authentic teacher identified by Thomas and Schubert (2001) (they prefer the more expansive term of educator). Commenting on the American equivalent of the NPST (for graduate teachers), known as the Interstate New Teacher Assessment and Support Consortium of the Council of Chief State School Officers (INTASC) (1995), they argue that the teacher identity provided in certification standards is limited and needs to be expanded in at least three directions. First, teachers should be '*engaged in philosophic enquiry*', that is, 'investigating the value assumptions of their students, their colleagues, and their own metaphysical, epistemological, and axiological convictions' (p. 234). Second, teachers need to develop as '*democratic connoisseur[s]*' or 'critical interpreters of existent curriculums and creators of new curriculums, novel forms of instruction, and appropriate methods of assessment' (p. 235). Third, teachers should see themselves as '*progressive activist[s]*' committed to 'democratic practice understood as ... public advocacy for social policies that attempt to redress injustice and public criticisms of state actions that oppress or institutionalize inequality' (p. 235). By incorporating these socially critical principles into certification standards, Thomas and Shubert (2001) believe 'a more dynamic, vital understanding of the educator's craft' is possible (p. 235). Significantly, it opens up dialogue around the question of what kinds of teacher standards are desirable in these dangerous times (see Smyth Chap. 2). To organise this discussion, I shall consider each of the seven NPST standards by providing a brief summary of each standard and then suggesting how we might advance a more socially critical conversation.

## *NPST Standard 1: Know Students and How They Learn*

Graduate teachers are required to demonstrate knowledge and understanding of the physical, social and intellectual development and characteristics of students and how these may affect learning especially as it relates to students from diverse cultural, linguistic, socio-economic and religious backgrounds (NPST, 2011, pp. 8–9).

This standard is geared to using the insights of developmental psychology and what is known about cultural differences to create appropriate teaching strategies for a range of students. No doubt, knowing students and how they learn is absolutely pivotal to effective teaching and learning. This is indeed important work and preoccupies the time and energy of teachers searching for inventive methods of instruction to engage students in mastering the content of academic disciplines. From this perspective then, the purpose of knowing students and how they learn is primarily limited to a conservative/traditionalist/behaviourist view of student engagement, one that is 'goal driven', with engaged students dutifully 'attending classes', trying hard, completing their homework and not cheating (McMahon & Portelli, 2004, p. 62; see Smyth et al., 2008, pp. 4–5).

What is missing in this interpretation of teaching is recognition of the normative assumptions and values underlying the structural and cultural processes of 'doing school' (Pope, 2001), for instance, large class sizes, rigid timetables, hierarchical structures, didactic pedagogies, punishments and rewards, deficit thinking, testing, grading, streaming, standardisation, competitiveness, vocationalism and irrelevant curriculum (Pope). As a consequence, the social institution of schooling perpetuates its primary function of sifting and sorting students and maintaining social order and control in ways that are mostly unwitting and unconscious. This is achieved on the back of a number of fundamental assumptions about teaching and learning derived from (mis)understandings of individual psychology and motivational theory and socially constructed notions of intelligence, meritocracy, gender, race and class (Down, 2006). As a consequence, 'the momentum of traditional practice is left to speak for itself' (Sizer, 2004, p. 78).

In contrast, a socially critical orientation to teacher standards is interested in pursuing 'a pedagogy of expansion—expanded social agency, civic activism, intellectual and academic identities' (Cannella, 2008, p. 190). To this end, teachers are willing to ask more troubling questions about how students are known and how they learn. For example: What assumptions and values inform my views about teaching and learning? Where do these views come from? Who benefits and loses? How do these views restrict student capacities for self-reflection and critical engagement? How does my teaching acknowledge and value student experience, language, culture and interests? What gets in the way of knowing students well? What does it mean to be educated? What needs to change?

## NPST Standard 2: Know the Content and How to Teach It

Graduate teachers are required to demonstrate knowledge and understanding of the concepts, substance and structure of the content and teaching strategies of the teaching area. This involves organising content, lesson plans, assessment and reporting as well as integrating literacy, numeracy and ICT into the curriculum (NPST, 2011, pp. 10–11).

In light of the recently announced Australian Curriculum, there has been considerable public debate about the role and place of academic subjects in the school curriculum. The Australian Curriculum, Assessment and Reporting Authority (ACARA) which is an independent statutory body established by the Federal Government to oversee the development and implementation of the national curriculum has so far developed four subjects—Mathematics, Science, History and English—with additional learning areas to be developed at a later stage. Whilst this is not the place to provide a full critique, it is suffice to say that the national curriculum is fraught with difficulties including a limited rationale, the disconnect between the stated goals of the curriculum and the curriculum itself, the lack of coherence and integrity across subjects, a return to the past in terms of curriculum design and failure to address questions of equity and social justice (Reid, 2009). Many of these criticisms are reflected in comments made by the former conservative Prime Minister John Howard when he declared:

> I am an avowed education traditionalist. I believe in high academic standards, competitive examinations, and teacher-directed lessons based on traditional disciplines . . . .and strong but fair policies on school discipline (Gratten, 2007, p. 4).

Ted Sizer (2004), founder of the Coalition of Essential Schools, argues that such views are widely shared in the broader community. Ask most adults what high school is for and you will get a similar response, he says. High school is *'where you learn English and math, and that sort of thing'*. For students, it's the same, 'High school is to "teach" these "subjects"' (p. 80). Thus, '[t]aking subjects' in a systematized, conveyor-belt way is what one does in high school' (p. 83). Whether the subject actually makes sense, engages students or leads to worthwhile learning is beside the point (Postman, 1996). George Wood (2005), principal of Federal Hocking High in Ohio, America, makes the point that teacher talk 'sounds surrealistically similar from classroom to classroom … the teacher summarizes and simplifies the material, provides a few examples or stories, and ends presenting the class with a neat little package that leaves scant, if any room for questions or interpretation' (p. 83).

In addressing this problem, a socially critical orientation to standards would expect teachers to not only have a strong grasp of the disciplines but also be willing to ask more penetrating questions about the nature of knowledge and how it is produced. As Freire (2004) points out, 'education is always a certain theory of knowledge put into practice' (p. 71). Therefore, in addition to understanding subject matter and academic skills which feature so prominently in the NPST, teacher scholars would ask 'more complex and compelling questions' as suggested by Kincheloe (2010): How knowledge is produced? Where does it come from— who produced it? How does it find its way into the curriculum? Who benefits from students parroting it back to the authorities? In what ways does it serve the needs of the neoliberal empire? What is the role of interpretation in the confrontation with this knowledge, what does it mean, what does it tell us about the worldview of those who produced it? How does such knowledge relate to who we are now and who we might become? What are the alternatives to such information that come from other places and ways of seeing the world? How do we produce better informed, more rigorous knowledge? (p. 4).

## NPST Standard 3: Plan for and Implement Effective Teaching and Learning

Graduate teachers should be able to set learning goals, plan lessons, develop a range of teaching strategies, incorporate a range of resources including ICT, demonstrate a range of verbal and non-verbal communication strategies, evaluate programmes and involve parents/carers in the process (NPST, 2011, pp. 12–13).

When taking classes on critical teaching, one is inevitably confronted by the question, 'yes, this is all very interesting but when are you going to tell us how to teach'. As a critical teacher educator, you inevitably come across prospective teachers who want to be given the 'right' teaching methods, strategies or pre-packaged curricula that will work with all students irrespective of context. Whilst gaining access to useful methods and resources is certainly desirable and a necessary first step to being an effective teacher, it is insufficient. The recipe approach to teaching, whether around content, instruction, values, motivation, ICT or behaviour management, reflects a much deeper view of teaching as method. Here, I share Bartolome's (1994) view that 'a myopic focus on methodology often serves to obfuscate the real question—which is why in our society, subordinated students do not generally succeed academically at school' (p. 174). Throughout this chapter, I have argued the pedagogical importance of moving beyond 'a narrow mechanistic view of instruction' because it is both politically and educationally naïve to divorce teaching from the broader socio-historical and political context in which it occurs (Bartolome, 1994, p. 123).

Instead of focusing on teaching methods that serve to 'control, instruct, monitor, reward and punish students as they acquire appropriate content' (Riveria & Poplin, 1995, p. 225), socially critical standards attempt to develop new insights and understandings by 'troubling knowledge' by which Kumashiro (2004) means 'to complicate knowledge, to make knowledge problematic' (p. 8). In this context, 'troubling' means 'to work *paradoxically* with knowledge, that is, to simultaneously use knowledge to see what different insights, identities, practices, and changes it makes possible while critically examining that knowledge (and how it came to be known) to see what insights and the like it closes off' (pp. 8–9). This kind of critical intellectual work is important because it provides teachers with an opportunity to 'de-familiarise present practices and categories', thus making everyday habits, routines, behaviours and practices seem 'less self-evident and necessary' (Ball, 2006, p. 62). In this sense, teaching is always partial, incomplete and contradictory (Kumashiro, 2004, p. 15). And as Freire (2000) reminds us, human beings are always in the 'process of becoming—as unfinished, uncompleted beings in and with a likewise unfinished reality' (p. 84). With this is in mind, attempts to predetermine teacher standards and what it means to be a 'good' teacher is far more complex and problematic than suggested by the NPST.

My argument is that by adopting some of these theoretical insights, teachers are better placed to provide a more expanded understanding of what it means to plan for and implement effective teaching and learning, for instance, pursuing classroom practices that are grounded in the lives of our students; critical; multicultural; anti-racist, pro-justice; participatory, experiential; hopeful, visionary; activist; academically rigorous; and culturally and linguistically sensitive (Bigelow, 2006, p. 7).

## NPST Standard 4: Create and Maintain Supportive and Safe Learning Environments

Graduate teachers should be able to identify strategies to support inclusive student participation and engagement, demonstrate the capacity to organise classroom activities, provide clear directions and understand the ethical use of ICT (NPST, 2011, pp. 14–15).

This principle recognises the importance of creating inclusive, participatory and engaging classrooms where all students are made to feel safe and welcome. From the point of view of students, their requirements are minimal, they want 'respect from their teacher; they want a classroom pedagogy relevant to their interests; and they want a teacher with enthusiasm and openness' (Margonis, 2004, p. 51). No doubt, teachers who can build close connections with their students, who 'know what matters to their students, what strikes their interest, [and] what would take them beyond the routine' are more likely to engage young people in learning (Wood, 2005, p. 56). Elsewhere, my colleagues and I have described in detail how the values of respect, trust and care are at the heart of the 'relational school' (Smyth et al., 2010). When these values are not apparent, for whatever reason, then students are more likely to 'disconnect, disengage and "drop out" of school' (p. 37).

If we are really serious about addressing the growing numbers of students who are not engaging with schooling, then there is an urgent need to develop socially just ways of thinking about student participation and engagement. The emphasis clearly needs to be on 'a schooling system that includes everybody' (Lynch, 2002, p. 12) and that actively works against both historical and contemporary forces of exclusion. Thus, socially critical teacher standards seek to address those aspects of existing curriculum, pedagogy, assessment and organisation of schools that may unintentionally sustain, marginalise, alienate and exclude some young people. In particular, it attempts to dismantle those individualising and pathologising approaches to schooling that serve to perpetuate social and educational inequalities (Valencia, 2010). At heart, therefore, socially critical standards demand a new kind of respect capable of not only 'dismantling hierarchies' and challenging the language of 'inhibition' and 'dutiful compliance' but creating 'respectful relationships' based on 'desire and commitment' (Lawrence-Lightfoot, 2000, p. 10).

## NPST Standard 5: Assess, Provide Feedback and Report on Student Learning

Graduate teachers should be able to demonstrate understanding of assessment strategies, feedback to students, assessment moderation, interpretation of data and reporting to parents/carers (NPST, 2011, pp. 16–17).

In a world dominated by the orthodoxy of standards, accountability and transparency teachers are increasingly compromised by the ascendency of standardised tests over authentic assessment practices. Not only has high stakes testing changed the culture of schools but it has seriously eroded the professional autonomy of teachers to make pedagogical decisions based on the best interests of their students. Commenting on the American experience, Roselli (2005) argues that the 'senseless frenzy of testing' and the 'race to show achievement gains [is] not winnable [and] ... speaks to a serious flaw in American education and a serious defect in the delivery of sound curriculum, instruction, and assessment within schools' (p. 53). Kincheloe et al. (2000) express similar concerns:

The proficiency test movement appears to be reducing the curriculum to a small body of inert information disconnected from the contextual experiences of the learning process. Disaffected students lose interest in school and drop out. Teachers who are already under extreme pressure lose interest in and enthusiasm for academic investigation and experientially based learning. Teaching and learning in an environment like this become an assembly-line function devoid of critical inquiry and investigation (p. 314).

In tackling this problem, socially critical standards promote authentic assessment practices that are real, fair, rigorous and meaningful (Kohn, 2004; Wiggins, 1999). Such approaches encourage 'rich and dialogic interactions' (Gallagher, 2007, p. 8) between teachers, students, families and community. The emphasis is on developing 'reciprocity and mutuality' for the purpose of promoting learning, not just reporting on it (p. 56).

## NPST Standard 6: Engage in Professional Learning

Graduate teachers should be able to demonstrate an understanding of the role of the NPST, identify appropriate sources of professional learning, seek and apply constructive feedback and explain the rationale for continued professional learning (NPST, 2011, p. 18).

In the context of the arguments mounted so far, this standard fails to provide any inkling of what it means to be an authentic teacher as envisaged by Thomas and Schubert. It fails to comprehend the qualities of 'philosophic enquiry', 'democratic connoisseur' or 'progressive activist'. As a result, we end up with an impoverished view of professional learning confined to technical and practical rather than emancipatory interests (Grundy, 1987). As Giroux and McLaren (1986) explain it, '[t]eachers as intellectuals treat their students as critical agents, question how knowledge is produced and distributed, utilize dialogue, and make knowledge meaningful, critical, and ultimately emancipatory' (p. 215). Thus, critically reflective practitioners are concerned with the moral question of 'why things are the way they are, how they got that way, and what set of conditions are supporting the processes that maintain them' (Simon, 1988, p. 2; Smyth, 1989). Unless professional learning standards are expanded to encompass all three levels of reflection (technical, practical and emancipatory), then there is little chance that teaching standards will move beyond the mundane.

## NPST Standard 7: Engage Professionally with Colleagues, Parents/Carers and the Community

Graduate teachers should be able to understand and apply the principles described in the codes of ethics and conduct for the teaching profession, understand the relevant legislative, administrative and organisational policies and processes, understand strategies for working effectively with parents/carers and understand the role of external professionals and community representatives (NPST, 2011, p. 19).

Again, this standard is locked into a narrowly conceived understanding of relationships and the connections between schools and communities. It is embedded in bureaucratic codes, rules and regulations designed to guide, monitor and control the boundaries of acceptable conduct between stakeholders. Whilst graduate teachers certainly need to know the various codes of professional conduct, there is scope to offer a more expansive understanding of school-community connections. Smyth et al., (2010) explain it this way:

> Young people's identities are shaped by social and cultural influences that lie outside the perimeters of the school. Yet, all too often an institutional barrier operates between schools and communities. Where schools see themselves as a part of the community, there is a greater likelihood of creating the right kind of cultural settings that will bring parents into the educational lives of their children. This is a twofold process. Schools are significant neighbourhood assets with the resources to promote civic engagement and strengthen the social and cultural fabric of local communities. Equally, communities have funds of knowledge that can enhance student engagement and school retention (p. 204).

What is being advanced here is a 'different kind of politics' whereby school and community activists rather than outside agencies and experts work with the community around 'a common vision of how schooling can work for all, including those most marginalized and excluded' (Smyth, Angus, Down, & McInerney, 2009, p. 131).

## Concluding Comments

In this chapter, I have argued that teacher standards are neither neutral nor impartial. On the contrary, standards are part of a wider set of culturally conservative and neoliberal discourses designed to refashion education in the interests of global capitalism. A key argument here is that discursive constructions of teacher standards are a powerful force in shaping how people either consciously or unconsciously think and act in schools. In this context, I have attempted to expand, challenge and unsettle taken-for-granted technical instrumental understandings of teacher standards in the hope that it might provoke a different kind of conversation, one that acknowledges not only the complexity and contested nature of teaching but the values of democracy and social justice.

## References

Apple, M. (2000). *Official knowledge: Democratic education in a conservative age*. New York: Routledge.
Apple, M. (2001). *Educating the "right" way: Markets, standards, God and inequality*. New York: RoutledgeFalmer.

Australian Institute for Teaching and School Leadership. (2011). *National professional standards for teachers.* Carlton, Australia: MCEECDYA.

Ball, S. (1989). Inside/out: The school in political context. In B. Cosin, M. Flude, & M. Hales (Eds.), *School, work and society* (pp. 135–153). Sydney, Australia: Hodder & Stroughton.

Ball, S. (1993). Education policy, power relations and teachers' work. *British Journal of Educational Studies, 41*(2), 106–121.

Ball, S. (2006). *Education policy and social class: The selected works of Stephen Ball.* New York: Routledge.

Bartolome, L. (1994). Beyond the methods fetish: Toward a humanizing pedagogy. *Harvard Educational Review, 64*(2), 173–194.

Bigelow, B. (2006). Getting to the heart of quality teaching. *Rethinking Schools, 20*(2), 6–8.

Braverman, H. (1998). *Labor and monopoly capital: The degradation of work in the twentieth century* (25th anniversary edition). New York: Monthly Review Press.

Brosio, R. (1994). *A radical democratic critique of capitalist education.* New York: Peter Lang.

Bullough, R., & Gitlin, A. (1991). Educative communities and the development of the reflective practitioner. In B. Tabachnick & K. Zeichner (Eds.), *Issues and practices in inquiry-orientated teacher education* (pp. 35–55). New York: The Falmer Press.

Cannella, C. (2008). Faith in process, faith in people: Confronting policies of social disinvestment with PAR as pedagogy of expansion. In J. Cammarota & M. Fine (Eds.), *Revolutionizing education: Youth participatory action research in motion* (pp. 189–212). New York: Routledge.

Connell, R. (1989). The labour process and division of labour. In B. Cosin, M. Flude, & M. Hales (Eds.), *School, work and society* (pp. 123–134). Sydney, Australia: Hodder & Stroughton.

Dewey, J. (1997). *Experience and education.* New York: Touchstone. (Original work published in 1938).

Down, B. (2006). Educational science, mental testing, and the ideology of intelligence. *Melbourne Studies in Education, 42*(1), 1–23.

Down, B. (2009). Schooling, productivity and the enterprising self: Beyond market values. *Critical Studies in Education, 50*(1), 51–64.

Fielding, M. (1999). Target setting, policy pathology and student perspectives: Learning to labour in new times. *Cambridge Journal of Education, 29*(2), 277–287.

Freire, P. (1998). *Pedagogy of freedom: Ethics, democracy, and civic courage.* New York: Rowman & Littlefield Publishers.

Freire, P. (2000). *Pedagogy of the oppressed* (30th anniversary edn.). New York: Continuum. (Original work published 1975).

Freire, P. (2004). *Pedagogy of indignation.* Boulder, CO: Paradigm Publishers.

Gallagher, C. (2007). *Reclaiming assessment: A better alternative to the accountability agenda.* Portsmouth, NH: Heinemann.

Garrett, P. (2011, February 9). *NPST press release.* Retrieved February 2, 2011, from: http://www.aitsl.edu.au/

Giroux, H. (1988). *Teachers as intellectuals: Toward a critical pedagogy of learning.* New York: Bergin & Harvey.

Giroux, H. (2004). *The terror of neoliberalism: Authoritarianism and the eclipse of democracy.* Boulder, CO: Paradigm Press.

Giroux, H. (2005). *Schooling and the struggle for public life: Democracy's promise and educations' challenge.* Boulder, CO: Paradigm Publishers.

Giroux, H., & McLaren, P. (1986). Teacher education and the politics of engagement: The case for democratic schooling. *Harvard Education Review, 56*(3), 213–238.

Grattan, M. (2007, May 15). Quality education demands choice, claims Howard. *The Age,* p. 4.

Greene, M. (1995). *Releasing the imagination: Essays on education, the arts, and social change.* San Francisco: Jossey-Bass.

Grundy, S. (1987). *Curriculum: Product or praxis?* London: Falmer Press.

Hinchey, P. (2006). *Becoming a critical educator: Defining a classroom identity, designing a critical pedagogy.* New York: Peter Lang.

Interstate New Teacher Assessment and Support Consortium (INTASC). (1995). *Model standards for beginning teacher licensing and development.* Washington, DC: Council of Chief State School Officers. Retrieved May 6, 2011, from: http://www.ccsso.org/Resources/Programs/Interstate_Teacher_Assessment_Consortium_(InTASC).html

Jenesick, V. (2001). The standards movement: Issues, problems, and possibilities. In J. Kincheloe & D. Weil (Eds.), *Standards and schooling in the United States, Vol. 1* (pp. 159–167). Santa Barbara, CA: ABC-CLIO.

Kincheloe, J. (1993). *Toward a critical politics of teacher thinking: Mapping the postmodern.* Westport, CT: Bergin & Garvey.

Kincheloe, J. (2001a). *Getting beyond the facts: Teaching social studies/social sciences in the twenty-first century.* New York: Peter Lang.

Kincheloe, J. (2001b). Hope in the shadows-reconstructing the debate over educational standards. In J. Kincheloe & D. Weil (Eds.), *Standards and schooling in the United States, Vol. 1* (pp. 1–103). Santa Barbara, CA: ABC-CLIO.

Kincheloe, J. (2010). *Knowledge and critical pedagogy: An introduction.* Dordrecht, The Netherlands: Springer.

Kincheloe, J. (2011). Meet me behind the iron curtain: The struggle for a critical postmodern action research. In K. Hayes, S. Steinberg, & K. Tobin (Eds.), *Key works in critical pedagogy Joe Kincheloe* (pp. 85–99). Rotterdam, The Netherlands: Sense Publishers.

Kincheloe, J., Slattery, P., & Steinberg, S. (2000). *Contextualizing teaching: Introduction to education and educational foundations.* New York: Longman.

Kohl, H. (1994). *"I won't learn from you": And other thoughts on creative maladjustment.* New York: The New Press.

Kohn, A. (2004). *What does it mean to be well educated? And more essays on standards, grading, and other follies.* Boston: Beacon.

Kumashiro, K. (2004). *Against common sense: Teaching and learning toward social justice.* New York: RoutledgeFalmer.

Lawrence-Lightfoot, S. (2000). *Respect: An exploration.* Cambridge, MA: Perseus Books.

Lortie, D. (2002). *Schoolteacher* (2nd ed.). Chicago: The University of Chicago Press (Original work published 1975).

Lynch, T. (2002). *Full service schooling: Building stronger relationships with schools and communities.* Melbourne, Australia: Myer Full Service School Project.

Margonis, F. (2004). From student resistance to educative engagement: A case study in building powerful student-teacher relationships. In C. Bingham & A. Sidorkin (Eds.), *No education without relation* (pp. 39–53). New York: Peter Lang.

McMahon, B., & Portelli, J. (2004). Engagement for what? Beyond popular discourses of student engagement. *Leadership and Policy in Schools, 3*(1), 59–76.

Ohanian, S. (1999). *One size fits few: The folly of educational standards.* Portsmouth, NH: Heinemann.

Phelan, A. (2009). A new thing in an old world? Instrumentalism, teacher education, and responsibility. In F. Benson & C. Riches (Eds.), *Engaging in conversation about ideas in teacher education* (pp. 106–116). New York: Peter Lang.

Pope, D. (2001). *"Doing school": How we are creating a generation of stressed out, materialistic, and miseducated students.* New Haven, CT: Yale University Press.

Postman, N. (1996). *The end of education: Redefining the value of school.* New York: Vintage.

Ravitch, D. (1995). *National standards in American education: A citizens guide.* Washington, DC: The Brookings Institution.

Ravitch, D. (2010). *The death and life of the great American school system: How testing and choice are undermining education.* New York: Basic Books.

Reid, A. (2009). Is this really a revolution? A critical analysis of the Rudd government's national education agenda. *Curriculum Perspectives, 9*(3), 1–13.

Rivera, J., & Poplin, M. (1995). Multicultural, critical, feminine, and constructive pedagogies seen through the eyes of youth: A call for revisioning of these and beyond: Towards a pedagogy for the next century. In C. Sleeter & P. McLaren (Eds.), *Multicultural education: Critical pedagogy and the politics of difference* (pp. 221–244). New York: University of New York Press.

Roselli, A. (2005). *Dos and don'ts of education reform: Toward a radical remedy for educational failure*. New York: Peter Lang.

Shor, I. (1992). *Empowering education: Critical teaching for social change*. Chicago: University of Chicago Press.

Simon, R. (1988). For a pedagogy of possibility. *Critical Pedagogy Networker, 1*(1), 1–4.

Simon, R. (1992). *Teaching against the grain: Texts for a pedagogy of possibility*. New York: Bergin & Garvey.

Sizer, T. (2004). *Horace's compromise: The dilemma of the American high school*. New York: Houghton Mifflin Company. (Original work published 1984).

Smyth, J. (1989). A critical pedagogy of classroom practice. *Journal of Curriculum Studies, 21*(6), 483–502.

Smyth, J. (2001). *Critical politics of teachers' work: An Australian perspective*. New York: Peter Lang.

Smyth, J., Angus, L., Down, B., & McInerney, P. (2008). *Critically engaged learning: Connecting to young lives*. New York: Peter Lang.

Smyth, J., Angus, L., Down, B., & McInerney, P. (2009). *Activist and socially critical school and community renewal: Social justice in exploitative times*. Rotterdam, The Netherlands: Sense Publishers.

Smyth, J., Down, B., & McInerney, P. (2010). *'Hanging in with kids' in tough times: Engagement in contexts of educational disadvantage in the relational school*. New York: Peter Lang.

Smyth, J., & Shacklock, G. (1998). *Re-making teaching: Ideology, policy and practice*. New York: Routledge.

Thomas, T. P., & Schubert, H. (2001). Reinterpreting teacher certification standards: Locating limitations and possibilities. In J. Kincheloe & D. Weil (Eds.), *Standards and schooling in the United States, Vol. 1* (pp. 229–243). Santa Barbara, CA: ABC-CLIO.

Valencia, R. (2010). *Dismantling contemporary deficit thinking*. New York: Routledge.

Weil, D. (2001). Goals of standards: World class standards? whose world, which economic classes, and what standards. In J. Kincheloe & D. Weil (Eds.), *Standards and schooling in the United States, Vol. 2* (pp. 505–533). Santa Barbara, CA: ABC-CLIO.

Wiggins, G. (1999). *Assessing student performance: Exploring the purpose and limits of testing*. San Francisco: Jossey-Bass Publishers.

Wood, G. (2005). *Time to learn: How to create high schools that serves all students*. Portsmouth, NH: Heinemann.

# Chapter 6
# Teachers as *Classed* Cultural Workers *Speaking Back* Through Critical Reflection

**John Smyth**

One of the most enduring albeit occluded aspects of teaching is its classed nature—who does it, how it occurs, to whom and with what effects—all of which hold quite profound implications for the nature of social divisions in the wider society. The irony is that the more we try to hide it, as scholars on the left have done through resorting to notions of 'the third way', and those on the right, by denying that differences exist except in terms of meritocracy, then the more class becomes glaringly apparent (Aronowitz, 2003; Freie, 2007; Gorz, 1982; Joyce, 1995; Lareau & Conley, 2008; Marshall, Swift, & Roberts, 2002; Savage, 2000; Skeggs, 2004). Social cleavages exist in respect of all aspects of schooling, especially the way schools are organised and have become complicit in the working through of educational policies of high-stakes testing, national curriculum, school choice, privatisation, marketisation and the like. This has had the effect of exacerbating the distance between the educational 'haves' and the 'have nots'—something Roberts (2009) raises as a pertinent but frequently unexamined question when he says:

> Most writing on education and social class proceeds with the domain assumption that it would be a better world if working class . . . children did better in education leading to more upward social mobility. (pp. 649–650)

If we think of teaching as a variant of sociological work, then, as Roberts (2009) correctly points out, 'sociologists have never given up on class', and the production of scholarly books with an emphasis on class has been 'unrelenting' (p. 647). As I have argued extensively elsewhere (Smyth, Down, & McInerney, 2010), schooling is an intensely relational social activity, and what flows from this is that 'few sociologists will need much persuading that class remains a fundamental organiser of social experience', (Roberts, 2009, p. 647) particularly in respect of schooling. The challenging part, as Roberts notes, is that 'restoring class to its once central

J. Smyth (✉)
School of Education, University of Ballarat, Mt Helen, VIC, Australia
e-mail: j.smyth@ballarat.edu.au

B. Down and J. Smyth (eds.), *Critical Voices in Teacher Education*, Explorations of Educational Purpose 22, DOI 10.1007/978-94-007-3974-1_6,
© Springer Science+Business Media Dordrecht 2012

position in the sociology of education will depend on there being something new to say, opening up new vistas of change' (p. 647)—which is the primary challenge of this bookend chapter to the introductory section of this book.


## 'How Class Works' in *Schooling*

Social class is very much alive and well in our education systems and is deeply entrenched, sometimes in ways that are not always immediately obvious or apparent to us (Anyon, 2005). As social institutions, schools are quintessentially middle-class institutions that do their classed work by appealing to and feeding the aspirations of children and families that most closely reflect the norms of compliance, docility, individualism, assiduousness and deferred gratification. These are qualities that are deeply encrypted into the way schools think about themselves and what subsequently transpires, and they are hallmarks that are constantly being recognised, reinforced and affirmed in all kinds of ways individually and collectively. Middle-class parents have become particularly astute and adept at recognising and responding to these cultural cues put out by schools. Governments around the world have also been quick to endorse 'school choice' as a policy option enabling the middle class to seemingly capitalise even more on benefiting the most from what schools have on offer to improve the life circumstances of their offspring. The whole marketised and self-promotional response of schools in order to secure 'market share' dramatically feeds and illustrates this ideology.

It would not be putting too fine a point on it to say that, at least in the past, the middle class have been especially adroit in working out how to ensure that schools provide the 'best deal' for their children—and any schools that fail to understand that reality and fail to deliver will feel the harsh effects of middle-class consumer sovereignty as they 'shop' their children around to secure positional advantage. This is a process that has been underway for some time, but in recent times it has become powerfully sedimented into the public imagination—almost as an article of faith—albeit disguised under the rubric of supposedly making schools 'accountable' and 'responsive' (see for example: Smyth, 2011a).

At one level, teachers have become important policy actors through which the socially classed relay of schooling operates. Dimitriadis (2008) argues that this has occurred through a 'full-scale assault on the pedagogical imagination' that has profoundly shaped and delimited the way teachers 'understand and interact with their students' (p. 261). His claim is that teachers have become thoroughly enmeshed in a 'discourse of control and containment' especially in the way 'cultural knowledge is increasingly deemed as superfluous when set against . . . measures of accountability' (p. 261). In other words, as long as the terrain of schooling is presented as if it were allegedly neutral (but in reality, it constitutes a highly reductive and very tilted playing field) in respect of matters of educational achievement, attainment and outcomes, then discussions can be kept away from more complex issues of multiplicity and difference through 'a managerial language which looks to contain difference, rather than engage it in productive ways' (p. 261). What also gets put aside with respect to this perspective is the 'tide of difference . . . that flourishes in the everyday lives of youth outside of the school', thus allowing such issues to be swept into 'a technocratic framework of institutional control' (p. 261). The challenge for Dimitriadis, as for this chapter, is how to encourage teachers to work 'against the grain of contemporary logics in education', in ways that 'wrestle with the complex worlds of young people' so as to necessarily raise class issues by putting the focus squarely on 'how oppression works in systematic ways' (p. 261)—but more about that shortly.

## Three Particular Instances: Relationships, Knowledge and Curriculum

The point being made so far in this chapter, and that is well put by Dimitriadis (2008), is that 'notions of class are thick and deep' (p. 267) in schools. While it is generally the case that class saturates 'the lives of all social actors across the class spectrum, with life and death consequences' (p. 267), what goes on in schools is certainly character forming and reinforcing in ways that have enduring consequences for young people, their lives and communities. Social class differentiations are not simply economic and material—they are more than that. Social gradients reach into the way a society constructs the nature of interactions, the substance of those relationships, and how 'goods, services and culture are produced' (Anyon, 2008, p. 190).

It is clear from a range of studies (Ball, 2003, 2006; Connell, 1993; Lareau, 2000, 2003; Reay, 2006, 2007; Reay & Lucey, 2000, 2004; Rothstein, 2004; Weis, 2008) that when it comes to the nature of pedagogical relationships in schools, the way in which knowledge is conceived and thought about, and the nature and style of curriculum provided—then these differ markedly depending upon the context in which schools are located, and the communities from which young people come.

Anyon's (2008) seminal study of these matters in the late 1970s seem to have changed little over time and may have even solidified further with the passage of time. She studied four archetypical schools:

> What she found in the *working class school*—with parents, mostly fathers, who were unskilled or semi-skilled occupational groups—was a prevailing emphasis on drill and skill approaches with a focus on the basics, simple skills, recall of facts, and with students involved in compliant and passive forms of learning, with teachers who viewed them as incapable of learning, 'lazy' and who needed to be kept 'busy' (p. 191). Knowledge was seen as constituting 'fragmented facts, isolated from context and connection to each other or wider bodies of meaning', and of a 'practical' 'rule-governed behaviors' that involved learning procedures with which to carry out tasks. (p. 193)

In the *middle-class school*—with parents who were well-paid blue and white collar workers including teachers, social workers and middle managers—Anyon (2008) found knowledge to be regarded as 'being made by experts' and regarded as 'more important or legitimate than what one discovers of attempts to define for oneself' (p. 194). The pedagogical consequence was that there was more 'flexibility' in teaching approaches, teachers 'explained how to do' things often in 'several' different ways, and overall there was 'less emphasis on retention of facts . . . and more emphasis on children's understanding of the generalizations' (p. 194).

In the *affluent professional school*—where parents were highly paid professionals such as doctors, lawyers and executives—the knowledge emphasis was on 'individual discovery and creativity' and 'personal activity on the part of the student' (p. 196). Teachers worked relationally with students to 'immerse them in ideas', getting them to 'make sense' of their learning experiences through questioning techniques that had students go beyond recall and regurgitation. Approaches included questions of the kind: 'How should I do this? [to the students]; 'What does this mean?'; 'You decide!'; 'What do you think?'; and 'Figure that out for yourself' (p. 196).

In the *executive elite school*—where parents were vice presidents or executives of multinational corporations—knowledge was constituted as an 'intellectual process' of 'reasoning and problem solving', of 'understanding the internal structure of things' (p. 202) and as having an 'opinion' (p. 201), with teachers regarding themselves as being primarily responsible for creating an environment in which students could be decision makers and problem solvers. The relational emphasis was on 'thinking things through' with students being challenged with 'open-ended questions' for which there were 'no set answers' (p. 199).

In each of these school archetypes, Anyon (2008) found there was a defining motif or dominant theme. For example, in the working-class school, the dominant defining response was around various forms of '*student resistance*'—from 'active sabotage' of the classroom environment either physically or behaviourally, or 'passive' in the form of withholding enthusiasm or attention. In the middle-class school, the theme was one of a '*sense of possibility*'—meaning, 'if one works <u>hard</u> in school (and life), one will go far' (p. 195). The affluent professional school was defined by a sense of '*narcissism or extreme individualism*' (p. 198) that could manifest itself in an 'emphasis on thinking for oneself' (p. 198), or equally, it could externalise as 'a resource for social good' (p. 199). The executive elite school had a prevailing emphasis on '*excellence*' seen to lie in 'the necessity of preparation for being the best for top-quality performance' (p. 202). The pressure here was 'to perform' in order to get into the 'best' universities and colleges (p. 202).

## Teaching as a 'Class Act'

The title of this section is not meant to be simply a flippant play on words. The intent is to try and cast a little light, in a very small way, on an issue that keeps surfacing in the literature, disappearing, re-appearing, but never actually vanishing completely. There is an extensive literature trail in education on teachers and social class (see for example Acker, 1999; Connell, 1985; Ginsburg, 1995; Lawn, 1987;

Lawn & Grace, 1987; Ozga, 1988; Robertson, 2000; Smyth, 2001; Smyth, Dow, Hattam, Reid, & Shacklock, 2000; Smyth & Shacklock, 1998; Waller, 1932). Harris (1982), however, provides one of the most interesting, fascinating, comprehensive and informative commentaries through his framework of the 'economic', 'political' and 'ideological' identification of teachers. Harris argues that teachers occupy a contradictory class location—on the one hand, they bear lots of similarities to the working class, but on the other hand, they do not really fit at all neatly into it. The work teachers do makes them far from innocent in the process by which the state produces and reproduces inequalities, social hierarchies and social stratification among students and in society in general. Being implicated in reproducing inequality is not an attribute that rests easily with a working class ethos. Yet on the other hand, teachers are also caught up in this web of complexity in the way in which they do not have autonomous control over their work, which is being largely determined at a distance from classrooms through centrally devised and imposed curriculum frameworks, standards, testing and other accountability regimes. In other words, teaching is increasingly being shaped and controlled by a managerial class that receives its ideological orders from global predators like the OECD, World Bank, IMF, which then warehouse these ideas through business councils and roundtables who constitute the major source of consultancy and educational advice to governments. Harris makes the point that 'it seems feasible that teachers in general get a personal buzz out of being in control of others (the pupils) in the workplace' (p. 132)—although it is a moot point as to whether many teachers would agree with him on that.

There are several ways in which teaching can be argued as constituting working-class work. At a fundamental level, teachers are paid a wage or a salary, and to that extent they have no direct control over their remuneration other than what they can garner through collective bargaining. Another key indicator is the way in which the work of teaching is increasingly being scripted and prescribed—and while not yet like factory work in terms of its menial nature—the refrain from teachers is that they often feel like schools have been converted into some kind of educational 'sausage' factory.

At a more complex level, it is very clear that for some considerable time, schools have been constructed as compliant annexes to the economy. When the economy falters, when it overheats or when there are outbreaks of student resistance in the form of truancy, 'dropouts' or declining retention rates, then teachers are focussed upon as the 'defective' link in the educational chain and become the butt of media outrage and draconian policy remedies. Interestingly, the ultimate futility of this was captured recently in a debate in Australia around the need to get welfare recipients off the public purse and into employment—the fact that teaching was not directly invoked was more oversight than anything else. The media headline, in an uncharacteristically nuanced way, captured it nicely when it said: 'Waving policy sticks won't swell workforce' (The Age, 2011, p. 10).

We get into somewhat more sophisticated territory on this topic when we follow Brown, Lauder and Ashton's (2011) recent revelation of the great capitalist scam of the educational hoax and its concomitant appropriation of teachers into it. What they reveal is that education and schooling is deeply implicated in fabricating the myth of the connection between education, jobs and incomes—in a context in which there is a ruthless global 'auction for cut-price brain power' in the intensified competition for decent, well-paying middle-class jobs. Brown et al. (2011) put their argument most succinctly around the storyline of:

> ...the breakneck speed at which China and India, along with other emerging economies across Asia, South America, and Eastern Europe, have geared up to compete for high-value goods and services. This is shattering the view that the economic world would remain divided into *head* nations, such as America, Britain, and German and *body* nations, including China, India, and Vietnam. Such ideas fail to understand how the global economy allows emerging economies to leapfrog decades of industrial development to create a high-skill, low-wage workforce capable of competing successfully for hi-tech, high-value employment. (p. 3)

The hoax is glaringly exposed in the way students are continuing to be schooled in the 'neoliberal opportunity bargain..[of] learning equals earning' (p. 5), but in a context in which students and their families are grossly ill-prepared 'to meet the challenges posed by the era of knowledge capitalism because they are caught up in a gale of creative destruction that makes it difficult to find individual solutions to changing economic realities' (p. 5). To put Brown et al.'s (2011) argument in its sharpest form, in America (and we can likely bracket in the UK, Australia and other countries in here as well), 'most of those with a university degree...have not witnessed an increase in income since the early 1970s' with the result that the promised 'path to individual and national prosperity though education, has been torn up' (p. 5) and completely rendered by the global forces of knowledge capitalism. The point being made here is that teachers are being unwittingly co-opted as operatives into the perpetuation of this upward mobility scam that is likely to come crashing down on all of us.

On a slightly different but related issue, Condron (2011) has recently highlighted yet again, the accumulating evidence that while the USA 'is one of the most affluent countries in the world ... U.S. students' average achievement tends to lag behind that of students in other affluent countries' (p. 47). Yet, at the same time, the USA 'is the most economically unequal ... [with] income and wealth ... more unevenly distributed ... than in any other affluent country' (p. 47). This also fits with Wilkinson (2005) and Wilkinson and Pickett's (2009) evidence that unequal societies are more unhealthy than more equitable societies (see: Smyth et al., 2010, pp. 69–70 for an elaboration). While associational evidence of this kind does not 'prove' connections, it certainly points an accusing finger in a direction that can no longer be denied, namely, that 'economic inequality shapes achievement' (Condron, 2011, p. 53).

Brantlinger (2008), also alluding to US schools (and the argument translates equally to other affluent countries that have bought into the neoliberal agenda), argues that they not only produce some of the largest educational disparities in the industrialised world, but possibly even more significant is the fact that it is not only the poor who are damaged through the perpetuation of such inequities:

> . . . school inequities do not result from unintended or uncontrollable forces, but rather from deliberate collaboration between educated classes responsible for determining the nature of schooling and capitalists with an interest in controlling the minds and actions of citizens. (p. 243)

Brantlinger's line of reasoning is that schools 'play to middle-class self-interest', and it is this that gives them their dominant position over what transpires in schools and how success and failure (and blame) are defined:

> . . . although middle-class people have little direct contact with low-income people, they glibly narrate stories about their deficiencies in intellect and work ethic. Without access to evidence to the contrary, they *know* in their gut that the playing field is level and that their version of *Others* is accurate. They find reasons to blame working-class and low-income people for class discrepancies and hold themselves up as models to emulate. (p. 243)

Brantlinger (2008) proffers three persuasive arguments as to why it is in the interests of the middle class to re-think the paradoxical space they have manoeuvred themselves into. First, 'highly stratified and competitive schooling is socially and emotionally damaging to *all children*, including the supposed middle-class winners in the system' (p. 245, my emphases). The individual pathology argument about disengaged, tuned out and switched off kids coming from lower-class dysfunctional families does not fit with the evidence—'many violent, depressed, and stoned students come from 'good', two-parent, middle class families' (p. 246). We have to look elsewhere to the meaningless and abstract learning that is being driven by commodification and individual goals, that is producing this debilitating 'toxic. . . .alienation' among students regardless of their class location (p. 246)— but its primary driver is the middle-class meritocracy game. Underlying this is the 'societal competition' and the 'Darwinian survival of the fittest mentality' (p. 247) that in reality produces nothing more than 'student and teacher commodification, exploitation and alienation' (p. 247). Second, there is the widening income gaps between rich and poor that Brantlinger refers to as 'Brazilianization' (which in essence is what Brown, Lauder and Ashton were referring to), which is having the effect of rather than aligning the middle class with the elite ruling classes whose interests are in keeping wages low and profits high, turning the middle class into the new working poor. And, third, inequity is ultimately unsustainable. In times of national and international stress, uncertainty and upheaval that we currently live in, there can be no other way to go other than that of 'social reciprocity'. In other words, if we think we can weather crises by leaving the weakest behind, then we are delusional. In times of crisis, as we saw in the immediate aftermath of the GFC, the only way to operate is inclusively because the issues are too complex and interwoven to try and 'go it alone'—so too is the message educationally. Academic intensification, fuelled by the view that a few can succeed and insulate and cloister themselves from 'damage', while the rest can be allowed to fail, is fanciful thinking. When a few fail, we are all vulnerable.

Where Brantlinger (1993, 2003) is leading us with all of this is going beyond an 'impoverished' competitive view of how those who are already advantaged need to conduct themselves. She makes the point that confronting status hierarchies 'is a job for scholars' (Brantlinger, 2003, p. 194) and doing this constitutes an activist imperative based on a wider view of 'social reciprocity morality' (Brantlinger, 2003, p. 193).

## Where Are the Spaces from Which Alternative Social Practices Can 'Speak Back'?

I can best start this section with an anecdote, because it illustrates the delusional state we are in educationally. Today as I sat down to write, I had one of those moments where I questioned the accuracy of my eyes and my own sanity. I encountered a newspaper item in an Australian newspaper (Topsfield, 18 April, 2011) indicating that the government was searching for a business to invent and manufacture an 'attention sustaining drink' for 12–19-year-olds to be dispensed to schools in the Western Metropolitan region of Melbourne (an especially socially disadvantaged area) to 'sustain their attention throughout the day' (Business Victoria, 2011). It was to cost less than $1 a serve, and the total for the project was to be less than $1 million—in a context in which schools are to cut $338 million from their education budgets! It seemed that all my research around the social and cultural lives of young people and their educational and pedagogical milieu for 40 years had been totally on the wrong track. All that is required is to find the right elixir and dispense it—it has nothing at all to do with an engaging curriculum, or pedagogically switched on teachers, or the complexity of young lives. This is akin to Postman and Weingartner's (1969) 'vaccination theory of education'—that all you need in education is to have something, like a 'subject', and once you have 'had it, you are immune and need not take it again' (p. 32).

It was my intention to lead into this section by invoking Postman and Weingartner's (1969) timeless educational classic *Teaching as a Subversive Activity*, except the anecdote overtook me. Postman and Weingartner's opening point in their book is the 'essential mindlessness' of bureaucracies summarised in the motto 'carry on regardless', carefully avoiding 'why' questions and only countenancing 'how to' questions (p. 24). It is beholden upon schools, therefore, to be 'subversive' in developing in young people 'the attitudes and skills of social, political and cultural criticism' (p. 16). Invoking Ernest Hemingway's retort to a reporter about the characteristic of a 'good writer'—his reply—'have a built-in, shockproof crap detector' (p. 16), and so too we might argue for the 'good teacher'. To put it in more polite language, schools and teachers have a moral and non-negotiable social responsibility to cultivate in young people that most subversive of intellectual dispositions—'the anthropological perspective . . . that allows one to be part of his [sic] own culture and, at the same time, to be out of it' (p. 17). In other words, 'to recognise when reality begins to drift too far away from the grasp of the tribe' (p. 17), which seems be what we are having an overabundance of at the moment in education, and to do something about it.

The kind of subversive/anthropological approach necessary as an antidote to puncture the pomposity and stupidity of ideas that are a being allowed to intrude uninterrupted into schools and classrooms from outside, is the approach of 'being critical'—in particular, ensuring that teachers operate as 'critically reflective practitioners' (Smyth, McInerney, Hattam, & Lawson, 1999). This is a disposition and a process that involves a more than being negative or carping, although confronting and naming nonsense has to be a part of it. The larger agenda is one of constructing an alternative in which teachers adopt an orientation within their teaching that is attuned to the kind of social class and political dispositions towards schooling canvassed in the earlier part of this chapter. It means being a courageous political activist (Smyth, Angus, Down, & McInerney, 2009) working with/for students, parents, families and communities towards *Critically Engaged Learning* (Smyth, Angus, Down, & McInerney, 2008), by which I mean foregrounding and being an advocate for issues that are demonstrably in the best interests of students, schools and communities—and not the interests of 'uncouth interloper' (Adorno, 1974, p. 23) and managerialist discourses and practices that have no rightful place in schools.

If we take as an example, one of the centrepieces of the neoliberal project, the notion of 'standards' that are allegedly collapsing around us in schools. What governments, educational systems and their cottage welfare industry of 'expert' consultants argue is required to restore public confidence are muscular forms of managerialism, accountability and teacher appraisal schemes that will panel beat recalcitrant teachers back into shape and magically restore sagging international economic competitiveness. If only it were that simple! Never mind the shattering effects on lives of the tectonic plates of global capitalism that are shifting around, over which we have no control, and that are determining our destiny in invisible and distant ways, as alluded to earlier by Brown et al. (2011).

Turning these kinds of tsunami forces around from within schools is a well-nigh impossible task, but if schools are characterised by one thing above all, it is a passionate belief in 'hope' and 'possibility'. As educators, we have to believe that we can work for collective betterment, that 'dark forces' can be put under the glare of scrutiny, named and exposed for the counterfeits and frauds they are and that more just, inclusive, democratic alternatives can be inserted in their place. That is what it means to be a critically reflective educational practitioner!

Taking on this Herculean task is the anthesis of quick-fix technical 'solutions' that are rampant at the moment and being inflicted on schools. The socially critically reflective alternative that I am talking about involves having an articulate philosophical disposition that says, in effect, there is something fundamentally wrong with the current functionalist fix-it mentality, that it lacks commonsense and that a better alternative is one that is solidly rooted in the dialogical and relational ways people live their lives, pursue their aspirations of themselves and their children and, in the process, use their intellects—rather than having them demeaned, denigrated and laminated over, as is occurring in the current dominant approach towards school reform.

So, what does this socially critical reflective disposition look like? To be blatantly honest—like nothing officially on offer in schools. It starts out with a number of quite *simple but very uncommon propositions*, like:

- A belief that 'questions' are more important than 'answers'—quite the opposite of the current dominant infatuations with 'solutions' to problems that are totally misunderstood (or wilfully misrepresented) or, that at best, have only been explored at the most superficial level.
- Starting from the stance that conventional ways of looking at issues to do with how schools are organised largely serve the wrong interests—for example, testing, school choice, league tables, performance-driven school self-management, outcome targets, standards, league tables, leadership, teacher effectiveness and almost any of the other imposed agendas we choose to focus on in schools. These are the policy relays of international capitalism in its race to the bottom in the unremitting quest for the cheapest per unit cost of labour. What has to happen is that these interlopers have to be robustly confronted and interrogated with a single question:

  > How is this (xxx) going to demonstrably improve the learning opportunities and life chances of these children and the communities they live in?

  The responses to this question will be startling and alarming. They will reveal that most of what has been insinuated into schools in living memory are not serving the interests they allege to be, and they ought to be jettisoned as collateral rubbish. Quite simply, they will fail the test question above.

  As a newspaper headline I encountered today so incisively put it, in its 180° deflection or rotation: 'State flunks its own literacy, numeracy tests' (Harrison, 2011)—a story about how the State government of Victoria in Australia failed half of the 34 targets it set itself, met only 6 targets and made some progress on 11. What is interesting is the positioning of the 'failure' here—not students, teachers or schools, but the State itself, and we could argue for good reason, because it has been co-opted into the futile international game of 'targetology' in which there can only ever be losers.
- It believes, contrary to the prevailing conventional view, that the people who know best about the obstacles/impediments/inferences to learning in schools (especially those labelled as the most 'disadvantaged') happen to also be the ones existentially closest to the issues—teachers, students, parents and community workers—and they have to be the front runners and leaders in explicating the issues and complexities and devising locally owned and locally sensitive solutions. The role of outsiders, if there is one at all, is in providing the resources by which local solutions can become a reality. In other words, there is a complete inversion here—even the most 'disadvantaged' communities are regarded for the strengths they have, rather than their alleged deficits, failings and pathologies, and are instead inextricably implicated in making sense of their situations and how they came to be the way they are, and devising new directions to satisfy unfulfilled aspirations.

Some of the *touchstone questions* that animate socially critical practitioners, include:

- Where did this idea come from?
- Who does it seem to work for, or whose interests are served? And concomitantly, whose are silenced or denied?
- How are the most marginalised (students/families) made to feel the most welcome/included here?
- Who says the current state of affairs have to be the way they are—and what interests are they serving?
- How can this school work in ways to include and listen to the most excluded?
- How can a curriculum be devised that is engaging, fun, rigorous as well as inclusive of the diversity present in most classrooms?
- How can assessment and reporting be developed that is demonstrable of strengths, successes, development and growth and that properly acknowledges inequities—rather than apportioning blame, being demeaning, punitive or retributive?
- How can we treat teachers as if they are intellectuals with something valuable to say about teaching and learning, rather than as if they were robotic unthinking technicians required to follow orders?
- How can teachers be encouraged to take the risks necessary for authentic learning to occur, and how can students be enthused with this same passion?
- How can students be given an authentic voice and ownership of their learning around big ideas that fire their imagination?

There are some very big and courageous questions in this, and they are not ones for the faint-hearted, but they are questions of the order of magnitude that need to be taken on if schools are to benefit *all children*, not just the already advantaged, and if teaching and learning is to be reclaimed from the impoverished and diminished set of ideas that have been allowed to hijack schools over the past 30 years.

The bookkeeping and accounting mentalities that have been behind these manoeuvres, and which have masqueraded as so-called regimes of accountability and transparency, may well have been doing what they have been for what they consider to have been the 'right' reasons, but the paradigm that has captured and animated them is one that is completely blind to the true purpose of schooling.

The reclamation process I am referring to needs to be as I have indicated around the larger sociological and political questions of what is happening to schools, but these need to be nested in a range of not unrelated questions at the level of the pedagogy of teachers in classrooms. As I expressed it on an earlier occasion, some possible candidates that might be the focus of critically reflective teachers in their daily teaching might include:

- Who talks in this classroom?
- Who gets the teacher's time?
- How is ability identified and attended to here, and what is the rationale?
- How is the unequal starting points of students dealt with here?

- How are instances of disruptive behaviour explained and handled?
- Is there a competitive or a co-operative ethos in this classroom?
- Who helps who here?
- Whose ideas are the most important or count most?
- How do we know that learning is occurring here?
- Are answers or question more important in this classroom?
- How are decisions made here?
- How does the arrangement of the room help or hinder learning?
- Who benefits and who is disadvantaged in this classroom?
- How is conflict resolved?
- How are rules determined?
- How are inequalities recognised and dealt with?
- Where do learning materials come from?
- By what means are resources distributed?
- What career aspirations do students have, and how is that manifested?
- Who determined standards, and how are they arrived at?
- How is failure defined, and to what is it ascribed? Who or what fails?
- Whose language prevails in the classroom?
- How does the teacher monitor his/her agenda?
- How does the teacher work to change oppressive structures in the classroom?
- What is it that is being measured and assessed in this classroom?
- Who do teachers choose to work with collaboratively, on what and under what circumstances (Smyth, 2011b, pp. 37–38)?

In situ questions like these, when asked against the wider background in which schools are operating, enables the focus to be put much more squarely on the forces that are shaping schooling and, thus, take negative attention away from those parts of the teaching/learning process that ought to be receiving more assistance in what they are doing.

## So, 'What Then Is to Be Done?'

The concluding section of this chapter invokes Lenin's famous line from his 1902 pamphlet *What is to be done?* in which he argues that battles over wages and economic matters on their own are unlikely to produce lasting or profound changes—rather, what has to occur is that people (like educators) have to become 'political' in the sense of understanding the workings of the knowledge sphere of relationships in *all of society*.

What the arguments in this chapter have sought to do is move somewhat in that direction. Teachers are caught up in their personal biographies and professional work in a struggle over social stratification, and the issues are deep, pervasive, enduring and complex. There is no likelihood that the top-down approaches that have significantly contributed to the situation described in this chapter in the first place have the political will or imagination to do anything about it.

The process for action, as I am calling it, will have to occur locally, in classrooms, in schools, among schools and with communities—by reflecting on the kind of issues in an active way that constructs alternatives. At a broad level, there are four moments (or steps) that have to be initiated for critical reflection to have a possibility of succeeding:

1. *Solidarity*: Very little is possible in terms of major change when we act individually. Social change of any consequence comes about through collective commitment to ideas or social solidarity. For educators committed to examining the kind of changes discussed in this chapter, a group of like-minded colleagues needs to affiliate in order to provide and receive the kind of support needed to be courageously analytical and supported in doing that . . . and for that to become a reality, there needs to be . . .
2. *Relational Space*: This refers to the safe place in which to dialogically examine through conversation with others what is going on, to engage in deep learning, to listen to the voices of those closest to the issues and, in the process, to gather the evidence from within educational settings on matters that are professionally unsettling or producing perplexity. Once a point of shared dissatisfaction is reached with the existing state of affairs and there is some clarity about what needs to be changed, then what is about to happen amounts to an . . . .
3. *Interruption*: By this stage, arguments, issues, dissatisfactions and possibilities about how things might be different will have been given a thorough airing, and not doing something differently is not an option. Making a change amounts to an act of interruption—and such changes will have been countenanced in the light of what is prudent and any expected obstacles, interferences and impediments. Knowledge will also have begun to be acquired as to what happened when changes are made, how things are different, what lessons have been learned for the future . . . and how these learnings might be used to inform or enthuse others . . .
4. *Celebrating/sharing successes*: Stepping back and assessing what has been accomplished is a natural thing to do—as is the desire to want to draw others into this circle of enthusiasm, to show and tell them what has been done and its benefits so as to be similarly informed from the experience. So, the process starts all over again . . .

Changes of the kind being argued for throughout this chapter are of a very different kind from those being leveraged from outside, for example, by demanding conformity to rules and regulations or by trying to engender improvements by means of inducements like performance indicators. As one cryptic observer put it, 'people aren't donkeys, so . . . put away the carrot and stick' (Gittins, 2011). What is occurring instead here are socially critically informed improvements that are profoundly embedded in *Practical Wisdom* (Schwartz & Sharpe, 2010)—which is the essence of what teachers as cultural workers do (Freire, 1998) because of the way they exercise judgement in respect of what is morally the right thing to do.

# References

Acker, S. (1999). *The realities of teachers' work: Never a dull moment.* London/New York: Cassell.
Adorno, T. (1974). *Minima moralia: Reflections from damaged life.* London: Verso.
Anyon, J. (2005). *Radical possibilities: Public policy, urban education and a new social movement.* New York: Routledge.
Anyon, J. (2008). Social class and school knowledge. In L. Weis (Ed.), *The way class works: Readings on schools, family and the economy* (pp. 189–209). London/New York: Routledge.
Aronowitz, S. (2003). *How class works: Power and social movements.* New Haven, CT: Yale University Press.
Ball, S. (2003). *Class strategies and the education market: The middle classes and social advantage.* London: Routledge/Falmer.
Ball, S. (2006). *Education policy and social class: The selected works of Stephen J. Ball.* London: Routledge.
Brantlinger, E. (1993). *The politics of social class in secondary schools: Views of affluent and impoverished youth.* New York: Teachers College Press.
Brantlinger, E. (2003). *Dividing classes: How the middle class negotiates and rationalizes school advantage.* New York/London: Routledge/Falmer.
Brantlinger, E. (2008). Playing to middle-class self-interest in pursuit of school equity. In L. Weis (Ed.), *The way class works: Readings on school, family and the economy* (pp. 243–259). London/New York: Routledge.
Brown, P., Lauder, H., & Ashton, D. (2011). *The global auction: The broken promises of education, jobs and incomes.* Oxford: Oxford University Press.
Business Victoria. (2011, 13 April). *Attention sustaining drink.* Technology Requirement Specification (TRS).
Condron, D. (2011). Egalitarianism and educational excellence: Compatible goals for affluent societies? *Educational Researcher, 40*(2), 47–55.
Connell, B. (1993). *Schools and social justice.* Toronto, Canada: Our Schools/Our Selves Education Foundation.
Connell, R. (1985). *Teachers' work.* Sydney, Australia: Allen & Unwin.
Dimitriadis, G. (2008). Class, teachers and teacher education. In L. Weis (Ed.), *The way class works: Readings on school, family and the economy* (pp. 261–272). New York: Routledge.
Freie, C. (2007). *Class construction: White working-class student identity in the new millennium.* Lanham, MD: Rowman & Littlefield.
Freire, P. (1998). *Teachers as cultural workers: Letters to those who dare to teach.* Boulder, CO: Westview Press.
Ginsburg, M. (Ed.). (1995). *The politics of educators' work and lives.* New York/London: Garland Publishing.
Gittins, R. (2011, April 20). People aren't donkeys, so best to put away the carrot and stick. *The Age,* Melbourne, p. 19.
Gorz, A. (1982). *Farewell to the working class.* London: Pluto Press.
Harris, K. (1982). *Teachers and classes: A Marxist analysis.* London: Routledge Kegan & Paul.
Harrison, D. (2011, April 19). State flunks its own literacy, numeracy tests. *The Age,* Melbourne, pp. 1 & 2.
Joyce, P. (Ed.). (1995). *Class.* Oxford: Oxford University Press.
Lareau, A. (2000). *Home advantage: Social class and parental intervention in elementary education.* Lanham, MD: Rowman & Littlefield.
Lareau, A. (2003). *Unequal childhoods: Class, race and family life.* Berkeley, CA: University of California Press.
Lareau, A., & Conley, D. (Eds.). (2008). *Social class: How does it work?* New York: Russell Sage.
Lawn, M. (1987). *Servants of the state: The contexted control of teaching 1900–30.* Lewes, UK: Falmer Press.
Lawn, M., & Grace, G. (Eds.). (1987). *Teachers: The culture and politics of work.* Lewes, UK: Falmer Press.

Marshall, G., Swift, A., & Roberts, S. (2002). *Against the odds: Social class and social justice in industrial society*. Oxford: Clarendon.

Ozga, J. (Ed.). (1988). *Schoolwork: Approaches to the labour process of teaching*. Milton Keynes, UK: Open University Press.

Postman, N., & Weingartner, C. (1969). *Teaching as a subversive activity*. Harmondsworth, UK: Penguin.

Reay, D. (2006). The zombie stalking English schools: Social class and educational inequality. *British Journal of Educational Studies, 54*(3), 288–307.

Reay, D. (2007). 'Unruly places': Inner-city comprehensives, middle-class imaginaries and working-class children. *Urban Studies, 44*(7), 1191–1201.

Reay, D., & Lucey, H. (2000). Children, school choice and social differences. *Educational Studies, 26*(1), 83–100.

Reay, D., & Lucey, H. (2004). Stigmatised choices: Social class, social exclusion and secondary school markets in the inner city. *Pedagogy, Culture and Society, 12*(1), 35–51.

Roberts, K. (2009). Review of Weis, "The way class works: Readings on school, family and the economy". *British Journal of Sociology of Education, 30*, 647–651.

Robertson, S. (2000). *A class act: Hanging teachers' work, the state and globalisation*. New York/London: Falmer Press.

Rothstein, R. (2004). *Class and schools: Using social, economic, and educational reform to close the black-white achievement gap*. New York: Economic Policy Institute.

Savage, M. (2000). *Class analysis and social transformation*. Buckingham, UK: Open University Press.

Schwartz, B., & Sharpe, K. (2010). *Practical wisdom*. New York: Riverhead Books.

Skeggs, B. (2004). *Class, self, culture*. London: Routledge.

Smyth, J. (2001). *Critical politics of teachers' work: An Australian perspective*. New York: Peter Lang Publishing.

Smyth, J. (2011a). The disaster that has been the 'self-managing school'—Its genesis, trajectory, undisclosed agenda, and effects. *Journal of Educational Administration and History, 43*(2), 95–117.

Smyth, J. (2011b). *Critical pedagogy for social justice*. London/New York: Continuum.

Smyth, J., Angus, L., Down, B., & McInerney, P. (2008). *Critically engaged learning: Connecting to young lives*. New York: Peter Lang Publishing.

Smyth, J., Angus, L., Down, B., & McInerney, P. (2009). *Activist and socially critical school and community renewal: Social justice in exploitative times*. Rotterdam, The Netherlands: Sense Publishers.

Smyth, J., Dow, A., Hattam, R., Reid, A., & Shacklock, G. (2000). *Teachers' work in a globalising economy*. London/New York: Falmer Press.

Smyth, J., Down, B., & McInerney, P. (2010). *'Hanging in with kids' in tough times: Engagement in contexts of educational disadvantage in the relational school*. New York: Peter Lang Publishing.

Smyth, J., McInerney, P., Hattam, R., & Lawson, M. (1999). *Critical reflection on teaching and learning*. Adelaide, Australia: Flinders Institute for the Study of Teaching.

Smyth, J., & Shacklock, G. (1998). *Re-making teaching: Ideology, policy and practice*. London/New York: Routledge.

The Age (Editorial). (2011, April 15). *Waving policy sticks won't swell the workforce*, Melbourne.

Topsfield, J. (2011, April 18). Government U-turn on 'weird' plan for school drink. *The Age*, Melbourne, p. 1.

Waller, W. (1932). *The sociology of teaching*. New York: Wiley.

Weis, L. (Ed.). (2008). *The way class works: Readings on school, family and the economy*. New York: Routledge.

Wilkinson, R. (2005). *The impact of inequality: How to make sick societies healthier*. New York: The New Press.

Wilkinson, R., & Pickett, K. (2009). *The spirit level: Why more equal societies almost always do better*. London: Allen Lane.

# Part II
# Teaching Class, Race, Gender and Student Activism

# Chapter 7
# Unsettling Class: Standpoint Pedagogies, Knowledge and Privilege

Jane Pearce

Imagine a sociology of education tutorial, taking place on the campus of an Australian university. There are 20 or so students in the group of mixed age and gender and of diverse social class backgrounds. All are in their third year of a 4-year Bachelor of Education degree. I have taught all of them before, but we have never looked at this subject together.

'So', I begin, 'What impact do you think social class has on a child's capacity to engage with education?'

It's a big question. The class sits, pondering.

'Well, I guess if you're working class you might not have the money to go on school trips and do extra-curricular stuff, and you might not have good equipment like other kids', offers Kelley.

'Being working class means never having enough money, never being sure of your job, always worrying about where the next meal's coming from and always having to move round because you can never afford your own home'. Chris confidently ticks the list off on her fingers.

'Yeah, and teachers don't like you if you're working class', says Lindy. 'I never had the right pencils and books, and used to go to school without shoes. You'd think the teachers would be extra sympathetic, but they just put me in a corner and ignored me'.

'And it doesn't stop with school', Shane says. 'Look at me—I'm 45 and still trying to finish my education at uni. Remember when I had to take a year off and went back to the buses to earn some money so I could carry on and finish?'

Monique, young and private school-educated, stares round-eyed at the group. 'I never knew you guys had such a bad time! Nothing like that ever happened to me. I s'pose that makes me, er ... really privileged?'

The others look at her. There is a tense silence; these are indeed difficult conversations. The group has become unsettled and, I sense, may be about to take sides on the basis of who is and who is not privileged. I am not sure how to proceed.

I make a mental note to tackle the topic differently next time.

J. Pearce (✉)
School of Education, Murdoch University, Perth, Australia
e-mail: j.pearce@murdoch.edu.au

B. Down and J. Smyth (eds.), *Critical Voices in Teacher Education*, Explorations of Educational Purpose 22, DOI 10.1007/978-94-007-3974-1_7,
© Springer Science+Business Media Dordrecht 2012

## The Importance of Social Class

In this chapter, I explore some of the ways I have attempted to do that, by bringing issues of social class to the fore in teacher education through pedagogies such as biography, critical inquiry and a 'standpoint' approach. Underpinning these attempts is the belief that it is vital for future teachers to develop a consciousness of how social class both opens up and closes down educational opportunities, so they can not only better understand and critique the practices that sustain class privilege but also demonstrate how they might use this knowledge to adopt more socially just alternatives. With the insights of Chris, Lindy, Shane and Monique as a guide, I have tried to find new ways to enable students of teaching to take up class-conscious positions in their own teaching, based on a deeper knowledge of the ways that the lives of us all are shaped by social class. In particular, I am interested in exploring how teachers might come to know or see social class in such a way as to help them understand their own students' experiences and orientations to education, and then engage with an institution that tends to be colonised by middle-class culture and values (Green, 2003; Hooks, 1994; Preston, 2007).

Social class remains a powerful predictor of success in education (Alfaro, 2008; Archer, Hutchings, & Ross, 2003; Ball, 2010). Issues associated with social class and access to education 'play an important role in ensuring either the reproduction of (middle-class) privileges or (working-class) disadvantages' (Archer et al., 2003, p. 5). The persistence of educational inequities, based on social class, bears this out, as McGregor (1997) explains:

> Being in the working-class is a synonym for underprivilege. Working-class people in general earn less than other groups, own less, have a poorer education, have less access to the goods of the society they live in, and have less opportunity for a good life: equal opportunity simply does not exist in Australia (p. 186).

In Australia, if inequalities can be defined in terms of access to higher education, there appears to have been no reduction in social group inequalities over the past two decades. Here, the proportion of students from low SES students enrolled in Australian universities remains unchanged at 15–16%, even though this group makes up 25% of the broader Australian population (Clancy & Goastellec, 2007; James, Blexley, & Maxwell, 2008). In the UK, there are indications that recent education reforms aimed at raising standards have had little or no impact on the gaps in performance between social groups (Ball, 2010). So while standards may have been raised overall, the gap persists. Ball suggests that such inequities can be explained partly in terms of the 'classist' nature of education policies and the class bias of schools, which operates through institutional procedures and teacher expectations 'for the interests of some and against those of other categories of children' (p. 157). Thus, while class may have become a part of our cultural and political 'unconsciousness' (Aronowitz, 2003, p. 25), it remains a salient and powerful category in understanding the cultural processes of advantaging and disadvantaging of students in education.

In view of suggestions that teachers themselves are implicated in such 'classist' practices, it seems essential that teacher educators bring to the fore issues of class in such a way that future teachers are able to develop a form of class consciousness. In other words, teacher educators should work with their students to make evident the dominant ideologies that 'inform our perceptions and treatment of subordinated students' (Bartolomé, 2008, p. x). To do this, we need first to be able to recognise that class is 'a major feature of subjectivity … central to us all, even if we do not feel impeded by it or choose not to recognize it, or to avoid it through disidentifications and dissimulations' (Skeggs, 1997, p. 7). However, as the events of the tutorial showed, talking about social class is risky. It 'makes us all tense, nervous, uncertain about where we stand' (Hooks, 2000, p. vii). Accordingly, matters of class power are 'sanitized and its powerful effects on the life chances of working-class students is denuded or made invisible' (McLaren & Farahmandpur, 2005, p. 8). In my teaching, I look for ways to explore the complexities of day-to-day experiences of social class to allow us to move beyond more simplistic and sanitised understandings to make salient the troubling and unsettling nature of class power, yet without placing students in position where they might feel embarrassed when their privileged or underprivileged status is unmasked during these processes.

As McLaren says, paraphrasing Marx, 'human beings act on and in the world in situations not entirely of their own making' (2004, p. xvii). Such situations, among which I include social class, have a particular affect on our behaviour as social beings. However, even though our social class is not of 'our own making', it does not mean our behaviours are necessarily circumscribed by it. Giddens' notion of the reflexive self is useful here, as it brings together ideas about the self and ideas about action. He suggests that 'reflexive awareness', which is the process of constantly monitoring the circumstances of individual action, is 'characteristic of all human action' (Giddens, 1991, p. 35). The following story, based on a childhood experience, is an example of using storytelling for reflexive awareness. It shows how it is possible to identify the values and ideologies hidden beneath the events and illustrate how the personal and the political are intertwined. I have used the story in my teaching to model critical inquiry and to explain how I first became aware of my own class privilege. Now, when teaching this unsettling issue, I begin by framing myself as a person of 'class', through the story of my association with Cathie.

## Cathie's Story

I learned early in my life as a school student how institutional habitus works to legitimise the dominant values of the school community (Reay, David, & Ball, 2001). I look back to my first days at school and remember how those students who were 'different' in their orientation to school (because they did not look after their pencils and books, were not eager to please the teacher, were not punctual) were seen as deficient. I can see now how I was made complicit in this process since

I was not 'different'. On the contrary, I had all the necessary and valued attributes to be seen as successful and could therefore be held up as an 'example' (as a teacher might hold up a piece of work to show the rest of the class what to do).

My identification with the teachers was to receive public confirmation when, as an older child, I began to be asked to help teach other children. At first, it was on an ad hoc basis, but later, I was sent to work on a regular basis with a child in another class who could not read. 'Cathie' was about 3 years younger than I, and she was sweet: friendly, pretty, chatty and sociable, but came from an extremely 'disadvantaged' family. I quickly became enthusiastic and very committed to making a difference for Cathie. I would go and listen to her read in class most days, and increasingly I spent time with her at lunchtimes too. I loved 'helping'; and the more she told me about her life, the more I wanted to help. I developed a fascination for Cathie, sensing how different her life was from mine, and began more and more to see her as a victim who needed to be rescued (by me). I relished my role as a saviour. Then one day, Cathie invited me to her house for tea.

She lived five minutes' walk away from me. There was her mother, in the grease-splattered kitchen. She was cooking chips for our tea. It looked as if they ate nothing else. The grease ran down the chip pan and covered the stove. It had formed a solid layer on the kitchen wall behind the cooker. It had splashed on the floor and been trodden in and was now integral with the floor covering. The sink was overflowing with unwashed dishes. There was little furniture in the living room, and what was there was broken and filthy. The house had a pungent smell. Cathie's mother was young and thin. She greeted me deferentially and apologised for the mess. I was a 10-year-old child.

After the tea, I went home in shock. I had never imagined that people could live like that. The contrast between what I had and what Cathie had was stark. I was devastated.

From memory, my friendship with Cathie waned from this point. I felt too guilty (of privilege) to invite her to my home and no longer took pleasure in being her 'teacher' once the deep gulf between her life experiences and my own became apparent. I had thought of us as friends, but could no longer relate to her in ways that were not confronting. As an adult, and as an educator, I find this memory sobering and difficult. I now see that my privilege was what made her oppression; only because of my privilege could I engage in her life, and she would never have been in a position to engage in mine in the same way.

I now understand how Cathie revealed to me new perspectives on the socially constituted nature of my privilege. She showed how, although we all live 'classed' lives, we are often unconscious of it. I look back and catch myself in the act of being subjectified as the 'norm' at school, becoming the 'other' to Cathie and her family. My social class situation, though indeed not entirely of my own making (McLaren, 2004), had nevertheless given me 'advantage'. As a future teacher, in what was in effect part of my 'apprenticeship of observation' (Hatton, 1998, p. 6), I had already been exposed to that idea that when teachers practise, they are engaged in a performance that is 'plotted within grids of power relations and social norms' (Alexander, Anderson, & Gallegos, 2004, p. 2).

## Critical Inquiry: Social Class and Habitus

In telling the story of Cathie, I have focused on the intensely personal and emotional side to the experience. However, the story also reminds us of the role of institutions in cementing social difference, and that to move away from feelings of guilt, our focus must move from the personal to the 'larger sociopolitical contexts' in which students experience education (McLaren, 1995, p. 153). Bourdieu's understanding of class, using the concepts of 'habitus' and 'field' (Bourdieu & Passeron, 1977, 1996), allows for such an analysis. As Ball (2006) explains, it is all about how 'class is *achieved* and *maintained* and *enacted* rather than something that just is!' (p. 8, my emphasis). Bourdieu suggests it is the interaction between objective structures or the 'field' (such as schools and other education institutions) and personal experiences or histories (such as those of students in schools) that culminates in a person's acquired habitus.

'Habitus' describes the way in which we behave and live our daily lives in response to the way that the field might organise us. Our habitus appears to us to be common sense and natural; it becomes a space that we regulate and is of our own making, but made unselfconsciously (Bourdieu, 1990). Individuals within the field are so caught up with that field's practices, both emotionally and intellectually, that as they live within the confines of the field and its values, they begin to inhabit the field 'like a garment' (Bourdieu, 2000, p. 143), comfortable inside it and displaying their own identity through the wearing of it. The field, constituted by those who participate in it, reflects the habitus of its constituents (Jenkins, 2002). The presence of middle-class values and habitus in the field of education renders it predominantly middle class. Not only that, agents in the field (such as teachers) incorporate the knowledge that will enable them to continue to constitute the field. 'The existence of a field presupposes and … creates a belief on the part of participants in the legitimacy and value of the capital which is "at stake" in the field' (Jenkins, 2002, p. 85). Cultural capital, social capital and symbolic capital are particularly at stake in the field of education. Here, since 'the education system is socially and culturally biased' (Reay et al., 2001, p. 5), the knowledges of the white middle class are valued over all other knowledges. Thus, institutional habitus legitimises the dominant values and the prevailing cultural capital of society (Lareau, 2000).

It is by engaging reflexively with the institutions that mould us that we can reveal our habitus. The field and habitus are intimately linked, almost inextricably so, unless we make a conscious, reflexive effort to understand their interconnections. Misrecognition is one of the consequences of not fully understanding the way in which we operate in the field (Danaher, 2002), but by exploring the concept of misrecognition, it is possible to make social class habitus more visible to students of teaching. By framing the story of my connection with Cathie in terms of the institutional contexts or field that led to the association in the first place, the political dimensions of the personal experience can be recognised. From this perspective, it can be seen how my habitus (which produced certain attitudes to other people as a well as particular personal identities) was a product of both my social class background and the institutional field that legitimised the values that I held. Through story, complex sociological concepts can be translated into experiences that are more easily recognised.

## Deficit Readings

Not only does Cathie's story bring out the role of institutional habitus in shaping individual habitus, it also shows how easily we slip into the dangerous reading of social class that views working-class students as 'disadvantaged', 'vulnerable' or 'at risk' (Shields, Bishop, & Mazawi, 2005, p. 9), and that places students and their families in deficit, with debilitating consequences. Another story of another 'disadvantaged' student, but seen this time through my eyes as a teacher, demonstrates how, by taking the student's standpoint, it is possible to turn the tables and place us, the teachers, in deficit.

I was reminded again of Cathie many years later when I was teaching in a large comprehensive school in a northern English city. The school drew students from socially mixed areas, yet many were students who experienced the chronic poverty and disadvantage found in areas of high unemployment. In some families, the experience of long-term unemployment had spanned three generations, and many students lived in sole parent families.

Edna was small for her age, skinny and always slightly unkempt. The dark circles under her eyes spoke of irregular hours, her grubby uniform and cheap shoes of the neglect that so often accompanies deep and unrelenting poverty. Edna's frail looks were deceptive. She had a steely determination, and little time for teachers who 'do her head in' by making unrealistic demands of her. By her fifth year in the school, Edna had garnered a notoriety that made even the toughest teachers approach her warily. She was the kind of kid whose absence from class will make a teacher's day less fraught.

Edna was in the 'bottom' class in her year. Classes were broadly streamed and named in an alphabetical hierarchy starting with J (the 'high flyers') and ending with T. Edna was in 5T. It was her last year in school, but she was hardly ever absent. Teachers said of her, 'I don't know why she's still coming in. What's the point?' In these ways, Edna's future was decided; she was already a reject, on the outer, wasting her (and our) time by her persistent attendance. So she was always in trouble, and suddenly in double trouble when she started not turning up for the after-school, hour-long detentions she seemed to receive daily. I was her form tutor. I had to do something.

Next morning, there she was: present as usual. During a lull in the early morning business of record keeping, I approached her.

'Edna, did you know you had a detention for Mrs. Williams last night?'
   'Yeah, Miss.' *(What are you going to do about it?)*
   'You know you should go to detention. It only makes it worse if you don't, in the long run'.

'Yeah, but I can't go'.

'What do you mean, can't go?'

'I just can't'. *(And what business is it of yours anyway?)*

'Edna, tell her!' Debbie chimes in. 'She's looking after Billy, Miss'.

'Thanks Debbie, but this is between me and Edna'.

'Yeah, but Miss...'

'Okay, Debbie. Thanks. That's enough'.

Edna was looking daggers at Debbie. This was something serious. I needed to rethink.

'Okay Edna. If it's something serious I understand, but it will be much easier if you can tell me, then I can speak to Mrs. Williams. We'll leave it for now, but come and see me at break'.

No response.

It was a usual, busy morning: Shakespeare with my favourite class then a struggle through a drama lesson. Morning break, cuppa in hand, I answered the knock on the staffroom door. It was Edna. I had forgotten.

'Oh, Edna. Come into the classroom where it's quiet. So—what have you got to tell me?'

'Well Miss, Debbie thinks I'm stupid for doing this, but I've been looking after Billy next door after school. He's a Down Syndrome boy and his mum works until 6. The bus drops him after school so he needs someone to look after him. I said I would. I really like it, and I can't let his mum down, and that's why I can't do the detention'.

So this was Edna out of school, a new and very different Edna to the one we had become familiar with. This was the mature, organised, responsible, good citizen Edna. And as I saw Edna in this new way, I began to glimpse us—the teachers and the school we represented—in new ways too, perhaps as Edna might see us: irrelevant, uncaring, incapable of understanding, uninterested, oppressive, meaningless, ridiculous. Why would someone like Edna want to engage with what we represented?

But Edna was in school every day—what if she *did* want to learn and was hanging in there, waiting for us to help her make some useful connections between what we (in our positions of authority) knew was important and the life she was living? What if that was it? That made it even worse.

Edna's story makes clear the contradictions between what education espouses (via ideas about the 'good citizen' and being 'responsible' and 'mature') and the actual practices that marginalise and shut out those very students who stand to benefit most from what education ought to offer. In Edna's case, the sorting process that she has been subject to, that placed her in the 'bottom' class and predisposed teachers to see her as 'hopeless' and wonder why she persisted in coming to school, has worked against the possibilities of her making any connections between real life and what the school had to offer. As teachers, we failed to 'see' her for what she was. This standpoint, shaped as it was by our institutional habitus that privileged certain kinds of students and formed 'deficit' readings of others, created this blindness. Had we observed the need to make visible and study critically the 'hegemonic ideologies that inform our perceptions and treatment of subordinated students' (Bartolomé, 2008, p. x), we might have recognised Edna's 'difference' more positively.

In the practices that placed her in the 'bottom' class, we can see the enactment of hidden scripts of 'competition', 'failure' and 'sorting' that are central in shaping relationships between teachers, families and students in schools (Gallegos, 2004).

Students who do not fit the dominant model of the 'good' student, such as Edna, are particularly susceptible to the negative impact of scripts of competition and failure when the practices of schooling ensure that 'only a small proportion of participants will attain rewards' (Alexander et al., 2004, p. 7). Gallegos (2004) suggests that scripts such as 'smart' and 'unsmart' are 'assigned' to students very early in their schooling (p. 108). Such scripts then provide the contexts for interactions between individuals throughout their 'performance of everyday life' in the school (Goffman, in Gallegos, 2004, p. 107). Significantly, in the context of schooling, it is much worse to be treated like a slow learner than it is to be labelled as one (Gallegos, 2004, p. 108). Once again we see the role of middle-class values and habitus in assigning the 'slow learner' script to Edna. Her cultural capital (shown in such things as her commitment to supporting Billy and his family) did not have the same legitimacy as the predominantly middle class forms of capital that had value in the school (which included forms of social capital and symbolic capital that Edna did not have). Edna's story reveals the ways that institutional habitus legitimises the dominant values and the prevailing cultural capital of society (Lareau, 2000).

Irrespective of the reasons behind Edna's placement in the 'bottom class', once she had been located in this marginal space, Edna's opportunities to perform alternative roles became extremely limited, since the scripts for those alternative roles were never made available to her. The practice of placing her in that particular group in the school provided a permanent and embodied reminder of her status as one of the school's 'slow learners'. And having been assigned the 'slow learner' script, it is not surprising that this was the script she continued to perform. As we see from Edna's story, there is strong evidence that this particular script failed miserably to reflect what she was actually capable of. However, being subject to those hegemonic ideologies which taught her that people like her were of no value and of no interest to the institution that was supposed to prepare her for life after school, it was no wonder that she resisted.

## Resisting Technical Solutions: A Standpoint Approach

Students of teaching are themselves subject to hegemonic ideologies. Particularly powerful are those ideologies that purport to identify what is worth knowing for apprentice teachers. The tendency to 'embrace technical solutions' and to dismiss 'discussions of ideology and its possible influences on teaching and learning' (Bartolomé, 2008, p. xi) is reinforced by pre-service teachers' anxieties about 'doing it right' in classrooms. These anxieties are further solidified by contemporary neoliberal discourses that emphasise competition, accountability and performance management for teachers in a 'high stakes' testing environment (Bartolomé, 2008; Connell, 2009; Gardner, 2010; Smeed & Bourke, 2010). In such a competitive environment, it is not surprising if both pre-service and in-service teachers are resistant to studying units that have 'nothing to do' with teaching or focus on social theory, preferring a focus on 'technical knowledge and skills' (Bartolomé, 2008, p. xi).

By making explicit my own 'apprenticeship of observation', my intention is to make clear both how teachers' beliefs, attitudes and approaches to classroom interaction reflect their particular ideological orientations (Bartolomé), and that pre-service teachers' beliefs are already in place before they are exposed to formal teacher education. The concept of 'standpoint pedagogy' is a useful way in to help students of teaching understand the particular standpoint they bring with them from this apprenticeship of observation.

The standpoint approach has been invoked on behalf of students who are marginalised in educational settings by their gender, social class, ethnic, racial or cultural backgrounds (Singh, 1998). This approach aims to place those students who are the least privileged by normalised education discourses at the centre of the learning process. In this respect, it works against those normalised pedagogies that unreflectingly promote the interests of students (such as myself) who are most privileged. It is a powerful concept and has particular relevance for students who are in the process of becoming teachers. A 'standpoint' approach can bring issues of social class to the fore by exposing the ways that students of teaching are 'blinded' to social class and its effects on learners. In this respect, a standpoint approach is akin to Brookfield's (1995) idea that in order to develop a critical pedagogy, teachers need to 'find some lenses that reflect back to us a stark and differently highlighted picture of who we are and what we do' (1995, pp. 28–9). Brookfield suggests autobiography is the best place to begin to 'discover the influences that shape teachers' lives and move teachers' actions' (p. 49). The concept of standpoint provides a starting point for the kind of critical enquiry that Brookfield refers to.

## Unsettling Class

I began this chapter by saying I was unsure how to proceed when next tackling the unsettling question of social class. My solution has been to use biography and take up a critical stance to explore the socially constituted nature of my own privilege and, in so doing, illustrate the persistence of ideologies about who is and is not deserving of education. I now begin with my own stories. I use them as examples of ways in which students themselves might reflexively engage with incidents in their own life histories, but also because it would be wrong to give the impression that I was somehow immune to the processes that shape social class privilege. The stories are a first stage in showing how students themselves might take up class-conscious positions that will critically inform their future work as teachers. By showing how these stories have shaped my pedagogy and informed my intentions to work against the debilitating practices that frame 'different' students in the ways they do, I hope to demonstrate the limitations of a default view of teaching that privileges technical know-how and skill development. Kincheloe's (2008) point that we need to develop a pedagogy that prevents students from being hurt should be justification enough for examining the ideological basis of what we do.

The stories represent a snapshot of my own apprenticeship of observation as a future teacher. The early experiences provide a frame for the later development of my standpoint as a teacher, with Edna's story an example of a later re-articulation of ideas about privilege and the practices of marginalising and pathologising students who differ from the norm. They form part of the complex network of experiences that make up my standpoint as a teacher and hence continue to shape my pedagogy. The stories are painful to remember and even more painful to tell in public. They reveal my complicity with the pathologising practices of education (Shields et al., 2005) that attend so many encounters between teachers and students who do not 'fit in' in the ways teachers would like them to. They are not stories of teaching successes, but are all the more important to tell because of that. They illustrate the messy and hurtful nature of the day-to-day struggles of teaching. These stories show how I learned about my privileged position in the classroom, and how I began to understand some of the consequences of that privilege. The power of the experiential framing of what we do may not be explicitly articulated in our day-to-day interactions with others. If our possibilities for action are constrained by habitus, a standpoint approach that addresses the problem of misrecognition frees us to explore different ways to act. When taking a standpoint approach, it is first necessary to clear our own social class blind spots before engaging in the reflexive processes of identifying our own marginalising practices. Storytelling is a way to begin this process.

As I have begun to use stories as a starting point for unsettling class, I have become aware that students are very willing to share their own stories of class and use them to frame the way they explore ideas about teaching. This suggests both that it is possible to make social class more visible by engaging in reflexive processes such as looking back and reinterpreting experiences in terms of the ways they have constituted us as social beings, and that this is valuable and illuminating. Such sharing requires risk taking and takes place most productively in classrooms where an emotionally safe learning environment is promoted. Safe spaces are more easily sustained when everyone observes three simple 'rules of engagement'. These are:

- What is said in the room stays in the room.
- Challenge the idea not the person.
- Use language carefully—make sure your words are chosen so as not to cause unintended hurt.

I have found that students readily observe such rules when it is clear that they are in place for the benefit of everyone.

I leave the final words to one of the students of teaching, Natalie, who was a member of a tutorial group where we spent time unsettling class in the ways I have described. Her comments reflect her new understandings about how her knowledge 'has been attained from information given to me from the white dominant culture'. She wrote:

Pedagogy is certainly a word which has been thrown around throughout my university career. When I began the degree I must say I had never heard of the word and it certainly got some getting used to being able to pronounce and use it. We have been encouraged along the way to develop our own pedagogy, our own teaching style, the way we will teach our students. Many units have discussed my future students and we have researched the different needs for all children, however this unit has encouraged me to look at me as the teacher, what am I taking in to my classroom; no longer is it just my 'teaching style' it is determining why and what I am teaching and whose voice is being heard, it is about critical pedagogy.

Prior to beginning this unit all my ways of improving my lessons would be superficial, perhaps an extra five minutes for that activity, decide upon groups before starting etc. In essence, if I was asked to improve my lesson, automatically it would be classroom management strategies that I would employ. It had not yet occurred to me that the big factor on improving student learning is actually context and content. So gone is the elaborate fluffy lesson plan that we are so trained to develop. My ideas need to come in much closer to home, my ideas need to be developed by my students.

I wish I had known these things at the start of my teaching career.

# References

Alexander, B., Anderson, G., & Gallegos, B. (2004). *Performance theories in education*. Mahwah, NJ: Lawrence Erlbaum.

Alfaro, C. (2008). Developing ideological clarity: One teacher's journey. In L. Bartolomé (Ed.), *Ideologies in education: Unmasking the trap of teacher neutrality* (pp. 231–249). New York: Peter Lang.

Archer, L., Hutchings, M., & Ross, A. (2003). *Higher education and social class: Issues of exclusion and inclusion*. London: Routledge Falmer.

Aronowitz, S. (2003). *How class works: Power and social movement*. New Haven, CT: Yale.

Ball, S. (2006). The necessity and violence of theory. *Discourse, 27*(1), 3–10.

Ball, S. (2010). New class inequalities in education. *International Journal of Sociology and Social Policy, 30*(3/4), 155–166.

Bartolomé, L. (2008). *Ideologies in education: Unmasking the trap of teacher neutrality*. New York: Peter Lang.

Bourdieu, P. (1990). *The logic of practice*. Palo Alto, CA: Stanford University Press.

Bourdieu, P. (2000). *Pascalian meditations*. Palo Alto, CA: Stanford University Press.

Bourdieu, P., & Passeron, J. C. (1977). *Reproduction in education, society and culture*. London: Sage.

Bourdieu, P., & Passeron, J. C. (1996). *Reproduction*. London: Sage.

Brookfield, S. (1995). *Becoming a critically reflective teacher*. San Francisco: Jossey Bass.

Clancy, P., & Goastellec, G. (2007). Exploring access and equity in higher education: Policy and performance in a comparative aspect. *Higher Education Quarterly, 61*(2), 136–154.

Connell, R. (2009). The work of teaching. *History of Education Review, 38*(2), 9–16.

Danaher, G. (2002). *Understanding Bourdieu*. Crows Nest, Australia: Allen and Unwin.

Gallegos, B. (2004). Performing school in the shadow of imperialism: A hybrid (coyote) interpretation. In B. Alexander, G. Anderson, & B. Gallegos (Eds.), *Performance theories in education* (pp. 107–126). Mahwah, NJ: Lawrence Erlbaum.

Gardner, S. (2010). Female students teachers' experience of contemporary and professional demands. *Redress, 19*(2), 18–21.

Giddens, A. (1991). *Modernity and self identity: Self and society in the late modern age*. Stanford, CA: Stanford University Press.

Green, A. (2003). Learning to tell stories: Social class, narratives, and pedagogy. *Modern Language Studies, 33*(1/2), 80–89.

Hatton, E. (1998). *Understanding teaching*. Sydney, Australia: Harcourt Brace.

Hooks, B. (1994). *Teaching to transgress*. New York: Routledge.

Hooks, B. (2000). *Where we stand: Class matters*. New York: Routledge.

James, R., Blexley, E., & Maxwell, L. (2008). *Participation and equity: A review of the participation in higher education of people from low socioeconomic backgrounds and Indigenous people*. Canberra, Australia: Universities Australia.

Jenkins, R. (2002). *Pierre Bourdieu*. New York: Routledge.

Kincheloe, J. (2008). *Critical pedagogy*. New York: Peter Lang.

Lareau, A. (2000). *Home advantage: Social class and parental involvement in elementary education*. New York: Rowman & Littlefield.

McGregor, C. (1997). *Class in Australia: Who says Australia has no class system?* Melbourne, Australia: Penguin.

McLaren, P. (1995). *Critical pedagogy and predatory culture*. London: Routledge.

McLaren, P. (2004). Foreword. In B. Alexander, G. Anderson, & B. Gallegos (Eds.), *Performance theories in education*. Mahwah, NJ: Lawrence Erlbaum.

McLaren, P., & Farahmandpur, R. (2005). *Teaching against global capitalism and the new imperialism: A critical pedagogy*. New York: Rowman & Littlefield.

Preston, J. (2007). *Whiteness and class in education*. Dordrecht, The Netherlands: Springer.

Reay, D., David, M., & Ball, S. (2001). Making a difference? Institutional habituses and higher education choice. *Sociological Research Online. 5*(4). Retrieved October 10, 2007, from http://www.socresonline.org.uk/5/4/reay.html

Shields, C., Bishop, R., & Mazawi, A. (2005). *Pathologizing practices: The impact of deficit thinking on education*. New York: Peter Lang.

Singh, M. (1998). Multiculturalism, policy and teaching: Defending democratic principles and practices. In E. Hatton (Ed.), *Understanding teaching* (pp. 319–331). Sydney, Australia: Harcourt Brace.

Skeggs, B. (1997). *Formations of class and gender*. London: Sage.

Smeed, J., & Bourke, T. (2010). Curriculum change in testing times. *Teacher, 216*, 28–31.

# Chapter 8
# Critical Engagement with Whiteness: Beyond Lecturing on the Evils of Racism

Nado Aveling

## Introduction: What Colour Are Your Eyes?

> ... over thirty years ago, Jane Elliott devised the controversial and startling, 'Blue Eyes/Brown Eyes' exercise. This, now famous, exercise labels participants as inferior or superior based solely upon the color of their eyes and exposes them to the experience of being a minority. Everyone who is exposed to Jane Elliott's work, be it through a lecture, workshop, or video, is dramatically affected by it (http://www.janeelliott.com/)

I first learned about Jane Elliott's work (Elliott 2006) during my first teaching appointment in a multiethnic school in the late 1970s. I cannot remember whether I actually saw the film *A Class Divided* that depicted Elliott's work with a class of fourth graders or whether I read about it somewhere. I do remember, however, that I was 'dramatically affected' by her approach just as the quotation above suggests. I also remember wondering whether such an exercise would work with my own class of 10 year olds who were not averse to name-calling and making racist observations under the guise of sharing certain 'facts' about indigenous people in this country. I had found that just talking to my students about name-calling and discrimination worked only as long as I was within earshot. Reports from tearful students indicated that racial 'teasing' continued sporadically during recess and lunchtime. Clearly, a different approach to just talking about hurtful racist name-calling was called for. One morning, we played *Blue Eyes/Brown Eyes*. The specific details of the exercise with that particular class escape me, but I vividly remember choruses of 'but that's not fair'.

Certainly, the memory of *Blue Eyes/Brown Eyes* has stayed with me, and when I made the transition to university teaching, I began to trial simulation games—with a specifically Australian focus—with teacher education students within the context

N. Aveling (✉)
School of Education, Murdoch University, Perth, Australia
e-mail: n.aveling@murdoch.edu.au

B. Down and J. Smyth (eds.), *Critical Voices in Teacher Education*, Explorations of Educational Purpose 22, DOI 10.1007/978-94-007-3974-1_8,
© Springer Science+Business Media Dordrecht 2012

of a second-year, mandatory, undergraduate unit titled *Education for Social Justice*. Successive cohorts of students with whom I have 'played the game' have told me that they hated the game, hated me and hated the ways in which they played the game but ultimately that they had learnt much. Over the years, I have experimented with incorporating different simulation exercises into the structure of my teaching, not as a stand-alone game but as exercises that 'fleshed out' the readings for each week and informed the key points with which I wanted students to grapple. I have found that this more integrated approach works well.

Hence, in this chapter, I want to tell the story of a group of Australian teacher education students from the 2010 cohort, as they explored prejudice and discrimination, and the workings of white privilege through a series of simulation exercises grounded in 'what-if' situations. I also take the opportunity, as a white female teacher educator, to reflect on my teaching/learning journey for as Fishman and McCarthy (2005) have pointed out if we are not 'self-reflexive about [our] own White biases' then 'productive talk about race' (p. 347) is not likely to eventuate with our students.

## Racism in Education

The national study *The Impact of Racism upon the Health and Wellbeing of Young Australians* (Mansouri, Jenkins, Morgan, & Taouk, 2009) revealed that schools were the primary setting for the experience of racism among young people. The study further found that racism impacted not only on students' education but also on their health and well-being. While these findings may not be particularly new or indeed startling, they confirm what the literature has documented for some time; that the existence of racism in schools is largely denied (see, e.g. Aveling, 2007; Cahill, 1996; Gillborn, 1996; Hatcher & Troyna, 1997; Martino, 2003; Nieto, 2004; Rizvi, 1993; Ryan, 2003). It is, therefore, not surprising that teachers tend not to be well equipped to deal with the more covert expressions of racism especially if we are not at the receiving end of racist practices (Groome & Hamilton, 1995; Lipman, 1998; Raby, 2004; Ryan, 2003). Certainly, my students have been heard to say that they abhor the idea of racism, but many also downplay the effects of racism with comments like 'They should just ignore it' or 'We don't mean anything by it'. They contend, moreover, that apart from isolated incidences of name-calling in the heat of the moment, racism is something that happens in countries other than our own. Students tend to be, not surprisingly, perturbed even sceptical of the statement that:

> Racism can often only be perceived by those who are its victims. Therefore it is reasonable to contradict the majority view and affirm that there is racism in Australia. Given Australia's colonial history this is not a surprising conclusion. (Human Rights and Equal Opportunity Commission, 1996, p. 1)

Not only do they not experience racism but many also believe that just because it does not happen to them, it does, *ipso facto*, not exist. As a teacher educator, this has long been of concern, for '... of all the schooling factors it is teachers and their pedagogies, which contribute most to better learning outcomes for all, particularly for students from disadvantaged backgrounds' (Lingard, 2005, p. 166).

One of the key points in understanding racism is an understanding of how we as 'whites' tend not to define ourselves by our skin colour and subsequently experience ourselves as non-racialized (Levine-Rasky, 2000; Roman, 1993; Scheurich, 1993). If future teachers are to engage their own students in anti-racism, then they themselves must not only learn that racism is real for those who are its victim but also actively explore how their own racial identities have been shaped within a broader racist culture. It is only then that teachers are able to engage their students in a meaningful and constructive way to address the everyday racisms that occur in schools. Hence, in working with teacher education students, it is my aim not only to prepare them to achieve optimal educational outcomes for all students but also to challenge them to examine how the boundaries of ethnicity, 'race' and power make visible how whiteness functions as a social construction, which if left unexamined:

> perpetuate a kind of asymmetry that has marred even many critical analyses of racial formation and cultural practice ... critical attention to whiteness offers a ground not only for the examination of white selves ... but also for the excavation of the foundations of all racial and cultural positionings ... critical analyses of whiteness are vital concomitants of engagements with racial subordination (Frankenberg, 1997, pp. 1–2).

Thus, with my students—most of whom are 'white'—I endeavour to invert the gaze and to explore the profound social consequences that the construction of whiteness holds for indigenous peoples and peoples of colour. It has been my experience that it is only when we are 'willing to dismantle knowledge, values, and so forth that are taken for granted, mainstream, status quo, quite secure, familiar and known, or a threat' (Berry, 2000, p. 132) that we can begin to understand that rather than being simply about skin colour, whiteness is 'about the *discursive practices* that privilege and sustain the global dominance of white imperial subjects and Eurocentric world views' (Shome, 1999, pp. 108–109).

For me, the critical engagement with whiteness is part of a larger project of anti-racism in education because for too long we have focused on the differences/shortcomings perceived in the 'other' and equated race with 'studying down' in the power structure. We need to turn the gaze around, and instead of remaining mired in deficit thinking and attempting to 'fix' indigenous students and other students of colour, explore ways in which teachers can become part of the solution rather than being part of the problem.

## Teaching Against the Grain: Some Considerations

Given that good teaching is more than good classroom management and sound content knowledge, then excellence in teaching must be based on more than cognitive competence, and indicators of what makes an excellent teacher ought to include not only knowledge about but also a deep understanding of and commitment to the principles and practices of social justice pedagogy. As McGee Banks and Banks (1995) have pointed out:

> ... it is not sufficient to help students to read, write and compute within the dominant canon without learning also to question its assumptions, paradigms and hegemonic characteristics. Helping students become reflective and active citizens of a democratic society is at the essence of our conception of equity pedagogy (p. 152).

In a similar vein, Mortiboys (2005) has suggested that excellence in teaching rests less on demonstrating the requisite procedures and skills than on attitudinal traits such as open-mindedness, empathy and a willingness to appreciate other people's point of view. If excellent teaching is indeed as much about attitudes as it is about cognitive excellence, then Kay's argument (1989) that the use of games or simulation exercises are an effective vehicle for achieving affective objectives comes into play. Exercises like *Blue Eyes/Brown Eyes* move towards engaging our feelings and attitudes as they force us to interrogate our own racialized, gendered and class-based assumptions.

Teaching against the grain in this way is not simply a matter of teaching as one would any other 'subject'; exploring 'race' and racism with white students goes to the core of our socially constructed identities (Aveling, 2006). Certainly, as human subjects, we tend to find it much simpler to talk about social justice than to 'do' social justice. 'Doing' social justice often finds us 'too close to home, the past, family, or friends [and take us into experiences] that will shock, scare or sicken' (Berry, 2000, p. 132). While it is simpler to stick to the 'facts', I remain convinced that pedagogies that engage the whole person are more productive because as Byrne and FitzGerald (1998) have suggested:

> When we explore the workings of prejudice and discrimination, it is immediately obvious that it is not only an attitude or a cognitive construct with which we are dealing. Powerful emotions can be involved. People can feel their cherished values under threat and instinctively resist any pressure to change since so much of their sense of self can feel bound up with the views and behaviours they have brought to the course. For this reason a 'sermon' on the evils of racism will not be effective, nor will information alone (p. 4).

Certainly, over the years, my students have exhibited all the symptoms listed above: they have become emotional, they felt threatened, they became angry and they resisted. As I have argued elsewhere (Aveling, 2006), when teaching about race and racism and how we as 'whites' are racialized, we are 'hacking at the very roots' of the ways in which students have conceptualized their subject position in terms of being non-racialized and non-racist. Many of my students, whatever their gender, social class position or cultural background, have told me that they have had to struggle to get to university, that they have experienced hardships, even discrimination and that they are not racist; that their whiteness has definitely not conferred privileges of any kind. Yet at the same time, students have talked about how 'eye opening' and 'life changing' the unit has been. Others, of course, have told me in no uncertain terms that I needed to change my ways:

> I would never have done this course if I wasn't forced to and find it offensive that I need to pay for the privilege.
>
> I felt I was forced to take on her views, otherwise I would not get anywhere with my marks.
>
> Anti-racist content needs to be changed to ensure that white students are not affronted.

The feelings that these students expressed are not peculiar to my students. As Cochran-Smith (1995) has pointed out:

> When we unleash unpopular things by making race and racism explicit parts of the curriculum, responses are often strongly emotional, and resistance, misunderstanding, frustration, anger, and feelings of inefficacy may be the outcomes (p. 542).

Thus, the dilemma with which I continue to be faced is to find a balance between my conviction that experiential learning has immense potential for dismantling racism on the one hand and my experiences of student resistance on the other. Given that the 'resisters' are also likely to graduate and teach the nation's children, my priority continues to be to find an approach that is less confronting but equally effective without, however, 'watering' down the curriculum or pandering to 'white' sensibilities. There are no 'silver bullet' solutions, and I still encounter resistance, but I also have a sense that my more 'softly-softly' approach of integrating exercises into the curriculum is more productive. It is, therefore, to a group of 13 students from the 2010 cohort to which I now turn to illustrate how the experiential learning component works out in practice.

## Education for Social Justice: Issues and Dilemmas

*Education for Social Justice* is a unit that is grounded in critical theorizing that attempts to move 'beyond interpretation to change' (Pinar, Reynolds, Slattery, & Taubman, 1995, p. 255) and that links the teacher education curriculum to the critical study of power, language, culture and history. For me, it is the approach of choice through which to challenge teacher education students to disrupt discursive practices of whiteness and Eurocentric views. Given that I am currently working on a 10-week semester schedule, I have divided the 30 teaching hours available to me into one lecture per week followed by a film with the third hour being set aside for discussion and 'what-if' activities.

Despite the fact that some students resist engagement, it is these activities that students seem to enjoy most. I definitely enjoy teaching in ways that are more immediate and more fun. I also enjoy the contact I have with small groups because it allows us to get to know each other while tackling tricky questions and exploring issues of concern. Most weeks, I come away feeling positive, and each year, I have a sense that this was the best group with whom I have ever worked. The 2010 group was no different. I hope that they have enjoyed our time together; they were certainly generous in giving me permission to use their work as I saw fit. Thank you.

As a group, they consisted of 12 female students and one sole male; one woman identified as Aboriginal, while the other 12 were of non-Aboriginal, European background; some had reasonably recently left school, and others had had more life experiences and had entered university through alternative entry pathways; some had children, others did not. All were studying to be primary school teachers and told me that they were committed to being the best teachers they could possibly be. In other words, the group was reasonably representative of teacher education students nationwide (Whitehead, 2007). Given that most of the students in this group were white, having an Aboriginal student—who chose the name Melody as a pseudonym—in my class concerned me initially because all too often the needs of:

> systematically privileged students are tended to without consideration of the needs of marginalized students who have the right to be able to be educated in a safe environment free from overt and covert forms of discrimination (Applebaum, 2010, p. 106).

I have certainly been in a situation when students have prefaced their comments with phrases like 'I'm not racist, but ...' (Aveling, 2002) only to let loose with racist diatribes of startling proportions. As I did not want to replicate 'the racist dynamics of the larger society' (Elias cited in Applebaum, 2010, p. 107), I knew that I needed to be particularly vigilant and use my power to silence students, when and if necessary, in order to ensure that white students did not monopolize the discussion, listened carefully and without interruption when Melody contributed and did not make unthinking racist comments. However, there appeared to be none of the underlying resistance in this group that I have almost come to expect, and we negotiated confronting ideas and discussions quite successfully. I do not really know why this was so: perhaps it was due to Melody's personality, possibly this was a really fantastic group or maybe I was particularly vigilant and good at forestalling any potentially harmful situations before they arose. Perhaps it was a combination of all of the above. It is the nature of the beast that I may never know. Whatever the reasons, Melody seemed to enjoy 'the shoe being on the other foot' and having an audience to listen to her point of view.

Over the years, I have collected diverse exercises (see, e.g. Adams, Bell, & Griffin, 1997; Craven, 1996; NSW Department of School Education, 1995; Savdié, n.d.) and adapted them in ways that seem to me to best add experiential dimensions to the readings I provide for students and the films we view. Depending on group dynamics, some of the activities have worked better than others; however, the consensus in the 2010 group seemed to be that overall; the activities were worth doing even though responses ranged from 'lukewarm' endorsement to 'fire-in-the-belly' enthusiasm:

> I did find the role-play exercises very useful. It is a teaching strategy that I can relate to.
>
> I have found that the various activities cement my learning in a more personal way. I have been able to have a taste of the feelings of others and this given an emotional link to the academic learning. ... Having to reflect on activities helps me become more reflective in other situations.
>
> It really opened my eyes to how I would have behaved in the past ... I never realized before that some of my actions and even words can come across as discriminating ...

## Teaching Against the Grain: Tackling 'What-If' Scenarios

Week 1 begins with an introductory activity focusing on identity that challenges students to position themselves in terms of their gender, their cultural background and their socioeconomic status as well as other axes of social dis/advantage. For many students, this is the first time they have to think beyond naïve individualism that positions them as 'just normal' in terms of cultural background and 'somewhere in the middle' in terms of social class. This is also the first time many of them think in terms of their whiteness; that their lives have unfolded in particular ways because of their skin colour and the benefits that this might have conferred. In sharing their understandings with the rest of the class, I was particularly careful not to make this mandatory because I wanted students to have a sense of being able to think about their positionality without feeling that this was necessarily open to scrutiny. Most, but not all, students opted to share key aspects of their lives with their peers. It was particularly illuminating for the class to hear Melody speak about her Aboriginality. I had a sense that they were genuinely appreciative of hearing about experiences that differed quite substantially from their own. I also wondered if any of them had ever really talked with or listened to an Aboriginal person.

Another activity deals with cultural diversity in the classroom. This activity allocates particular roles to students and asks them to move one step forward or to remain in place, depending on how they think their character might feel in response to a specific situation. It is certainly a powerful visual way to see how whiteness seems to allow students to move forward much more easily. Some students commented in their journal:

> I was one of the characters who took the most steps forward. What shocked me was that there were still people on the starting line … it really struck me how large the gap is in our society between different people and their life chances. All of the students should have been able to step forward as far as me but they couldn't. The class of around 13 of us was spread all over the classroom. This also made me realize just how varied our schools are not just by race or by socioeconomic status but other things as well.
>
> The simulation this week was role-playing students within a classroom of varying ages, genders, ethnic background and socioeconomic background. We were all given a person to be and respond to the questions accordingly. Out of all of us only 2 reached the finish point in being happy, achieving and successful at school. This raised the issue that as teachers how do we identify what motivates our students to not only come to school but also want to learn. In some cases our students have to deal with a bunch of challenging life issues before they can even think about applying themselves to their learning environment.

What struck students to begin with was the diversity to be found in classrooms. The fact that some students succeed because of their whiteness did not come up in discussion until much later in the piece when I asked 'How was your "character" different from you?' Little by little, the meaning of 'life chances' and what constitutes 'the gap' in terms of educational outcomes between Aboriginal and non-Aboriginal students becomes more of a reality as students made the connection between their own relatively privileged status and the status of the 'character' in whose shoes they attempted to walk for a while. Melody was again happy to comment on why some 'characters' were unable to move forward.

Perhaps the most powerful of exercises is the one which focuses on the effects of government policies on the lives of Aboriginal peoples. Unfortunately or fortunately (as the case may be), Melody was absent that day. This is an exercise that I approach with some trepidation as it requires me to suspend my natural inclination to be a 'nice' person and to take on a persona that is quite different from how I like to think of myself. Speaking softly, I invite students to come and choose a piece of coloured paper and some coloured pens. I tell them that we will do a drawing exercise, but that their drawing skills are unimportant and that stick figures and doodles are quite acceptable. When students have settled back at their desks, I continue: 'Close your eyes and think about your family; think about what is important to you. What do you treasure? Who are the people in your life that nurture and support you? What is most meaningful to you?' Continuing in a soothing monotone, I exhort and reassure intermittently, until I have a sense that students are satisfied with the representations of people and things they most value. It is then that I change from kindly Dr. Jekyll to cruel and insensitive Mrs. Hyde. As I move from desk to desk to peruse students' work, I speak little but make a point of showing my disdain for their efforts, culminating with the act of physically picking up one piece of work and after voicing my displeasure, tearing the paper to shreds. A shocked silence follows. It is a silence that, I hope, allows the enormity of my actions to sink in and connections to be made.

The discussions are slow to get started. The mood is subdued. Students are shell-shocked. Gradually, one or two hands are raised. Responses to my next question 'How did you feel?' were tentative at first:

> I felt shocked.
> My stomach turned.
> I was hoping you wouldn't tear up my drawing of my mum.
> I thought 'What the hell is going on here?'
> I felt scared.
> I was hoping you wouldn't see me.
> I thought 'She's a liar'.

The drawing they had so lovingly (if hesitantly) drawn seemed to represent more than images on coloured paper. Indeed, I had a sense that the images had almost come to represent the real thing, and a threat to the image was perceived to be almost as dire as a threat to the real thing. Of course, debriefing is crucial in an exercise such as this; how they felt, what the exercise reminded them of and how it related to our topic for the week. Later, students wrote:

> After being given enough time to complete this task Nado went around the class and at random ripped up selected peoples' pieces of paper. The class' reaction was varied, some people gasped out loud but no one laughed. I felt a mixture of fear (please don't take away my pictures of mum) and shock at the invasive and offensive nature of the action. The exercise did what no textbook could, no matter how personal its account of experience. It made me think directly about my mother, my cousins, about my home, not as vague notions but as actual people and places being taken away from me. It was such a horrifying feeling that I went home and called my parents to make sure they knew how much they mean to me.

> The activity was obviously regarding the Stolen Generations. It was a very affecting activity ... I feel like it is the first thing that has really brought home the message of the Stolen Generations.
>
> Nado got us all nice and relaxed to reflect on something that was important to us, and then drew our thoughts. Then all of a sudden Nado's voice changed and started to order us around, criticizing our work, ending with tearing up someone's paper. This exercise was for us to feel what it is like to be degraded and belittled. The rest of us just sat there quietly, not game to say a word in case she picked on us. It was a great exercise to feel what it was like to have no voice and to fear speaking out: to have an authoritative figure dictate to you what to do. Something I would not like to experience too often!

It is certainly not an activity that I would want to do too often either; I feel for the students and am frequently left with a headache. Nevertheless, it is an activity that I repeat each year because it demonstrates in a very real way what generations of Aboriginal people have experienced on a regular basis. It is an activity that generates empathy in ways that reading about *The Stolen Generations*[1] cannot do. This simulation exercise complements students' reading because without the knowledge of historical events, the exercise would lose meaning. It is only when the two come together that empathy and knowledge produce deep understanding.

A final exercise on which I want to comment is grounded in Peggy MacIntosh's (1997) discussion of the invisible knapsack of white privilege. I have found that we can talk about white privilege and read about it, but to actually experience how white complicity in racism (Applebaum, 2010) is enacted is more difficult. While we are able to talk about walking through shops without being followed by store detectives or seeing 'people like us' represented in popular TV shows, discussions invariably raise the question: 'How does that make *me* complicit in systemic racism?' (Applebaum, 2010, p. 27). Applebaum suggested that such questions are not unusual, and my students have certainly voiced their puzzlement in this regard. Why indeed are they meant to be personally responsible for the fact that Aboriginal people or people of colour are routinely telling us that they are harassed disproportionately compared with their non-Aboriginal peers? It is certainly not 'we' who do the harassing nor do we have control over the hiring practices of major television studios; it is those 'bad' whites who do not know any better. 'We', who know better, are 'good' because we know that our whiteness confers unearned privileges, and we do not, moreover, commit acts of racial violence. We should, therefore, not be tarred with the brush of being complicit in institutional racism. However, as Applebaum argued, such privilege cannot be discarded as one would take off a knapsack to find a fully fledged anti-racist underneath because '[t]he emphasis on personal awareness ... overshadows the need for understanding and challenging the system of power that support white privilege' (p. 31). Moreover, as Applebaum further argued, the links between 'privileges that benefit white people and how such benefits *sustain* systems of oppression' are frequently resisted (p. 33).

---

[1]The term *The Stolen Generations* refers to the systematic and legal practice of removing children from their families and communities. This was designed to assimilate Aboriginal children into white society. It was a practice that continued into the 1960s.

My students are no different in this regard. However, I have not yet learned how to take the next step and effectively explore 'white ways of being in the world' (Applebaum, 2010, p. 30) and ultimately actually 'do' something about racism. This 'doing' needs to happen, not from the perspective of a 'good' white but from a perspective of ongoing vigilance because as Yancy (2008) has argued, dismantling whiteness is a continuous project; it is 'a project in process, always becoming, always in need of another step' (Warren cited in Yancy, 2008, p. 238).

While I do not know with any degree of certainty how my students' professional lives will unfold or indeed the extent of their 'deep' learning, I have the hope that they will go out and teach the next generation of students in ways that are truly socially just. Interestingly, just a few weeks ago, a student from the 2011 cohort posted a comment on the unit's discussion board that alerted me to the fact that sometimes simulation is no substitute for noticing things in the 'real world':

> I was at my local shopping centre and having worked there a number of years ago, you quickly learn how to spot who is the undercover security person. So while I was there I had noticed that the security person was following an Indigenous couple around the store. ... There was absolutely no reason for security to be following them, other than the colour of their skin. ... It absolutely disgusted me, and through studying this unit, I actually feel bad for not saying something to the security guard at the time, but my 'whiteness' wasn't something I was aware of at the time. ... I know at that point if I had wanted to, I more than likely could have walked out of that shop with pockets full of goods without so much as a second glance.

Despite the fact that there are no 'foolproof' ways of ensuring that my approaches have the outcomes I desire, my students can no longer plead ignorance. What they will do with the knowledge and understandings they have gained is outside my sphere of influence. Will it all be too hard? Will it disappear through the cracks as the 'realities' of schooling, such as classroom management and standardized testing takes over every available minute of the day? Will they succumb to pressures from their colleagues to toe the line?

## Concluding Comments: Giving Students a Place to Start

At the conclusion of *Education for Social Justice*, I expect students to acknowledge that Australia's history is not merely something that happened a long time ago, that it is, indeed, something that has ongoing implications for indigenous people and people of colour and by inference, for them as educators. While I want them (us) to own their (our) whiteness and to become aware of white race complicity, at the same time, I believe that it is important to provide future teachers with strategies and resources that enable them to move beyond feelings of guilt, fear and alienation that critically examining whiteness frequently engenders. Over the years, I have become much more explicit with my students about:

the fact that changing 'Whiteness' is not the issue, that guilt and shame are not the end of our curriculum but, rather, our joint thoughtfulness about how our society might dismantle its historical practices of social injustice (Gillespie, Ashbaugh, & DeFiore, 2002, p. 249).

This is a point that I have to reiterate throughout the semester. I have found that it is not enough to say once: 'This is not about making you feel guilty. This is about understanding how being white has shaped us as well as provided us with unearned privileges, and armed with this understanding, to do something about racism' (or words to that effect).

I continue to 'tinker around the edges' of the material that I teach—and the ways in which I teach it—as I continue to read and learn and evaluate what other teacher educators tell me of their experiences. I also continue in my belief that despite an inability to simulate all of life's experiences, 'affective attainment is as important in learning … as cognitive achievement' (Montalvo, 1989, p. 95). The responses from my students tend to vindicate this position. Their responses also indicate a certain enjoyment in learning in this way, despite the fact that such learning is invariably unsettling. Occasionally, I receive e-mails from past students to tell me how they are using what they have learned in workshops at the chalk-face of their daily lives. Such e-mails are gratifying because they remind me that the work is worth doing.

> … it is easy to start feeling guilty about what our ancestors have done. I believe this is why some people choose to close their eyes rather than reach out because the wrongs are so monumental … this unit is already challenging my thinking and giving me a place to start.

# References

Adams, M., Bell, L. A., & Griffin, P. (1997). *Teaching for diversity and social justice: A sourcebook*. New York/London: Routledge.

Applebaum, B. (2010). *Being white, being good: White complicity, white moral responsibility, and social justice pedagogy*. New York: Lexington Books.

Aveling, N. (2002). Student teachers' resistance to exploring racism: Reflections on 'doing' border pedagogy. *Asia-Pacific Journal of Teacher Education, 30*(2), 119–130.

Aveling, N. (2006). "Hacking at our very roots": Re-articulating white racial identity within the context of teacher education. *Race, Ethnicity and Education, 9*(3), 261–274.

Aveling, N. (2007). Anti-racism in schools: A question of leadership? *Discourse: Studies in the Cultural Politics of Education, 28*(1), 69–86.

Berry, K. S. (2000). *The dramatic arts and cultural studies: Acting against the grain*. New York: Falmer Press.

Byrne, M., & FitzGerald, H. (1998). *Blue eyed training kit on discrimination and prejudice for use in an Australian context*. Loganholme, Australia: Marcom Projects.

Cahill, D. (1996). *Immigration and schooling in the 1990s*. Belconnen, Australia: Australian Government Publication Service.

Cochran-Smith, M. (1995). Uncertain allies: Understanding the boundaries of race and teaching. *Harvard Educational Review, 65*(4), 541–570.

Craven, R. (Ed.). (1996). *Teaching the teachers: Indigenous Australian studies for preservice teacher education: Model core subject manual*. Sydney, Australia: School of Teacher Education, The University of New South Wales.

Elliott, J. (2006). *Blue eyes, brown eyes exercise*. Retrieved February 2, 2011, from: http://www. janeelliott.com/

Fishman, S., & McCarthy, L. (2005). Talk about race: When student stories and multicultural curricula are not enough. *Race, Ethnicity and Education, 8*(4), 347–364.

Frankenberg, R. (1997). Introduction: Local whiteness, localizing whiteness. In R. Frankenberg (Ed.), *Displacing whiteness: Essays in social and cultural criticism* (pp. 1–2). Durham, NC/London: Duke University Press.

Gillborn, D. (1996). Student roles and perspectives in antiracist education: A crisis of white ethnicity. *British Educational Research Journal, 22*(2), 165–179.

Gillespie, D., Ashbaugh, L., & DeFiore, J. (2002). White women teaching white women about white privilege, race cognizance and social action: Toward a pedagogical pragmatic. *Race, Ethnicity and Education, 5*(3), 238–253.

Groome, H., & Hamilton, A. (1995). *Meeting the educational needs of aboriginal adolescents* (NBEET Commissioned Report, No. 35). Canberra, Australia: Australian Government Publishing Service.

Hatcher, R., & Troyna, B. (1997). Racialization and children. In C. McCarthy & W. Crichlow (Eds.), *Race, identity and representation in education* (pp. 109–125). London: Routledge.

Human Rights and Equal Opportunity Commission. (1996). *Understanding racism in Australia*. Canberra, Australia: Australian Government Publication Service.

Kay, L. (1989). Painting the classroom with the reality of role playing. In I. L. Sonnier (Ed.), *Affective education: Methods and techniques* (pp. 157–161). Englewood Cliffs, NJ: Educational Technology.

Levine-Rasky, C. (2000). The practice of whiteness among teacher candidates. *International Studies in Sociology of Education, 10*(3), 263–284.

Lingard, B. (2005). Socially just pedagogies in changing times. *International Studies in Sociology of Education, 15*(2), 165–186.

Lipman, P. (1998). *Race, class and power in school restructuring*. Albany, NY: SUNY Press.

Mansouri, F., Jenkins, L., Morgan, L., & Taouk, M. (2009). *The impact of racism upon the health and wellbeing of young Australians*. Deakin University Institute for Citizenship and Globalisation, Burwood, Australia. Retrieved February 2, 2011, from http://www.fya.org.au/wp-content/uploads/2009/11/Impact_of_Racism_At-A-Glance.pdf

Martino, W. (2003). 'We just get really fired up': Indigenous boys, masculinities and schooling. *Discourse: Studies in the Cultural Politics of Education, 24*(2), 157–172.

McGee Banks, C., & Banks, J. (1995). Equity pedagogy: An essential component of multicultural education. *Theory into Practice, 34*(3), 152–158.

McIntosh, P. (1997). White privilege and male privilege: A personal account of coming to see correspondences through work in women's studies. In R. Delgado & J. Stefancic (Eds.), *Critical whiteness studies: looking behind the mirror* (pp. 291–299). Philadelphia: Temple University Press.

Montalvo, F. (1989). Affective instruction in cross-cultural social work education. In I. L. Sonnier (Ed.), *Affective education: Methods and techniques* (pp. 91–95). Englewood Cliffs, NJ: Educational Technology.

Mortiboys, A. (2005). *Teaching with emotional intelligence*. London/New York: Routledge.

New South Wales Department of School Education, Multicultural Education Unit. (1995). *Whole school anti-racism project*. Sydney, Australia: New South Wales Department of School Education, Multicultural Education Unit.

Nieto, S. (2004). *Affirming diversity: The sociopolitical context of multicultural education* (4th ed.). Amherst, MA: University of Massachusetts.

Pinar, W. F., Reynolds, W. M., Slattery, P., & Taubman, P. M. (1995). *Understanding curriculum: An introduction to the study of historical and contemporary curriculum discourses*. New York: Peter Lang.

Raby, R. (2004). There's no racism at my school, it's just joking around: Ramifications for anti-racist education. *Race Ethnicity and Education, 7*(4), 367–383.

Rizvi, F. (1993). Children and the grammar of popular racism. In C. McCarthy & W. Crichlow (Eds.), *Race, identity and representation in education* (pp. 126–139). New York: Routledge.

Roman, L. G. (1993). White is a color! White defensiveness, postmodernism, and anti-racist pedagogy. In C. McCarthy & W. Crichlow (Eds.), *Race, identity and representation in education* (pp. 71–88). New York: Routledge.

Ryan, J. (2003). Educational administrators' perceptions of racism in diverse school contexts. *Race Ethnicity and Education, 6*(2), 145–164.

Savdié, T. (n.d.) Speak up: It starts with you. *Anti-racism training kit for educators.* Penrith, Australia: Nepean Migrant Access.

Scheurich, J.J. (1993, November 5–16). Towards a discourse on white racism. *Educational Researcher, 22*(2), 5–10.

Shome, R. (1999). Whiteness and the politics of location. In T. Nakayama & G. Martin (Eds.), *Whiteness: The communication of social identity* (pp. 107–128). Thousand Oaks, CA: Sage Publications.

Whitehead, K. (2007). Addressing social difference with prospective teachers who want "to make a difference. *Asia-Pacific Journal of Teacher Education, 35*(4), 367–385.

Yancy, G. (2008). *Black bodies, white gazes: The continuing significance of race.* Lanham, MD/Boulder, CO/New York: Rowman & Littlefield Publishers, Inc.

# Chapter 9
# 'Undoing' Gender and Disrupting Hegemonic Masculinity: Embracing a Transgender Social Imaginary

**Wayne Martino**

## Introduction

Some years ago, when I was still an English teacher in a secondary school in Western Australia, I wrote a paper entitled, 'Deconstructing Masculinity in the English Classroom' (Martino, 1995). It represented my attempt to think through the implications of poststructuralist feminist theories for my classroom practice and was influenced strongly by Bronwyn Davies' concerns about oppressive gender binaries and how they came to inform her understanding about the role of storylines or narratives in their capacity to both reinforce and interrupt *the discursive production of male/female dualism in school settings* (Davies, 1989). What I got from reading Davies' work at the time was that the stories we tell and make available to children in classrooms are informed by certain discourses and patterns of desire, which define the limits and possibilities for understanding ourselves as gendered, raced, classed and sexual subjects. In other words, built into storylines are subject positions from which we are able to make sense of ourselves as gendered beings. Moreover, the revelation that we could choose to make available to our students other imaginative possibilities for thinking about gender, and specifically masculinity, beyond the limits of binary and dualistic regimes of thought and truth was, and still is, very appealing to me. However, how I have come to understand this pedagogical project has been informed further by my engagement with other theories and particularly by the work of transgender and genderqueer scholars, such as Butler (2004), Connell (2009), and Stryker (2006), who raise important questions about *transgender phenomena* as they relate to the political significance of gender embodiment and positionality.

W. Martino (✉)
Faculty of Education, The University of Western Ontario, London, ON, Canada
e-mail: wmartino@uwo.ca

B. Down and J. Smyth (eds.), *Critical Voices in Teacher Education*, Explorations
of Educational Purpose 22, DOI 10.1007/978-94-007-3974-1_9,
© Springer Science+Business Media Dordrecht 2012

Initially, as a grad student, it was my engagement with feminist poststructuralist theory that was the foundation for my critical interventionist work in the English classroom. In this sense, *coming to theory*, as Hooks (1994) explains, became a means for me to grasp a deeper understanding of and knowledge about personal experience and of being and living in the world, particularly with regards to the role that dominant or hegemonic discourses about gender and sexuality played in setting limits to embracing a social imaginary beyond dualist and essentialist thinking about masculinity (Petersen, 1998). Moreover, Connell's work (1995) further provided me with a theoretical arsenal for further understanding the construction and interplay of masculinities in the everyday lives of men and boys. Such frameworks enabled me to recognize 'the relations between different kinds of masculinity' and how these in turn were structured by economic, social and institutional forces of dominance and subordination, as well as practices 'that exclude and include, that intimidate, exploit, and so on' (p. 37).

This history of my engagement with theory is important because it helps to provide both a context and basis for understanding the critical pedagogical work that I believe is still necessary in embracing the political project of *undoing* hegemonic masculinity as an oppressive force in the lives of both boys/men and girls/women (Martino & Pallotta-Chiarolli, 2005). Hence, my focus in this chapter is on thinking through the significance of addressing hegemonic masculinity in schools as part of a broader political project of gender justice and gender democratization. In so doing, I draw on some of the transgender and genderqueer scholarship to illustrate how it has influenced my thinking about the political project of addressing the limits of hegemonic heterosexual masculinity in boys' lives in schools, with its implications for 'undoing' the power relations at play in such configurations of practice and embodied power relations. The work of both Judith Butler (2004) and Susan Stryker (2006) has provided a fruitful epistemological basis for reflecting on the politics of transgender studies and its pedagogical implications. In light of such theoretical insights, my aim is to examine the specific role of teachers and teacher educators in making available imaginative possibilities for students to embrace a politics of gender that is committed to social justice in conservative times. My starting point is a consideration of the project of *deconstructing masculinity* as a basis for critically reflecting on the politics of *undoing gender* as a pedagogical intervention in the English classroom. As I attempt to illustrate in this chapter, this political project is not so much committed to *gender abolition* as it is to *gender democratization* in schools (Connell, 2009).

## Deconstructing Masculinity in the English Classroom

Some time ago, Davies (1989) highlighted the usefulness of using stories and texts in the English classroom to disrupt binary thinking about gender, and her insights are still relevant today, particularly in terms of their pedagogical implications. Her focus on how children imaginatively position themselves in response to the stories they read in the classroom, and how such positioning needs to be understood in terms of both the discourses about gender to which they have access and which are mobilized by the author in the writing of the text, signalled possibilities for me as teacher in terms of thinking about how specific texts might be used to interrupt hegemonic masculinity. This knowledge is still useful in helping teacher education students to think through the uses and implications of feminist poststructuralist theories in the literacy classroom, both in terms of text selection and reading practices. For example, Davies highlights how choosing certain feminist-inspired texts such as *The Paper Bag Princess* enable educators to introduce to students in the classroom counter-hegemonic narratives which function to interrupt dominant constructions of masculinity and femininity. An alternative to the master narrative of the prince saving the princess and living happily ever after is provided, with the latter rushing to save the former from a dragon, which not only burns her castle and clothes, but also abducts the prince. However, Davies shows that while the narrative provides alternative subject positions for students to take up vis-à-vis the positioning of the princess as *active heroic agent* and female hero, many students refused to read the story in these feminist terms (p. 231). For example, the lure of dragon, with all its associations of hegemonic masculinity, features strongly in the students' reading of the text. They refuse to see Elizabeth as empowered—she loses her prince in the end, not because of her own decision to leave him, but because she lacks virtue. With burnt clothes and wearing a paper bag, she does not measure up as a princess and is therefore unworthy of his attention.

Through such examples, Davies highlights that, while texts may provide or encourage alternative ways of thinking about gender, this does not necessarily mean that readers will actively embrace such imaginative possibilities. Many students, in fact, may resist such positioning. However, reading Davies work, as an English teacher at the time, made me think more strategically and consciously about using particular texts in the classroom to introduce students to a critique of hegemonic masculinity and to consider the various readings that might be generated in response to such texts. In this way, I was able to conceptualize texts as a pedagogical site for investigating the impact and significance of hegemonic masculinities in their lives. The idea that texts could be used to make available alternative discourses about masculinity and to create imaginative possibilities for students to refuse the old or familiar ones was (and still remains) an exciting pedagogical venture for me. For example, the focus on deconstructing the ways in which masculinity is represented in texts enabled critical attention to be drawn to the costs and limits of subscribing to a version of masculinity that relies on the denigration and devaluation of 'the feminine'. This critical project may serve as a starting point for making available alternative ways of knowing for boys in schools, which do not have to be governed by the terms set by an oppressive binary logic of male and female dualism.

The text I chose and which I wrote about in 1995 as a pedagogical basis for realizing such a textual political practice in the English classroom was a short story about father who disapproves of his son playing dolls with is his younger sister, an activity which leads to the former's developing masculinity being brought into question. Mr. Murray, the father, treats his son's gender non-conforming behaviour as unacceptable and insults him by referring to him as a 'poofter' and a 'moping poet'. For example, the father indicates one evening at the dinner table that he does not want his son to turn into a 'lily-livered poofter'. In order to meet up to his father's expectations, David (the son) eventually feels constrained to shoot a possum to prove his manhood: 'He was still with terror, the horror of shooting it convulsed his stomach, his bowel, he could already hear his sister's hysteria' (Keyte & Baines, 1982, p. 115; Martino & Mellor, 1995). The violent act leads him to feel sick, and, finally, the text presents the reader with an image of a boy who has been numbed by his experiences, a boy forced to repress his sensitivity and emotionality in order to be accepted by his father who considers disparagingly such traits to be feminizing and emasculating attributes. David is described at the end of the story playing cricket, 'like an automation figure on a mechanical dock, chiming futile time in the flat emptiness of eternity' (Keyte & Baines, 1982, p. 116).

The story highlights the costs for those who step outside of traditional gender stereotypes or norms and raises critical questions about the policing of boys' masculinity. In this capacity, it opens up tremendous possibilities for initiating important discussions about hegemonic masculinity, gender non-conformity and the role of homophobia and *gender bashing* in the lives of boys. Namaste (2006), for example, distinguishes between *gender* and *queer bashing* in highlighting the extent to which 'a perceived transgression of normative sex/gender relations', or rather what she terms 'the perception of gender dissidence', can result in violence, with males, for example, judged to be effeminate being subject to verbal abuse and physical attack (p. 585). Namaste's point is that many individuals are victimized and targets of violence, 'not because of their sexual orientation, but because of their visible gender presentation which is perceived to be threatening to male and heterosexual domination of public space' (p. 584). Such a text, therefore, opens up a space in the English classroom within which dominant versions of masculinity and their workings can be analysed, critiqued and deconstructed. While such discussions or use of texts provide no guarantee that students will embrace such critical readings of the hegemonic gender order, they do provide access to counter positions and alternative social imaginaries of masculinity for boys. For example, while some boys in my English classes at the time resisted and rejected the invitation of the text to embrace David—that is, they rejected Mr. Murray and his abusive treatment of his son, but still tended to read David in disparaging terms as a 'poof'—they were still being exposed to alternative readings as a basis for reflecting on their own positioning within hegemonic discourses. Just the idea of making available other points of view which challenge dominant thought about the heteronormative constraints of gender expression and masculinity is a start and carries with it productive possibilities for examining 'the production of our own sense of who we are, of our subjectivity' in response to texts that make available a consideration of what it might mean for boys and girls who transgress acceptable limits of self-presentation, as it relates to gender expression and particularly the imposition of hegemonic masculinity (Davies, 1989, p. 229).

As Davies reiterates, such a pedagogical practice involves students 'learning to recognize the constitutive force of the images and metaphors through which sex-gender is taken up as their own, and to make choices about refusing the discursive practices and structures that disempower them or that constitute them in ways that they do not want' (p. 240). While there are some limits to such a practice of deconstruction in terms of undoing hegemonic masculinity, there are clear pedagogical benefits to making available counter narratives and critical framework, with their potential for interrupting normalizing impulses and tendencies that continue to inform approaches to boys' education well into the millennium. For example, the following strategies continue to characterize the pedagogical reform agenda at the heart of policy making related to boys' education and, for the most part, are governed by a neoconservative social imaginary that is more committed ideologically to recuperating gender binaries that dismantling them (Froese-Germain, 2006; Lingard, Martino, & Mills, 2009; Martino & Kehler, 2007; Titus, 2004):

1. The need for a more boy-friendly curriculum, which is considered to be inclusive of boys' distinctive interests and learning needs
2. The need for more male teachers who, as a consequence of being male, are supposedly better equipped to relate to boys and to address their learning needs
3. The need for single-sex classes in English where boys do not have to worry about girls and where teachers can more easily cater for boys' interests and learning styles

These political reform agendas highlight the need for more progressive social imaginaries that refuse the hegemonic limits of such binary categorizations and the problems they create for both boys and girls in schools (Martino & Rezai-Rashti, in press).

## From Representation to the Reality of Material Embodiment

Davies (1989) also refers to an incident that took place in a preschool in Ohio involving a deaf boy, Michael, who painted his nails bright read. The children had found some nail polish in their teacher's belongings and had started playing with it in class. The next day, he returned to class with an angry note from his father stipulating that he did not want his son to play with nail polish. Michael explained to the researchers that that he was 'a good boy' and that 'good boys do not wear nail polish'. When the researchers tried to explain that while boys generally do not wear nail polish, some boys like to do so, 'just for fun', Michael insisted, 'I am a boy, a boy, a boy'. In response, the researchers acknowledged that he was a boy, but still insisted that it was ok for boys to engage in such practices, at which point he proceeded to pull down his pants and to point to his genitals, impatiently asserting, 'Here look, I am a Boy!' This incident highlights how gender norms get lived and experienced as biological differences that are grounded in sexed bodies. As Butler (2004) points out, conditions of intelligibility for understanding and recognizing ourselves as gendered and sexed subjects are 'composed of norms and practices have become presuppositional' (p. 56). For Michael, it is 'the constraining of bodily norms' (p. 4) and categorization of his gender in terms which reduce it to a form of 'anatomical essentialism' that emerge as the problem. As Butler points out, it is the 'staging and structuring of affect and desire' which helps us to understand how 'norms work their ways into what feels most properly to belong to me'. The possession of a penis and what it has come to signify forcibly defines the limits of Michael's intelligibility as a gendered subject, the terms of which have been clearly set by his father. Such considerations lead to a question of the significance of a transgender politics for creating a more gender-just social imaginary that moves beyond merely representational politics to a consideration of the material and embodied experiences of gender. In other words, such a critical practice cannot be understood solely within the limits of a politics of representation in terms of engaging with 'narrative forms, the metaphors, the visual and auditory images, through which stories are told and lived out, through which individuals discursively position themselves and are positioned and re-positioned' (Davies, 1989, p. 237).

As Stryker (2006) points out, transgender studies offer both epistemic insights and different critical practices that I believe move us beyond the political signifi-cance of deconstruction to a consideration of important questions of embodiment and positionality, as they pertain to understanding gender diversity: 'It is as concerned with material conditions as it is with representational practices, and often pays particularly close attention to the interface between the two' (p. 3). In this sense, transgender studies provide analytic frameworks for interpreting gender, desire, embodiment and identity that disrupts while simultaneously reartic-ulating the normative relations that are assumed to exist between the 'biological specificity of the sexually differentiated body, the social roles and statuses that a particular form of body is expected to occupy, the subjectively experienced relationship between a gendered sense of self and social expectations of gender role performance, and the cultural mechanisms that work to sustain or thwart specific configurations of gendered personhood' (p. 3). In this sense, transgender identification needs to be understood in all of its complexity and not as a crude form of transvestism or a drag performance that simply parodies an exaggerated femininity. Stryker, for example, talks about 'the cross dressing farces that litter the landscape of popular culture' and further adds that 'deliberate misrepresenta-tion of the relationship between representation/gender and referent/sex' has dire consequences, with transgender people who interrupt the correlation of a particular biological sex with a particular social gender simply being considered to have got it wrong—their gender expression is seen to be a lie or 'a false representation of an underlying material truth' rather than as a legitimate and valid expression of gender (p. 9). It is in this sense that transgender theorizing involves an examination of the individual's relationship and understanding of their embodied experiences of gender identification and is, therefore, 'more attuned to questions of embodiment and identity than to those of desire and sexuality' (p. 7). Thus, transgender analytic frameworks are not incompatible with a political project of *undoing gender* in the sense that they can be deployed to draw attention to the limits and justification of a politics of hegemonic masculinity, as it relates to enforcing a dimorphic system of gender that reduces the expression of masculinity to a crude form of biological essentialism and sex differences—a recuperative masculinity politics which characterizes much of the reform agenda pertaining to the field of boys' education (see Lingard et al., 2009 for a critique of such gender reform agendas).

Stryker (2006), for example, highlights the limitations of conceiving of gender identification in these terms—it is not as stable a referent as many seem to think: 'Gender is simply what we call bodily sex when we see it in the mirror of representation—no questions asked, none needed' (p. 9). But boys are never just simply boys or girls simply girls! And in this sense, Stryker argues that transgender phenomena 'call into question both the stability of the material referent "sex" and relationship of that unstable category to the linguistic, social, and psychical categories of "gender"' (p. 9). Thus, gender expression and identification are always a mediated and embodied experience that cannot be reduced uniformly to what is typically called *the sex of the body*. However, as the case of Michael (the deaf boy to whom Davies refers in her paper) illustrates, and as Butler (2004) points out, a politics of truth about sexed bodies is implicated in particular regimes of knowledge/power relations that govern ways of knowing our bodies and relating to them which 'forcibly define intelligibility' (p. 55): 'This is what Foucault describes as the politics of truth, a politics that pertains to those relations of power that circumscribe in advance what will and will not count as truth, which order in certain regular and regulatable ways, and which we come to accept as the given field of knowledge' (Butler, 2004, p. 55).

Such transgender analytic frameworks and insights can further inform our understanding of the political project of what Connell (2009) terms *gender democracy* as opposed to embracing a strategy of *degendering*, which she claims is committed to the 'abolition of gender wherever it is found' (p. 146):

> The real alternative to de-gendering, it seems to me, is a strategy of gender democracy. This strategy seeks to equalize gender orders, rather than shrink them to nothing. Conceptually, this assumes that gender does not, in itself, imply inequality. (p. 146)

The focus, hence, becomes undoing a gender binary system that is committed to embracing a hegemonic social order which is built around the legitimation and valorization of hegemonic masculinity. Cooper (2004), for example, is interested in the strategic possibilities of countering or dismantling 'the hierarchy between men and women, and the divide which naturalizes fixed dimorphic genders', while still endorsing a kind of gender fluidity and polymorphic alternative that is at the heart of trans-activist politics, with its focus on affirming the centrality of choice and voluntary gender identity' (p. 85). As Stryker (2006) argues, transgender studies call attention to the complexity of how gender is 'lived, embodied, experienced, performed and encountered' in ways that point to the limits of a dominant binary sex/gender ideology of Eurocentric modernity to account for its various expressions (p. 3):

> [Transgender studies] helps correct an all-too-common critical failure to recognize 'the body' not as one (already constituted) object of knowledge among others, but rather as the contingent ground of all our knowledge, and of all our knowing. By addressing how

researchers often fail to appreciate the ways in which their own contingent knowledges and practices impact on the formation and transformation of the bodies of others, transgender studies makes a valuable contribution towards analyzing and interpreting the unique situation of embodied consciousness. (p. 12)

This focus on embodied experience leads clearly to a question of subjugated knowledges of transgender people and the political significance of their insurrection in terms of marking out both ontological and epistemic legitimacy for their insights and claims on the basis of their embodied experiences and 'of their relationships to the discourses and institutions that act upon and through them' (Stryker, 2006, p. 13).

## What Is to Count as a Legitimate or Viable Gendered Personhood

Butler (2004) provides some useful analytic insights into the politics of gendered personhood through her focus on the experience of one transgendered individual, David, who was born with XY chromosomes and, at the age of 8, underwent surgery to correct phimosis, a problem with the tightness of the foreskin which prevents retraction over the glands. During the procedure, a significant portion of his penis was severely burned and damaged. Butler recounts how David's parents, while watching television one evening, encountered John Money, who was discussing transsexual surgery and advocating the view that after such surgery the child, through socialization, could adapt to the new gender and live a happy, *normal* life. David underwent the surgery—his testicles were removed and preliminary preparation to create a vagina was also undertaken so that David, who was subsequently named Brenda, could decide to complete the process when she was older. The case is interesting in that it highlights the important role that parents and the medical professional play in embracing certain norms and the very criterion by which a person is judged to be a gendered being, a criterion which, Butler argues, 'posits coherent gender as a presupposition of humanness' (p. 58). In short, David's parents turned to medical professionals to correct what they considered to be potential effects of the blotched surgery for hampering the recognizability of their son as a legitimate gendered subject.

What is interesting about the case is that David, while determined unequivocally to be a boy at birth, was designated by the medical profession as a girl and became Brenda a few months later. However, subsequently, in his teens, he decided to become a man. This latter decision was supported by the intervention of a group of psychiatrists and endocrinologists who intervened in the case, believing that a mistake had been made. They espoused a hormonal basis for gender identity, which conflicted with the social constructionist position espoused by those professionals at John Money's *Gender Identity Institute*, who initially treated David before he became Brenda. The basis for the second surgical intervention was Brenda's own refusal to conform to traditional behaviours associated with being a girl—she simply refused the socialization that was imposed and rather found herself developing the desire to play with certain gender-differentiated toys, such as guns, and even preferred to urinate standing up despite the fact that she had no penis. Butler adds that when she was caught urinating in this position, other girls at the school threatened to *kill* her! This detail highlights the politics of gender normalization and embodiment in terms of how it is policed and imposed in school contexts through regimes of violence (Wyss, 2004).

The point of David's refusal to live as a girl and to act like one, however, was used to refute Money's position about the cultural malleability of gender identity—that is, that conventional patterns of masculine and feminine behaviour are not fixed and could indeed be altered. His refusal to *act* as a girl, therefore, served to confirm the views of certain endocrinologists that *biology is indeed destiny*—that David's 'deep-seated sense of gender' was indeed linked to his 'original set of genitals', understood as 'an internal truth and necessity' that govern intelligibility of gendered personhood (Butler, 2004, p. 62): 'Whereas the Money Institute enlists transsexuals to instruct Brenda in the ways of women, and *in the name of normalization*, the endocrinologists prescribe the sex change protocol of transsexuality to David for him to resume his genetic destiny, *in the name of nature*' (p, 64) [original emphasis]. Thus, malleability is 'violently imposed' on David by the medical establishment via castration and forced to become a girl, while his naturalness as a boy subsequently has to be 'artificially induced' (p. 66).

However, Butler uses the case to draw attention to the complexity of the relation of gender identity to anatomy—it is much too simplistic to read the configuration of gendered personhood in terms of 'the biological specificity of the sexually differentiated body' (Stryker, 2006, p. 3). Such relations and identifications cannot be understood in reference to the biological sexed body as a stable material referent for grounding an ultimate or essential truth about gender. These relations are often rearticulated and psychically mediated in ways that cannot be reduced merely to the anatomical body. For example, Butler points out that:

> This body becomes point of reference for a narrative that is not about the body, but which seizes upon the body, as it were, in order to inaugurate a narrative that interrogates the limits of the conceivably human. What is inconceivable is conceived again and again, through narrative means, but something remains outside the narrative, a resistant moment that signals a persisting inconceivability. (p. 64)

Butler further claims that this notion of an essential gender core, which is tied irreversibly to anatomy in a biologically determinist sense, is unable to capture the complexity of David's relation to his body and how 'he allegorizes transsexuality in order to achieve a sense of naturalness' (p. 65). She highlights that David's understanding of his own gender identity neither confirms nor denies gender essentialism, or for that matter, a theory of social construction. In short, Butler argues that David's own feelings about his *true* gender have to be understood within the apparatus of knowledge/power relations to which he has been subjected. David, for instance, is quoted as confirming his own sense of being a male. As Brenda, he would look at himself, the types of toys he was being given, his clothes, his lean body, and thought he was a 'freak'—there was a profound disconnect between imposed signifiers of femininity and his own sense of male gender identity. David asserts, 'I mean there [was] nothing feminine about me' (Butler, 2004, p. 68).

Butler is careful not to deny David's self-assertions, but frames them in terms of 'linguistic fragments', which she situates within analytic frameworks that highlight the extent to which 'a description of the self that takes place in language' is already saturated with norms' that govern how we inscribe or speak ourselves into existence (p. 68–69). For example, Butler claims that his claims about feeling different— how 'there were little things from early on'—need to be understood in terms of broader regimes and apparatuses for installing him as a legitimate gendered subject. His own self-understandings about his gendered personhood are also implicated in certain normative judgments—such understandings are not simply inscribed on a black slate:

> He seems clear that norms are external to him, but what if the norms have become the means by which he see, the frame for his own seeing, his way of seeing himself? What if the action of the norm is to be found not merely in the ideal that it posits, but in the sense of aberration and of freakishness that it conveys? Consider where precisely the norm operates when David claims, 'I looked at myself and said I don't like this type of clothing'. To whom is David speaking? And in what world, under what conditions, does not liking that type of clothing provide evidence for being the wrong gender? For whom would that be true and under what conditions?... But in what world precisely, do such dislikes count as clear or unequivocal evidence for or against being a given gender? Do parents regularly rush off to gender identity clinics when their boys play with yarn, or their girls play with trucks? Or must there already be a rather enormous anxiety at play, an anxiety about the truth of gender which seizes on this or that proclivity of dress, the size of the shoulder, the leanness of the body, to conclude that something like a clear gender identity can or cannot be built from scattered desires, these variable and invariable features of body, of bone structure, of proclivity, of attire? (p. 70)

This analysis is not meant to lead readers to draw a conclusion about the truth or falsity of David's gender or about surgical transformation in this particular case. Butler, in fact, asserts that this is not her intent. Rather, her point is to produce a more complex understanding of the systems and regimes of normalization at play in determining what is to count as viable gendered personhood. For instance, she argues that David's first surgery was instigated by his parents and medical professionals in an attempt to correct the problem of his ablated penis. It was based on a certain ideal or normative construction of biological male bodies. However, his second surgery, Butler points out, was based on behavioural and verbal indicators, which conflicted with an imposed female identity. Both surgical interventions, however, as Butler argues, rely on certain inferences and normative judgments about biological bodies in relation to how gender is expected to work. In fact, David ultimately comes to deeply disrespect the first set of doctors who performed the initial surgery. He rejects their rationalization and justification for the surgery on the basis that he would be *picked on* and that he would not *find anybody* unless he had vaginal surgery: '... it dawned on me that these people gotta be pretty shallow if that's the only thing they think I've got going for me; that the only reason why people get married and have children and have a productive life is because of what they have between their legs' (Butler, 2004, p. 71).

As Butler points out, David refuses to have his personhood and worth reduced to what he has between his legs:

> David does not trade one gender norm for another, not exactly. It would be wrong to say that he has simply internalized a gendered norm (from a critical position) as it would be to say that he has failed to live up to a gendered norm (from a normalizing, medical position), since he has already established that what will justify his worth will be the invocation of an 'I' which is not reducible to the compatibility of this anatomy with the norm ... Something exceeds the norm, and he recognizes its unrecognizability. (p. 72)

There is something intelligible to David that lies outside of those medical professionals who have sought to fix and ground his gender in a stable relation to his biological anatomical body. As Butler argues, he disrupts their politics of truth and the limits of their knowledge by 'making use of his desubjugation within that order of being to establish possibility of love beyond the grasp of the norm' (p. 74).

Butler's analysis of David's case is important because it provides further knowledge and understanding about gender expression and identity that 'call into question both the stability of the material referent sex and the relationship of that unstable category to the linguistic, social and psychical categories of "gender"' (Stryker, 2006, p. 9). It highlights the need for teachers and teacher educators to provide analytic frameworks that build a deeper understanding about gender variance, with the spirit of embracing a more gender-just social imaginary in which gendered personhood is not simply reduced to a stable biological referent or a form of *anatomical essentialism*. Rather, gender expression is better understood in terms of its complexity in its interrelationship with the body, gender role performance, apparatuses of knowledge power relations and the cultural mechanisms at play that 'work to sustain or thwart specific configurations of gendered personhood' (Stryker, 2006, p. 3).

## Implications: Towards a Trans-imaginary Politics of Gender Justice in Schools

Transgender studies and the analytic frameworks it elaborates provide the epistemological and conceptual grounding for both policy making in education and for building pedagogical practices and understandings of gender diversity and gender variance in school communities. Sykes (2004), for example, argues that gender profoundly impacts on our lives, politics and subjectivities—common sense notions that *girls will be girls* and *boys will be boys* are simply inadequate and fail to account for how students experience and embody their gender identities:

> Within schools especially, teachers need to become familiar with students' 'gender-queer' identities that are proliferating within alternative youth culture. Masculinity may not be restricted to male identity, nor femininity to female identity. People may identify with both masculinity and femininity, perhaps as bi-gendered or intersexed. (p. 21)

The body can and should no longer be posited in essentialist and deterministic terms as the biological referent for gender expression, without understanding the complex interrelationships of sex and gender, biology and culture that underscore 'specific configurations of gendered personhood' (Stryker, 2006, p. 3). It is in this sense that the 'biological sexed body guarantees nothing: it is necessarily there, a ground for the act of speaking, but it has no deterministic relationship to performative gender' (Stryker, 2006, p. 10). The examples of (1) Michael, the deaf boy who wore nail polish (Davies, 1989); (2) David, who enjoyed playing with dolls (Martino, 1995); and (3) David, who had sex reassignment surgery, serve as very useful cases for both introducing trans-analytic frameworks and for raising important questions with our teacher education students about gender variance and the embodied and performative experience of gender. As Namaste (2006) points out, while related phenomena, it is important to distinguish between the gender and queer bashing.

There are clearly social justice implications for schools, school boards and teacher education faculties in failing to incorporate a focus on gender variance and expression into the curriculum and in system-wide policy making committed to addressing bullying and safety for all students (Taylor & Peter, 2009; Wyss, 2004). As I have attempted to illustrate in writing this chapter, the English classroom is an ideal site for introducing and dealing with narratives of gender variance and transgender phenomena, especially given its pedagogical focus on textuality and multi-mediated representation as pivotal to the project of critical literacy (Muspratt, Luke, & Freebody, 1997). Embracing texts which deal with transgender phenomena are central to expanding the horizons of hope, particularly with regards to embracing an imaginary that incorporates a more gender-just politics. For example, videos such as *Princess Boy* (2010) and short films such as *A Christmas Story* (Saul, 2004) are very useful as discussion pieces in classrooms and as a means by which to address issues related to the limits of hegemonic masculinity, gender non-conformity, gender expression and transgenderism in schools. *Princess Boy* involves a segment from a talk show in Seattle, which focuses on a young boy who likes to dress up like a princess, and how his family and school has reacted to his gender non-conformity. It presents both a family and school community who embraces his gender variance and does much to build a social imaginary committed to gender justice. *A Christmas Story* is set in 1969 and involves an off-screen father filming his family opening their Christmas presents. The son, however, is more interested in the sister's gifts than the more *manly* ones he receives. This short film highlights the particular family dynamics at play in enforcing hegemonic masculinity, gender conformity and the consequences of refusing to embrace it. The two texts work well together in showing how two very different family contexts contribute to either thwarting or sustaining gender variance and gender justice in children's lives. Such narratives make available positions from which to embrace possibilities beyond gender binaries and to interrogate the imposition of such binaries on boys' expression of personhood.

## Conclusion

In this chapter, I have attempted to build knowledge and theory regarding the necessity of *undoing gender* as a political project that is central to imagining a more socially just world. Central to such a politics, as I have illustrated in drawing on the early work of Bronwyn Davies, is the critical deconstructive work around interrogating hegemonic masculinity in the English classroom. In addition to endorsing such a critical practice, I have argued for the need to incorporate an analytic focus on transgender phenomena as a basis for building a more comprehensive understanding of gender embodiment and performativity. By drawing on the work of Susan Stryker and Judith Butler, in particular, I have attempted to unravel what I see as being the implications of such frameworks and knowledge for teacher educators and teachers in schools, particularly in terms of raising critical and ethical questions about what is to count as a viable, gendered personhood. Through discussing various examples provided in this chapter, which focus, to a certain degree, on gender non-conformity in young boys' lives, what I have tried to illustrate is the necessity of embracing a transgender social imaginary, which refutes gender essentialism, as central to a political project of gender justice. Moreover, by engaging with such theories and their practical implications for including texts which deal with transgender phenomena in the English classroom, I have tried to demonstrate that the project of deconstructing hegemonic masculinity is not incompatible with embracing a transgender social imaginary. Central to fostering such imaginative possibilities is the introduction of narratives and texts in the classroom that make available imaginative possibilities for thinking about gender beyond the limits imposed by biological essentialism and binary regimes of thought which cite the body as a stable referent for gender expression.

## References

Butler, J. (2004). *Undoing gender*. New York/London: Routledge.

Connell, R. (1995). *Masculinities*. Sydney, Australia: Allen & Unwin.

Connell, R. (2009). *Gender*. Cambridge, UK: Polity.

Cooper, D. (2004). *Challenging diversity: Rethinking equality and the value of difference*. Cambridge, UK: Cambridge University Press.

Davies, B. (1989). The discursive production of the male/female dualism in school settings. *Oxford Review of Education, 15*(3), 229–241.

Froese-Germain, B. (2006). Educating boys: Tempering rhetoric with research. *McGill Journal of Education, 41*(2), 145–154.

Hooks, B. (1994). Theory as liberatory practice (Chapter 5). In B. Hooks (Ed.), *Teaching to transgress* (pp. 59–76). New York/London: Routledge.

Keyte, B., & Baines, R. (Eds.). (1982). *The loaded dice*. Melbourne, Australia: Nelson.

Lingard, B., Martino, M., & Mills, M. (2009). *Boys and schooling: Beyond structural reform*. London/New York: Palgrave.

Martino, W. (1995). Deconstructing masculinity in the English classroom: A site for reconstituting gendered subjectivity. *Gender and Education, 7*(2), 205–220.

Martino, W., & Kehler, M. (2007). Gender-based literacy reform: A question of challenging or recuperating gender binaries. *Canadian Journal of Education, 30*(2), 406–431.

Martino, W., & Mellor, B. (1995). *Gendered fictions*. Cottesloe, Australia: Chalkface Press.

Martino, W., & Pallotta-Chiarolli, M. (2005). *'Being normal is the only way to be': Adolescent perspectives on gender and school*. Sydney, Australia: University of New South Wales Press.

Martino, W., & Rezai-Rashti, G. (in press). Neo-liberal accountability and boys' underachievement: Steering education policy by numbers in the Ontario context. *International Journal of Inclusive Education*.

Muspratt, S., Luke, A., & Freebody, P. (1997). *Constructing critical literacies*. Sydney, Australia: Allen & Unwin.

Namaste, V. (2006). Genderbashing: Sexuality, gender, and the regulation of public space. In S. Stryker & S. Whittle (Eds.), *The transgender studies reader* (pp. 584–600). New York/London: Routledge.

Petersen, A. (1998). *Unmasking the masculine*. Thousand Oaks, CA: Sage.

Princess Boy. (2010). http://thesocietypages.org/socimages/2010/10/17/princess-boy-addressing-childrens-gender-non-conformity/

Saul, M. (2004). A Christmas story. In: *True love: An anthology of seven short gay films* (Produced by Brian nelson). http://www.michaelsaul.com/MichaelSaul.com/Films.html

Stryker, S. (2006). De-subjugated knowledges: An introduction to transgender studies. In S. Stryker & S. Whittle (Eds.), *The transgender studies reader* (pp. 1–17). New York/London: Routledge.

Sykes, H. (2004). Genderqueer: Transphobia and homophobia in schools. *ORBIT Magazine, 34*(1), 21–23.

Taylor, C., & Peter, T. (2009). *Youth speak up about homophobia and transphobia: The first national climate survey on homophobia in Canadian schools. Phase one report*. Toronto, Canada: Egale Canada Human Rights Trust.

Titus, J. (2004). Boy trouble: Rhetorical framing of boys' underachievement. *Discourse, 25*(2), 145–169.

Wyss, S. (2004). 'This was my hell': The violence experienced by gender non-conforming youth in US high schools. *International Journal of Qualitative Studies in Education, 17*(5), 709–729.

# Chapter 10
# Strategic Confrontation: Within and Against Conservative Refusals

Lisa J. Cary

## Introduction: The Critical Incident

*Setting: A doctoral unit in a College of Education in a large research university in central Texas, USA. The title of the unit was Curriculum Theory and the focus for this week was Critical Theory in Curriculum.*

*Action: The small group presenting on the work of Michael Apple finished their presentation. As usual I stood up to fill in any gaps and talk about related issues. I was not totally happy with the presentation so I felt I had a lot of ground to cover to explain a Critical approach to understanding curriculum. As usual I responded to questions and statements from the students in the class. It is possible that I was a tad tired—I'm just saying. So, when one of the students refused to consider that the 'playing field was not equal', well... I just lost it. I gave an impassioned speech/lecture/rant on how hegemonic forces work to conceal the effects of power and how only someone who benefited from the system could refuse to see the 'truth' of the situation.*

*I was justifiably horrified that I had lost it and couldn't sleep that night. I had learned over many years of teaching topics with a Critical lens on schooling and social justice that you had to be very subtle about the content. I had learned to teach in a less-oppositional manner—saying things like 'this school of thought suggests...' and 'we have an ethical imperative to teach these theories to centre the rights of all students to life opportunities and successful educational experiences'....*

*So, in the next class I handed out a survey I had created that asked the students to reflect on the 'impromptu lecture' I had given last week and how they had felt*

L.J. Cary (✉)
School of Education, Murdoch University, Perth, WA, Australia
e-mail: l.cary@murdoch.edu.au

B. Down and J. Smyth (eds.), *Critical Voices in Teacher Education*, Explorations of Educational Purpose 22, DOI 10.1007/978-94-007-3974-1_10,
© Springer Science+Business Media Dordrecht 2012

*about it afterwards. Surprisingly, the vast majority said they found it very useful
and informative. One response, however, was as follows:*

> *I'm so sick of hearing about Critical Theory and social justice in every unit I take for my
> doctorate. I think we should be talking more about how to teach ALL students.*

*This respondent is not alone in his/her desire to leave all that depressing stuff
behind and just get on with teaching. I consider this to be a conservative refusal.*


## Theoretically Speaking . . .


This chapter is an explication of thoughts and theories I have drawn together over
25 years of teaching issues of social justice. I will use a number of different
approaches to the same question—how do we teach within and against conservative
refusals and resistances. I see this as an attempt to interrupt hegemony at work, in
much the same way as I did when I wrote about the refusals of citizenship much
earlier in my career (Cary, 2001). At that time I was interested in the socio-historic
construction of citizenship as a way into discussions regarding redemptive notions
of the good teacher and worthy students (Popkewitz, 1998). This work has led me
to work on cultural outcasts as a way of highlighting the erasure of bad girls in
social institutions (Cary, 2003). However, throughout these theoretical journeys into
understanding, I have also been a teacher of difficult knowledge. By this I mean,
I teach on issues that confront the status quo. These confrontational issues also
require more than just 'good teaching'. In fact, I have moved from a quite angry
and opposition place early in my career to a much more complicated postmodern
space in my efforts to work within and against conservative refusals and resistance
to critical social justice issues (Cary, 2006).

In my recent work, I have developed a postmodern approach to researching how
we know—discursively produced epistemological spaces—I call this Curriculum
Spaces Research Theory (Cary, 2006). I find it a useful way to think about the
texts of teaching. Curriculum Spaces is an approach to investigating epistemological
spaces as discursive productions from a poststructural/postmodern perspective.
It draws upon the notion of discourse as an absent power that gives authority,
validation and legitimization. 'A discourse author-ises certain people to speak and
correspondingly silences others, or at least makes their voices less authoritative.
A discourse is therefore exclusionary' (Usher & Edwards, 1994, p. 90). It moves
the field of Curriculum from studying the self and the desire to 'give voice' to
others to a more complicated understanding of how we are all framed by these
historical, social and cultural discourses that, in effect, produce the possibilities of
being. However, this effect of power is not linear, nor deterministic. Curriculum
Spaces draws upon the Foucauldian notion that power circulates and actively
produces knowledge and ways of being. This approach studies the manifestation of
relationships within the social network. Therefore, the theory and research presented
in this chapter consider social relationships and 'how we know' individuals, reform

movements and educational and social discourses, as a vital undertaking. As such, these relationships should be investigated to produce a complicated understanding of subjectivities and thus move us beyond deterministic, simplistic desires for voices and stories.

Therefore, this chapter will use two main avenues of approach to this topic. First, I will present a brief discussion of the nature of teachers in film as a way into the simulacra of 'good teaching'. Second, I will outline a discussion of teaching as cultural performance to lead to a more complicated understanding of teaching in conservative times.

## The 'Good Teacher' as Simulacra

I have used the concept of simulacra of teacher to frame this section as it is a 'useful' way of studying the subject position of the 'good teacher' without falling into traditional notions of teacher image. Lather (1991) describes it as a copy without an original, drawing on the Baudrillardian argument that there has been a shift from a culture of representations to a culture of simulacra. Thus, the simulacra of teacher embrace 'epistemological insufficiency can generate practices of knowing that put[s] the rationalistic and evidentiary structures of science under suspicion in order to address how science betrays our investment in it' (Lather, 2001, p. 3).

Some of the questions I have asked in my classes on Curriculum Theory included: (1) What do we desire as teachers? (2) What are we allowed to desire? and (3) How is desire produced in this text and in the classroom? In previous work, I have used the notion of desire as one way of studying what it means to be teacher (Cary, 2001). The work of Deborah Britzman (1998) and Alice Pitt (1998) was central to this analysis as they suggest a move towards a complicated understanding of research and educational practices and away from a wish for heroism and rescue through research. This has been particularly useful for rethinking the representation of 'teacher' in this chapter as a way to 'unseat the authority of the humanist subject by insisting upon the notion of the unconscious' (Pitt, 1998, p. 537). Analysing the film texts in terms of objects of desire enables a different discussion to take place—one that insists on the role of the unconscious (Pitt). The previously unexplored aspect of desire in the simulacra of teacher opens up the analysis of the layers of discursive organization as constructing (and deconstructing) ideals of 'good teacher', 'popular teacher', 'teacher as friend', and 'teacher in social relationship' (Foucault, 1977; McWilliam, 1999; Popkewitz, 1998). In this way, we can consider the 'difficult knowledge' of education by exploring the question, status and directionality of interference, and issues of love, hate and transference (Britzman).

Building on previous work on vintage films (Cary, 2006; Cary & Reifel, 2005), the aim is to consider the implications of studying teacher as simulacra, as a layered, complex actor who is not reduced to the normative, reductive spaces of being a 'teacher' in the current educational/professional climate. The purpose is to disrupt and add to conceptions of teacher and teaching, as reflected in existing disciplinary research on teaching (Lortie, 1975; Popkewitz, 1998). This move enables us to avoid generating a model of the 'good teacher' that is built on normative generalizations of teacher practice, a generalization that is provided as a truth claim. Rather, this work aims to reveal another way of analysing what it means to be a teacher and what it means *not* to be a teacher (i.e. what is said and unsaid). The question addressed was: What does it mean to be a 'good' teacher, a 'bad' teacher or a 'dangerous' teacher? And, according to Ellsworth (1997), who does the film think you are? In other words, how does the normalized construction of what we know as a 'good teacher' interact with the portrayals, for example, of the charismatic and dangerous teaching of Miss Jean Brodie in 'The Prime of Miss Jean Brodie'? How do our notions of 'good' teaching interact with the portrayal of the dangerous and inspiring teaching presented in 'Dead Poets Society'? And, even more interesting, do we see ourselves in the Brodie character or the John Keating character? Is this a possibility—why and why not?

Many questions emerge when you consider the way the role of the teacher is presented in film. I think this is important to consider when we are talking about teaching difficult knowledge in the face of conservative refusals because, when we analyse the danger of the pedagogy used by these 'dangerous teachers', we also reveal our assumptions about teacher and teaching in general (Labaree, 1992, 1995, 1996). I also think this work would be most useful in undergraduate preservice teacher preparation programmes as a way to deconstruct our 'apprenticeship of observation' as outlined by Lortie (1975). It is time to prepare teachers who have a complicated understanding of their profession and who can work to interrupt populist constructions of that profession in the media (possibly even in dangerous and inspiring ways).

The approach presented above is one way of allowing us to sustain rigorous questioning of the 'truth' embodied in educational work in order to disrupt the 'natural' (neutral) foundations of the dominant discourses in the field (Popkewitz & Brennan, 1998). Truth, according to Foucault, is played out in the three-dimensional space of knowledge, subjectivity and power (Simola, Heikkinen, & Silvonen, 1998). This is an important point to consider when studying the dominant discourses in teacher education as the 'truth' of the discipline can be deconstructed as might the ways in which the 'subject'/the 'good' citizen/the 'good' student is constituted and constitutes himself/herself. An investigation of the production of 'truth' and the 'subject' reveals the ways in which the field (and Hollywood's representations of teachers) has excluded and silenced marginal (and dangerous) discourses. Once we recognize that we exist within the tensions of the modernist knowledge project/redemptive project that has shaped the dominant discourse of the field, we can create spaces, places and suggestions for the re-conceptualization of the field through an understanding of how discourses and governing practices (Foucault's governmentalities) are produced within a populist rhetoric of redemption:

> Curriculum as a governing practice becomes almost self-evident as we think of the 'making' of the proper citizen. This citizen is one who has the correct dispositions, sensitivities and awareness to act as a self-governing individual in the new political, cultural and economic

contexts. Current reforms that focus on 'constructivist pedagogy' and teacher education reforms that considered the 'beliefs' and 'dispositions' of the teacher are the secularization of the confessional systems of self discipline and control. (Popkewitz, 1998, p. 89)

Lather (1996) opens this space for discussion when she states:

Critical appropriations of postmodernism focus on the regulatory and transgressive functions of discourses that articulate and organize our everyday experiences of the world. To both confirm and complicate received codes is to see how language is inextricably bound to the social and the ideological. This moves social inquiry to new grounds, the grounds of 'discourse', where the ways we talk and write are situated within social practices, the historical conditions of meaning, the positions from which texts are both produced and received. (p. 360)

By focusing on the ways we know and speak about teaching difficult knowledge in conservative times, we can probe the manifestations of the relations of the power of 'truth' as distinct from the forms of dominance. 'A discursive structure can be detected because of the systematicity of the ideas, opinions, concepts, ways of thinking and behaving which are formed within a particular context, and because of the effects of those ways of thinking and behaving' (Mills, 1997, p. 17). The study of discourse practices in this project utilizes both a poststructural perspective and a postcolonial perspective to shift the focus away from the critical realist interpretation to a more complicated study of the formation of the subject/culture by looking at the way we live out our lives in this contested terrain of contradictory positions and symbolic exchanges (Lather, 1996).

## Understanding the Social Construction of Teaching as an Ethical Issue

Another way into this discussion is to consider the act of teaching as a cultural performance within and against the social construction of teaching. I have learned over the years that oppositional pedagogy is like 'preaching to the choir'. It seems to inspire only those students who agree with a Critical perspective. So, in my current teaching life, I attempt a more strategic and interruptive pedagogy. This approach is built upon the many different postmodern theories I have studied as a way into a more sophisticated pedagogy, one informed by theory, that puts theory into practice. By stepping away from an oppositional position, I now highlight the agenda for teaching about social justice as an ethical move in an enlightened citizenry. I strongly believe this is an important strategic decision. Of course, in the Critical Incident presented at the beginning of the chapter, I totally lost it and stepped right back into an oppressive oppositional teaching position. And it is this realization that made me so uncomfortable and led to the survey of the students.

A number of authors centre this issue of understanding social difference in their work in teacher education. For example, Sleeter (1994), McLaren (1997), and Frankenberg (1993) all highlight the need for the study of the underlying epistemological assumptions of anti-racist and multicultural education to work against the assimilationist tendencies of institutionalized efforts. Drawing upon the works of these respected scholars, we can examine positions of privilege and power in teaching, or in this specific case, the teacher and the resistant student in the teacher education classroom. By utilizing this ethical move, we can work towards addressing the ways these constructions reproduce the oppression and dominant erasure of difference in order to interrogate the ways in which we know ourselves.

Along the same lines, Lincoln (1998) also suggests we interrogate the modernist knowledge project that has created a culturally normative space from which the dominant culture has performatively engaged and subordinated all other ways of knowing and being in the world. One way into this interrogation is the work of Parker Palmer (1993). Palmer presents epistemology as a communal act, in a sense as a culturally performative act in the classroom as a living, ongoing experience. He also highlights that 'we cannot amend our pedagogy until our epistemology is transformed' (Palmer, 1993, p. xvii). Along the same lines, Audre Lorde (1984) sums it up when she states 'the oppressors have maintained their position and avoided responsibility for their actions' (p. 115). By making invisible the ways in which the dominant position has been reinscribed and reproduced through even well-intentioned pedagogical reforms, we can interrogate the position of exclusivist social constructions of difference of race, class, gender and sexuality, for example. When it comes to race, John Hope Franklin (1993) believes that the reason we have failed to create a colour-blind society is because it is not in our (white people's) best interests to do so. He calls for an investigation of our past, our race, our dominant whiteness. Therefore, it is a strategic and ethical move to talk back as a position of power from the margins (Hooks, 1989). This move puts counter-hegemonic discourse to work and calls for a collective effort in teacher education classrooms.

One way of doing this would be to reveal the power at play in the silence of whiteness. Frankenberg (1993) suggests that studying and troubling whiteness will allow whites involved in anti-racist and multicultural education to reconceptualize their place in the process. 'We have been well socialized as racist … we know a lot about racism. I want White people to articulate, examine, question and critique what we know about racism' (Sleeter, 1994, p. 5). Defining whiteness is paramount to any discussion that attempts to trouble the social construction of difference. McLaren (1997) defines it as follows:

> Whiteness is a socio-historical form of consciousness, given at birth at the nexus of capitalism, colonial power, and emergent relationships among dominant and subordinate groups. Whiteness is a refusal to acknowledge the ways in which whites are implicated in social relations of privilege and power through domination and subordination. (p. 9)

Sleeter (1994) argues, 'by white racism (or white supremacy) I am referring to a system of rules, procedures, and tacit beliefs that allows white people to collectively maintain control of the wealth and power of the nation, and of the world' (p. 6). By defining something previously unarticulated, whiteness may be revealed as a standpoint of privilege, a structural advantage and a place from which to other all those considered non-white (Frankenberg, 1993).

Understanding the social construction of difference as an oppressive and exclusivist force is vital in teaching in conservative times. This chapter calls for teacher educators to interrupt positions of raced, classed or gendered privilege and to provide spaces from which to work against normalizing institutional and pedagogical practices that reinforce the epistemological position of dominance. This is not an easy task. Cornel West (1993) highlights the magnitude of this issue when he states that conservative behaviourists talk comfortably about attitudes and values as if they are quite separate from political and economic structures. Gloria Ladson-Billings (1995) supports this position when she talks of the ways in which courses that work to interrupt the dominant culture face major hurdles. Such work often face unexpected resistance, and they actually 'engender resistance and reinforce stereotypes ... are seen as lacking intellectual rigor ... to mollify those racialized others' (p. 9). I see these courses as oppositional in nature.

In order to move beyond oppositional stances to a more strategic space of understanding how the social construction of difference works, I have drawn upon the work of Homi Bhabha (1994) in *The Location of Culture*. He highlights the reinscription of hegemonic discourse through the relativistic discourse of diversity. He suggests that by highlighting the hybridity of cultural performance, we may move beyond essentialist discussions of race and culture. Culture, according to Bhabha, is developed performatively through discursive processes. Bhabha aims to disrupt the epistemological assumptions of the hegemonic discourses that silences and erases issues of race from any discussion of culture. He especially highlights the need to focus on the performative culture of difference rather than on diversity which has become a culturally relativistic position—a white solution to the black problem. In all of these representations of the social and cultural understanding of difference, I think a move must be made to move beyond oppositional pedagogy to a more strategic confrontation, within and against, the conservative refusals of the powerful dominant culture.

## Moving from Oppositional Pedagogy to Strategic Confrontation

The resistance of that one white female student in the Critical Incident outlined at the beginning of the chapter is an example of a tangible and concrete hegemonic force. How do we move such students beyond/around/underneath/over resistance? The pedagogical strategies outlined below aim to provide a learning space that enable and encourages all students to become aware and enabled to recognize the ways in which their race is culturally performed/engaged in teaching. In this way, it is my hope that they will use this awareness to become conscious of the ways in which they must work both within and against the normalizing tendencies of schools, and act politically and personally to become visible in society in general. We must bring together our understandings of the social construction of difference to interrogate and disrupt the hegemonic discourses that continue to work in teacher education. By engaging in the following pedagogical strategies as teacher educators and teachers, we may make visible these oppressive constructions of difference, these positions of privilege and power.

To disrupt these normalizing and silencing tendencies of dominant discourses that have effectively co-opted teacher education and made it a safe and convenient place to reinscribe the status quo, a pedagogy that interrupts the comfort of refusals must also engage and make visible the cultural performance of teachers and students alike, as they consciously work towards a position of personal and political action. The ways in which this may be done include the development of a community of truth (although I want to trouble the unitary tendencies of this concept), dialogue (again wanting to trouble the idealist foundations of this concept), use of narrative and personal histories and personal/political action.

## *Contemplative Spaces for Collective Projects*

We can begin by creating contemplative spaces for silence and dialogue, learning spaces to interrupt the ways in which silence and culturally normative spaces reinscribe difference. Working within and against the total institution as Ladson-Billings (1995) highlighted, we may bring to consciousness the ways in which we depend upon the very institutions that attempt to silence and co-opt counter-hegemonic education. This can be achieved by developing an anti-essentialist epistemological move that highlights partiality, incoherence, ongoing and communal knowing. It is a *collective* project in which we must engage personally and professionally, through coalitions and classrooms (Hooks, 1994; West, 1993). All approaches must be framed within a spiritual professional commitment to love, humility and comradeship (Freire, 1970; Palmer, 1993) and engage in an epistemological investigation as recent pedagogical reforms focus only on technique and 'the underlying epistemology remains unexamined and unchanged' (Palmer, 1993, p. 30). By formally creating spaces within curriculum and syllabi, these spaces will not just be 'teachable moments' but planned and focal parts of the learning experience. Spaces can be created through time for personal reflection, response to readings and feedback for critical self-reflection through journaling (Ford & Dillard, 1996). Deconstructing self through critical self-reflection is paramount also and can occur by using personal histories, autobiographies and narratives of individual's journeys that highlight how we perform our understandings of difference. This is demonstrated in the Critical Incident when I engaged in safe discussion of the pedagogical event through confidential surveys. Silence (which we often face as teacher educators raising issues of race in classrooms or conferences) may be a place racial bonding and reinforcing inequitable epistemological positions. Thus, Sleeter (1994) calls for a positionality in teacher education that will interrupt racial bonding patterns that occur through dialogue. Throughout this process, the ongoing and partial nature of cultural understanding must be highlighted as a place for growth and constant cultural performance.

## *Developing a Community of Truth*

According to Palmer (1993), a community of truth is a 'rich and complex network of relationships, in which we must both speak and listen, make claims on others, and make ourselves accountable' (p. xii). To develop this in a classroom, you must immediately make central the concerns and issues raised by the students by providing pedagogical spaces for their involvement. Moving beyond the transmission or critical arrogance of a transformative perspective, a community of truth means the teacher educator makes central the personal stories and histories of the students as a common place from which to start deconstructing their raced, classed and gendered positionality. Palmer states that brief personal introductions as we see in most teacher education classes immediately signify the centrality of the teacher's voice and the unimportance of personal student experience. Students must feel safe yet challenged to respond to other's stories and receive feedback on their own. Learning is not necessarily a comfortable process. 'A learning space needs to be hospitable not to make learning painless but to make painful things possible' (Palmer, 1993, p. 74).

## *Personal Stories and Journaling*

Creating spaces for the critical analysis of required readings highlighting the 'othered' experiences of non-white teachers, students and critical thinkers is most important (Palmer, 1993). Personal stories and histories, such as mentioned briefly above, are vital:

> Analyzing the connections between white daily lives and discursive orders may help make visible the ways in which white stability—as a location of privilege; a culturally normative stance; and a standpoint—are secured and reproduced. These accounts then legitimate exploitative 'practice politics', even when those that develop them have good intentions. (Frankenberg, 1993, p. 242)

In their work on 'becoming multicultural', Ford and Dillard (1996) state that 'teachers and students alike bring personal histories that influence their perceptions of self, and in turn, their social interactions in any learning or schooling context' (p. 232). Strong connections exist between Freire's (1970) conceptualization of problem-posing education where teachers become teacher/student and students become students/teachers 'as they become jointly responsible for a process in which they all grow' (p. 67) and Ford and Dillard's stages of becoming multicultural. The four stages are (1) Consciousness of Self as Subject, (2) Deconstruction through Critical Self Reflection, (3) Critical Social Consciousness and (4) Critical Social Political Action. Using personal histories and stories and having students present them to the class is one way of working through these stages. Feedback and critical self-reflection is most important—from peers and from the instructor or teacher educator.

Hooks (1994) also highlights the importance of dialogue: 'Dialogue is the simplest process by which teachers, scholars, and critical thinkers can cross boundaries, barriers that may or may not be constructed by race, class, gender, professional standing or other differences' (p. 130). How would I use dialogue in the classroom? Small groups, required readings, group presentations on issues and areas of literature (theoretical and poetic) are a few specific ways to engender discussion. There is always the difficulty of moving beyond simplistic discussions of difference, and, thus, the choice of the readings is vital and the preparation of the teacher educator central.

## *Personal and Professional Critical Political Action*

However, most important is what we do as teachers with all of this discussion and dialogue about difference. Well, we have to act—for 'our actions speak louder than our words as we strategically formulate, plan and implement teaching methods that are based on egalitarian and multicultural ideals .... In acting politically, the individual breaks down the walls of invisibility and silence of their personal self, creating discomfort in others' (Ford & Dillard, 1996, p. 236). It is vital that as teachers committed to confronting conservative refusals, we embody our epistemological and ethical standpoints by the way we know and act in the world (Palmer, 1993).

## Conclusion

Throughout my experiences as a teacher and student of Social Justice curriculums in Australia, Canada and the United States, the most personally transformative experiences I recall were when space had been allocated in the curriculum or course syllabus for personal journeying and responding to both the students' and the teacher's journey towards understanding the social construction of difference. It is the people I have met and loved that have enabled me to see my own colour, class and gender and the way these positions play out in the dominant society. My personal and professional actions speak louder than any words as I teach using a number of strategic planned and unplanned ethical moves in my classes that include autobiographical presentations, journaling with responses from fellow students and myself as teacher educator and spaces and places for discussion of those sacred readings (Palmer, 1993) where individual stories and poems, music and lyrics take us beyond our comfortable places of privilege.

# References

Bhabha, H. K. (1994). *The location of culture*. New York: Routledge.

Britzman, D. P. (1998). *Lost subjects, contested objects: Toward a psychoanalytic inquiry of learning*. New York: State University of New York Press.

Cary, L. J. (2001). The refusals of citizenship: Normalizing practices in social educational discourses. *Theory and Research in Social Education, 29*(3), 405–430.

Cary, L. J. (2003). Unhomely spaces and deviant subjectivity: The socio-historical homelessness of juvenile female offenders. *International Journal of Qualitative Studies in Education, 16*(4), 579–594.

Cary, L. J. (2006). *Curriculum spaces: Discourse, postmodern theory and educational research*. New York: Peter Lang.

Cary, L. J., & Reifel, S. (2005). Cinematic teacher landscapes. *Action in Teacher Education, 27*(3), 95–109.

Ellsworth, E. (1997). *Teaching positions: Difference, pedagogy, and the power of address*. New York: Teachers College Press.

Ford, T. L., & Dillard, C. B. (1996). Becoming multicultural: A recursive process of self- and social construction. *Theory into Practice, 35*(4), 232–238.

Foucault, M. (1977). *Discipline and punish*. Translated from French by Alan Sheridan. New York: Vintage Books.

Frankenberg, R. (1993). *White women, race matters: The social construction of whiteness*. Minneapolis, MN: University of Minnesota Press.

Franklin, J. H. (1993). *The color line: Legacy for the twenty-first century*. Columbia, MO: University of Missouri Press.

Freire, P. (1970). *Pedagogy of the oppressed*. New York: Seabury Press.

Hooks, B. (1989). *Talking back: Thinking feminist, thinking black*. Boston: South End Press.

Hooks, B. (1994). *Teaching to transgress: Education as the practice of freedom*. New York: Routledge.

Ladson-Billings, G. (1995). *It's never too late to turn back: A critical race approach to multicultural education*. American Educational Research Association annual conference, San Diego, CA.

Labaree, D. (1992). Power, knowledge, and the rationalization of teaching: A genealogy of the movement to professionalize teaching. *Harvard Educational Review, 62*(2), 123–134.

Labaree, D. (1995). A disabling vision: Rhetoric and reality in *Tomorrow's Schools of Education. Teachers College Record, 97*(2), 166–205.

Labaree, D. (1996, Summer). The trouble with ed schools. *Educational Foundations, 10*(3), 27–45.

Lather, P. (1991). *Getting smart: Feminist research and pedagogy with/in the postmodern*. New York: Routledge.

Lather, P. (1996). Troubling clarity: The politics of accessible language. *Harvard Educational Review, 66*(3), 525–545.

Lather, P. (2001). Postmodernism, poststructuralism and post(critical) ethnography: Of ruins, aporias and angels. In P. Atkinson & S. Delamont (Eds.), *The handbook of ethnography* (pp. 477–492). London: Sage Publications.

Lincoln, Y. (1998). From understanding to action: New imperatives, new criteria, new methods for interpretive researchers. *Theory and Research in Social Education, 26*(1), 12–29.

Lorde, A. (1984). *Sister outsider: Essays and speeches*. California: Crossing press; Freedom.

Lortie, D. C. (1975). *Schoolteacher*. Chicago: University of Chicago Press.

McLaren, P. (1997, Fall). Decentering whiteness: In search of a revolutionary multiculturalism. *Multicultural Education, 5*(1), 4–11.

McWilliam, E. (1999). *Pedagogical pleasures*. New York: Peter Lang.

Mills, S. (1997). *Discourse*. New York: Routledge.

Palmer, P. J. (1993). *To know as we are known: Education as a spiritual journey*. San Francisco: Harper San Francisco.

Pitt, A. (1998). Qualifying resistance: Some comments on methodological dilemmas. *International Journal of Qualitative Studies in Education, 11*(4), 535–553.

Popkewitz, T. S. (1998). The culture of redemption and the administration of freedom as research. *Review of Educational Research, 68*(1), 1–34.

Popkewitz, T. S., & Brennan, B. (1998). Restructuring of social and political theory in education: Foucault and a social epistemology of school practices. In T. S. Popkewitz & M. Brennan (Eds.), *Foucault's challenge: Discourse, knowledge, and power in education* (pp. 3–35). New York: Teachers College Press.

Simola, H., Heikkinen, S., & Silvonen, J. (1998). A catalog of possibilities: Foucaultian history of truth and education research. In T. S. Popkewitz & M. Brennan (Eds.), *Foucault's challenge: Discourse, knowledge, and power in education* (pp. 64–90). New York: Teachers College Press.

Sleeter, C. (1994, Spring). White racism. *Multicultural Education, 1*(4), 5–8.

Usher, R., & Edwards, R. (1994). *Postmodernism and education*. London: Routledge.

West, C. (1993). *Race matters*. Boston: Beacon.

# Chapter 11
# Studying Culture Jamming to Inspire Student Activism

Marilyn Frankenstein

When I was hired in 1978 at The College of Public and Community Service (University of Massachusetts/Boston), without a PhD and with my only publication being a basic algebra textbook, I was told that my work would be sufficient for getting tenure. Then, after my pre-tenure review, it was clear I would have to publish a theoretical article for my tenure file. At first I resisted, thinking the heart of my work is in my curriculum development and my teaching practice, and it was a waste of time to sit and reflect. But, I decided to be practical since I loved my job, audited one of Henry Giroux's radical education classes at Boston University, and, with the help of colleagues (particularly James Green and Kathleen Weiler), learned what it meant to think about my work in theoretical terms. The process of writing this article taught me about the value of reflection (Frankenstein, 1983).

And, in a personal way, it also brought the world into my life. In 1986, when my life seemed to be closing down, after surgery for a cancer with a difficult prognosis, and with a desire to see the world before it was too late, I got a letter from a Brazilian scholar, Ubi D'Ambrosio, asking to translate my article into Portuguese. That started a process of my getting connected with many scholars around the world, including my long-term coauthor, Arthur Powell. With Arthur and Marty Hoffman I attended my first international conference in 1988 (ICME in Budapest); through John Volmink, Cyril Julie, Mathume Bopape, and others, I spent 2 months giving talks in South Africa; through Paulus Gerdes, I gave talks in Mozambique; through Europe Singh, Rupee Singh, and Les Scafe, I gave talks in London; through Gelsa Knijnik, Ubi D'Ambrosio, and others, I spent a month giving talks all over Brazil.

M. Frankenstein (✉)
College of Public and Community Service (CPCS), The University of Massachusetts,
Boston, MA, USA
e-mail: marilyn.frankenstein@umb.edu

B. Down and J. Smyth (eds.), *Critical Voices in Teacher Education*, Explorations    151
of Educational Purpose 22, DOI 10.1007/978-94-007-3974-1_11,
© Springer Science+Business Media Dordrecht 2012

Now, over 30 years later, I feel I have made my contribution to critical mathematics education,[1] particularly to establishing a theoretically based practice in critical mathematics literacy education. I will eventually publish a collection of my articles and curricular materials, which will include relevant political and professional and visual autobiographical collage, and will introduce the next direction of my work.

My interdisciplinary work now involves understanding arguments, media literacy, and economic literacy, as well as critical mathematics literacy. A recent manuscript "Which Measures Count for the Public Interest?" (Frankenstein, 2011) draws on all these areas. I am currently planning a long-term community project on tax policy education, moving from teaching university students in an activist academic environment to teaching people in communities, in the streets, with the goal of education for activist participation in social justice. As this project moves forward, I will use what I learned from my initial work and find some time to sit and reflect. This project will involve active, cultural intervention to change community discourse. To develop these ideas, I wrote a teacher resource guide for the film *The Yes Men Fix the World* http://theyesmenfixtheworld.com/guide/Main_Page. This chapter draws from that guide.

I did not personally know The Yes Men when Andy asked me to write this teacher guide for their new movie, *The Yes Men Fix the World*.[2] And they did not know me. But I had e-mailed them that my students loved their first film, *The Yes Men*, as part of learning about the actions of the World Trade Organization, and they needed someone to write a guide. I wound up writing a 65,000-word interdisciplinary resource guide that uses the movie to study satire, the politics of knowledge, media literacy, economic literacy, and art and activism. The guide[3] uses these studies to inspire students to "fix" some piece of the world through connecting with existing social change groups and thinking together of creative ways to stop business as usual.

Below is a glimpse of the culture jamming and other artistic interventions that can be studied to inspire students to participate in struggles for justice. I will briefly discuss the work of The Yes Men, outline the structure of the teacher resource guide, and present a framework for thinking about the myriad kinds of artistic interventions that "jam up" our taken-for-granted assumptions and detail some specific interventions.

---

[1] When Arthur Powell and John Volmink and I formed the Criticalmathematics Educators Group (CmEG) in 1991, following a conference we organized in October 1990, we decided to use one word to describe critical mathematics because of our hope that one day all mathematics education will be critical. In the future, we intend to create a website for the group, which will include the archive of the five CmEG Newsletters we distributed 991 and 1997.

[2] www.bullfrogfilms.com/catalog/yes.html.

[3] http://theyesmenfixtheworld.com/guide/Main_Page.

## The Yes Men

We need to be devious in order to achieve a condition of honesty.

The Yes Men

The Yes Men, political performance artists whose work stems from their tactical media skills, characterize much of their satire as "identity correction— impersonating big-time criminals in order to publicly humiliate them." And by "criminals" they mean corporate criminals "who put profits ahead of everything else." Further, The Yes Men view their work as a "form of collaboration with journalists" since issues that the corporate media ignores get reported when The Yes Men perform their interventions.

In their first movie, *The Yes Men*, they explain that economically and politically powerful institutions like the World Trade Organization characterize their work as benevolent and just. In spite of the evidence that their collective actions have led to catastrophe for hundreds of millions, and possibly billions, of people, these organizations speak as if they are promoting social justice. The Yes Men, by impersonating officials who speak *for* those organizations, and speaking from the evidence of the havoc wrecked *by* those organizations, are correcting the identity of these groups, showing how hideous, how far from any concept of justice, the consequences of their actions really are. The trouble is The Yes Men's audiences, most of whom are connected to those organizations, and many of whom are implicated in perpetrating those consequences, do not get it. They see The Yes Men's recounting of those organizations' activities as good and clever and just.

*The Yes Men Fix the World* explores why our world is broken, why those who broke it do not see the shattered people and planet, why those of us who do see should not be silent, and what can we do other than scream. The movie gives examples of what The Yes Men think is broken—the continuing toxic poisoning in Bhopal, the continuing post-Katrina racial "cleansing" in New Orleans, and the increasingly catastrophic consequences of climate disruptions. Using satire, they are anything but silent. And, they address specific outrages as interconnected consequences of structures that value profits over people. The movie, then, is a wonderful vehicle for teaching about these connections and for encouraging activism that turns up the volume.

## Brief Overview of the Resource Guide

The first part of the guide suggests learning activities to prepare students to understand the movie at a deeper level by thinking about satire and its uses in addressing political issues and about the different kinds of underlying frameworks— conservative, liberal, and left—people can use to make sense of what is going on in the world. The second part of the guide focuses on student reactions to the film and their reflections on some of the major themes in the film—media literacy, the real-world consequences of an unfettered free-market world view, whose intellectual work "counts" as worth considering in fixing the world, and activist art interventions by various social justice groups—all leading to student involvement in a process of fixing some small piece of their world.

Howard Zinn argues that a key part of an education for social justice is talking about the promises that are made in documents such as *The Universal Declaration of Human Rights* and the gap between those promises and the realities of our world. "And therefore suggest in varying degrees of persuasion that that gap should be filled."[4] What I tried to do in this teacher's guide is clearly not neutral. Rather, I suggest a conceptual framework for understanding the gap Zinn names and why it exists, using *The Yes Men Fix the World* as the central learning experience, and the philosophy of my dear friend, Ashanti Pasha, as the central goal of the learning experience: to "re-claim the construct of Service, and return it to its rightful social purpose of helping people correct wrongs, and not abate them."[5]

## A Few Examples from Selections of the Resource Guide

Although the focus of this article is on the art and activism part of the guide's curriculum, the entire interdisciplinary curriculum uses art as one way to explore the various topics. For example, in the resources listed to explore satire, I include the parody video response to Garth Brooks agreement to sell his music exclusively through Wal-Mart,[6] as well as a fairly liberal music video Brooks made in the early 1990s[7] that was banned by some country stations, and was "the first Brooks single in three years to fall short of the Top 10."[8] Other examples of satire connected to the arts include Native American novelist Sheman Alexie on the Colbert Report,[9] and Damali Ayo's "How to Rent a Negro" website.[10] Broadly speaking, all satire can be considered a form of arts and activism. As George Orwell, stated: "Every joke is a tiny revolution [because . . . ] it upsets the established order." "To be funny," Orwell argued, "you have got to be serious."[11]

---

[4] Schivone (2009), p. 53.

[5] E-mail communication with the author, June 26, 2009.

[6] http://www.WalmartWorkersRights.org/.

[7] The original link I had rotted, although the embedded video still works in the online guide: http://theyesmenfixtheworld.com/guide/Satire#Selling_Wal-Mart. If that link does not work, try: http://www.singingfool.com/Title.aspx?publishedid=395355. The title of the Garth Brooks liberal song is "We Shall be Free."

[8] http://articles.latimes.com/1992-10-29/entertainment/ca-909_1_country-music.

[9] http://www.colbertnation.com/the-colbert-report-videos/189691/October-282008/sherman-alexie.

[10] http://www.rent-a-negro.com/.

[11] Quote from Woodside (2001).

Art can also be used to explore how numbers are and can be used politically in the media. One example involves discussing the meaning and power of artist Chris Burden's "The Other Vietnam Memorial"[12] which refers to the famous memorial in Washington, D.C., by artist Maya Lin which lists the names of 57,939 Americans killed during the Vietnam War. Chris Burden etched 3,000,000 names onto a Rolodex-type structure that, standing on its end, fills the entire room in which it is displayed. The names represent the approximate number of Vietnamese people killed during the US war on Vietnam. Since many of their names are unknown, Burden created variations of 4,000 names taken from Vietnamese telephone books. Also, the museum notes comment that by using the form of a common desktop object that (before the computer) was used to organize professional and social contacts, Burden underlines the unrecognized loss of Vietnamese lives in US memory. Does this art work jam up the way people generally think of who and how many died in our war on Vietnam?

## The Yes Men as Culture Jammers

The Yes Men interventions stop business-as-usual. In one action, for example, The Yes Men cleared a fancy business luncheon after 300 oilmen attendees lit up their *Vivoleum*© candles, which The Yes Men-as-ExxonMobil-Men presented as solutions to global climate disruptions. The candles, ostensibly made from the flesh of humans whose lives were disrupted by industrial climate catastrophes, were supposedly illustrating a new sustainable energy source. And they smelled convincing. So, business was stopped; The Yes Men had jammed up the "culture of capitalism."[13,14]

Mark Dery, who popularized the term "culture jamming" in articles In *The New York Times* and *Adbusters*, quotes Stuart Ewen, a critic of consumer culture:

> We live at a time when the image has become the predominant mode of public address, eclipsing all other forms in the structuring of meaning, yet little in our education prepares us to make sense of the rhetoric, historical development or social implications of the images within our lives.[15]

Dery asks, how, then, can we resist? "How to box with shadows? In other words, what shape does an engaged politics assume in an empire of signs?" His answer is through culture jamming—the art of interrupting and disrupting prevailing cultural signals and codes: "introduc[ing] noise into the signal as it passes from transmitter

---

[12]This work is in the collection of the Museum of Contemporary Art in Chicago, IL, and can be viewed at http://www.archinode.com/wtcmwj.html.

[13]http://theyesmen.org/hijinks/vivoleum.

[14]The Yes Men are currently planning to extend their work through *The Yes Lab* (http://theyesmen.org/lab.), where activists can participate in "brainstorms and trainings to help [them] carry out Yes-Men-style projects of their own." We are discussing the possibility of doing workshops for teachers, using the resource guide discussed in this article.

[15]Dery (1993) http://www.markdery.com/archives/books/culture_jamming/#000005\%23more.

to receiver, encouraging idiosyncratic, unintended interpretations. Intruding on the intruders, [culture jammers] invest ads, newscasts, and other media artifacts with subversive meanings; simultaneously, they decrypt them, rendering their seductions impotent." He argues they re-create a public discourse and have fun while doing it; he says they are "Groucho Marxists."

## Culture Jamming to Stop Business as Usual

> When you pray, move your feet.
>
> – African Proverb

Frances Fox Piven, in Challenging Authority: How Ordinary People Change America (2006) argues that

> ordinary people exercise power in American politics mainly at those extraordinary moments when they rise up in anger and hope, defy the rules that ordinarily govern their daily lives, and, by doing so, disrupt the workings of the institutions in which they are enmeshed. The drama of such events, combined with the disorder that results, propels new issues to the center of the debate, issues that were previously suppressed by the managers of political parties that depend on welding together majorities. When the new issues fracture or threaten to fracture electoral coalitions, political leaders try to restore order and stem voter defections by proffering reforms. (pp. 1–2)

In some ways, all actions that disrupt business-as-usual, that challenge the taken-for-granted ways our world works, actions such as writing alternative histories or whistle-blowing or participating in the solidarity economy,[16] jam up the status-quo culture. But, for this chapter, I will focus on artistic actions that put new, disruptive ideas into public awareness. The complete guide contains additional ways that people can disrupt the taken-for-granted, such as developing educational materials, creating alternative journalism, and participating in civil disobedience. The categories I use to organize this material overlap because the actions are all interconnected and interdisciplinary.

What follows is a glimpse of different kinds of cultural interventions through the arts, ones that I know about and that I find powerful, that could be used to jam up things in our work of "fixing" the world.[17] But, of course, there are tons more out there, and tons more your students could create. In different ways, to me, these actions reflect Romare Bearden's view that art celebrates the victory of life over suffering and hardship. Further, James Baldwin contends: "The purpose of art is to lay bare the questions which have been hidden by the answers."[18] And, even further, Booker T. Washington, in his inaugural address to the 1896 season of the Brooklyn Institute of Arts and Sciences (which today is the Brooklyn Museum) argued: "The

---

[16]http://www.populareconomics.org/ussen/.

[17]When I had to cut because of space, I tried to include art activists that might not be as well known as others, such as Paul Robeson and Pete Seeger, who are also included in the teacher resource guide.

[18]Quoted on the website of The Actor's Gang: http://www.theactorsgang.com/.

study of art that does not result in making the strong less willing to oppress the weak means little."[19]

## Billboards, Posters, Flyers, and Other Street Actions

A group of ACT UP[20] members formed the Gran Fury artistic collective that, in the early 1990s, produced some of the memorable visual work of that movement.[21] The name refers to both their outrage at the reactions of the media, the corporations, the government, and the general public to the AIDS epidemic and to the name of the car model that the New York City police used at the time. One of their posters "Kissing Doesn't Kill: Greed and Indifference Do" "mimics the codes of capitalist pleasure and visual seduction to capture the viewer's attention and direct it to the AIDS crisis" and also "affirms the power of queer desire in the face of an ongoing epidemic."[22] Although Gran Fury was able to display the poster on the sides of buses in various cities, they had to accept a compromise eliminating the original side panel which stated "Corporate Greed, Government Inaction, and Public Indifference Make AIDS a Political Crisis."

Courtesy: Gran Fury

Two of their artistic interventions, early precursors to The Yes Men actions, were fake money scattered around Wall Street and a production of *The New York Crimes* newspaper. For an ACT UP demonstration on Wall Street in March 1988, they printed up leaflets that looked like various money denominations on one side and on the other had strong messages:

---

[19]Copied by the author from a plaque in the Brooklyn Museum.

[20]The ongoing ACT UP Oral History Project (http://www.actuporalhistory.org/index1.html.) is a collection of interviews which can be watched online that presents a "comprehensive, complex, human, collective, and individual pictures of the people who have made up ACT UP/New York." The project's coordinator's hope is that these oral histories will "de-mystify the process of making social change, remind us that change can be made, and help us understand how to do it."

[21]http://digitalgallery.nypl.org/nypldigital/dgkeysearchresult.cfm?num=0&word=gran\ %20fury&s=1&notword=&d=&c=&f=&k=0&lWord=&lField=&sScope=&sLevel=&sLabel= &imgs=20&pNum.

[22]Meyer (1995), p. 52.

Courtesy: Gran Fury

For an ACT UP demonstration at New York City Hall in 1989, Gran Fury created a four-page fake newspaper, *The New York Crimes*, printed in the same fonts and style of *The New York Times*, with articles highlighting the terrible handling of the AIDS crisis in the city and locating "the root cause of the worsening crisis not in HIV infection or unsafe sex but in the government neglect and inaction." They distributed these papers by purchasing one "real" paper from the newspaper machines, which allowed access to the entire stack, and then wrapping their *Crimes* paper around all the other "real" papers.[23]

The Billboard Liberation Front's (BLF) manifesto, "The Art and Science of Billboard Improvement: A Comprehensive Guide to the Alteration of Outdoor Advertising," is a political response to the saturation of our visual environment where, as they put it, "Billboards have become as ubiquitous as human suffering, as difficult to ignore as a beggar's outstretched fist.... Larger than life, subtle as war, they assault your senses with a complex coda of commercial instructions, the messenger RNA of capitalism.... You can't run and you can't hide, because your getaway route is lined to the horizon with signs..." It outlines techniques developed over more than 20 years of "experience executing billboard improvements professionally, safely, and (knock wood) without injury or arrest."[24]

And there are different kinds of "billboards," like The Nixon Stamp Envelope,[25] and the Mud Stencils developed by Milwaukee-based artist Jesse Graves as a way to avoid toxic paints, in an "environmentally friendly street art."[26]

Courtesy: Santa Cruz Comic News www.thecomicnews.com

---

[23]Meyer (1995), pp. 73–74.

[24]http://www.billboardliberation.com/guidebook.html.

[25]Now that people can make their own stamps (http://www.usps.com/postagesolutions/customizedpostage.htm.), all sorts of possibilities emerge... Although some may run into issues, like Jonah Peretti when he tried to personalize his Nike sneakers with the word "sweatshop." (http://www.thenation.com/article/my-nike-media-adventure and http://www.shey.net/niked.html)

[26]http://mudstencils.com/.

CODEPINK, named to play with the Bush color-coded homeland security terrorist alerts (which would never include such a "feminine" color; their online magazine is called the PINKTANK), was organized in the USA in 2002 to fight against the wars on Iraq and Afghanistan and to stop new wars and to "re-direct our resources into healthcare, education, green jobs and other life-affirming activities."[27] It is now an international network of people who organize to directly confront the warmongers. They have sent peacemaking delegations to Iran, Pakistan, Syria, Beirut, Iraq, Italy, the war tribunal in Turkey, Britain's Stop the War assembly, a gathering in Thailand of women worldwide, and the World Social Forum in Brazil and Venezuela. They do not have official membership:

> We don't require official affiliation to speak, act, or protest with CODEPINK. People committed to creative protest against militarism and injustice are CODEPINK. People who want to influence a shift in the focus of world society and governments from militarism to life-affirming endeavors are CODEPINK. People who are not ashamed to wear a big pink button, and thereby encourage conversation are CODEPINK. People who are not afraid to be unreasonable or to be called un-patriotic in the name of peace and social justice are CODEPINK. People who realize that you must be the change you want to see in this world are CODEPINK.

One of their latest campaigns, "Stolen Beauty,"[28] which they situate in the "Boycott, Divestment and Sanctions (BDS)" movement that aims to end Israel's occupation of Palestinian lands, calls for boycott action against Ahava cosmetics.[29] Their website plays on Ahava's campaign slogan, "Beauty Secrets from the Dead Sea," to expose the underlying secret that Ahava "products actually come from stolen Palestinian natural resources in the Occupied Territory of the Palestinian West Bank, and are produced in the illegal settlement of Mitzpe Shalem.... The Hebrew word 'Ahava' means love, but there is nothing loving about what the company is doing in the Occupied Palestinian territory of the West Bank." Their website contains a step-by-step action guide for those interested in participating in the campaign, including how to organize a street theater "muddy" picket on the sidewalk outside stores that carry Ahava products.

## Visual and Written Texts

Jay Smooth is an educator and the founder of New York's longest running hip-hop radio show, Underground Railroad (WBAI), whose *Ill Doctrine* video blog[30] addresses controversial issues with philosophical hip-hop presentations. His vlogs

---

[27]http://www.womensaynotowar.org/article.php?list=type&type=3.

[28]http://www.stolenbeauty.org/article.php?id=4951.

[29]As of this writing, Costco has stopped carrying Ahava cosmetics.

[30]http://www.illdoctrine.com/.

address issues such as "How to Tell Someone they Sound Racist,"[31] "An Old Person's Guide to 'No Homo'," a brilliant critique of homophobia in the hip-hop community,[32] and "If Bill O'Reilly was a Rapper."[33]

"The Real Cost of Prisons Project Graphic Texts"[34] has created popular education materials to "explore the immediate and long-term costs of incarceration on the individual, her/his family, community and the nation." A number of graphic artists created three comic books documenting real stories and data: *Prison Town: Paying the Price* tells the story of how the financing and site locations of prisons affect the people of rural communities in which the prison is built. It also tells the story of how mass incarceration affects people of urban communities where the majority of incarcerated people come from. *Prisoners of the War on Drugs* includes the history of the war on drugs, mandatory minimums, how racism creates harsher sentences for people of color, stories on how the war on drugs works against women, three strikes laws, obstacles to coming home after incarceration, and how mass incarceration destabilizes neighborhoods. *Prisoners of a Hard Life: Women and Their Children* includes stories about women trapped by mandatory sentencing and the "costs" of incarceration for women and their families. Also included are alternatives to the present system, a glossary, and footnotes. The book in which all the comics are reprinted (available through the website) includes information about how the comics have been used by organizers and activists inside and outside prison by ESL teachers, high school teachers, college professors, students, and health care providers around the USA.

## *Visual and Oral Texts (Film and Theater)*

Bamako is a fictional account of a village in Mali that decides to put the World Bank on trial.[35] A review states: "*Bamako* is mostly potent speeches from African teachers and writers who expose the regressive and destructive nature of privatization, who point to the complete and utter failure of an imported economic strategy, and who tell stories of suffering and struggle caused by or exacerbated by such policy. Do not be fooled, there is little pity to be found in all this: the vigorous speeches set a fiery tone of anger, resistance and regeneration that should cause even the odd republican

---

[31] http://www.youtube.com/watch?v=b0Ti-gkJiXc.

[32] http://www.youtube.com/watch?v=YJnlPP7jm5s. and also check out Jay Smooth's "The Gay Hip-Hop Book" http://www.youtube.com/watch?v=n9HgxFuzVaQ&NR=1.

[33] http://www.youtube.com/watch?v=q6kIMiNJQRY.

[34] http://www.realcostofprisons.org/.

[35] Abderrahmane Sissako, New Yorker video, 2006, 117 min, trailer at http://www.youtube.com/watch?v=onRjl8yLsy0.

bow-tied banker on Wall Street to at least exercise the imagination in seeing numbers as real, lived consequences. Bamako is after all, a film that personalizes policy without pulling any punches."[36]

The Winter Soldiers were Vietnam veterans who testified about their experiences in that war, showing that atrocities such as My Lai were not unique. These whistle blowers were named in contrast to Thomas Paine's 1776 statement: "These are the times that try men's souls. The summer soldier and the sunshine patriot will, in this crisis, shrink from the service of his country; but he that stands it now deserves the love and thanks of man and woman." Their stories were investigated and corroborated by the media. The film *Winter Soldier*[37] consists mostly of the raw footage of this investigation, conducted by Vietnam Veterans Against the War (VVAW) in Detroit, Michigan, in the winter of 1971. The film *Winter Soldier* was shown and praised in Europe, but was largely overlooked in the USA. One of the filmmakers has written: "One common theme in what the veterans testified about, that stood out as extraordinary, is that the war in Vietnam was being waged largely against civilians."

The Iraq Veterans Against the War Winter Soldier Project is in the process of creating a documentary about hearings they conducted in March 2008 with veterans of the war on Iraq and the war on Afghanistan. Currently, it is a web series "This is Where We Take Our Stand."[38] When this group of Winter Soldiers were asked what they hope viewers of their testimony will come away with, they replied: "We hope they'll have a sense that it is everyone's responsibility to confront the wars that are being carried out in our name, no matter who is president."

*The Actor's Gang* is an educational theatrical institution, "with a mission to make theater more accessible to a broad and diverse audience" with a goal of inspiring their viewers "to feel, think and above all, question."[39] Their "'Dead Man Walking' Play Project" "engages students in theology, philosophy and law classes that address the moral issues and complexities of the death penalty in an open forum centered around the performance of a play." They work with schools in Los Angeles and around the United States and also provide in-prison theatrical training to inmates "fostering nonviolent expression." Artistic Director Tim Robbins discusses their recent production of Father Daniel Berrigan's *The Trial of the Catonsville Nine*, one of the historic anti-Vietnam War protests by Catholic peace activists, on the news show "Democracy Now!"[40]

---

[36]http://artthreat.net/2007/04/bamako-film-puts-the-world-bank-on-trial-and-wins/.

[37]http://video.google.com/videoplay?docid=3846752822614629443#.

[38]http://thisiswherewetakeourstand.com/?p=22.

[39]http://www.theactorsgang.com/.

[40]http://www.democracynow.org/2009/8/27/actor_director_tim_robbins_takes_up.

## *Visual and Conceptual Texts (Conceptual Art)*

Adrian Piper, who holds a doctoral degree in philosophy from Harvard University, has created many political conceptual art projects.[41] A number of her earlier art interventions resemble what happened with The Yes Men—she was trying to shock people into a reflection on their racism, and instead, people either agreed with the racist sentiments she presented or were silent. Instead of provoking rational thought and counterreaction, her 1980 installation, *Four Intruders Plus Alarm Systems*, "featuring photos of black men accompanied by recordings of voices engaged in rambling, anti-black monologues," provoked several viewers to thank her for "expressing their views so eloquently" (Shatz, 1998, p. 41). Piper, a Black American with light skin who could "pass" for white, has experienced the way white people talk when they think they are only among other whites. In 1986, after someone had made a racist remark at such gatherings, she passed out a business-size card:

> Dear Friend,
>
> I am black.
>
> I am sure you did not realize this when you made/laughed at/agreed with that racist remark. In the past, I have attempted to alert white people to my racial identity in advance. Unfortunately, this invariably causes them to react to me as pushy, manipulative, or socially inappropriate. Therefore, my policy is to assume that white people do not make these remarks, even when they believe there are no black people present, and to distribute this card when they do.
>
> I regret any discomfort my presence is causing you, just as I am sure you regret the discomfort your racism is causing me.
>
> Sincerely yours,
> Adrian Margaret Smith Piper

John Sims describes his work as interdisciplinary conceptual art "interested in the intersecting worlds of mathematics, art and political activism."[42] The political work he does jams the culture of racism. For example, one of the works in his *Recoloration Proclamation Project* is a Confederate flag, recolored in African colors of black, red, and green. Because the work is so controversial, it has had an impact on more than the people who see it in art galleries. In 2004, he planned an outdoor installation for the lawn of Gettysburg College in Pennsylvania, "The Proper Way to Hang a Confederate Flag." The Sons of the Confederate Veterans and the Ku Klux Klan were successful in pressuring the college to reduce the scale of the exhibit and present it indoors. So, Sims boycotted his own opening, having a film crew tape it for use in the film he is making as part of this project. Three years later, the Brogan

---

[41] http://www.adrianpiper.com/.

[42] http://www.johnsimsprojects.com/.

Museum of Art and Science in Tallahassee, Florida, did not succumb to similar pressures and included the Confederate flag, hung from a 13-ft gallows as Sims orig- inally intended. In this exhibit, AfroProvocations, the museum also included Sims' 2007 "Official Ballot for the Afro Confederate Flag," which "depicts six versions of the Confederate flag on what resembles the Florida presidential election ballot of 2000. Instead of the traditional Confederate battle flag, though, the flags depicted are black, green and red" (Sexton, 2007). Ironically, the museum is across the street from the state Capitol building that, until 2001, flew a Confederate flag. To conclude his multiyear *Recoloration Proclamation* project, Sims has issued a "Call to Artists, Poets, and Community Organizers" "to help in a multi-state burial of the flag."

Courtesy: John Sims

Wafaa Bilal[43] is an Iraqi American artist and professor of photography and imaging at the New York University who grew up in Iraq under Saddam Hussein, spending time in refugee camps in Kuwait and Saudi Arabia. Two years after his brother was killed by an unmanned aircraft at a US checkpoint in Iraq in 2005, Bilal, who had been allowed to enter the USA as a refugee, was watching the news and saw a report on a woman whose job it was to remotely control and detonate bombs in Iraq from a console in Colorado. Realizing that it could have been this woman, or someone very similar to her, who pressed the button that killed his brother, he created an interactive art installation to force viewers to confront what it is like to live in the midst of war. Bilal lived in a small room in an art gallery in Chicago for

---

[43]http://www.wafaabilal.com/ and also see *Democracy Now!* March 9, 2010 for an interview with Bilal http://www.democracynow.org/2010/3/9/105_000_tattoos_iraqi_artist_wafaa.

a month. In person and virtual visitors could shoot at him with a remote-controlled paintball gun. Over 60,000 paintballs from 138 countries were shot at him. While still in Iraq, he began to realize "that art is more of an encounter than a technique of skill, and that the piece of artwork itself can only be completed by the involvement of the audience."[44]

## *Sound Texts (Music)*

Ayman Meghames, a Palestinian literature major and organizer of a recent talent competition for Palestinian rappers, feels that "making music is a form of resistance to war and occupation, and also a tool to communicate the reality of life in Palestine. 'Most of our lyrics are about the occupation... Lately we've also started singing about the conflict between Hamas and Fatah. Any problem, it needs to be written about." Rapper Chuck D, from the group Public Enemy, once called rap music the CNN for Black America. For Ayman and his friends, music is their weapon to break media silence. "Most of the world believes we are the terrorists... And the media is closed to us, so we get our message out through Hip-Hop."[45]

Palestinian hip-hop and rap is also the subject of the documentary film, *Slingshot Hip Hop*, that interweaves stories about particular rappers, both those living inside Israel and in the Occupied Territories, with reporting about the occupation, from the perspective of the Palestinians.[46] For a perspective on the film from a woman studying to be a rabbi, who spent the 2008 summer in Jerusalem, see the Velveteen Rabbi blog,[47] which also contains a number of videos of Palestinian and Israeli rappers, and various links with more information. She writes about how the film insists "on the part of the rappers and also their parents (who seem bemused by their kids' strange styles of dress and modes of singing, but also seem on the whole very proud) that violence is not the answer: speech is the answer. The artists go into Palestinian youth centers, where they're largely idolized, and preach the gospel of using your voice instead of stones."

Serj Tankian was born in Beirut, Lebanon, in 1967 to Armenian parents. The family emigrated to Los Angeles in 1975. He graduated from California State University as a Marketing and Business major and was running his own accounting software, when, in 1995, he cofounded the rock band *System of a Down* with three Armenian American friends. This is a multiplatinum, Grammy-award winning rock band "with a conscience, a message, and a desire to constantly evolve."[48] The film

---

[44]Pascarella (2008), pp. 40–42.

[45]Flaherty (2009).

[46]There are a number of different trailers on YouTube: http://www.youtube.com/watch?v=1rdS8zNp3ow&feature=related.

[47]http://velveteenrabbi.blogs.com/blog/2009/05/slingshot-hiphop.html. (May 2009).

[48]http://www.systemofadown.com/main.html.

*Screamers*[49] documents "the band's efforts to persuade both the British and U.S. governments to recognize the Armenian genocide. *Screamers* also traces the history of modern-day genocide—and genocide denial—from the first occurrence in the twentieth century in Turkey, to today in Darfur. Commentary and interviews with Pulitzer prize-winning author Samantha Power (*A Problem from Hell: America and the Age of Genocide*), survivors from Turkey, Rwanda and Darfur, FBI whistle-blowers, and the recently assassinated Hrant Dink, who was murdered in Turkey after appearing in this film, shed light on why genocides repeat." The website also contains information about activism to stop genocide and materials for educators.

# Conclusion

## *Making Connections and Maintaining Hope*

> Do not pray for an easy life; pray to be a strong person.
>
> – Prayer from India

At one point in *The Yes Men Fix the World*, Mike says: "We'd done all we could to show people how it sucked if we let greed run the world; instead of freaking out they just take our business cards." We won't be able to find the time and the emotional and intellectual energy to act if we think we will just be adding to Mike and Andy's collection of business cards.

To me personally, two things stand out as very hopeful from The Yes Men's movies: because those in fairly powerful positions go along with the horrors without thinking very deeply about the issues (they seem to be just looking for opportunities to hand out their business cards), there is hope that a real education could change their ideas and actions, and, even now, not everyone goes along, particularly when someone else (in this case, The Yes Men) offers an alternative idea. In their first film, *The Yes Men*, they disbanded the World Trade Organization so that the WTO could rethink its policies which had brought so much misery to so many people in the world, and many in the audience said they thought it was a bold, good idea. In *The Yes Men Fix the World*, the contractors in New Orleans applaud the "hoax" government reopening/not-tearing-down of public housing. And many people were happy at the "dream" news reported in the fake *New York Times* that The Yes Men created and distributed with headlines such as "Iraq War Ends," "Court Indicts Bush on High Treason Charge," and "Nationalized Oil to Fund Climate Change Efforts."[50]

The hope is that when we see that the irrationality and silences of those in power can be manipulated by The Yes Men's interventions, we can become more

---

[49]http://www.screamersmovie.com/. Carla Garapedian, Armenian Recordings/Columbia Music Video, 2007, 95 min.

[50]http://theyesmen.org/hijinks/newyorktimes.

confident to be more active participants in decision-making in our democracy. We can realize that we are not "stupid," and begin to think about the connections between knowledge and power and how we might use our knowledge to become more powerful, to intervene in influencing and creating public policies that can fix some part of the world.

The hope is that when we understand that not everyone goes along, when we study some of the many ways people have and are continuing to resist the exploitative actions of those in power, we can realize that our efforts to resist injustice and create more justice in the world matter.

Howard Zinn (2004) cites specific examples of how history has many surprises, some of them victories for justice, so "it's clear that the struggle for justice should never be abandoned because of the apparent overwhelming power of those who have the guns and the money and who seem invincible in their determination to hold on to it. That apparent power has, again and again, proved vulnerable to human qualities less measurable than bombs and dollars: moral fervor, determination, unity, organization, sacrifice, wit, ingenuity, courage, patience—whether by blacks in Alabama and South Africa, peasants in El Salvador, Nicaragua and Vietnam, or workers and intellectuals in Poland, Hungary and the Soviet Union … The future is an infinite succession of presents, and to live now as we think human beings should live, in defiance of all that is bad around us, is itself a marvelous victory."

In the tradition of all progressive cultural activists, Gandhi described the process of social change as: "First they ignore you. Then they laugh at you. Next they fight you. Then you win."[51]

# References

Dery, M. (1993). Culture jamming: Hacking, slashing and sniping in the empire of signs. *Open Magazine Pamphlet Series*. http://www.markdery.com/archives/books/culture_jamming/#000005%23more.

Flaherty, J. (2009). Resistance in Gaza: Young Palestinians find their voice through hip-hop. *Left Turn: Notes from the Global Intifada*, June 10. http://electronicintifada.net/content/young-palestinians-gaza-find-their-voice-through-hip-hop/8286

Fox Piven, F. (2006). *Challenging authority: How ordinary people change America*. Lanham, MD: Rowman & Littlefield.

Frankenstein, M. (1983). Critical Mathematics Education: An Application of Paulo Freire's Epistemology. *Journal of Education*, 165(4), 315–339, reprinted recently in the *Philosophy of Mathematics Education Journal* (Number 25, October 2010, online at http://people.exeter.ac.uk/PErnest/pome25/)

Frankenstein, M. (in press). Which measures count in the public interest? In L. J. Jacobsen, J. Mistele, & B. Sriraman (Eds.), *Mathematics teacher education in the public interest*. Charlotte, NC: Information Age.

Goodman, A., & Goodman, D. (2008). *Standing up to the madness: Ordinary heroes in extraordinary times*. New York: Hyperion.

---

[51] Attributed to Gandhi; found in Goodman and Goodman (2008).

Meyer, R. (1995). This is to enrage you: Gran Fury and the graphics of AIDS activism. In N. Felshin (Ed.), *But is it art? The spirit of art and activism* (pp. 51–83). Seattle, WA: Bay Press.

Pascarella, M. (2008). Out of your comfort zone: Meet Iraqi American artist Wafaa Bilal. *The Progressive*, October, pp. 40–42.

Schivone, G. M. (2009). A joyful insurgency: Resistance education and the celebration of dissent. *Z Magazine*, July/August, pp. 53–55.

Sexton, C. J. (2007). Southern group protests a depiction of the Confederate flag. *The New York Times*, March 17. (http://www.nytimes.com/2007/03/17/us/17confederate.html?_r=1& oref=slogin&ref=us&p.)

Shatz, A. (1998). Black like me. *Lingua Franca, 8*(8), November, 39–54.

Woodside, S. (2001). *Every joke is a tiny revolution: Culture jamming and the role of humour.* Masters thesis, University of Amsterdam, Media Studies, December. (sven.woodside@student,uva.nl)

Zinn, H. (2004). The optimism of uncertainty. *The Nation*, September 4, http://www.thenation.com/doc/20040920/zinn.

# Part III
# Contesting the Curriculum

# Chapter 12
# Big Expectations for Little Kids: The Crisis in Early Childhood Education

Libby Lee-Hammond

## Introduction

Last week, my son brought his homework to the kitchen whilst I was preparing dinner. It was a worksheet requiring him to classify nouns and verbs. Whilst completing this task with some help from across the room from me, he surreptitiously wrote in perfectly executed cursive writing '*this sucks*' on his homework and photographed it on my iPhone™; he quickly erased his comment before I could see it and left his sophisticated evaluation of his homework on my smartphone. What a telling sign of the times when homework has so many possibilities to be engaging and even enjoyable, yet kids continue to be assigned tasks that they quite openly tell us really do 'suck'. My son's facility with technologies has no place in the homework regime. And why is the dry and decontextualised learning of nouns and verbs a priority in schools? Because children sit tests that rate them against all the other children their age in our entire nation. This in turn places their teachers under the microscope, the results of the school are published on a government hosted publicly accessible website entitled My School (ACARA, 2011), and parents, as consumers of education, can and do. look up the site to make comparisons between schools in their area when deciding where to send their children to be educated. Under the guise of school improvement, the site offers parents and communities detailed information of all the schools finances and testing results, and Barry McGaw, as Chair of the Australian Curriculum, Assessment and Reporting Authority (ACARA), in his welcome letter to the site, boldly declares that the site enables higher-achieving schools the opportunity to act as a valuable resource for lower-achieving schools by creating opportunities for them to share their successful policies and practices (McGaw in ACARA). In this chapter, I will

L. Lee-Hammond (✉)
School of Education, Murdoch University, Perth, Australia
e-mail: L.Lee@murdoch.edu.au

B. Down and J. Smyth (eds.), *Critical Voices in Teacher Education*, Explorations
of Educational Purpose 22, DOI 10.1007/978-94-007-3974-1_12,
© Springer Science+Business Media Dordrecht 2012

critique the view that national testing and the publication of results is a step towards educational improvement. Indeed, I will argue that the very foundations of education are undermined by such practices and that the deprofessionalisation of teachers, the demise of childhood and the absence of meaningful learning are the outcomes of such practices (Alquist, Gorski, & Montaro, 2011; Noddings, 2005; Stobart, 2008).

As an early childhood teacher educator, I despair at the impact of national testing and programmes delivered under the guise of 'early intervention' on the ever-shortening childhoods of Australian children. Even more, I despair that the really engaging and worthwhile teaching and learning that I prepare my students to undertake is quickly forgotten in the 'reality' of what is required of them in schools. One dilemma I face is how best to prepare students to utilise play-based pedagogies in a testing and standards-oriented school system. Despite play-based pedagogies being enshrined in the national framework for early years learning (Commonwealth of Australia, 2010), it is proving extremely difficult for graduate teachers to make a case for play when there are tests to prepare for and pressure from the parents and the principal to prepare children for formal learning and the national tests. Why is play vanishing in the institution of schooling? Why after 11 years of teaching in university and graduating thousands of students are they not able to legitimately utilise play as a medium for learning? Why is Australia taking the same disastrous path as the UK and the USA when there are rich early childhood education models available to us in various European countries that offer children a chance to experience freedom and creativity in childhood *and* an excellent formal education?

I encourage my students to think critically and to take risks and, in turn, be in a position to enable children to take risks and think critically (Thomas & Kincheloe, 2006). I encourage my students to be prepared to be spontaneous, to follow children's lead and to create learning environments where higher-order thinking skills (Bloom, 1956) and pedagogies for multiliteracies (Yelland, Lee, O'Rourke, & Harrison, 2008) are valued, encouraged and indeed part of the everyday activities in the learning environment. Instead, what students repeatedly report back to me after their practical experience in schools is that preparation for testing, formal learning and the dominance of paper- and pencil-based literacy and numeracy activities dominate the school day. I advocate for transformative teacher education that 'requires more than simply being programmed to teach particular things in particular ways; there must be a sense of openness . . . not predetermined by a tertiary institution, or government, and that the purpose of education is necessarily one of forming an identity' (Gibbons, 2011). What identities can I assist undergraduate early childhood teachers to form in a tightly controlled regime where they are not free to create curriculum that is responsive to children's socio-cultural contexts, interests and identities?

In this chapter, I want to explore the broader dilemmas of preparing student teachers to enact internationally recognised pedagogical approaches in early childhood education in an environment where the economy drives our education and social policies, national testing looms large and children, teachers, principals and parents are under scrutiny. This scrutiny is based on what Thompson describes as a 'mechanism of control' (2007, p. 10) exercised over schools and teachers and based on the performance of children in a single national test. The National Assessment Program Literacy and Numeracy (NAPLAN) is undertaken at intervals in year 3, 5, 7 and 9. More recently, another on-entry test is used to measure children's literacy and numeracy performance in the first year of school. Thompson (2007) notes that not only is testing in this manner problematic from the point of view of being fair and accurate but also detrimental to students and educators. He (2007) explains that 'there is increasing anecdotal evidence that despite the "common sense" explanation of NAPLAN as a fair and accurate measure of student abilities, it seems to be deployed and experienced more as a mechanism of control than an innovative revolutionary initiative. It is a modulatory machine that produces fearful staff and student dispositions' (p. 10). And fearful they are, the same child mentioned above who told me his homework sucks, at the tender age of 8, was in tears the night before his year 3 NAPLAN test, telling me he was worried that everyone would 'find out I'm dumb'. We have a crisis in Australian education.

## Reforms in Early Childhood Education and Care in Australia

Two major reforms in early childhood education have taken place in recent years. The first is the introduction of a national framework for early years learning and the second is the introduction of a national curriculum. In this section, I will examine each of these documents and explain how, despite their purported intentions, they each undermine the stated goal of our political leaders to promote excellence in Australian schooling (Ministerial Council on Education, Employment, Training and Youth Affairs [MCEETYA], 2008, hereafter referred to as MCEETYA, 2008).

### *The Early Years Learning Framework for Australia*

The Australian Early Years Learning Framework, known as the EYLF (Department of Education, Employment and Workplace Relations [DEEWR], 2009), acknowledges the significance of early childhood education in shaping children's identities and understandings of their world, creating opportunities for them as individuals to realise their potential. The EYLF is framed around three noble motifs:

- *Belonging*: emphasising first a child's identity as a member of a family, a cultural group and a community
- *Being*: 'the significance of the here and now ... engaging in life's joys and complexities' (DEEWR, p. 7)
- *Becoming*: the process of change that occurs as children learn and grow

The EYLF states that 'the early childhood years are not solely about preparation for the future but also about the present' (ibid, p. 7). The notion of being 'in the moment' in childhood is a refreshing one and one that values childhood as a time to explore and engage with the world.

Five learning outcomes are identified in the EYLF for children participating in early years learning programmes from birth to 5 years; these outcomes are intended to reflect the Melbourne Declaration on Education Goals for Young Australians (MCEETYA, 2008) that 'all young Australians become successful learners, confident and creative individuals and active and informed citizens' (Commonwealth of Australia, 2009, p. 5; MCEETYA, 2008, p. 8). Drawing on examples from current policy and practice in early childhood education in Australia, I want to argue that the emphasis on testing and accountability is counterproductive to advancing the stated goals of official policy pronouncement. Hursh (2008) explains 'preparing students to pass the tests, rather than to obtain a complex and sophisticated understanding of the world' (p. 3) leads to a diminished view of young children's education.

The Early Years Learning Framework emphasises that early childhood education is ultimately an investment in human capital formation. An argument repeated in many forums is that for every dollar spent in early childhood, society saves up to 16 dollars in later life (Calman & Whelan, 2005; Fitzgerald, 2010). I find this formula particularly distasteful as it unashamedly takes a position that the economy is the main beneficiary of quality early childhood education. Calman and Whelan (2005) note in their report titled *The Economic Impacts of Childcare and Early Education: Financing Solutions for the Future* that 'investments in quality child care and early childhood education do more than pay significant returns to children—our future citizens. They also benefit taxpayers and enhance economic vitality' (p. 1).

More recently, Fitzgerald (2010) writes of the social and economic benefits of early childhood education:

> Children provided early childhood education are more likely to proceed through school at grade level, have skilled jobs, attend college and earn more money. These children are less likely to spend time on welfare and in the legal system, use marijuana, and be regular smokers. Early childhood education is a financial boon for the entire state (Minnesota). It can realize a return on investment of as much as $16 for every dollar spent. Annual benefits of universal early childhood education would pay for themselves within 17 years. (p. 3)

Economic arguments for early childhood education, such as the two examples above, are at the heart of my dilemma as an early childhood teacher educator. My passionate belief is that if we continue to measure, standardise and shift control of our pedagogical work away from students, families and teachers to legislators, we risk sacrificing the complexity, breadth and intellectual rigour of teaching and learning. Testing requirements undermine student academic success, and more particularly, that despite the rhetoric, they only contribute to a widening gap between middle-class students and those from racial and ethnic minorities and students living in poverty (Hursh, 2008; Lareau, 2000; Stobart, 2008).

## *A National Curriculum*

The Australian Curriculum is the first national document to set out detailed content descriptions for use in schools from preschool (foundation) to year 12. In line with my earlier discussion regarding the neoliberal construction of early childhood education as an economic exercise, Ditchburn (2011) recognises 'the introduction of an Australian curriculum is intentionally positioned and designed from the "top down" to meet the needs of global markets and the economy, rather than necessarily the needs of students or teachers' (p. 2). Because this chapter focuses on early childhood education, and for the sake of discussion, I use elements of the English curriculum to demonstrate the absurdity of prescribed curriculum for preschool children. I also argue, along with other scholars (Reid, 2009), that the stated goals of the curriculum are actually undermined by the curriculum itself.

A major criticism of the National Curriculum is that it is heavily prescribed and does not afford educators an opportunity to respond to students in a range of socio-economic contexts. Ditchburn (2011) further notes that the curriculum is 'disconnected from local realities ... and adopted a one-size-fits-all approach' (p. 3). My own research (Lee, 2006) with early childhood programmes in remote Australian Aboriginal communities provides one such context as an example of how the current reforms further marginalise an already marginalised group, a discussion I will elaborate upon later in this chapter.

The rhetoric of ACARA (2011) is that 'it is intended that jurisdictions, systems and schools will be able to implement the Australian Curriculum in ways that value teachers' professional knowledge, reflect the local contexts and take into account the individual's family, culture and community background' (p. 1). Such a notion is laudable and would provide student teachers with ample opportunity to create curriculum that is innovative, contextually relevant and tailored to the competencies of particular cohorts of children. However, the following statement of content provides a clear indication of the level of prescription regarding content and a view of literacy that is particularly narrow:

> Students <u>write</u> one or more simple <u>sentences</u> to retell events and experiences for a known <u>audience</u>. Their writing is connected appropriately to illustrations and images produced as part of the <u>text</u>. They link two or more ideas or events in written and spoken <u>texts</u>. They use and understand familiar vocabulary, <u>predictable text</u> structures and common visual patterns. The short <u>texts</u> they produce show <u>understanding</u> of <u>concepts about print</u> including letters, words and <u>sentences</u>. They use left to right <u>directionality</u>, <u>return sweep</u> and spaces between words. (ACARA, 2011, original emphasis)

The level of linguistic sophistication required of children in the foundation year is quite extraordinary compared to curriculum offered to children in this age group a decade ago and is the topic of much discussion among early childhood professionals. For example, I subscribe to an online discussion forum for Australian early childhood educators (P-3 discussion) who are frequently debating the issues around the requirement for preschool children to construct a sentence in writing, a requirement that was previously reserved for the more formal learning that takes place in year 1. The concern, which I share, expressed by numerous teachers in this forum is about prematurely introducing written sentence structure to children who may not have had adequate exposure to pre-literacy experiences. Such an approach may well have long-term detrimental consequences for a child who is continually required to produce evidence of literacy skills that they are simply not ready to achieve. Children who have had insufficient opportunity to develop pre-literacy skills in oral language are at particular risk (Roskos, Tabors, & Lenhart, 2009).

## Social Pedagogical Approaches

There are numerous examples from Germany, Finland, Norway and Hungary to attest that there is no long-term benefit to starting formal reading and writing earlier. Children in Scandinavian countries routinely commence school at least 2 years later than Australian children, yet their performance on international tests in secondary school show they are among the most literate populations in the world (OECD, 2011). The pedagogical approach generally adopted in Scandinavian and some European countries may be described as a social pedagogy tradition whereas Australia, the UK and the USA have taken a teacher-directed, sequential approach. A major point of divergence exists in approaches to curriculum and the view of the child as a protagonist in their learning (Malaguzzi, 1993) and is explained by the OECD thus: 'In curricular design terms, the difference in approach may be characterised as the adoption of a sequential learning approach in pre-primary classes, while the social pedagogy tradition favours more holistic learning' (OECD, 2006, p. 137).

Van Kuyk (cited in OECD, 2006), writing about the holistic approach offered in the Netherlands, critiques the sequential approach:

> The sequential approach is primarily teacher directed and offers limited opportunities for children to develop self-regulation. Activities often fail to tap into children's intrinsic motivation, because they do not authentically meet the needs and interests of children. When this intrinsic motivation is missing, the teacher will have to work harder to engage the children in learning ... learning becomes artificial and uninteresting. In the holistic approach, all developmental areas are addressed through play and broad project work that encourage active learning and multiple experiences in the major developmental domains. With the help of experienced teachers (and parents and older children), young children can choose their activities and organise the projects, an excellent experience in self-regulation and agency, and one that is highly motivating. (p. 137)

European nations adopting social pedagogy have amply demonstrated the effectiveness of this approach in terms of long-term student outcomes. Unfortunately, this model seems to have been overlooked by our Australian policymakers, thus making the work of preparing students to teach in the current context in Australian schools frustrating to say the least. The influence of politicians of various persuasions on the development of education policy has clearly had a detrimental impact. A recent example of this occurred when I was asked to give evidence at a parliamentary inquiry into literacy and numeracy education in Western Australia. A state government minister, who was chairing the inquiry, reported by way of analogy to 'fixing' literacy problems that when she takes her Audi motor vehicle to the mechanic for a service, the technician refers to a manual to fix the problem. She asked me in all sincerity why teachers cannot do that for children and why I was not preparing them better to be able to do that. I replied that children are not cars and teachers are not technicians. Her perspective on the issue of what constitutes learning and teaching was made more alarming because of her power to influence and shape legislation, policy and provision of Australian education.

## Multiliteracies

As discussed above, the Australian National Curriculum, in my view, offers a narrow interpretation of what it means to be literate, since for over a decade, leading researchers in literacy education have been investigating a broader focus of literacy in schools to reflect the multimodal and digital texts so integral to life in the twenty-first century. The literacies required in the digital age have been described in the literature as multiliteracies (Cope & Kalantzis, 2000; Yelland et al., 2008). The multiliteracies framework (New London Group 1996) defines print literacy and a variety of multimodal communication as different kinds of literacies. Multiliteracies is a term used to encompass interrelations between linguistically and culturally diverse print, visual and audio texts, and the term includes the communicative skills of speaking, writing and reading. However, it appears that the new curriculum ignores the multiple modalities afforded to children in the twenty-first century (Harrison, Lee, O'Rourke, & Yelland, 2009; Yelland et al., 2008).

So what does a critically reflective teacher do? Early childhood teacher educators spend a significant amount of time exploring with students the ways that they can come to know the children they teach in terms of their competencies and strengths. Through play-based pedagogies, they are able to enrich and extend children's learning in complex and engaging ways. Students explore a range of devices for observing and documenting children's learning in inclusive, relationship-based environments and play contexts. This deep knowledge of children's ways of knowing seems to be irrelevant in the current climate of performance-based education. How then do I prepare my students to function in a professional environment that requires them to ignore their own professional judgements about children's 'readiness' and the international evidence of the benefits of learning through play, to simply teach the curriculum as prescribed by legislators? I cannot and I will not, and that is what concerns me. For me, it is an ethical issue and a dilemma. I am simply not prepared to teach students in this way, but then again, if I do not, they will drown in the system. So my best hope in this crisis in education is to assist students to think critically, to be political and to advocate for authentic learning and teaching. The best tool I can give them is to help them cultivate an identity as a critical professional educator rather than a deskilled worker who delivers programmes and performance outcomes for a government wedded to neoliberal policies.

## On-Entry Testing in Australian Schools

In 2006, the Council of Australian Governments (COAG) agreed that an 'on-entry' assessment programme be introduced across all states and territories. In Western Australia, children entering pre-primary (the first full-time year of school) will undertake an 'online interview' between weeks 4 and 8 of the first term of school. According to the Department of Education WA, 'The main objective of the program in Western Australia is to provide information to assist teachers in developing informed and intentional teaching for PLAY BASED [sic] programs, reflective of each child's needs – those that may require or benefit from early intervention, consolidation or extension' (DOE, 2011). The capitalisation of the words PLAY BASED on the Department website suggests that there are individuals within the bureaucracy who see great potential for the online interview to lead to a formal academic programme that jeopardises play-based learning, and although bureaucrats are obliged to enforce the will of the government of the day, they have some influence on how information is provided to the public and can and do make clear their concerns.

It is the content of the online interview that is most concerning, since it organises and compartmentalises learning into subject areas at the earliest point in children's schooling. On entry to school, children are asked to respond to a series of questions and tasks to measure their knowledge and skills. In the literacy interview, they are asked to respond to tasks in speaking, rhyming words, concepts of print, words, sounds and letters, listening and recalling and 'having a go' at writing. Whilst the numeracy interview focuses on the number sequence, counting, partitioning (seeing numbers in parts), comparing and ordering length and shapes and positional language (DETWA, 2011).

Traditionally, early childhood education has been viewed as emphasising a process orientation over finished products and providing correct answers to closed tasks and questions (Krieg, 2011); however, in the neoliberal era, a shift has taken place to measure children's content knowledge in literacy and numeracy in order to provide intervention for those who do not reach certain standards on entry to school. Krieg problematises the place of the newly emerging emphasis on subject knowledge in early childhood education and rightly notes that content knowledge is contestable and unfinished and that the EYLF foregrounds particular subject areas such as mathematics and maintains the 'privileged position of some ideas over others' (2011, p. 50).

Earlier work by Moll, Amanti, Neff, and Gonzalez (2005) poses a very different model to the commencement of schooling whereby teachers are encouraged to familiarise themselves not with content knowledge but with children's 'funds of knowledge'. This refers 'to the historically accumulated and culturally developed bodies of knowledge and skills essential for household or individual functioning and well-being' (p. 133). The funds of knowledge approach affords teachers an opportunity to become teacher researchers and to tap into the rich resources that children bring from their home and community. These resources can be utilised by teachers to provide a curriculum that is responsive and relevant to students. Such an approach has great merit in developing relationships with children in which they feel valued as contributors to the classroom endeavour (Bingham & Sidorkin, 2004). The commitment to children's funds of knowledge and the relationship of children's learning to their family, home and community are now famously demonstrated by the educational project in the Reggio Emilia schools in Italy. Relationship-based pedagogy and the notion of education as a continuing research process are the hallmarks of the Reggio Emilia schools (Gandini, 1993; Malaguzzi, 1993), and they provide a refreshing contrast to what I see as the demise of authentic early childhood education in Australia.

## Voices from the Field

So what do practitioners make of this shift? To encourage exchange of professional dialogue among students and the profession, I recently set up a Facebook® Community Page titled Early Years Learning (Lee-Hammond, 2011). I posted a link to a story about an American mother suing a preschool for putting her child's Ivy League chances at risk by not teaching sufficient formal academic skills (Martinez, 2011). Following this post, a discussion took place between practising teachers and some of my students who voluntarily subscribe to the page. The discussion between them highlights the very things I discuss in this chapter, the dilemmas that practising teachers face in a changing educational landscape and the frustration of students who know there is a different and preferable approach but have few opportunities to see or implement in practice. Some excerpts from that conversation reinforce the arguments advanced in this chapter:

> Teacher 1: In my district there is very little play in Prep, there is mostly skill-based rotations. After studying my Masters, I find it very disappointing to see early years education going down a road of mostly behaviourist approaches to meet District expectations. I believe we are headed in this direction for a number of reasons including NAPLAN focus and comparison of States and schools and pushes from people above who do not necessarily have an understanding of current research in early years education. Another concern for me is that because there are benchmarks being introduced (such as how many sight words need to be recognised, reading levels etc), many pre-literacy experiences are not being offered to children (e.g. simply singing nursery rhymes to develop an understanding of rhythm and rhyme) due to pressure. Many children in my District do not have access to these early experiences prior to school and do not have the phonological skills that can be helpful in literacy learning later. Overcrowded curriculum, huge expectations and a move toward results rather than learning to love learning are many contributing factors in my opinion.

> Teacher 2: I agree, I am in the Kimberley and have seen this push on Indigenous kids, who are ESL/D learners.

> Student: My concern was exactly what you have been discussing here ... that the push to improve literacy and numeracy outcomes has resulted in a declining incidence of play-based opportunities for learning. Surely it is possible to address these outcomes within a play-based curriculum????

> Teacher 3: I'm a year 1 teacher who is back part time after having children. I am finding the formal instruction in early years alarming!!!

> Teacher 4: Me too I feel stressed and I know the kids are too!

This conversation is happening in classrooms and schools around the nation, and the accountability machine is sucking the life out of our best and brightest teachers. I recently visited a school where I had worked on an action learning project with a group of early childhood teachers a couple of years ago. When I inquired about a particular teacher who was one of the most outstanding early childhood educators I have ever encountered, her dismayed colleagues informed me that she had suffered a breakdown. Her colleagues believed this was a direct result of the strain of working in a system that did not allow her to teach in the ways she knew were the most successful, rich and meaningful for young children. She has since left the profession.

Another teacher working in the pre-primary at the same school confided that she was having fortnightly 'accountability' meetings with her principal to present her programme in order to demonstrate that what she was doing was going to improve the summative test scores of her class of 5-year-olds.

This teacher openly discussed her programme with me explaining that teaching to the test is the only way that she can guarantee the level of improvement in test scores required by her principal. She expressed concern at having to introduce number sentences in addition (i.e. $4 + 2 =$) to children who were not ready. She believed they should be experiencing a range of rich numeracy tasks in concrete addition situations before the addition symbol was introduced (most commonly, this is not introduced until year 1). However, despite her training and knowledge of appropriate practice in early numeracy, she is under fortnightly pressure from her principal to teach this particular equation in order to improve class and school performance.

Like other Catholic schools, this school is required by the Catholic Education Office to adopt the PIPS (Performance Indicators for Primary Schools) test as an on-entry test for children entering pre-primary (typically 5-year-olds), and the teachers are expected to demonstrate an improvement in student learning via a 'post test' at the end of the year. The data is centrally recorded, and principals have their own performance indicators directly aligned with student performance on these tests. The name of the test itself is terminology more usually found in the business world where performance indicators are routinely used to measure productivity, these are not usually terms associated with young children's learning in early education. Performance indicators that predict student trajectories contradict the vast literature spanning many decades in psychology and education research regarding the impact of teacher expectations on self-fulfilling prophecies and student performance (Jussim & Eccles, 1992; Rist, 2009).

## Student Feedback

Like most academic staff in a university, I routinely undertake student evaluations of my teaching and have done so for over 12 years. This year, for the first time I received a comment from an undergraduate early childhood teacher that stated 'while I agree with the play based and children's interest approach, I'm worried it won't meet government demands', and this is further evidence that decades of research in early childhood education are under serious threat due to the global impact of neoliberalism as it penetrates the Australian education system in the wake of the No Child Left Behind Act (Carr & Porfilio, 2011; United States Government, 2001). As Hursh (2008) notes, the reforms in school curriculum and pedagogy are now firmly focussed on teaching students skills and knowledge for a productive workforce and a globally competitive economy. According to Hursh, this is the most blatant attempt in history to support and 'visibly promote neoliberal theories and policies, which promote economic profit and growth over all other social goals' (p. 4).

## Equity for Australian Aboriginal Learners in Early Childhood

In the above extract from the Facebook page, one teacher introduces a dimension to this debate that I wish to explore briefly. Equity and disadvantage are not only perpetuated but reinforced in the neoliberal regime where test scores count and 'funds of knowledge' (Moll, Amanti, Neff, and Gonzalez 2005) are irrelevant (Au, 2008; Hursh, 2008). An example from my research in Aboriginal early childhood education (Lee-Hammond, 2010) highlights how in everyday practices teachers in the early years, under pressure to teach formal literacy and numeracy skills, are missing the mark with students and perpetuating the 'gap' in educational outcomes between Aboriginal and non-Aboriginal children.

In 2009, I interviewed a 7-year-old Aboriginal boy who I will call Harry. He lives in a remote Western Australian Aboriginal community. I asked him to tell me what happens during a typical day at school. Whilst hearing stories about playing soccer, swinging on the monkey bars, taking the lunch orders to the canteen and being 'Star of the Day', he told me 'the teacher says "we're gonna (sic) do hard things now" and that's when she hands out all the papers'. This comment resonated with and saddened me as I had observed Harry in class and noticed his demeanour change instantly when formal paper and pencil work was brought into the programme. During my visit, he was being taught the letter 'V' in isolation. The teacher was using resources from the dominant non-Aboriginal culture including photocopied pictures of violins and violets that had little or indeed no relevance or connection to his Aboriginal culture, family and community. His very sound funds of knowledge were ignored. A teacher under pressure has little time to think of ways to enable children like Harry to access their home and community knowledge to make sense of phonology, phonics, semantic knowledge and syntax essential in the orchestration of reading and writing (Hudson, Pullen, Lane, & Torgesen, 2009).

Similarly, children from low socio-economic or disadvantaged backgrounds, refugee or migrant children with English as a second language and children with English as a second dialect are at a significant disadvantage in the testing regime. Their command of the basics is prioritised by the system at the cost of meaning, relevance and contextualisation.

The disadvantage afforded to minority children is highlighted by Hursh (2008) who notes that in the USA, some low-performing students have been encouraged to skip a day at school when the tests are being taken or to drop out, thereby serving the schools need to score well on the tests. Similar stories are reported in the Australian media at the time of our national testing each year. By pushing the neoliberal agenda and assigning economic benefit to test scores, our system is failing the very students it is designed to serve. It is a brutal system that rewards the middle class as well as children with learning difficulties and punishes those groups in our community who are disadvantaged on a whole range of measures. It is a system in which I find myself constantly in conflict as a teacher educator.

## Conclusion

As an exercise whilst writing this chapter, I located my own Kindergarten report from 1973 when I attended school in NSW. It consisted of a one-page document with hand-drawn figures of children learning to share and to take care of their belongings and doing up buttons and zips. The stated intention of this document was to introduce children to school as 'a happy learning place'. I was rated on this report as either developing at a satisfactory rate, requiring further help or performing with ease. In light of the massive changes that have occurred in early childhood education in my lifetime, I decided to contact my former school and ask for a copy of their current Kindergarten report. I was not surprised that in 2011, I was sent a seven-page document with detailed information in each of the key learning areas, and within each there were strands with detailed descriptors of achievement. Students in 2011 are rated as achieving at a standard that is Outstanding, Satisfactory or Basic. Times have certainly changed, but it is not a flash in the pan. We are in danger of losing the very essence of what it means to teach and learn because we are entrenched in a political system wedded to neoliberalism as if there is no other choice. I would like to argue there is a choice, and it involves the profession taking a unified position to boycott national testing and to lobby at the local and federal level to expose the inadequacies of a system that purports that testing and standards are the only way to improve learning. Such claims are nonsense. As Hursh argues 'we must become politically engaged in changing education policies. It is not enough to work in our own classrooms and schools; we must educate the public about the purposes of democratic schooling and the harm that the recent reforms have caused to those goals' (2008, p. 11).

I liken the situation in early childhood education in Australia to the nursery rhyme about the Incy Wincy Spider; young children in our nation strive to climb the water spout of our schools, but there is a struggle to reach the top, with formalised curriculum, standards and tests, and if children do not succeed, then the rain washes them back down. We can only hope that with resistance from critically reflective practitioners, some sunshine will come to dry up the rain.

# References

Alquist, R., Gorski, P., & Montaño, T. (2011). *Assault on kids: How hyper-accountability, corporatization, deficit ideologies, and Ruby Payne are destroying our schools.* New York: Peter Lang.

Au, W. W. (2008). *Unequal by design: High stakes testing and the standardization of inequality.* London: Taylor & Francis.

Australian Curriculum, Assessment and Reporting Authority (ACARA). (2011). *My school.* Retrieved April 26, 2011, from http://www.myschool.edu.au/

Bingham, C. W., & Sidorkin, A. M. (Eds.). (2004). *No education without relation.* New York: Peter Lang.

Bloom, B. S. (1956). *Taxonomy of educational objectives, handbook I: The cognitive domain.* New York: David McKay Co Inc.

Calman & Whelan (2005). *Early childhood education for all: a wise investment: Recommendations arising from the economic impacts of child care and early education Financing Solutions the Future Conference.* New York: Legal Momentum's Family Initiative and the MIT Workplace Center.

Carr, P. R., & Porfilio, B. (Eds.). (2011). *The phenomenon of Obama and the agenda for education: Can hope audaciously trump neoliberalism?* Charlotte, NC: Information Age Publishing.

Commonwealth of Australia. (2009). *Belonging, being and becoming: The early years learning framework for Australia.* Canberra, Australian Government Department of Education, Employment and Workplace Relations for the Council of Australian Governments.

Commonwealth of Australia. (2010). *Educators belonging, being and becoming.* Canberra, Australian Government Department of Education, Employment and Workplace Relations for the Council of Australian Governments.

Cope, B., & Kalantzis, M. (Eds.). (2000). *Multiliteracies: Literacy learning and the design of social futures.* London: Routledge.

DETWA (2011). *Educational measurement: On entry.* Retrieved November 7, 2011, from http://www.det.wa.edu.au/educationalmeasurement/detcms/portal/

Ditchburn, G. (forthcoming). Anational Australian curriculum: In whose interests? *Asia Pacific Journal of Education.*

Education Department of Western Australia. (2011). *On entry program: An overview for parents.* Retrieved April 5, 2011, from www.det.wa.edu.au/educationalmeasurement

Fitzgerald, J. (2010). *Early childhood education: Upfront investment, lifetime gain.* Minnesota. Retrieved June 6, 2011, from http://www.mn2020.org/issues-that-matter/education/early-childhood-education-upfront-investment-lifetime-gain

Gandini, L. (1993). Fundamentals of the Reggio Emilia approach to early childhood education. *Young Children, 49*(1), 4–8.

Gibbons, A. N. (2011). The incoherence of curriculum: Questions concerning early childhood teacher educators. *Australian Journal of Early Childhood, 36*(1), 9–15.

Harrison, C., Lee, L., Yelland, N., & O'Rourke, M. (2009). Maximising the moment From Preschool to School: The place of multiliteracies and ICT in the transition to school. *International Journal of Learning, 16*(11), 465–474.

Hudson, R. F., Pullen, P. C., Lane, H. B., & Torgesen, J. K. (2009). The complex nature of reading fluency: A multidimensional view. *Reading & Writing Quarterly: Overcoming Learning Difficulties, 25*(1), 4–32.

Hursh, D. (2008). *High-stakes testing and the decline of teaching and learning: The real crisis in education.* Lanham, MD: Rowman & Littlefied.

Jussim, L., & Eccles, J. S. (1992). Teacher expectations: II. Construction and reflection of student achievement. *Journal of Personality and Social Psychology, 63*(6), 947–961.

Krieg, S. (2011). The Australian early years learning framework: Learning what? *Contemporary Issues in Early Childhood, 12*(1), 46–55.

Lareau, A. (2000). *Home advantage: Social class and parental intervention in elementary education* (2nd ed.). Lanham, MD: Rowman & Littlefield.

Lee, L. (2006). Curriculum in early childhood in Australia. In R. New & M Cochran (Eds.). *Early Childhood Education* (pp. 894–897). Westport, CT: Greenwood.

Lee-Hammond, L. (Producer/Director). (2010). *Mungullah best start kids go to school* [DVD] Co-produced by Jeff Asselin and Libby Lee-Hammond for the Aboriginal Education and Training Council of Western Australia. Perth: Kulbardi Productions.

Lee-Hammond, L. (2011). *Early years learning facebook community page*. Retrieved April 26, 2011, from http://www.facebook.com/earlyyearslearning

Malaguzzi, L. (1993). For an education based on relationships. *Young Children, 49*(1), 9–12.

Martinez, J. (2011). Manhattan mom sues $19K/yr. preschool for damaging 4-year-old daughter's Ivy League chances. *NY Daily News*, March 14. Retrieved May 2, 2011, from http://articles.nydailynews.com/20110314/local/29149269_1_ivy-league-public-school-music-and-physical-education

Ministerial Council on Education, Employment, Training and Youth Affairs. (2008). *Melbourne declaration on educational goals for young Australians*. Melbourne, Australia: MCEETYA.

Moll, L., Amanti, C., Neff, D., Gonzalez, N. (2005). *Funds of knowledge for teaching: Using a qualitative approach to connect homes and classrooms*. Mahwah, New Jersey: Lawrence Erlbaum Associates, Inc.

Noddings, N. (2005). *The challenge to care in schools: An alternative approach to education*. New York: Teachers College Press.

Organisation for Economic Co-operation and Development. (2006). *Starting strong II*. Paris: OECD Publications.

Organisation for Economic Co-operation and Development. (2011). *Finland takes number one spot in OECD's latest PISA survey, advance figures show*. Retrieved June 8, 2011, from http://www.oecd.org/document/60/0,3343,en_2649_201185_39700732_1_1_1_1,00.html

Reid, A. (2009). Is this really a revolution? A critical analysis of the Rudd government's national education agenda. *Curriculum Perspectives, 9*(3), 1–13.

Rist, R. C. (2009). HER classic reprint: Student social class and teacher expectations: The self-fulfilling prophecy in ghetto education. *Harvard Educational Review, 70*(3), 257–302.

Roskos, K., Tabors, P. O., & Lenhart, L. A. (2009). *Oral language and early literacy in preschool: Talking, reading, and writing*. Newark, DE: International Reading Association.

Stobart, G. (2008). *Testing times: The uses and abuses of assessment*. London: Routledge.

Thomas, P. L., & Kincheloe, J. L. (2006). *Reading, writing, and thinking: The postformal basics*. Rotterdam, The Netherlands: Sense Publishers.

Thompson, G. (2007). *Modulating power and 'new weapons': Taking aim at the 'Education Revolution'*. Conference Presentation. Philosophy of Education Society of Australasia.

United States Government. (2001). No child left behind act of 2001. *Public Law*, 107–110, 107th Congress. Retrieved June 19, 2011, from http://www2.ed.gov/policy/elsec/leg/esea02/index.html

Yelland, N., Lee, L., O'Rourke, M., & Harrison, C. (2008). *Rethinking learning in early childhood*. London: Open University Press.

# Chapter 13
# Whispering to the Hippopotamus About the 'Literacy Boomerang': Literacy Wars and Rumours of Wars

**Cal Durrant**

According to *The Quotations Page* website, it was during the fourth century BC that the Greek dramatist Aeschylus first coined the phrase 'In war, truth is the first casualty' (2010). Given that in any conflict, at least two sides see the 'truth' from very different perspectives, this phrase is perhaps less surprising than we might think at first. Since my appointment to an academic post in the early 1980s, I am struggling to remember a time when English literacy levels were not publicly perceived to be in a state of crisis and/or under heavy media fire.

The noted English writer George Orwell's disdain for his generation's English literacy levels is strikingly stated in his *Mankind in the Making*, published by Harper Bros in 1903. While positioned in the context of what he anticipated might happen during his imagined New Republican movement, Wells suggested that 'Only a very small minority of English or American people have more than half mastered the splendid heritage of their native speech … The speech of the Colonist is even poorer than the speech of the home-staying English' (Wells, 2004, pp. 80–81). Much of the blame for this situation he placed squarely with the teaching profession (apparently not an accusation that is the exclusive domain of the contemporary expert critic): 'It (English) is atrociously taught, and taught by ignorant men. It is atrociously and meanly written' (p. 81), and 'Schoolmasters as a class know little of the language. In none of our schools, not even in the more efficient of our elementary schools, is English adequately taught' (p. 85).

As for the average person, Wells suggested that:

> In spite of the fact that they will sit with books in their hands, visibly reading, turning pages, pencilling comments, in spite of the fact that they will discuss authors and repeat criticisms, it is as hopeless to express new thoughts to them as it would be to seek for appreciation in the ear of a hippopotamus. (p. 84)

C. Durrant (✉)
Director of the ACU Literacy Research Hub, School of Education, English Literacy,
Australian Catholic University, Sydney, Australia
e-mail: Cal.Durrant@acu.edu.au

B. Down and J. Smyth (eds.), *Critical Voices in Teacher Education*, Explorations of Educational Purpose 22, DOI 10.1007/978-94-007-3974-1_13,
© Springer Science+Business Media Dordrecht 2012

Orwell's opinions might easily be transferred to some of the current critics of literacy standards in Australia or indeed most countries around the globe. Literacy crisis talk is no respecter of international borders. Readers may recall the American crisis talk in the late 1950s, particularly after the Russians launched Sputnik in 1957. Rudolph Flesch's *Why Johnny Can't Read* (1955) had ignited a new round of educational concern in the United States and the falling behind in the space race fitted very neatly into a Cold War crisis view about abandoned or failed pedagogies and inefficient school systems. The *Newsweek* article 'Why Johnny Can't Write' had a similar effect in the mid-1970s, and we have seen the more recent debate that lead to the debacle that was George Bush's *No Child Left Behind* policy, complete with its conflicts of interest and widespread allegations of high level corruption.

In the United Kingdom, New Labour introduced a National Literacy Strategy in response to business and media pressure about falling standards of literacy during the 1990s. A central focus of this strategy was the Literacy Hour, a distinctly functional and traditional set of procedures that were examples of a top-down process that Labour announced in 2009 that it would scrap after persevering with it for over a decade. The United Kingdom has since ended prescriptive 'teacher-proof' teaching materials in favour of local school and teacher judgement as a means of progressing the nation's literacy achievement levels.

In South Africa, the government launched a six billion-rand programme in 2007 to tackle their 'literacy crisis', the *NGO pulse* commenting that 'the current literacy crisis is a thorny issue and a battlefield of self-interest' (NGO Pulse, 2008).

In early 2009, The Canadian Language and Literacy Research Network (CLLRN) called for a full Canadian government literacy strategy to combat the problems created by Canada's own 'literacy crisis'. As with many such calls for action, University of British Colombia research chair Victoria Purcell-Gates countered this assumption: 'Ignoring the fact that there is NO evidence of a literacy crisis in Canada, let's look at some of the solutions that are being proposed as if there were'. She then commented on some of the assertions made by the CLLRN:

> These solutions generally reflect a type of free-floating anxiety that Canadian teachers do not spend enough time teaching the 'basics' of reading. These include things like knowing the sounds of words (phonemic awareness), knowing how to sound out words (decoding), vocabulary knowledge, and how to understand what you are reading (comprehension strategy knowledge). More structured and systematic teaching of 'skills' is called for. (Quoted in Staffenhagen, 2009)

Here in Australia, we have had frequent and repeated iterations of a literacy crisis since very early in the twentieth century. For a detailed description of contemporary versions of these, I recommend that readers refer to Ilana Snyder's recent comprehensive treatment of what she refers to as *The Literacy Wars* (Snyder, 2008) and also *Debating Literacy in Australia* by Green, Hodgens and Luke (1994). Yet despite all of the rhetoric surrounding literacy crises, real evidence of such declines appears to be limited to occasional national or state/territory testing blips and anecdotal reports.

In the United States, the *No Child Left Behind* policy is being dismantled because of the enormous cost and the realisation that, despite the many billions of dollars spent on it, no statistically reliable improvement in literacy levels has resulted. Reading literacy levels have remained much the same, according to the National Endowment for the Arts (NEA) 2007 report, *To Read or Not To Read: A Question of National Consequence*. Nine-year-olds jumped seven points on a 500-point measurement scale of reading ability between 1988 and 2004, while 17-year-olds fell by five points over the same period (NEA, 2007, p. 10). Presumably, those same 9-year-olds will score higher if/when they are tested at age 17, but even if they do not, these sorts of rises or falls on a 500-point measurement scale hardly represent statistically reliable evidence of a crisis in reading levels in the United States. Further, as Steven Johnson pointed out in his article in Britain's *The Guardian* newspaper:

> ... when you look at prose literacy levels in the adult population: in 1992, 43 percent of Americans read at an intermediate level; by 2003 the number was slightly higher at 44 percent. 'Proficient' readers dropped slightly, from 15 percent to 13 percent. In other words, the distribution is basically unchanged – despite the vast influx of non-native English speakers into the US population during this period. (Johnson, 2008)

Despite this, the NEA report's discourse reads as an alarming wake up call to the nation, as implied by its title, and in much the same fashion as similar reports in Australia (Rowe, 2005) and the United Kingdom (Rose, 2009). Chairman Dana Gioia stated in his Preface:

> The story the data tell is simple, consistent, and alarming. Although there has been measurable progress in recent years in reading ability at the elementary school level, all progress appears to halt as children enter their teenage years. There is a general decline in reading among teenage and adult Americans. Most alarming, both reading ability and the habit of regular reading have greatly declined among college graduates. These negative trends have more than literary importance. As this report makes clear, the declines have demonstrable social, economic, cultural, and civic implications (NEA, 2007, p. 3).

As Johnson's opening quip in his *Guardian* piece highlights, 'We've been hearing about the decline of reading for so long now that it's amazing a contemporary teenager can even recognise a book, much less read one' (Johnson, 2008). Indeed, some might suggest that the most significant statement in the NEA's Executive Summary is contained in the final qualifying paragraph:

> Caution should be used in comparing results from the several studies cited in this publication, as the studies use different methodologies, survey populations, response rates, and standard errors associated with the estimates, and the studies often were designed to serve different research aims. No definite causal relationship can be made between voluntary reading and reading proficiency, or between voluntary reading, reading proficiency, and the reader characteristics noted in the report. (NEA, 2007, p. 20)

In the United Kingdom, the National Literacy Strategy referred to above has now headed in a very different direction towards teacher judgements about student learning, while here in Australia, we have seen very little concrete follow up to the numerous literacy reports commissioned by a succession of federal government agencies, apart from the introduction of nationwide standardised testing in the form of the National Assessment Program in Literacy and Numeracy or NAPLAN as it is known (see, e.g. Australian Language and Literacy Council, 1995; Freebody, 2007; Rowe, 2005).

Rather than revisit some of the recent debates about literacy and standards, I want to focus on how we might interpret such debates over time and in context, and to do this, I will commence with a relatively insignificant publication from the United States and expand both its relevance to literacy debates in this country as well as explore contemporary additions to the model outlined not long after my first appointment to a Faculty of Education, more than a quarter of a century ago.

In 1986, the then President of the Californian Federation of Teachers, Miles Myers, circulated a short discussion paper entitled *The Present Literacy Crisis and the Public Interest* (Myers, 1986). In his paper, Myers described six literacy standards that he believed had existed in the United States between 1800 and the present and argued why none except the last of these standards had required a professional teaching force in order to teach them:

| | |
|---|---|
| Oral literacy | Signature literacy |
| Recitation literacy | Sign literacy |
| Comprehension literacy | Inferential literacy |

Each of these literacy standards, he argued, was 'designed to meet a specific national need during a particular historical period, each required a different teaching style, each persists in the folklore of our society, and each became part of the foundation for later, higher standards of literacy' (pp. 1–2).

Myers described 'oral literacy' as being the first literacy stage in the USA and one that required that a citizen became a fluent speaker, based on what is known elsewhere as the great oral tradition. But by the middle of the nineteenth century, a new requirement emerged in response to a predominantly agrarian economy and a shifting population—from East to West—what he dubbed 'signature literacy'. Being able to sign your name enabled a person to 'borrow money, to claim and settle land, to inventory moving property, to certify births and deaths, and so forth' (p. 2). As Myers observed, 'signature literacy' could be taught by non-professionals, as it was the pedagogy of supervising silent copying and endlessly repetitious pen drills, thus requiring few real educational qualifications of its teaching force.

From about the 1880s through the early years of World War I, there was a major migration of Europeans into the United States, and according to Myers, this required a new 'recitation literacy' emphasis in the school system in order to 'socialise these new populations into the core culture of our country' (p. 3). By standing next to their desks and reciting poems and passages from the American core texts—along with Bible verses—students were absorbed into and by their new culture. Myers suggests that this particular literacy phase totally changed schools, firstly because such pedagogy required a differentiation of age/grade/ability levels and thus led to separate classrooms for students, and secondly—such student separation enabled rows of desks 'bolted to the floor' to define these new classroom spaces. However, by 1915, the proliferation of automobiles, the new industrial requirements, the strong shift to urbanisation and the mobilisation of an expanded armed force brought concomitant changes in literacy demands for the nation.

For the next half century, Myers asserts that the United States 'moved towards a standard of comprehension literacy for all its citizens' (p. 4). First, people needed to develop 'sign literacy', the understanding of the relationship between letters and sound and the accompanying ability to read simple signs and labels. Without such a general literacy competence, it was difficult to imagine how the organisation of 'armies, factories, streets, highways and large shopping markets' could be achieved (p. 4). For Myers, this was the first time that a type of unannounced literacy demand was placed on the American population. Up until now, authorities had uttered what it was students needed to learn and repeat, thus emphasising memory as a major learning mode. The unannounced text represented 'a radical departure from the familiar, pre-announced text in recitation literacy' for it now placed emphasis on letter-sound recognition and the principal learning repository shifted from the human memory to print storage (p. 4). Unsurprisingly, many believed that this would lead to a national loss of memory and a 'dumbing down' of the population, an argument that has persisted into twenty-first-century debates about education more broadly and English literacy in particular (see Donnelly, 2004, 2005, 2007).

Myers argues that the first noticeable step towards sign literacy in the USA was the introduction of tests for army draftees during World War I. Those who claimed to have been to school were given a written test, and 40% of them tested at the third grade level. Interestingly, by the time of the Second World War, 60% were identified as being at the third grade level, and by the Vietnam conflict, this had increased to 80%. But Myers suggests that a new literacy expectation came into effect around the time of the Sputnik launch in 1957, when sign literacy was deemed to be no longer sufficient (Myers, 1986, p. 5):

> 'Comprehension literacy' went beyond the simple recognition of signs; it took into account the ability to 'summarise the literal information of stories and newspaper reports' (pp. 4-5). By 1986, Myers points out that 95 percent of young American adults (aged 21 to 25) could read at the fourth grade level and approximately 80 percent at the eighth grade level. Added to this, more than 70 percent of the nation's seventeen year olds were still in school, whereas in 1940, this figure had been as low as 40 percent. (p. 5)

So what happened to teaching during this same time frame? Myers argues that in order to achieve both sign and comprehension literacy, educators introduced a crude behaviourist model of learning for both teaching and teacher preparation based on the work of Skinner. The result was teaching practices that emphasised 'slot-filling, sequenced drills, small pieces within small units, elaborate grading and reward systems and multiple-choice tests' (p. 6). Further, school systems adopted management models that worked along the lines of manufacturing; teachers were supplied with centrally prepared 'teacher-proof' materials; they provided reinforcement when the script said to do so and kept accurate records of every assessment item. In this model, the teacher was the principal's 'routine worker'. Of course, such methods achieved some success if students' literacy achievements were measured according to acts of memory and the literal meanings of words, but once again, the fully professionalised teacher was not required in such a scenario (Myers, 1986, p. 6).

At the 1986 Carnegie Forum on Education and the Economy, the Berkeley Roundtable concluded that for a nation to survive in current world markets, it needed a workforce with 'an education broad enough to enable workers to move flexibly among technological generations' (quoted in Myers, 1986, p. 7). Myers suggested that this was an education that moved beyond the vocational and required more complex processes than what either sign or comprehension literacy could provide. He listed the sorts of social needs that this new standard of literacy would have to meet:

- Students as citizens would need to be able to go beyond literal word meanings in order to interpret the meanings of texts, including assessing authorial intention.
- Students as workers would need to know how to learn and to problem-solve in order to be able to adapt to the new technologies and the reorganisation of old ones.
- Students as workers would have to be able to participate in decision making in the workplace, including the capacity to discuss and write (p. 8).

This new literacy capacity Myers framed 'inferential literacy' and its complexity called for students to not only interpret and respond to others' texts but to initiate and create their own. For Myers, previous forms of literacy represented a window on reality; texts were transparent revelations of the way the world is. Inferential literacy on the other hand looks at texts more as 'screens through which one sees the world but darkly'. The key concept for Myers was that one of the realities of inferential literacy was 'an awareness of how language both produces and labels reality' (1986, p. 9).

Such literacy practices also called for different ways of teaching students. The supply of teacher-proof materials was no longer workable or appropriate because the classroom became a negotiable space requiring the teacher to research his/her students in order to make fine-grain negotiations with them and judgements about their performance. It required an educator who can think on his/her feet in order to adapt to the changing learning pathways of his/her students and in order to also grow, to be able to make and learn from his/her own mistakes. Myers' argument 25 years ago was that with each new literacy achievement comes a public need and demand for ever higher standards and levels, and, thus, society could not blame any perceived literacy 'crisis' in the United States on the failure of the public school system, but rather on its accumulated successes, which he suggested were 'unmatched in the world' (1986, p. 16).

A decade has passed since Bill Green and I published 'Literacy and the new technologies in school education: Meeting the l(IT)eracy challenge?' (Durrant & Green, 2000). Much has happened at local school, department and state and federal government levels in relation to focusing on literacy over that 10-plus-year period. Some of the work that we drew on in that article included that of Chip Bruce, in particular his diagram outlining a visual representation of literacy development since early times (Bruce, 1998). In reviewing Miles Myers' outline of literacy developments in the United States, I have constructed a diagram that incorporates Bruce's model with that of Myers, along with what I see as the exciting developments and contributions that we have both seen and are yet to see via the realities and future potential of what are loosely called the Web 1.0, Web 2.0 and Web 3.0 technologies.

I have labelled this diagram the 'Literacy Boomerang', more from its shape than any deep, enduring metaphorical reference, though with the recursive nature of the so-called 'literacy wars' that tend to come back—repeatedly—there is perhaps more to the metaphor than I imagined. While I acknowledge the much older traditions of written forms such as Sumerian cuneiform and the Egyptian hieroglyphs, I have focused on recent literacy history where reading and writing moved out of the domain of the privileged classes towards being a societal expectation from about the end of the eighteenth century.

As readers will observe, the dates I have linked with the various literacy stages or developments are arbitrary ones, and are therefore representative rather than fixed, and quite likely are variable according to the geographical area or culture under examination. For example, 'signature literacy' time frames may well apply to the US history but not to the UK experience, though I suspect the insatiable search for new farming lands and successive gold rushes in Australia may well translate to a progressively more mobile and literate population there during the early tomid-1800s.

Perhaps a more fundamental issue with any kind of model or graphic representation of historical periods, social changes and technological developments is that of period shift. I do not pretend that each of these 'stages' happened in isolation or indeed separately from others. Bruce has connected literacy changes to newly available technologies—as does Myers, though in slightly different ways. In my opinion, it is this understanding that could do much to defuse some of the vitriol in contemporary critical comments from both traditional and progressive sides of the literacy fence. In the same way as the development of writing did not lead to the gradual demise of speech from the oral tradition, I do not believe that the keyboard will eventually render unnecessary the teaching of handwriting.

Literacy skills and societal expectations are rarely mutually exclusive; it is never a case of 'either this or that' but rather 'this—as well as that'. Each change in supply and demand of literacy over the past 250 years has built on the notions and affordances of the previously existing literacy, and there has rarely, if ever, been a case of where one form has stopped abruptly when another began. We only need to look at the developments of the past 25 years and the changes in communications habits and practices from Web 1.0–3.0. Many of us are still using technology as a source of entertainment, knowledge and understanding, in much the same way as I used an encyclopaedia as a child, but there are others who also use it as a social and economic medium to network, collaborate and produce goods and services (Web 2.0), while yet a small minority of others are pushing beyond these towards the promised benefits of virtual reality worlds where the boundaries between humans and technology become blurred, not in a dark, sinister way but at that point where

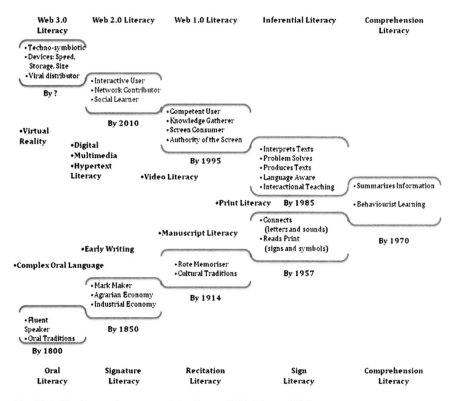

**Fig. 13.1** The literacy boomerang (after Bruce, 1998; Myers, 1986)

apps are distributed virally via phone, email and social networking sites and human and technological functions and affordances act as one, what some have termed techno-symbiosis (Brangiere & Hammes-Adele, 2011). In the evolution of literacy practices, previous forms and understandings have served as foundations for new and additional concepts of literacy, not as replacement ones (Fig. 13.1).

As Catherine Beavis so aptly observes 'Introducing the texts of the new technologies to the classroom need not mean the end of literacy curriculum as we know it, the exclusion of literature, or the loss of the capacity to think critically and aesthetically' (Beavis, 1998, p. 50). For me, what is interesting about the 'new literacies' associated with Web 1.0, 2.0 and 3.0 concepts and practices is that as we move further towards these high-tech literacies, the curve in the 'literacy boomerang' is taking us back along a parallel arc in the direction of many of the indicators of the oral tradition with its methods of storytelling and broader cultural communications embedded in different art forms, including the visual, musical and physical, often requiring advanced levels of cooperation and collaboration with large numbers of people. Not that this trend will call a halt to the literacy wars of course, but it will undoubtedly continue to shift the battle fronts.

Let me return to Miles Myers. It is not difficult to recognise the heavily progressive nature of his observations about teaching and learning in US schools in *The Present Literacy Crisis*. Of course, a quarter of a century later, his identified 'new literacy' pedagogy is often blamed for the educational, social and economic ills of western countries, and, hence, we come back to a new iteration of the so-called 'Literacy Wars'.

So why is it that each successive generation seems dissatisfied with the current educational achievements of the next?

This is not a new phenomenon by any means. Paul Brock reminded us of some of the criticisms of the literacy standards of previous generations of students in his wonderful discussion paper for the New South Wales Department of Education and Training, *Breaking Some of the Myths—Again* (1998), including:

- George Elliott, President of Harvard College, who wrote in 1871 that 'Bad spelling, incorrectness as well as inelegance of expression in writing, ignorance of the simplest rules of punctuation and almost entire want of familiarity with English literature, are far from rare among young men of 18 otherwise well prepared for college'.
- Andrew Sledd, Assistant Professor of English at Harold Washington College, who commented in 1988 that '... the discussion of this (declining standards myth) is not timely—it is timeless; for although Newsweek certified our crisis a mere decade ago ... no fewer than five consecutive generations have been condemned for writing worse than their predecessors. By now our students should hardly put processor to paper; it's a wonder they can write at all'.
- American historian Harvey Daniels, in examining George Puttenham's despair about the falling literacy standards of the youth of his day (1586), concluded: '... literacy has been declining since it was invented; one of the first ancient Sumerian tablets deciphered by modern scholars immortalised a teacher fretting over the recent drop in (standards of) students' writing' (quoted in Brock, 1998, p. 3).

In Australia, the story has been much the same. Sir Harold Wyndham observed in 1987 that 'the severest critics of our education system have selective memories and hark back to a golden age that never existed' (Wyndham, 1987, p. 15). Judith Goyen's study at Macquarie University in the early 1980s revealed that the highest rates of functional illiteracy in those Australians born in English-speaking countries were amongst those over the age of 60 (11.9%), products of the 'good old days' of knowledge-based education (quoted in Brock, 1990, p. 23).

So what are we to make of 'literacy crisis' talk and the so-called literacy wars?

Ilana Snyder points to the fact that literacy crises are frequently linked to 'socio-economic change of some kind' (Snyder, 2008, p. 7; see also McGraw, 2007). She also raises the issue of different definitions of literacy being part of the problem, particularly in relation to the difference between viewing literacy as a cognitive function rather than as a social practice (Snyder, 2008, p. 11). Peter Freebody (2007) wryly observes that some wars occur in order to prove that there must have been a crisis in the first place, but that there are two senses in which there is always a crisis in literacy education.

First, that we might interpret there being a crisis in literacy education to mean that there is 'a need for a turning point in literacy education due to institutional inertia in the face of rapidly changing communicational environments'. He goes on to point out that because school students are taught by teachers who in turn have been taught by teacher educators, that there is by definition a two-generational lag in the process, hence 'there is always an urgency about revisiting and revising literacy education practices in light of research on communicational, cultural, linguistic and economic conditions' (Freebody, 2007, p. 11). (It should be noted here that this assumes a degree of professional withdrawal by both teacher educators and teachers, which in itself is a highly contestable assumption.)

Second, there are always groups within society that have experienced long-standing critical relationships with schooling in general and literacy education in particular:

> Their literacy crisis may relate to sporadic access to schooling or access only to inadequate schooling, or substantial mismatches between their language repertoire and the language of use in schools, or other cultural experiences or lack of experiences for which the institutionalised schooling available to them is not adequately prepared. (Freebody, 2007, p. 12)

In 1994, Dennis Baron suggested that whether or not we define literacy in its narrow understanding of reading and writing or more broadly as the ability to operate effectively within a given culture or context: 'literacy must be regarded as a process of moving from outside to inside, from unknowing to knowing, and from foreign to familiar' (Baron, 1994, p. 2). And perhaps this gets to the heart of the matter. The creation and perpetuation of socio-economic capacity divisions within all societies has an alienating effect for both literacy 'insiders' and 'outsiders', and given that these are realised for any individual when one is relatively young and economically dependent, Andrew Sledd's wry observation is a generative one: 'There will always be a literacy crisis, if for no other reason than because the old never wholly like the young' (Quoted in Brock, 1998, p. 3).

With each successive generation, the evolution of new literacies enabled by new technologies and their affordances tends to rub uncomfortably with the previous generation, and if this brief examination of the 'literacy boomerang' is any indication at all, likely always will.

# References

Australian Language and Literacy Council. (1995). *Teacher education in English language and literacy.* Canberra, Australia: Australian Government Publishing Service.

Baron, D. (1994). *'The literacy complex', in the Newsletter of the Center for the Study of Cultural Values and Ethics.* Accessed June 9, 2011, from http://www.english.illinois.edu/-people-/faculty/debaron/essays/litcomplex.htm

Beavis, C. (1998). Pressing (the right?) buttons: Literacy and technology, crisis and continuity. *English in Australia, 123,* 42–51.

Brangiere, E., & Hammes-Adele, S. (2011). Beyond the technology acceptance model: Elements to validate the human-technology symbiosis model. In M. Robertson (Ed.),

*Ergonomics and health aspects of work with computers* (pp. 13–21). Berlin: Springer. Accessed on July 11, 2011, from http://books.google.com.au/books?id=x8vTk6tJWuUC& pg=PA15&lpg=PA15&dq=Technosymbiotic&source=bl&ots=pJR6PozJ6Y&sig= 7LwzwsbvGEYl4DT9vGhmHzYfm5M&hl=en&ei=nRUeTqWXAuSNmQWG14TrBw& sa=X&oi=book_result&ct=result&resnum=2&ved=0CB0Q6AEwAQ#v=onepage&q= Technosymbiotic&f=false

Brock, P. (1990). Five myths about literacy. *Queensland Teachers Union Professional Magazine*, October, pp. 22–27.

Brock, P. (1998). *Breaking some of the myths–again*. Sydney, Australia: NSW Department of Education and Training.

Bruce, B. (1998). New literacies. *The Journal of Adult and Adolescent Literacy, 42*(1), 46–49.

Donnelly, K. (2004). *Why our schools are failing*. Sydney, Australia: Duffy and Snellgrove.

Donnelly, K. (2005). Cannon fodder of the culture wars. *The Australian*, February 9, from http://www.onlineopinion.com.au/view.asp?article=3024&page=0

Donnelly, K. (2007). *Dumbing down: Outcomes based and politically correct, the impact of the culture wars on our schools*. Richmond, Australia: Hardie Grant Books.

Durrant, C., & Green, B. (2000). Literacy and the new technologies in school education: Meeting the l(IT)eracy challenge? *The Australian Journal of Language and Literacy, 23*(2), 89–108.

Flesch, R. (1955). *Why Johnny can't read*. New York: Harper & Row.

Freebody, P. (2007). *Literacy education in school: Research perspectives from the past, for the future*. Camberwell, Australia: ACER.

Green, B., Hodgens, J., & Luke, A. (1994). *Debating literacy in Australia: A documentary history: 1945–1994*. Melbourne, Australia: Australian Literacy Federation.

Johnson, S. (2008). Dawn of the digital natives. *The Guardian*, 7 February. Accessed on July 5, 2011, from http://www.guardian.co.uk/technology/2008/feb/07/internet.literacy

McGaw, B. (2007). Preface. In P. Freebody (Ed.), *Literacy education in school: Research perspectives from the past, for the future*. Camberwell, Australia: ACER.

Myers, M. (1986). *The present literacy crisis and the public interest* downloaded at ERIC: http://www.eric.ed.gov/ERICWebPortal/search/detailmini.jsp?_nfpb=true&_&ERICExtSearch_ SearchValue_0=ED288183&ERICExtSearch_SearchType_0=no&accno=ED288183

NEA. (2007). *To read or not to read: A question of national consequence*. Executive Summary. Accessed on July 2, 2011, from http://www.nea.gov/research/ResearchReports_chrono.html

NGO Pulse. (2008). *The literacy crisis*. Accessed on July 4, 2011, from http://www.ngopulse.org/ article/literacy-crisis

Rose, J. (2009). *Identifying and teaching children and young people with dyslexia and literacy difficulties*. Department for Children, Schools and Families (Now Department of Education, UK). Accessed on July 1, 2011, from https://www.education.gov.uk/publications/standard/ publicationdetail/page1/DCSF-006592009

Rowe, K., & National Inquiry into the Teaching of Literacy (Australia). (2005). *Teaching reading*. Accessed on April 22, 2011, from http://research.acer.edu.au/tll_misc/5

Snyder, I. (2008). *The literacy wars*. Sydney, Australia: Allen & Unwin.

Staffenhagen, J. (2009). Is there a literacy crisis in Canada? *The Vancouver Sun,* 24 March. Accessed on July 8, 2011, from http://communities.canada.com/vancouversun/blogs/ reportcard/archive/2009/03/24/does-canada-have-a-literacy-problem.aspx

The Quotations Page. (2010). Accessed on June 27, 2011, from http://www.quotationspage.com/ quote/28750.html

Wells, H. G. (2004). *Mankind in the making* (1903). Hazleton: Pennsylvania State University Electronic Classics Series. Accessed on June 18, 2011, from www2.hn.psu.edu/faculty/jmanis/ hgwells/Mankind-Making.pdf

Wyndham, H. (1987). Wyndham lashes at critics. *The Sunday Telegraph, 26*, 15.

# Chapter 14
# Critical Engagement with Literacy and Qualitative Research: Towards Socially Just Pedagogy in the Teacher Education Classroom

Wendy Cumming-Potvin

## Introduction

As the Australian political climate privileges a competitive approach to standardized literacy testing across states, neoliberal advocates have attempted to essentialize teacher education by arguing for the need to train literacy teachers who focus on the conventions of language and privilege a phonics-based approach to teaching reading. Juxtaposed against a postmodern world of deepening diversity and multiple literacies demanding innovation for understanding cultural, social and political contexts, this 'back-to-basics' approach to literacy is underpinned by a managerial philosophy in teacher education (see Doecke & Kostogriz, 2005). On the other hand, an increasingly complex range of literacy practices in the twenty-first century is associated with local diversity and global connectedness, which requires sophisticated explanations for understanding student achievement (see The New London Group, 2000) and designing pre-service teacher programmes. For more than a decade, educational researchers and practitioners committed to social justice have called for contemporary ways of 'doing literacy' to develop citizens who can deconstruct texts and participate in society through community, economic and public engagement (Healy, 2008; Luke & Carrington, 2002; Philp, 2006). From this perspective, the teaching and learning of literacy involves understanding multiple strands within complex and competing communities (see Bourdieu, 1973; Wenger, McDermott, & Snyder, 2002).

As a teacher educator concerned to implement literacy programmes emphasizing social justice, respect for others and critical enquiry (see Giroux, 2004), I draw on qualitative research to deconstruct some of my pre-service teaching experiences in Western Australia. After commenting briefly on the concepts of social justice

W. Cumming-Potvin (✉)
School of Education, Murdoch University, Perth, Australia
e-mail: W.Cumming-Potvin@murdoch.edu.au

B. Down and J. Smyth (eds.), *Critical Voices in Teacher Education*, Explorations of Educational Purpose 22, DOI 10.1007/978-94-007-3974-1_14, © Springer Science+Business Media Dordrecht 2012

and critical pedagogy in educational discourses, I describe how I used results from a qualitative literacy research project to facilitate pre-service teachers' critical reflection in a large compulsory English curriculum unit. Next, I reflect on how I conducted a qualitative research project aiming to deepen understandings about the teaching and learning of literacy for a group of pre-service teachers via engagement with on-campus, online and home communities. Finally, in the context of Australia's current neoliberal climate, my discussion highlights possibilities and limitations for developing pre-service and postgraduate reflective practitioners who are dedicated to teaching for social justice.

## Social Justice, Literacy Education and Critical Pedagogy

As a matter of principle, official education policies in Australia refer to the concept of social justice. The Melbourne Declaration on Educational Goals for Young Australians (Ministerial Council on Education, Employment, Training & Youth Affairs, 2008) recognizes the role of education in building a just, equitable and democratic society. Western Australia's Curriculum Framework (Curriculum Council, 2010) also acknowledges the concept of social justice through a set of shared values relating to social and civic responsibilities, common good and participation in cultural diversity and democratic processes. Despite these discourses, which position social justice as a collective responsibility for Australian education sectors and the broader community, numerous educational researchers have reiterated that many school philosophies and practices remain inequitable (Keddie & Nayler, 2006; Martino & Pallotta-Chiarolli, 2003; McInerney, 2007). As well, the Commonwealth government's emphasis on NAPLAN testing and publication of academic ratings on the My School website (http://www.myschool. edu.au/) have resulted in concern over pedagogy such as 'teaching to the test' (Rout, 2011), with a focus on educational product over process (Eacott, Wilkinson, Blackmore, Lingard, & Rawolle, 2010). Such concerns echo criticisms of the USA's No Child Left Behind Policy, which was deemed to dumb down curriculum by focussing on 'kill and drill' multiple-choice testing whilst disadvantaging English language learners and special education students with inappropriate testing (see Darling-Hammond, 2007). For literacy educators, these perceptions are aggravated by a mainstream political climate promoting a pre-packaged and step-by-step approach to the pedagogy of reading as a panacea for all students' academic success (see Ewing, 2006).

On a broader level, teacher educators must consider multiple factors when attempting to promote social justice and critical pedagogy, particularly in Western societies where increasingly results from standardized testing, such as PISA, are used to advance academic competition across countries, based on student performances, especially in literacy. First, in spite of the numerous references to social justice and critical pedagogy in educational discourse, the conceptual interpretations of the terms are multiple and often contested (see McLaren, 2003; Merret, 2004).

Second, the implementation of socially justice pedagogy is often perceived as an uncomfortable pathway, influenced by teachers' unique biographies, values and beliefs (Jordan Irvine, 2004). In this respect, Cochran Smith (2004) suggested that teacher education for social justice is problematic on both pedagogical and political levels, for it requires ongoing social structures and contextual support within higher education institutions. Finally, despite the imperative to develop teachers who ask compelling questions to go beyond a passive knowledge of banking (see Freire, 1970), in the first part of the new millennium, a technical approach to teaching has predominated in the Western world (Kincheloe, 2008).

Mindful of these challenges, especially in the mainstream managerial context of Australian education, I was keen to explore with my pre-service teachers the interwoven nature of social justice, critical pedagogy and literacy. Despite the multiple interpretations of social justice, preparing pre-service teachers to work across diverse socio-cultural contexts has been described as involving the examination of several concepts such as self-identity, ethnocentrism, privilege, racism and culturally appropriate curriculum (see Jones & Enriquez, 2009; Sleeter, 2008). From a Freirean perspective (1970, 1985), educating for social justice means creating a world with a fuller sense of humanity, which provides opportunities for learners to reflect with humility on assumed knowledge. To achieve social justice in the area of literacy education, Luke, Comber, and Grant (2003) argued that communities must collaborate to understand diversity and overcome economic exploitation and social discrimination. From a pedagogical viewpoint, Beavis and O'Mara (2006) recommended promoting a sense of community in pre-service literacy education by nurturing and challenging students' concepts about literacy and social justice, encouraging students to engage with the wider field of literacy (i.e. websites, government departments, libraries, bookshops, etc.) and presenting a range of texts for enjoyment, reflection and critical analysis. In this vein, I drew on the pedagogical work of Luke and Freebody (1999) and The New London Group (2000) to scaffold pre-service literacy teachers to build critical connections between theory and practice.

## Bridging the Chasm Between Pre-service Teacher Education and Primary Classrooms: Critically Reflecting on a Year 7 Boy's Literacy Progress

Whilst acknowledging my personal beliefs and biases as an educator/researcher (Ping-Chun, 2008), I aimed to develop rapprochement between literacy learning in the pre-service teacher programme and primary school classrooms. My purpose was to utilize qualitative research to support pre-service teachers in better understanding and negotiating their own pedagogies to develop a more equitable understanding of teaching contexts (see Miller, 2008) in Western Australia and abroad. My understandings of qualitative research were underpinned by concern to examine educational experiences from a holistic perspective, acknowledging the ambiguous and multilayered nature of reality (Kincheloe, 2003).

Initially, I drew on data from a qualitative study during which I had collaborated with a classroom teacher to scaffold the progress of a class of Year 7 students in a West Australian state school. In this Year 7 classroom, the scaffolding unfolded dynamically over time during reading circles (see Cumming-Potvin, 2008) and was mediated by context (small group or whole class), relationships (peers and/or adults) and learning tools (conventional and/or multimodal texts). Retrospectively, in the pre-service teaching classroom, the progress of 1 Year 7 boy (Art) was examined to provide opportunities for pre-service teachers in a large compulsory literacy unit to critically reflect on how to scaffold diverse primary students in a socio-culturally appropriate manner.

To scaffold my pre-service teachers' critical reflection, I employed a pedagogical process involving several steps. First, I presented pre-service teachers with information about socio-cultural factors, such as Art's literacy profile and the background to the research site. With a student population of more than 900, the primary school examined was located in an urban English-speaking neighbourhood and considered to be predominantly of middle socio-economic status, with a majority of students using English as a first language. Art was a member of a first-generation immigrant family who migrated to Australia from the UK and used English as a first language. Although he responded well to in-class scaffolding, Art was frequently absent from school. Ongoing teacher observations and standardized testing indicated that Art was dyslexic and at risk of not meeting minimal literacy benchmarks. During student interviews I conducted in the school, Art willingly acknowledged that he read little at home but indicated that he had multiple experiences and skills related to information and communication technology (ICT). Once aware of Art's educational context, my pre-service teachers were invited to reflect on how mediating factors outside the formal curriculum, such as absenteeism, social class and home environment, may influence a student's ongoing literacy progress.

Second, I offered my pre-service teachers explanations and opportunities to comment on the study's intervention process which used an action-reflection approach in the primary classroom to build on Art's knowledge of and interest in ICT; a proposed Year 7 literacy unit included scaffolded tasks designed around the four resources literacy model (Freebody, 2004; Luke & Freebody, 1999). In preparation for the unit of study, which was based on the novel 'Tuck Everlasting' (Babbitt, 1975) the classroom teacher and students designed a web page on which online messages could be posted to reading group members, the whole class or the teacher. Because I had already introduced Luke and Freebody's work in the pre-service classroom, as we learned more about Art's authentic journey in the primary classroom, I encouraged pre-service teachers to interrogate this model to connect the theory and practice of teaching and learning literacy. For example, I asked probing questions, such as: How do proficient readers develop? (Campbell & Green, 2006). How do you view the teacher's role in facilitating a holistic approach to reading? How might you scaffold the literacy development of a primary student who uses English as an additional language? What role might migration play in a primary student's literacy development?

Third, in the pre-service teacher classroom, by presenting transcripts gathered from literacy tasks involving Art's engagement with his peers and me, I used the following examples to deconstruct scaffolding in primary school contexts. Again, I emphasized the Luke and Freebody (1999) literacy model to illustrate a holistic approach to reading, particularly for working with children identified as challenged by the literacy curriculum. In this case, the analysis of several transcripts revealed that Art could be scaffolded to use a range of literacy roles, from code breaking to critical analysis. For example, as Art used a desktop computer in the school library to post a message about the novel Tuck Everlasting on the class discussion board, he spontaneously requested my assistance with the code breaking of language (see Luke & Freebody). Art asked: Is that how you spell 'reckon'? My response focussed on the relationship between spoken and written language: 'Well, reckon? (emphasizing the R sound)... Can you hear the sound?'

During the same task, when Art related his confusion about the text, I provided scaffolding aiming to deepen Art's comprehension. In the following extract, to facilitate meaning making, I encouraged Art to substantiate his statements with examples from the novel. As he learned to unpack these metacognitive processes, Art began to engage with the text participant practice (Luke & Freebody, 1999), which promotes links between the text and the student's life world.

11. Art: (Looks at the computer screen, then slowly reads his online message). Do any of you reckon this book is a bit boring? I also don't get the story. I think it's all out of order.
12. Researcher: Mmh. Out of order... What do you mean by out of order?
13. Art: Like it's not... it's all different parts of it.
14. Researcher: The different parts don't seem to be in order. Is that what you mean?
15. Art: Yeah.
16. Researcher: Like the sequencing of the days? O.K. Do you find that confusing?
17. Art: Yeah, it's like it's not really as though... it wouldn't really happen in real life... you wouldn't like be one place one moment and then another place in the next.
18. Researcher: O.K Can you give me an example of what happens in the book when that happens?
19. Art: Well, like it's as though they're like at the, umm, they're riding along and all of a sudden they're at the Tucks' house and then all of a sudden they're in this boat going down the stream and stuff... (Cumming-Potvin, 2008, pp. 41–42).

Towards the end of the pedagogical sequence, the interaction shifted towards text analyst (Luke & Freebody, 1999), a practice which refers to students reading between the lines; I encouraged Art to position himself as a critical reader by asking whether the author (Natalie Babbitt) had intentionally made these decisions about structuring the novel. As these transcripts were analysed, pre-service teachers asked questions such as:

• Which strategies might be used to promote the text analyst practice in the upper primary classroom?
• How can critical literacy be encouraged in the early childhood setting?

Finally, once these transcripts had been deconstructed, the pre-service teachers were invited to draw on the authentic example of Art to apply their knowledge about the teaching and learning of literacy. Aiming to link literacy learning in the 'practical' and 'professional' worlds of primary schools to pedagogy introduced in the tertiary setting, I invited pre-service teachers to critically reflect on their English school experience placement. Specifically, I encouraged pre-service teachers to consider how they might scaffold the literacy development of an 'authentic' student observed during primary school placements. I presented (Bain, Ballantyne, Mills & Lester 2002) framework of five R's as a holistic way of approaching this task: reporting, responding, relating, reasoning and reconstructing. As they planned strategies to scaffold the literacy learning of 'real' primary school students, the pre-service teachers were encouraged to reflect on mediating factors outside the formal curriculum, such as social class, race, language and health, which can impact significantly on students' academic progress.

## Deepening Understandings: Pre-service Teachers Engaging with a Pedagogy of Multiliteracies

In addition to examining data gathered in the primary school setting to promote critical reflection in teacher education classrooms, I conducted a qualitative research study aiming to deepen pre-service teachers' understandings of teaching and learning literacy. Assuming that knowledge is embedded in social, cultural and material communities of practice (see Lave & Wenger, 1991), the project was underpinned by The New London Group's (2000) pedagogy of multiliteracies; navigating the postmodern literacy landscape was linked to celebrating socio-cultural diversity and creating more socially just learning opportunities. The project focussed on a small group of pre-service teachers who voluntarily engaged with peers and researchers during on-campus focus groups and online discussions; at home, they engaged in shared literacy experiences with their children aged between 4 and 7 years.

To track literacy understandings during on-campus focus groups and online discussions, these pre-service teachers were invited to respond to open-ended questions such as 'How would you define literacy?' and 'How have you developed this definition of literacy?' As illustrated below in excerpts of the pre-service teachers' transcripts, Grace, Eva and Sally linked prior and present learning experiences to reflect on their expanding definitions of literacy, thus alluding to the New London Group's concept of *situated practice*. Grace, for example, suggested that recently she regarded literacy as involving more than books or conventional texts but also advertisements and visual media. Eva indicated that she currently viewed the term literacy as holistic and critical, which was very different to the way literacy had been presented to her as a child at school.

> ... we always used to think it was books, or reading, but probably even through this unit it's not just reading a book its reading everything, like you know visual things, reading advertisements books, reading like the media all that sort of thing so to me I think literacy is a lot more than I ever defined it as (Grace).

And added to that, I think it's more, what I've got out of the course that it's more, it's also making sense of it in a real holistic, I like to use the word [literacy] in a holistic sense, that you're being critical... That you, that you see where writers are coming from and why they've written the way they've written. Why newspaper articles are read, you know, portrayed the way they are and that sort of thing too. So I mean, I was never taught that at school, that was something that was definitely not there (Eva).

Moreover, as Eva and Sally elaborated their definitions of literacy, they referred to issues such as: Why are texts written? How they are written? And how can literacy be used to assist children to broaden life experiences and acknowledge social diversity? These questions relate to *critical framing* (The New London Group, 2000), whereby learners interpret historical, cultural and ideological contexts of learning.

...I agree with both the comments, but it's becoming more aware of how, it's not just about the book, it's how it connects with life ahm, especially with the theme of this one's families and stuff, so it's how it connects with the families and how it can relate to what happens in the book... to themselves and to other people .... I suppose it's just making the connection with life...and trying to put the child say in the place of another child so like...you know. We're in a single parent family so that's what we're used to, but then you see another family where there's lots of relatives around .... And vice versa for kids in different situations, so it's learning to broaden the horizons beyond what happens in the home and the school (Sally). (Cumming-Potvin, 2009, p. 88).

During these informal focus groups with peers and researchers, Sally was able to deepen her reflection about literacy to discuss political aspects linked to power and *critical framing*. In the extract below, for example, Sally commented:

Well I think it comes to this [power], this you know, being literate with [the power] and I think the more literate that you are and that's not just literate in terms of enjoyment but literate in terms of society then the more power you have, to be a citizen or do you know what I mean or to be a more active citizen in society.... obviously the more awareness you have of the wider things, then the more active a citizen you can be.

Concurrently to the focus groups, these pre-service teachers were studying a 14-week English curriculum course during which they developed pedagogical repertoires for future primary literacy school placements. Engaging with the on-campus focus groups, the pre-service teachers selected their preferred children's picture books from a recommended list examining the theme of diversity in families. As the home-based shared literacy experiences unfolded, the pre-service teacher participants extended the original list of picture books by suggesting personal favourites, children's preferences or librarians' recommendations.

Drawing on knowledge gained from shared reading experiences with children in informal settings, during subsequent focus group discussions, the pre-service teachers began to consider more socially just ways of using picture books during their formal pre-service teaching placements. This shifting of knowledge from one context to another is defined as *transformed practice* within the language of a pedagogy of multiliteracies (The New London Group, 2000). In the extract below, for example, Sally, Eva and Grace discuss utilizing picture books containing strong visual imagery, such as 'Let's Get a Pup' (Graham, 2003) and 'Love You

Forever' (Munsch, 2000) to discuss misconceptions and stereotypes about families' appearances, a practice often associated with critical literacy (see Luke & Freebody, 1999; Martino, 1999).

> 53. Sally: Because it does come to starts love, like if you are reading it ['Love You Forever'] to a large group of children.... I think you have to be really careful where your kids are coming from. Like if they don't come from ideal backgrounds or maybe mum and dad, or maybe if their background is ok, but not what you perceive as being the ideal childhood, I think you have to be really careful with these family related books as to what, 'cause if you say this is the way family, you're kind of saying this is the kind of way a family should be and if that is not the way their family is.... (Cumming-Potvin, 2009, p. 90).
> 54. Grace: (overlapping) It's almost racist. It could be couldn't it, if you weren't-
> 55. Eva: Or stereotypical.

Here, the pre-service teachers' comments about critiquing idealized conceptions of family aligned with those of literacy researchers who have argued for using picture books to explore content, ideology and non-mainstream issues with young children and adolescents (Dean & Grierson, 2005; O'Brien, 2001).

## Social Justice, Critical Pedagogy and Literacy: Tensions and Ambiguities

On one level, these pre-service teachers (Sally, Eva and Grace) drew on their acquired knowledge of children's literacy learning to agree that reading texts should be used to counter stereotyped images of families in the primary curriculum. However, during another focus group, tensions surfaced about the pre-service teachers' multiple interpretations of the educational discourse related to a pedagogy for social justice (see McLaren, 2003; Merret, 2004). For example, in turns 201 and 203 of the following transcript, whilst acknowledging her desire not to alienate parents, Sally argued for teachers to utilize critical literacy as a political strategy to inform and empower students to question the status quo. Although Eva agreed that assisting students to learn to read critically was significant, in line 202, she questioned the overtly political role of teachers and suggested that the process of becoming literate was innately empowering. Grace, on the other hand, in turn 205 suggested that teachers should distance themselves from their own values when aiming to empower students.

> 201. Sally: But I think that becomes our role as a teacher is to make people become a bit more aware of the social, of what's really going on not just. That's where all that critical literacy comes in. [-] I have to try and be careful I don't upset any parents. But I think you have to make people aware of what's happening in society ahm, and to be literate in that way. Do you know what I'm saying? Otherwise you can't be an empowered citizen if you're not really aware of what's going on, does that make sense?
> 202. Eva: But then the teaching role isn't to be political, it isn't political. Teaching is political but it's not your job to be political in the way you do it is it? But empowering.

> Empowering, teaching kids to be, to learn, to read to be literate and to, so they can be informed and then be empowered to do something should they feel.
> 203. Sally: And to question.
> 204. Eva: Yes. And to be able to be critical, like you are saying to be.
> 205. Grace: That's right, I guess you have to be careful that it's not your values coming across.
> 206. Eva: Yes absolutely. Yes, it's a fine line.
> 207. Sally: But you want to make children, but I guess that's what this critical literacy does. If you can get them to question text that they're reading, just a standard story, you know, a standard story, if you can get them to learn to question those, then they see something on the TV or they read the newspaper, as they're getting older they read the newspaper then hopefully those same questioning skills will kick in. Yeah, but yeah it's a fine line.

The tensions and ambiguities associated with Sally, Eva and Grace's discourses in relation to the teacher's role when implementing programmes for social justice can be explicated through the work of McInerney (2007). In his ethnographic study tracking the reforms in one Australian school, McInerney argued that teachers' acknowledgment of progress towards social justice was tempered with their awareness that the task was immense and beset with practical obstacles. In fact, the metaphor of the 'fine line' painted by Sally and Eva resonates with that of the 'tightrope', which McInerney utilized to depict teachers struggling to uphold an emancipatory position, whilst engaging creatively with a neoliberal discourse.

Notwithstanding these challenges, glimmers of hope can be discerned in Sally's intentions to develop critical literacy in the classroom as an avenue for students to critique a repertoire of conventional and popular texts (e.g. stories, newspaper articles or television programmes).

## Final Words: Challenges and Looking Towards the Future

Confronted by an Australian political landscape which supports a managerial approach to teacher education, with an emphasis on standardized testing, critics have called for a more sophisticated approach to literacy education. Against a backdrop of globalization and neoliberalism, it would appear paramount for educators of the twenty-first century to embrace the rapidly changing technological and socio-cultural factors which affect the values, skills, attitudes and practices required for active citizenship. With a deeper raison d'être than the acquisition of skills and knowledge about conventional spelling, grammar and handwriting, from a contemporary viewpoint, literacy represents a life-long dynamic process involving individuals within diverse and contending communities. Aiming for a socially just and critical pedagogy, a contemporary approach to literacy also embraces the complex multilingual and multimodal nature of communication, characterized by globalization and large-scale migration in the new millennium (see The New London Group, 2000).

Against this socio-political scenery, I have deconstructed in this chapter some key tertiary teaching experiences in West Australia, which drew on qualitative research and aimed to facilitate pre-service teachers' critical reflections about literacy whilst acknowledging the complex and ambiguous nature of reality. Linked to a compulsory literacy education unit and grounded in the theoretical work of The New London Group (2000) and Luke and Freebody (1999), the analysis maps my attempts to implement pre-service literacy tasks emphasizing social justice and critical pedagogy. Although historically many literacy theories have attempted to pinpoint the necessary components for students' academic success, it is impossible to pre-determine the expectations particular cultures or communities may hold for individuals' engagement with texts. Luke and Freebody (1999) argued that literacy expectations are interwoven with societies' normative conceptions, which underpin the necessity for literacy learners to interrogate and resist texts. In this sense, raising more critical questions than answers, my pedagogical work of modest scope is limited by the conceptual and structural challenges of developing socially just literacy programmes.

Of the multiple challenges relating to scaffolding critical pedagogy, it would be untruthful to veil the fact that emancipatory education is associated with contestations and tensions. Giroux (1985), for example, described social institutions as fragmented sites filled with complex forms of resistance. In schools, where the voice of mainstream power brokers is often increasingly dominant, it can be difficult for teachers to assume the role of leaders rather than followers. Although modelling socially just intellectual and moral stances may be valuable for teacher education, Jones and Enriquez (2009) argue that pedagogy is also influenced by a complex interplay of social, cultural, political and personal factors; it is impossible to predict how a pre-service teacher will apply, adapt or transform pedagogy in the classroom setting. Whilst pre-service teachers and graduate teachers are routinely encouraged to reflect on their classroom practice, the fear of critiquing 'authentic' teaching practice often stifles the level of analysis. During school experience placements, for example, many of my teacher education students expressed anxiety about using reflective journals to critique classroom pedagogy and/or school policies. Other pre-service teachers were fearful about professional repercussions for graduate teachers who critiqued educational practice in their school communities. Under these circumstances, the question remains unanswered about how to safely support pre-service teachers to engage productively as agents of social change in spaces involving contestation and resistance.

Another challenge to scaffolding socially just pedagogy relates to the socio-cultural composition of pre-service teaching cohorts. Educated in white, middle-class and monolingual English backgrounds, the majority of my pre-service teachers (including Sally, Grace and Eva) remain largely unrepresentative of Australia's broader multicultural society. Although these pre-service teachers may acknowledge their privileged status, it has been argued that many such candidates may begin education programmes with naïve pre-conceptions about classrooms, young children's acquisition of literacy and the world, more generally (see de Courcy, 2007). It has been further suggested that white graduate teachers may have little cross-cultural or racial knowledge and possess stereotypical beliefs about diverse students (Assaf & McMunn Dolley, 2006; Sleeter, 2001). Hence, a key question persists: How can we develop pre-service teachers' cross-cultural and racial knowledge whilst recruiting a greater number of candidates who more equitably represent the multicultural nature of Australian society?

Although Australian vernacular is associated with the concept of 'giving individuals a fair go', challenges on a broader level indicate that Australia is still an unequal society (McInerney, 2007). According to Jones and Enriquez (2009), it is widely recognized that schools operate for and perpetuate the mainstream power of white, English-speaking, patriarchal, heterosexual, middle-class and affluent groups. As school systems are increasingly governed by a centralized approach to education, with proposed Commonwealth strategies to promote excellence in teaching by offering cash rewards in the form of one-off teacher bonuses, universities are also increasingly entrenched in a managerial style approach to education. In this context, Freire's (1970) denouncement of bureaucracies and call to transform the rigid nature of student-teacher relationships in universities appears progressively more implausible. On a practical level, increasingly, the casualization of the academic work force coupled with large university class sizes lend themselves to a one-size-fits-all approach, making it difficult to attend to students' diverse needs (see Oliver, 2006).

Notwithstanding these challenges, it would be overly pessimistic to ignore the glimmers of hope for more socially just schools and teacher education that etch the world's horizon. 'Hopelessness is but hope that has lost its bearings .... When it becomes a program, hopelessness paralyses us, immobilizes us' (Freire, 1994, p. 2). For Freire, succumbing to hopelessness dissolves our strength to re-create a more socially just world. Whilst still vulnerable, hope for student empowerment in this chapter is symbolized by Sally, a pre-service teacher who, on the cusp of her graduation, was still passionate about the need to dispel stereotypes in the classroom and engage with literacy as an explicitly political process. This hope is reminiscent of Giroux's (2007) call for educators to embrace the political nature of pedagogy and empower students to understand that, although fraught with tensions, ambiguities and resistance, democracy is possible.

# References

Assaf, L. C., & McMunn Dooley, C. (2006). "Everything they were giving us created tension": Creating and managing tension in a graduate-level multicultural course focused on literacy methods. *Multicultural Education,* Winter, *vol. 14*(2), pp. 42–49.

Australian Curriculum, Assessment and Reporting Authority. (2010). *Australian curriculum.* Retrieved September 29, 2010, from http://www.acara.edu.au/curriculum.html

Babbitt, N. (1975). *Tuck everlasting.* London: Bloomsbury.

Bain, J. D., Ballantyne, R., Mills, C., & Lester, N. C. (2002). *Reflecting on practice: Student teachers' perspectives*, Post Pressed: Flaxton, Australia. Retrieved February 20, 2011, from http:www.lace.org.au/documents/Info_sheet_Reflection.pdf

Beavis, C., & O'Mara, J. (2006). Preparing English teachers for a changing world. In B. Doecke, M. Howie, & W. Sawyer (Eds.), *Only connect: English teaching, schooling and community* (pp. 349–369). Kensington Gardens, Australia: Wakefield Press in Association with The Australian Association for the Teaching of English.

Bourdieu. (1973). Cultural reproduction and social reproduction. In R. Brown (Ed.), *Papers in the sociology of education, knowledge education and cultural change* (pp. 71–112). London: Taylor & Francis.

Campbell, R., & Green, D. (2006). *Literacies and learners*. Frenchs Forest, Australia: Pearson Education.

Cochran-Smith, M. (2004). Defining the outcomes of teacher education: What's social justice got to do with it? *Asia-Pacific Journal of Teacher Education, 32*(3), 193–212.

Cumming-Potvin, W. (2008). Partners, pedagogy and technology: A year 7 boy's reading progress. *Curriculum Perspectives, 28*(3), 37–47.

Cumming-Potvin, W. (2009). Social justice, pedagogy and multiliteracies: Developing communities of practice for teacher education. *Australian Journal of Teacher Education, 34*(1), 82–99.

Curriculum Council. (2010). *Curriculum framework*. Osborne Park, Australia: Curriculum Council.

Darling-Hammond, L. (2007). Evaluating no child left behind. *The Nation*. Retrieved July 5, 2011, from http://www.thenation.com/doc/20070521/darling-hammond/print?rel=nof

Dean, D., & Grierson, S. (2005). Re-envisioning reading and writing through combined-text picture books. *Journal of Adolescent & Adult Literacy, 48*(6), 456–469.

de Courcy, M. (2007). Disrupting preconceptions: Challenges to pre-service teachers' beliefs about ESL children. *Journal of Multilingual and Multicultural Development, 28*(3), 188–203.

Doecke, B., & Kostogriz, A. (2005). Teacher education and critical inquiry: The use of activity theory in exploring alternative understandings of language and literacy. *Australian Journal of Teacher Education, 30*(1), 15–24.

Eacott, S., Wilkinson, J., Blackmore, J., Lingard, B., & Rawolle, S. (2010). These puzzling times: A critical lens on educational leadership. Australian Association for Research in Education, *AARE 2010 International Education Research Conference – Melbourne, Australia.*

Ewing, R. (2006). Introduction: A need to move beyond the 'Reading Wars'. In R. Ewing (Ed.), *Beyond the reading wars: A balanced approach to helping children to learn to read* (pp. 1–6). Newton, Australia: Primary English Teachers' Association.

Freebody, P. (2004). Hindsight and foresight: Putting the four roles of reading to work in the daily business of teaching. In: A. Healy, E. Honan (Eds.) *New resources for literacy learning* (pp. 3–17). Newtown, NSW, PETA.

Freire, P. (1970). *Pedagogy of the oppressed*. New York: The Continuum International Publishing Group Inc.

Freire, P. (1985). *The politics of education: Culture, power and liberation*. South Hadley, Mass (USA)

Freire, P. (1994). *Pedagogy of hope*. London: Continuum.

Giroux, H. (1985). Critical pedagogy, Cultural politics and the discourses of exprerience. *Journal of Education, 167*(2), 22–41.

Giroux, H. (2004). *The terror of neoliberalism: Authoritarianism and the eclipse of Democracy*. Boulder, CO: Paradigm Publishers.

Giroux, H. (2007). Democracy, education and the politics of critical pedagogy. In P. McLaren & J. Kincheloe (Eds.), *Critical pedagogy: Where are we now?* (pp. 1–8). New York: Peter Lang.

Graham, B. (2003). *'Let's get a pup'*. London: Walker Books.

Healy, A. (2008). Expanding student capacities: Learning by design pedagogy. In E. A. Healy (Ed.), *Multiliteracies and diversity in education: New pedagogies for expanding landscapes* (pp. 2–29). Melbourne, Australia: Oxford University Press.

Hsiung, P.-C. (2008). Teaching reflexivity in qualitative interviewing. *Teaching Sociology, 36*(3), 211–226.

Jones, S., & Enriquez, G. (2009). Engaging the intellectual and the moral in critical *literacy* education: The four-year journeys of two teachers from teacher education to classroom practice. *Reading Research Quarterly, 44*(2), 145–169.

Jordan Irvine, J. (2004). Foreword. In M. Cochran Smith (Ed.), *Walking the road-race, diversity and social justice in teacher education* (pp. xi–xiv). New York: Teachers College Press.

Keddie, A., & Nayler, J. (2006). Pedagogy as discursive practice: Enabling spaces for social justice. *Curriculum Perspectives, 26*(3), 1–10.

Kincheloe, J. (2003). *Teachers as researchers: Qualitative inquiry as a path to empowerment.* New York: Routledge Farmer.

Kincheloe, J. (2008). *Knowledge and critical pedagogy.* Dordrecht, The Netherlands: Springer.

Lave, J., & Wenger, E. (1991). *Situated learning: Legitimate peripheral participation.* New York: Cambridge University Press.

Luke, A., & Carrington, V. (2002). Globalisation, literacy, curriculum practice. In R. Fisher, M. Lewis, & G. Books (Eds.), *Raising standards in literacy* (pp. 231–250). London: Routledge Falmer.

Luke, A., Comber, B., & Grant, H. (2003). Critical literacies and cultural studies. In G. Bull & M. Anstey (Eds.), *The literacy lexicon* (2nd ed., pp. 15–35). Frenchs Forest, Australia: Pearson Education.

Luke, A., & Freebody, P. (1999). A map of possible practices: Further notes on the resources model. *Practically Primary, 4*(2), 5–9.

Martino, W. (1999). 'Cool boys', 'party animals', 'squids' and 'poofters': Interrogating the dynamics and politics of adolescent masculinities in school. *British Journal of Sociology of Education, 20*(2), 239–264.

Martino, W., & Pallotta-Chiarolli, M. (2003). *So what's a boy? Addressing issues of masculinity and schooling.* Buckingham, UK: Open University Press.

McInerney, P. (2007). From naive optimism to robust hope: Sustaining a commitment to social justice in schools and teacher education in neoliberal times. *Asia-Pacific Journal of Teacher Education, 35*(3), 257–272.

Mclaren, P. (2003). Critical pedagogy: A look at the major concepts. In A. Darder, M. Baltodano, & R. D. Torres (Eds.), *The critical pedagogy reader* (pp. 69–96). New York: Routledge.

Merrett, C. (2004). Social justice: What is it? Why teach it? *Journal of Geography, 103*(3), 93–106.

Miller, S. (2008). Book walk: Works that move our teaching forward: "speaking" the walk, "speaking" . . . . *English Education, 40*(2), 145–154.

Ministerial Council on Education, Employment, Training and Youth Affairs (2008). *Melbourne declaration on educational goals for young australians.* Retrieved Feb 29, 2012, from www.mceecdya.edu.au.

Munsch, R. (2000). *Love you forever.* Sydney, Australia: Red Fox, Random House.

O'Brien, J. (2001). Children reading critically: A local history. In B. Comber & A. Simpson (Eds.), *Negotiating critical literacies in classrooms* (pp. 37–55). Mahwah, NJ: Lawrence Erlbaum Associates, Inc.

Oliver, R. (2006). Exploring a technology-facilitated solution to cater for advanced students in large undergraduate classes. *Journal of Computer Assisted Learning, 22*(1), 1–12.

Ping-Chun, H. (2008). Teaching reflexivity in qualitative interviewing. *Teaching Sociology, 36*(3), 211–226.

Philp, K. (2006). *Media release: English teaching in the twenty-first century is a highly complex endeavour.* Australian Association for the Teaching of English (AATE). Retrieved June 30, 2006, from htt://www.aate.org.au/media/releases0/response_english_april.html

Rout, M. (2011). Gillard was concerned schools prepared for NAPLAN tests. *The Australian* (published April 13, 2011).

Sleeter, C. (2001). Preparing teachers for culturally diverse schools: Research and the overwhelming presence of whiteness. *Journal of Teacher Education, 52*(2), 94–106.

Sleeter, C. E. (2008). Preparing white teachers for diverse students. In M. Cochran-Smith, S. Feiman-Nemser, & D. J. McIntyre (Eds.), *Handbook of research on teacher education: Enduring questions in changing contexts* (3rd ed., pp. 559–582). New York: Routledge.

The New London Group. (2000). A pedagogy of multiliteracies: Designing social futures. In B. Cope & M. Kalantzis (Eds.), *Multiliteracies: Literacy learning and the design of social futures* (pp. 9–39). South Yarra, Australia: MacMillan Publishers Australian Pty Ltd.

Wenger, E., Mc Dermott, R., & Snyder, W. (2002). *Cultivating communities of practice: A guide to managing knowledge.* Cambridge, USA: Harvard Business School Press.

# Chapter 15
# Performing 'Hope': Authentic Story, Change and Transformation in Teacher Education

Peter Wright

Teaching is always a performance. There are actors who are present, an audience—usually, but not always students—and most importantly a dynamic that exists between them; this relationship being key to successful pedagogy. In short, teaching is relational work. In the best of all possible worlds, this dynamic is a relationship that is forward looking, has dignity and characterised by hope. Zournazi (2002, p. 9) describes hope as 'a space for dialogue ... exchange ... [for] voices to be heard' and risks for encounters with others 'that create possibilities for change'. It is this possibility that is important for education in the way that inducts young people into a world that is not yet known or fully formed.

This chapter describes a project conducted with pre-service teachers where a hopeful project was conducted through a one-semester unit—Learning Through the Arts—delivered in an intensive summer mode each day over 2 weeks. Hope as a concept was enquired into, imagined and embodied, and through arts practices, insights into hope were gained; this project thereby becoming an example of arts relationality (Keifer-Boyd, 2011) and arts-based research (Barone & Eisner, 2011; Knowles & Cole, 2008).

Key to these processes were the notions of voice and agency foregrounding engagement, action and performativity (Wright, 2011), where the personal, social and cultural were inextricably linked, thereby reflecting the world in which we live and 'the sensuous acts of meaning making' (Willis & Trondman, 2000, p. 9) that flow from it. Denzin (2001), for example, draws attention to the way that as we live in a 'performance-based, dramaturgical culture' (p. 26) and that as 'we know the world only through our representations of it' (p. 23), projects such as this can exist as a 'form of radical democratic process' (p. 23) uncovering both power dynamics and socially constructed lived experience.

P. Wright (✉)
Arts Education and Research Methods, Murdoch University, Perth, Australia
e-mail: p.wright@murdoch.edu.au

B. Down and J. Smyth (eds.), *Critical Voices in Teacher Education*, Explorations of Educational Purpose 22, DOI 10.1007/978-94-007-3974-1_15,

In this project, pre-service teachers with little or no prior experience of the arts were inducted into a performance troupe, or ensemble, and participated in a process of deep listening to each other's stories that were then embodied and expressed. Following the great theatre maker, Augusto Boal (2006), this ensemble could be thought of as being both analogical and complementary—analogical in the way that students were similar, but not identical, and complementary in the way that their differences and individual elements were brought together for a common purpose. This work that this ensemble engaged in then was to both shape and then *express* communication beyond the rational and precise into the sensual and aesthetic reflecting the dynamic embodied way we live in the world.

Engagement through and the development of arts skills and processes led to the development of a tangible product—*Performing Hope,* the final performance. These skills and processes reflected a focus on emotion, a tolerance for ambiguity or not knowing, a cycle of enquiry and reflection, and connection with others. It is these distinct characteristics that provide a powerful model for an education that is authentic and responsive, and where we prepare young people 'to see things as if they could be otherwise' (Greene, 1995, p. 15).

Key to these processes are the ability to imagine, see alternatives, represent and interpret our world and integrate personal and shared understanding (Davis, 2008). In a context of neoliberal and neo-conservative education where experience is homogenised and reductive and human, social and cultural capital is reduced to the goal of keeping the economy competitive; these processes are key if a critical and democratic education is to succeed (Apple, 2011).

This project culminated in a public performance where 'hope' as an organising construct was enquired into, engaged with through arts practices, the results of these processes performed for the benefit of others there present, thereby enhancing understanding; the notion of hope being one key principle that imbued the project with particular qualities and being essential for education. The public performance then became in and of itself a manifestation of hope highlighting the way that communication even the production of language—usually thought of as a purely cognitive act—is an embodied experience, Merleau-Ponty (1962) highlighting the way that all lived experience is grounded in the body and its relation to situated contexts. Consequently, Hope was *performed,* constituted through the enactment both showing and doing—this enactment existing in contrast to more formal forms of education that rely merely on telling (Kincheloe, 1999). In this way, hope became more than an intellectual idea; it was illuminated from multi-perspectives and was *sense-making* rather than knowledge-giving through performance with its amplifying and social power.

The second key principle was the importance of the arts in human lives. This principle reflects the ways that the arts are natural, normal and necessary for humans to flourish (Dissanayake, 2007). Consequently, to deny young people an education that is through the arts, with the arts, in the arts and for the arts is to deny them some of the most fundamental ways of knowing, doing and becoming, thereby diminishing their capacity to be fully functioning citizens.

*Performing Hope* was a group-devised performance that grew out of student's authentic stories, 'hope' being the theme that united them in times of increasing global inequality. Key to this performance was the student's lived experiences themselves and the relationships that developed them. As in any group, there are resources present within members—both individually and collectively—that help shape who they are and, in part, determine who they will be. It is also the group notion that is important where the rampant individuation of a market-driven consumerist economy leads to feelings of isolation and loneliness (Zournazi, 2002).

The social pedagogic artful processes through which performance was devised were important at a number of levels, first, through a process of building community or, in performance terms, an ensemble where the goal was to create a performance piece *between* us. In this process, there was recognition of both difference and what unites us. For example, this particular group of students was made up of a soldier recently retired from active military duty and seeking to retrain as an educator, a young woman from the West Bank in Palestine who 'escaped' the trauma of conflict with her family hoping for a more peaceful life, a young Muslim woman from Somalia who hoped for better things for her family, other mature-age first-generation higher education students and some students straight from school. What united each of this disparate group was a commitment to education, including enrolling at university to further their own learning journeys in formal ways, and those seeking to train as educators with a commitment to others through teaching as a profession.

Specific drama practices facilitated this process, for example, getting-to-know-you exercises teach everything from turn taking to providing each person with an opportunity to be playful with ideas, or simply to move or speak thereby developing their communication abilities. These processes are important in the way that they model democracy and active citizenship and move participants into multi-modal ways of knowing and doing. This means that as a group, students intentionally move away from the purely cognitive or the cerebral, recognising that whatever sources of information we use and draw on are also mediated through our bodies. This significantly helps participants to not only *do* and *be* in different ways but also break down the Cartesian dualism that permeates so much of education. Consequently, *Performing Hope* was also an identity work.

The processes of building trust and a group dynamic were also critical to this work. Each of these processes are contingent on the skill of the 'teacher', part of which is to create safe boundaries around the work, to metaphorically 'hold' the group as it develops thereby facilitating risk taking and by modelling dialogic processes, mutual respect and understanding. As Ayers (2002, p. 40) highlights: 'teaching can be, must be if it is to maintain its moral balance, a gesture toward justice'. The adjunct to this process is the teacher removing himself or herself as the 'font' of all knowledge within the group—the group itself having expertise and latent abilities within it. Paulo Freire (1972, p. 67) describes this beautifully:

> Through dialogue the teacher-of-the-students and the students-of-the teacher cease to exist and a new term emerges: teacher-student and students-teachers. The teacher is no longer

merely 'the one-who-teaches', but one himself taught in dialogue with then students, who, inturn, while being taught, also teach. They become jointly responsible for a process in which all grow.

What this means is that a space is created for knowledge exchange, rather than knowledge transfer in the way one may 'pour' knowledge from a full vessel into an empty one. This 'third space' (Bhabha, 1994), as a place of transition 'betwixt and between' (Turner, 1967), is one rich with potential for learning (Cook-Sathe, 2006; Wright, 2002). When one works more as artist or maker of theatre giving shape and form to ideas, this process is clear. In short, the key to these successful practices lies in foregrounding dignity in the relationship building both responsibility to others and oneself.

The second key practice lies in recognising, enlisting and strengthening each individual's—and the groups—creative dispositions. For example, participants are taught how to improvise and freed to be playful in ways that are informal, fun and consensual.

Play has been described as an attitude of 'throwing off constraint...' (Millar, 1968, p. 21) which might be physical, social, emotional or intellectual. It is through play, for example, and its practices in drama as improvisation that possibilities for greater freedom, interactivity and creative possibilities are developed. These dispositions are in stark contrast to outcomes based on education driven by systemic standardised testing.

The influential improvisation teacher Viola Spolin (1999, p. 11) reveals the potential power of this work:

> In spontaneity, personal freedom is released, and the total person, physically, intellectually, and intuitively, is awakened. This causes enough excitation for the student to transcend himself or herself—he or she is freed to go out into the environment, to explore, adventure, and face all dangers unafraid... Every part of the person functions together as a working unit, one small organic whole within the larger organic whole of the agreed environment.

Greene (2001, p. 142) also describes how teaching is comprised of 'moments of improvisation'. It is in these moments that freedom, responsiveness, relationality, creative possibilities and 'freeing [of] the imagination' become hopeful and indeed critical projects. For example, through these processes, students break free of their own socially determined location, boundaries that constrain them, and open up a space for imaginary play, that is, for learning, improved communication, and to be 'actors' or have agency in their own lives (Wright, 2011). Following Boal (2006), creativity demands the invention of alternatives.

Notions of play in all of its meanings are synonymous with performance, most importantly in a space apart from Western everyday life and a mechanistic rational worldview. Play theorist Sutton-Smith (1997, p. 221) describes some important characteristics of play as being 'adaptive variability... [and] flexibility, not admirable precision'. In addition, Goffman (1971) also highlights the different roles we play in everyday life. What *Performing Hope* did then was to potentially expand participant's role repertoires and potential freedom to 'play' them, thereby providing greater choices and flexibility in facing unknown futures. As Greene

(2001, p. 29) highlights: 'the more we know the more we are likely to see and hear'; the corollary being, the more we see and hear from 'other' perspectives, the more we are likely to know. Consequently, in developing each student's personal, social and cultural agency (Wright, 2009, 2011), we are more likely to move beyond 'instructional instrumentalism' and towards 'subjective and social reconstruction' (Pinar, 2004, p. 24; Pinar, 2006, pp. 109–120).

It is playfulness that makes this shift in attitude possible where participants can step outside of and then manipulate systemic frames of reference through an impulse towards freedom and connection. This lies in contrast to a focus on immediate instrumental objectives so prevalent in contemporary education driven by goals, a culture of accountability, and inhibited by fear. In short, it is imaginative play that produces possibilities—both deconstruction and reconstruction—and the potential for transformation.

It is from these possibilities and through these arts practices where consensual participation was key that artefacts were developed, in the case of this project, *Performing Hope*. What this means, then, is that in a project such as this, it is not enough to simply teach 'skills' in an individualistic and instrumental way—following government rhetoric 'to get a job', for example, there must be the freedom for these to be used in generative, as opposed to reductive, ways. It is the somatic engagement of participant's authentic stories, and the enactment of these through arts skills and processes, that gives such projects a particular saliency revealing the way we are interrelated, interconnected and continually called on to be different.

In a processual and performative way, stories were elicited from the group which then became the 'texts' used both to inquire into an individual's experience and perform for the benefits of others. For example, the young Palestinian woman recounted the fear she felt huddled together with her family in a bomb shelter during an air strike, then the mixed feelings experienced as she left extended family to seek a more peaceful life in an unknown place—hope being juxtaposed against anxiety. Each of these 'moments' was represented by students in an embodied way through frozen moments (still image) or tableau (Neelands, 1990).

What this process does is to 'crystallise' and then represent the key feeling at that moment so that ideas can be visualised and themes and patterns revealed. These both amplify the 'felt' or sensate dimension of participant's experience and move them away from cognitions or intellectual ideas to the kinaesthetic engaging multi-modal ways of knowing and validating experience.

This process further recognises that we do not live in the world in a purely rational way; we respond to, and are influenced by our feelings. Consequently, an education that is content driven and primarily concerned with the transmission of facts is impoverished (Freire, 1972). Megan Boler in a play on words calls this 'feeling power' (1999). Hence, by way of contrast with this 'transmission' model, *Performing Hope* resonated with both participants and their audience because it was *of* their experience with credibility and authenticity being markers of quality and utility value.

Identifying what was 'key' for participants provided a strong focus for this arts-based enquiry so that it could become generative in nature. For example, students were challenged to move from an embodiment of a single moment to add a sound that evoked or gave voice to what this moment might be. For example, beginning from a frozen image expressing a student's fear, a second was asked to find a way to join in, both looking at what was 'offered', then responding to it in gesture then a sound that gave 'voice' to what she saw—this process both witnessing and validating this 'lived experience' and adding to it. The composite of this was a tableau that was both representative and expressive of this group's experiences individually and collaboratively, and a performance of it—in short, documenting and bearing testament to other ways of living and hoping.

The results of this 'embodied enquiry' (Todres, 2007) then became a soundscape that could be shaped, framed and edited, engaging different sensory modalities— each 'language', movement and stillness, sound and silence—providing tools for expression that were not English language, or even word, dependent. In Sontag's words: 'text is one stopping point along a continuum that can also include visual communication, music, dance, theatre, even silence' (1967). This meant that anyone in this group, no matter what his or her ability, could contribute.

Next, a movement was added to the growing performance. This process, warmed up to through image and sound, added greater depth through an 'offer' made to others. For example, seeing one person's movement both showed one persons' interpretation of a 'moment' but also provided an invitation to join in, elaborate or critique and contribute. Consequently, this form of embodied learning acts as critical pedagogy, for a knowing from the senses—visceral knowing—as critical in the 'Freirean' sense, moving from an often one-dimensional image of knowledge into the transactional.

Each level of this task also implies a larger 'risk' for many participants where there is a greater degree of 'visibility' and potential for self-disclosure. For many, this presence represents challenge. Consequently, these processes were modelled, scaffolded, stepwise, shared and supported and subsequently became more effortless as the group developed its own identity and confidence grew.

Importantly, each of these processes is generative, social and aesthetic with each leading on to the next and in turn generating other responses. What this reveals is how questions have more than one answer (Eisner, 1997) and how there are many ways of knowing; one important pedagogical principle being the way each offer made or idea embodied was accepted and considered as something to be further extended or elaborated. In this way, *Performing Hope* as an aesthetic event both draws participants into the world with its varied viewpoints whilst also refracting it through one's own subjectivity—here being art's educative potential through an awareness of difference. For example, Gordon (2007) highlights the way play can be both a reflective and reflexive process through neither losing one's self in the world nor completing retreating from it into one's own subjectivity. When play and art are linked, the educative significance of these often parallel processes is revealed. For example, in Greene's words: 'The world perceived from one place is not the world' (1995, p. 20).

Each moment that was offered and story as it was shared became a 'pre-text' (Haseman, 1991) to be shaped and framed towards performance, thereby building confidence and group identity through shared tasks and processes. In addition, each performance provided opportunities for reflection and critique thereby building up a sense of 'connoisseurship' (Eisner, 1977) amongst participants offering teaching moments that were present for all to see.

For the ex-soldier, this meant relating a story told to him by his grandfather who had been an ANZAC at Gallipoli during the First World War. This story was told as a monologue, the young man becoming his grandfather for this performance. The story, told with a mixture of terror, pathos and humour, enabled others to both be witness to his familial experience—one that was part of Australia's heritage and indeed shaped his own life journey—and his own courage performing for the first time in a theatrical way. One student, for example, made the observation that a digger's hat[1] would both communicate to an audience who he is and add to the context helping them locate 'where' he was as he recounted this tale. What this process also revealed was the further pedagogical principle of 'working for someone else's success' foregrounding the way that education, at its best, is an act of service.

The third poignant story was that of the Somalian women arriving in Australia having survived both trauma in her homeland and Australia's border protection policies. As this story was performed through image, sound and movement in non-discursive ways, we as an audience to these authentic stories were able to see a series of leavings and arrivals, each driven by hope and the fears and aspirations that were attributes and dimensions of it. This notion also resonated more broadly with the student group as for many the broad motivation present within them for engagement with education was consistent with the idea of leaving a life, or chapter of one's life behind, in order to realise hope.

A unifying thread that ran through the performance was the Greek myth of Prometheus. In this story, Prometheus, against the wishes of Zeus, brought fire from the sun to woman/mankind so that she/he may no longer live in darkness. The Prometheus story then became key and was used as a theatrical device to link individual's stories and provide a dynamic and emotional thread to the performance as a whole. Also in the way that story begets story, fire and light became generative key metaphors to this project and for education encapsulated through W. B. Yeats often quoted phrase 'Education is not filling a bucket, but lighting a fire'. For example, Leonard Cohen's 2001 song 'By the Rivers Dark' became the opening prelude to the performance.

Growing from this metaphor and located within contemporary culture was the story of Rosa Parkes, the African American woman whose act of protest in 1955 involved claiming her right to a seat on a bus in Alabama in preference to a white woman. This act of protest became a key moment in the American civil rights movement as others looked to her act of courage for inspiration, the US Congress referring to her as 'the first lady of civil rights' and 'the mother of the freedom

---

[1] A digger's hat, made from rabbit's fur with its fold-up sides and ceremonial ostrich feather plume, is the essence of an Australian soldier's uniform and distinctive identity.

movement'.[2] This notion of standing up for what you believe in, and not be relegated to a position constrained by established societal position, resonated with numerous project participants, many of whom came from homes as the first in their family to undertake higher education. Hence, social justice became a powerful theme explored through our performative enquiry and performance-making processes.

It is the aesthetic ways in which these stories were performed—making learning visible—that gave form to feeling and (re)presented in aesthetic ways that what might not easily be 'said' in others. For example, different forms of representation are both enabling and constraining, thereby broadening the sense-making processes and the meanings we attribute to them—using a different array of referents— enlarging rather than narrowing our understandings. *Performing Hope* gave form to feeling of person, place and situation; it was an expressive form in the service of understanding. In short, *Performing Hope* makes available through performative means—communicative arts practices—what cannot be known through other discursive forms thereby enlarging our understanding (Eisner, 2003).

In addition, knowing how someone feels provides connection and builds relationship, and developing the skills and knowledge required to express it honours experience. What is true in education is true in life; 'it is harder to hurt someone when you know their story' (Wright & Palmer, 2009), and when the arts are employed in this way, they become relational dialogic work—competencies critical for an education that is *artful* in being with others.

It is in these ways, where the arts are used both as a means for enquiry and a way to represent the results of that enquiry, that the arts become a heuristic making visible the complex ways that we interact with the world and what 'hope' might mean. Through these practices, we move beyond propositional forms of knowledge—the precise, quantifiable, prescriptive and formulaic—and towards evocative and empathic participation with some deep meanings in human life. Consequently, *Performing Hope* becomes a celebration of what makes us human through enacting qualities of experience, using aesthetic means to make visible what is not yet noticeable or fully formed—to see, to feel and to know—thereby bringing hope into being and moving beyond 'reproductionist thinking' (Flecha, 2011).

*Performing Hope* was also a political process, first, through the way that it provided a public space where people could speak and be heard, and second, in its processes. For example, public intellectual Susan Sontag (1987) underscores that contestation, candour and pluralism—fundamental democratic virtues—are essential elements in any artistic endeavour. Third, the project highlighted the way that arts processes revealed that what happens in schools impacts on the social context in an iterative way. Fourth, many participants reported that they were drawn to education in the hope of 'making a difference' both individually and collectively. A common word for this politicised educational process being 'consciousness raising', and consciousness as Greene (1995) reminds us, always includes creativity and the imagination.

---

[2]http://www.gpo.gov/fdsys/pkg/PLAW-106publ26/content-detail.html.

Consequently, cycles of enquiry, reflection and action become both political acts and reflect good pedagogy and enquiry. In addition, these processes themselves, *enquiry, engagement* and *reflection,* on an issue that validates the lived experience of participants are consistent with the tradition of critical participatory action research in the way that Finley (2003) notes grows out of an ethics of human relationship. It is these concerns and processes that make education 'more than measuring' through including *presence, openness* and *flexibility.* In addition, they help us better understand the 'artfulness' of good teaching where the qualities of being a good teacher and good at teaching are understood to be in relationship with each other requiring constant awareness, responsiveness and adjustment (Flecha, 2011).

Finally, R.S. Peters, an English philosopher, described education as an attitude to be carried with you rather than a score to be achieved. In his words: 'to be educated is not to have arrived at a destination; it is to travel with a different view' (1967, p. 8). Consequently, encapsulated within a final multi-media montage of images and sound were the project participant's thoughts, wishes and aspirations for the future including 'there is always hope', that 'with hope anything is possible' and that 'hope is the dream of a soul awake'. It is this final sentiment that powerfully links the role of the arts with education and is captured in the description by Maxine Greene as a 'wide awakeness' or enlivening the senses in the service of learning (Greene, 2001). This enlivening, in contrast to anaesthetising or dulling the senses, is a hopeful project with rich metaphors and symbolic languages providing new ways of wondering about ourselves and our world.

# References

Apple, M. W. (2011). Democratic education in neoliberal and neoconservative times. *International Studies in Sociology of Education, 21*(1), 21–31.

Ayers, W. (2002). Creating the teacher and changing the world. In E. Mirochnik & D. C. Sherman (Eds.), *Passion and pedagogy: Relation, creation, and transformation in teaching* (pp. 37–51). New York: Peter Lang.

Barone, T., & Eisner, E. W. (2011). *Arts based research.* Los Angeles: Sage.

Bhabha, H. K. (1994). *The location of culture.* London: Routledge.

Boal, A. (2006). *The aesthetics of the oppressed* (A. Jackson, Trans.). London: Routledge.

Boler, M. (1999). *Feeling power: Emotions and education.* New York: Routledge.

Cook-Sather, A. (2006). Newly betwixt and between: Revising liminality in the context of a teacher education program. *Anthropology and Education Quarterly, 37,* 110–127.

Davis, J. H. (2008). *Why our schools need the arts.* New York: Teachers College Press.

Denzin, N. K. (2001). The reflexive interview and a performative social science. *Qualitative Research, 1*(1), 23–46.

Dissanayake, E. (2007). Pleistocene and infant aesthetics. In L. Bresler (Ed.), *International handbook of research in arts education* (pp. 783–798). Dordrecht, The Netherlands: Springer.

Eisner, E. W. (1977). On the use of educational connoisseurship and educational criticism for the evaluation of classroom life. *Teachers College Record, 78*(3), 325–388.

Eisner, E. W. (1997). The promise and perils of alternative forms of data representation. *Educational Researcher, 26*(6), 4–10.

Eisner, E. W. (2003). Concerns and aspirations for qualitative research in the new millennium. In N. Addison & L. Burgess (Eds.), *Issues in art and design teaching* (pp. 52–60). London: Routledge Falmer.

Finley, S. (2003). Arts-based inquiry in QI: Seven years from crisis to guerrilla warfare. *Qualitative Inquiry, 9,* 281–296.

Flecha, R. (2011). The dialogic sociology of education. *International Studies in Sociology of Education, 21*(1), 7–20. doi:10.1080/09620214.2011.543849.

Freire, P. (1972). *Pedagogy of the oppressed* (M. Ramos, Trans.). Harmondsworth, UK: Penguin Education.

Goffman, E. (1971). *The presentation of self in everyday life.* London: Penguin.

Gordon, G. (2007). *What is play? In search of a universal definition.* Retrieved January 17, 2010, from www.gwengordonplay.com/pdf/what_is_play.pdf.

Greene, M. (1995). *Releasing the imagination: Essays on education, the arts, and social change.* San Francisco: Jossey-Bass.

Greene, M. (2001). *Variations on a blue guitar: The Lincoln centre institute lectures on aesthetic education.* New York: Teachers College Press.

Haseman, B. (1991). Improvisation, process drama and dramatic art. *The Drama Magazine – The Journal of National Drama* (July), 19–21.

Keifer-Boyd, K. (2011). Arts-based research as social justice activism. *International Review of Qualitative Research, 4*(1), 3–20.

Kincheloe, J. L. (1999). Cultivating post-formal intra/interpersonal intelligence: Cooperative learning critically considered. In S. R. Steinberg, J. L. Kincheloe, & P. H. Hinchey (Eds.), *The post-formal reader: Cognition and education* (pp. 313–328). New York: Falmer Press.

Knowles, J. G., & Cole, A. L. (Eds.). (2008). *Handbook of the arts in qualitative research.* Thousand Oaks, CA: Sage.

Merleau-Ponty, M. (1962). *The phenomenology of perception* (C. Smith, Trans.). London: Routledge & Kegan Paul.

Millar, S. (1968). *The psychology of play.* Harmondsworth, UK: Penguin.

Neelands, J. (1990). *Structuring drama work.* Cambridge, UK: Cambridge University Press.

Pinar, W. F. (2004). *What is curriculum theory?*. Mahwah, NJ: Lawrence Erlbaum.

Pinar, W. F. (2006). *The synoptic text today and other essays: Curriculum development after the reconceptualization.* New York: Peter Lang.

Peters, R. S. (1967). *The concept of education.* London: Routledge and Kegan Paul.

Sontag, S. (1967). The aesthetics of silence. *Aspen no. 5+6, item 3.* Retrieved August 17, 2007, from http://www.ubu.com/aspen/aspen5and6/threeEssays.html#sontag.

Sontag, S. (1987). *A Susan Sontag reader.* Harmondsworth, UK: Penguin.

Spolin, V. (1999). *Improvisation for the theatre: A handbook of teaching and directing techniques* (3rd ed.). Evanston, IL: Northwestern University Press.

Sutton-Smith, B. (1997). *The ambiguity of play.* Cambridge, MA: Harvard University Press.

Todres, L. (2007). *Embodied enquiry: Phenomenological touchstones for research, psychotherapy and spirituality.* Basingstoke, UK: Palgrave MacMillan.

Turner, V. (1967). Betwixt and between: The liminal period in rites de passage. In V. Turner (Ed.), *The forest of symbols: Aspects of Ndembu ritual.* Ithaca, NY: Cornell University Press.

Willis, P., & Trondman, M. (2000). Manifesto for ethnography. *Ethnography, 1*(1), 5–16.

Wright, P. R. (2002). Playing 'betwixt' and 'between' learning and healing. Playback Theatre for a troubled world. In B. Rasmussen & A. Ostern (Eds.), *The IDEA dialogues 2001* (pp. 140–149). Bergen, Norway: International Drama Education Association.

Wright, P. R. (2009). Teaching in arts education. In L. J. Saha & A. G. Dworkin (Eds.), *International handbook of research on teachers and teaching* (pp. 1049–1060). New York: Springer.

Wright, P. R. (2011). Agency, intersubjectivity and drama education: The power to be and do more. In S. Schonmann (Ed.), *Key koncepts in theatre/drama education* (pp. 111–115). Rotterdam, The Netherlands: Sense Publishers.

Wright, P. R., & Palmer, D. (2009). Big *h*ART at John Northcott estate: Community, health and the arts. *The UNESCO Observatory, Refereed E-Journal. Multi-Disciplinary Research in the Arts, 1*(4). Retrieved from http://www.abp.unimelb.edu.au/unesco/ejournal/vol-one-issue-four.html

Zournazi, M. (2002). *Hope: New philosophies for change.* London: Routledge.

# Chapter 16
# A Socially Critical HPE (aka Physical Education) and the Challenge for Teacher Education

**Richard Tinning**

## Introduction

In the 1960s I trained as a physical education (PE) teacher at the University of Melbourne. Trained was the operative word. It was a training of the body and was heavily influenced by military-inspired pedagogies. What constituted PE itself seemed rather straightforward. But of course it was not and, like all school subject areas, PE has been shaped by contestation and power struggles (see Goodson, 1992). Over its history what stands for PE has been the result of ongoing tensions between the discourses of health, the military, nationalism, fitness and sport.

Forty years on, much of what stands for PE in schools has changed considerably. While still doing pedagogical work on physical activity, the body and health, the emphasis has changed as educational and societal contexts have changed. Currently, it is the discourse of health that is being privileged in PE. For example, in Australia, the 'new' HPE learning area has placed the pursuit of good health at the centre of focus. For example, according to the Queensland HPE Syllabus for years 1–10 (Queensland School Curriculum Council, 1999, p. 1):

> The key learning area provides a foundation for developing active and informed members of society, capable of managing the interactions between themselves and their social, cultural and physical environments in the *pursuit of good health.* (emphasis added)

Nowadays, in Australia and New Zealand, it makes no sense to talk about PE (in government schools at least) independent of health. Indeed, in both countries, the official curriculum area is called Health and Physical Education (HPE). However, combining physical education with health education seems to be a peculiarly Antipodean 'initiative', and PE still exists as a separate subject to health education

R. Tinning (✉)
School of Human Movement Studies, University of Queensland, Queensland, Australia

School of Critical Studies in Education, University of Auckland, Auckland, New Zealand
e-mail: rit@hms.uq.edu.au

B. Down and J. Smyth (eds.), *Critical Voices in Teacher Education*, Explorations
of Educational Purpose 22, DOI 10.1007/978-94-007-3974-1_16,
© Springer Science+Business Media Dordrecht 2012

in most other countries of the world (see Pühse & Gerber, 2006). In the UK, for example, the National Curriculum for PE includes no health education. Moreover, in the country that invented rugby, PE is still seen, both officially and in practice, mainly as sports and games. However, while nationalist and sport discourses dominate in the UK, there is, nevertheless, an implicit assumption that increased involvement in sports and games with make for a healthier nation state. The link is more explicit in many Asian countries (e.g. Singapore, Hong Kong, Taiwan) where school PE, although not including health education, is increasingly focused on the development of fitness with the assumption that fitter children will be healthier children.

According to contemporary Australian curriculum documents, HPE teachers have a 'responsibility to [teach] the socially critical liberal curriculum as defined by the State' (Macdonald & Kirk, 1999 p. 140). The HPE Curriculum Statement (Curriculum Council, 1994), on which various state curriculum documents have been developed, clearly articulates the principles of diversity, social justice and supportive environments as underpinning the HPE curriculum. The New Zealand HPE curriculum is underpinned by a similar logic.

As a long-time advocate of the socially critical curriculum (e.g. Tinning, 1987) and as an advocate for educative rather than instrumental purposes of physical education (e.g. Tinning, 1997), I should be delighted with the intent of these new HPE curricula. My enthusiasm for the new curricula is, however, somewhat measured. While they do offer new opportunities for physical education, they also present considerable challenges for teacher education.

In this chapter, I discuss some of the tensions and dilemmas that confront physical education teacher education (known as PETE) while recognising that the acronym should be (H)PETE. However, this is a new conceptualisation is not shared by many other countries so I will continue to use PETE. Within this chapter, I will refer mainly to the Australian and New Zealand context, recognising of course that, though the specifics might be different, there are some more general issues relating to teacher education for PE that tend to be recognisable across most countries.

In particular, I discuss the type of subject matter content knowledge that typically underpins such programmes and the significance of the body as a defining feature in identity making for those who choose HPE as their teaching area. In the face of conceptions of education as human capital and the juggernaut of increased prescription regarding competencies and standards, I contend that it is how HPE teachers *think* and *feel* about education, social justice, physical activity, bodies and health that will be their most important graduate attribute. In this regard, I offer a modest critical pedagogy as a way to develop emotional commitment to the socially critical project.

## Health and Human Capital

How we think about HPE must be located in the context of major contemporary educational and health discourses. Currently, in Australia, our educational system is charged with the task of educating for a 'clever country' in which future citizens are multi-skilled, competent with information technology, literate and numerate in order that they play a productive part in a globalised economy. Education is increasingly conceptualised and driven by a logic underpinned by 'a now internationally rampant vision of schooling, teaching and learning based solely on systemic efficiency at the measurable technical production of human capital' (Luke, 2002, p. 1). In addition, citizens of our 'clever country' should also be healthy citizens who are self-regulating, informed, critically reflective and capable of constructing their own healthy lifestyle and minimising risky behaviours. Healthy citizens are good human capital, they are more productive and they make fewer demands on health services.

We live in a social context that gives unprecedented attention to the body (see Petersen, 1997), to sport and physical activity (see Greneau, 1997) and to health (Lupton, 1995). Indeed, fitness, as one specific potential outcome of sport and physical activity, is now widely promoted as an opportunity to create the body you want and avert certain health risks. It is in this contemporary social context that HPE must teach students to manage their lifestyle such that health risks are avoided or reduced. Indeed, risk identification and management is a key tenet in the conception of 'the new public health' (Petersen & Lupton, 1996) underpinning contemporary HPE in Australia and New Zealand. HPE as a learning area is central to the mission of 'making' the healthy citizen (Tinning & Glasby, 2002). However, as corporate pedagogues (Steinberg & Kincheloe, 1997) and market logic (Kenway & Bullen, 2001) become increasingly influential in the lives of young people, the potential of HPE to realise this mission (deliver on its stated outcomes) becomes increasingly difficult.

Thinking about the work of HPE teachers as 'making' certain types of citizens is certainly not new. The purpose of the drill and mass exercises that characterised PE in the early twentieth century was explicitly to 'make' docile and healthy children (Kirk, 1993; Lawson, 1984). What is new within the Australian and New Zealand context, however, is the relatively recent (circa early 1990s) construction of the learning area of HPE which subsumes the previously separate subjects of health education, physical education, home economics and outdoor education within a framework that is underpinned by an explicit commitment to a social view of health and a socially critical orientation (Macdonald, Hunter, Carlson, & Penny, 2002).

The new HPE curriculum, the conditions of contemporary schooling and the nature of postmodern youth culture have meant that traditional ways of *doing* PE in Australia and New Zealand and of *being* a PE teacher are now unacceptable. The PE teacher is now the HPE teacher, and it is the responsibility of PETE to prepare them for this new reality.

## A Socially Critical Curriculum for HPE

As mentioned above, the new socially critical Australian and New Zealand HPE curriculum is a curriculum reform that offers a challenge to some of the taken-for-granted beliefs of many teachers of physical education. In a recent interview with an experienced head of an HPE department at a large Australian metropolitan high school, when asked what she considered to be the most frequent issues that she had to deal with as a teacher in HPE, her reply was 'relationships, peer pressure and sex'. She said issues relating to pregnancy, the pill, breakups with boyfriends, negotiating and mediating peer group disputes, etc. were dominant. In her words, 'HPE teachers are often the interface between kids and their parents in matters relating to personal development in general and sexuality education in particular'. Accordingly, Glover and Macdonald (1997, p. 24) contend that

> Tertiary programs [in (H)PETE] need to consider the increasing demands being placed on teachers with respect to broader health and social concerns of young people such as drug use, harmful drinking, child abuse, youth suicide and traffic safety to name just a few, but which require a multi-disciplinary input as suggested by the [HPE curriculum].

The contemporary HPE curriculum opens up the space for such issues to be engaged. Moreover, the new HPE curriculum expects that students will achieve outcomes related to personal development and health education *in addition* to physical activity and movement. For teachers who are interested primarily in teaching about sport and physical activity, this expectation to teach personal development and health education might be a serious challenge to their notion of what their job as a HPE teacher should be.

Underpinned by a social view of health (rather than a biological view) in which both the individual (agent) and the social structures have responsibilities and in which health is seen to be multidimensional including physical, mental, emotional and spiritual dimensions, the new socially critical HPE curriculum is at odds with the taken-for-granted beliefs of many PE teachers.

Significantly, the 'new' HPE curriculum is based on a view of health that challenges how many PE teachers think about health. For example, for many PE teachers, health is seen merely as a 'natural' by-product of participation in sports and games. The unquestioned assumption that sport and exercise = fitness = health is part of a cluster of beliefs that Crawford (1980) has called healthism. According to Crawford, healthism describes the tendency for health problems to be defined as essentially individual problems; that is, the individual is solely responsible for his/her own health. Moreover, in healthism, body shape is seen as a metaphor for health, and it is through the physical that health is manifest. These beliefs are compatible with the traditional PE conception of health as essentially biological and individualistic. It is therefore not surprising that Kirk and Colquhoun (1989) claim that healthism is the dominant ideology with PE and the broader field of human movement studies (HMS) and exercise science.

## Resistance

Glover and Macdonald (1997) found that some student teachers resisted the integrated nature of the HPE learning area. They argue that the possibility of resistance and knowledge disavowal (Ennis, 1994) by teachers who are not favourably disposed to the underpinning ideas of the curriculum must be seriously considered. It must also be recognised that there are some teachers who, although committed to the values of a socially critical curriculum and active advocates for social justice, nonetheless remain uncommitted to the logic of the integration of PE and health in the HPE learning area.

Glover and Macdonald (1997) suggest that this might be explained by the student teachers' relative lack of knowledge and understanding of the content, concepts and underpinning principles of the learning area, in particular those related to personal development, a social view of health and a critical orientation towards physical education. Significantly, Glover and Macdonald found that for most prospective HPE teachers, their primary area of interest was in physical activity and not with the other strands of the learning area.

Typically, contemporary HPE teacher education programmes now teach content and concepts previously found more commonly in health education courses (such as a social view of health, mental health and sexuality). This curriculum offers a considerable challenge to many student teachers that have come into these programmes expecting to find reinforcement of the things they already value. Accordingly, attempts to date by teacher educators to introduce HPE student teachers to some of the ideas and principles of the socially critical curriculum by means of critical pedagogy have been less than enthusiastically received (see, e.g. Gore, 1990; Macdonald & Brooker, 1999; Tinning, 2002). It seems that without a certain level of emotional commitment (Giddens, 1991) to the values underpinning the socially critical HPE curriculum, the success of teacher education will be marginal (Dowling, 2008).

In contemporary (H)PETE programmes, students are often also challenged by a critical perspective towards competitive sport. The story of Guillem, published in the *European Physical Education Review* (Vol. 5(2), 1999), provides a powerful example of how students can resist what challenges them. Pepe Devís-Devís, a teacher educator in Valencia, Spain, set a number of books for his PETE students to read. One expressed a liberal view of sport, another a subjective and participatory view of an athlete and the third a more socially critical perspective on sport in society. On reading *Sport, A Prison of Measured Time,* J.M. Brohm's (1978) classic Marxist analysis of sport, Guillem, a student who was described as having a strong athletic identity, was so challenged that he experienced a serious identity crisis. As he admitted, 'sport is my way of being and on this I have built my life', and after reading the book, he said 'I didn't feel happy with myself. I knew that [the reading] had subconsciously left me devastated' (Devís-Devís & Sparkes, 1999, p. 139). As a symbolic reaction to this crisis, Guillem actually burnt the book as an act of resistance and denial. Of course, many people may first resist that which challenges their cherished beliefs as a first stage in coming to change. The issue with Guillem was the severity of his resistance and the consequential emotional response. It exposes the power of identity in the PE teacher's life.


## Identity, the Body and Becoming a (H)PE Teacher

The late Garth Boomer was once reported as saying that 'you teach who you are'. While obviously an oversimplification, there is a strong strand of common sense in the statement. Who we are (our identity, our self) is integrally connected with our practices as teachers and teacher educators. Wexler (1992) argued some time ago that for young people, schooling is essentially about 'becoming somebody'. It is about constructing identity or rather constructing some new identities that offer a reinforcing space in which to be somebody. In their classic *Boys in White*, Becker et al. (1961) revealed how medical students take on the identity of doctors while they are in medical school. And so it is with teachers. For the student teacher, life is also a process of becoming (a teacher) in which identity making is a key feature.

But identity is not something constructed and then just polished up and finished. Rather, it is constitutive of the reflexive project of the self and it is constantly in process (Giddens, 1991). McLaren (1998) points out that identity formation is taking on new meanings in these 'postmodern times'. For example, as Kenway (1998) has noted, the biographical project of the self (becoming somebody) in postmodernity has become so strongly attached to the market that it is difficult to find an identity outside of it.

For HPE teachers in particular, one of the most significant manifestations of this market influence in the postmodern context is the increasing commodification of the body and physical activity (Tinning & Glasby, 2002). Given the centrality of the body to postmodern identity making and to life politics (Giddens, 1991; Shapiro, 2002), the making of HPE teacher identity exemplifies the 'spectre of life politics' (Shapiro, 2002) that haunts contemporary life. Moreover, it is at times difficult to 'distinguish life-political questions concerning self-identity from those that focus more specifically on the body' (Giddens, 1991, p. 217).

This is a complex 'space', and according to Kenworth-Teather (1999), the '[b]ody and self are inextricably folded within each other. Rather than a unity of body and self there is a doubling: an *embodied self*' (p. 9). Perhaps this observation has even more purchase for the identity of HPE teachers. The thesis advanced here is that as 'the politics of identity is increasingly wrapped around configurations of the body' (Elliott, 2001, p. 99), prospective HPE teachers' engagement with the ideas of the new HPE curriculum will be influenced by their embodied identities. A significant dimension of their teacher identity is shaped by the central place that physical activity, sport and the body plays in their daily lives. Understanding the role played by teachers' embodied identities is a significant issue in HPE teacher education.

## Who Becomes a (H)PE Teacher?

Regardless of whether or not PE is a stand-alone subject (as it is in the UK and most states of the USA) or part of HPE (as it is in Australia and New Zealand), its teachers have been found to have relatively similar discursive histories with respect to the central place that physical activity, sport and the body plays in their identity construction (Macdonald & Kirk, 1996; Templin & Schempp, 1989). Moreover, maintaining a physically active lifestyle is central to the identity of many PE teachers (e.g. Sparkes, 1999). To a certain extent, their identity as a PE teacher is based on their embodied identities as practical 'doers', physical activity seekers.

However, there is also evidence that many PE teachers are insensitive to social issues, elitist, sexist, 'pragmatic sceptics' and anti-intellectual (Dewar, 1989; Macdonald et al., 2002). Clearly this profile raises real concerns as to the extent to which such teachers will share an emotional commitment to the values that underpin the contemporary socially critical liberal HPE curriculum. Working with the possible tensions between student teachers' dispositions and emotional commitments and those underpinning a socially critical teacher education remains a significant challenge for teacher educators committed to the critical project.

While there are numerous reasons why young people might choose to pursue a career in the teaching PE, one significant factor is that they tend to be active 'mesomorphs' who enjoy sport and physical activity. A mesomorph is someone with a body type that is stocky, muscular and athletic. A career in PE is seen as a way to continue to be involved in the things they enjoy doing. It is compatible with their developed sporting *habitus* (Hunter, 2004).

According to Brown (1999), because HPE teachers have 'long-term personal investments into the dominant masculine arenas of PE and sport, their identities are strongly engrained with these characteristics by the time they begin Initial Teacher Training' (p. 155). Part of that culture is 'transmitted' by/through one's body. PE teachers communicate through their mesomorphic physical selves without saying a word, and conceptions of 'the good teacher' carry bodily judgments. For example, there is a strong historical legacy influencing what it means to be a good PE teacher. This legacy is represented in the expectation that 'one must, literally, look the part – mesomorphic, able-bodied, physically capable and physically fit' (Macdonald & Kirk, 1999. p. 132). Moreover, whether PE teachers like it or not, their lifestyle and their bodies are constantly under surveillance by the community and the students alike (Macdonald & Kirk, 1996).

While attributing personality characteristics to physical attributes has been around since the ancient Greeks and Romans ('Yon Cassius, he has a lean and hungry look; he thinks too much; such men are dangerous'[Julius Caesar]), care is needed in accepting such generalisations. Determinism can be a slippery slope. However, Hargreaves (1986) captures something of the history of sentiment towards mesomorphs when he reports that they are more likely 'to be unsympathetic to those who are perceived to be thin, fat or physically incompetent and are more likely to be conformist and authoritarian' (p. 170). Further, he suggests that 'the mesomorphic image resonates strongly with ideologically conservative notions concerning achievement, drive and dynamism, discipline, conformity, cleanliness, efficiency, good adjustment, manliness and femininity' (p. 170). Mesomorphism as ideology (Tinning, 1990) accepts muscularity and a toned body as 'good' and assumes that such a body shape actually represents control, efficiency, discipline and health.

Such characteristics, traits and dispositions are certainly not compatible with the principles of social justice, supportive environments and diversity that underpin the socially critical Australian and New Zealand HPE curriculum. Having said this, I hasten to add that there are many HPE teachers who are exceptions to the PE teacher caricature. However, if we take a system-wide view, the image of the PE teacher is not a positive one. Like it or not, the active mesomorph with a sporting habitus is going to continue to be the dominant group in all HPE teacher education programmes.

The challenge, therefore, is to use pedagogies that critique and disrupt the taken-for-granted assumptions and beliefs that tend to be associated with such a sporting habitus. Just because young people come into PETE programmes with particular dispositions, values and embodied histories with regard to their bodies, health, sport and physical activity does not mean that they cannot change.

## Possibilities for Change

To facilitate such change, I have been a long-time advocate of critical pedagogy within physical education teacher education (see Tinning, 1987). But critical pedagogy is no panacea and certainly has been subjected to considerable critique over the past few decades (e.g. Biesta, 1998). These criticisms have been concerned with both practical and conceptual issues. As Buckingham (1998) makes clear however, critical pedagogy has come under attack not just from the conservative Right but also from many feminists and others on the educational Left who might be expected to share similar political agendas to the critical pedagogues. In this category are the powerful critiques of Ellsworth (1989), Lather (1989, 1998), Gore (1993), Kenway (1989) and Luke and Gore (1992). However, while cognizant of the dangers of using categories such as Left and Right (see Giddens, 1994), the fact that critical pedagogy has been critiqued by many of its (earlier) advocates is, in my view, a healthy sign for those still committed to a social reconstructivist education.

Reflecting on her own experiences, Kohli (1998, p. 515) speaks clearly of the limitations of critical pedagogy:

> As more of us extolled the virtues of critical pedagogy we came up against its limitations, including its reliance on 'rational dialogue' ... It became clearer and clearer to me that one did not change deeply held political, social, and philosophical positions simply by acquiring new knowledge or new perspectives through conversations with others.

In this regard, I find myself drawn to Gur-Ze'ev's (1998) argument for a more sceptical, less utopian 'counter education that does not promise collective emancipation' (cited in Kohli, 1998, p. 517). As I will show below, such a concept is at the heart of my notion of 'modest critical pedagogy'.

The passion of countless critical pedagogues has been fuelled by what Giddens (1991) called 'emancipatory politics'. Emancipatory politics is ' ... a generic outlook concerned above all with liberating individuals and groups from constraints which adversely affect their life chances ... Emancipatory politics is concerned to reduce or eliminate exploitation, inequality and oppression' (Giddens, 1991, pp. 210–211). Significantly, however, this is not a politics that is central to the life of most of the student teachers of HPE (Tinning, 2004). For them, the discourse of emancipatory politics has never been dominant. Concepts such as conscientisation, ideology and emancipation were relatively unknown (at least at the professional level) to young physical education teachers of the 1970s, 1980s and 1990s. Physical education teachers (and HPE teachers) have arguably been more concerned with matters of lifestyle than with matters of life chances. Their interests are probably best described as reflecting a 'life politics' agenda. 'Life politics does not primarily concern the conditions which liberate us in order to make choices: it is a politics *of* choice' (Giddens, 1991, p. 214).

Some student teachers of HPE in Australia come to their course with an emotional commitment that might be said to be coherent with a socially critical agenda. For such students, there is a real possibility of making a 'connection'. For others (perhaps the majority), the intellectual rationale for a socially critical curriculum and a reconceptualist vision of schooling are insufficient to change their opinion or their practice. In this regard, according to Giddens (1991, p. 38), '[c]ognitive frames of meaning ... will not provide the sense of security in the coherence of day-to-day life unless there is a "corresponding level of emotional commitment"'.

For some HPE student teachers, engaging the socially critical perspective agenda of the HPE curriculum and critical pedagogy might confront their deep emotional commitment to their particular point of view or way of seeing the world. Macdonald and Kirk (1999), for example, found that for some committed Christian students studying to become the HPE teachers, the health 'content' they were required to teach (e.g. such issues as STD prevention, abortion and sexuality) represented a serious challenge to their belief system. This 'clash of belief systems' represented a serious emotional challenge for many of these students. It destabilised their ontological security (Giddens, 1991) and also created a particular challenge for the HPE teacher educators.

Giddens (1991) argues that in contemporary times the self 'is seen as a reflexive project for which the individual is responsible. We are, not what we are, but what we make ourselves' (p. 75). But this is not a simple task. Moreover, since the reflexive project calls for the 'ongoing reconstruction' of our identities, our ontological security may be threatened. Ontological security is important. If we need a reminder that unintended pedagogical work of critical pedagogy can have damaging effect on our ontological security, the story mentioned above of Spanish PE teacher educator José Devís-Devís and his student Guillem provides a powerful example.

We certainly need to be very careful of using pedagogical encounters that embarrass or degrade students' values, choices and commitments. As a result of their research into popular culture, schooling and young people, Kenway and Bullen (2001) argue that 'students do not tend to appreciate teachers [or professors] who make them feel ashamed about their choices and lifestyles all in the name of helping them' (p. 165). Indeed, 'deconstruction may have an emotional fallout' (ibid.). With similar sentiment about the limits of critique, Crowdes (2000) claims that in many classes in which critical pedagogies are used, students 'are often left with their fairly extensive sociological vocabularies and socially aware minds detached from their bodies and agency in matters of conflict resolution and change' (p. 25). Accordingly, she argues for the use of pedagogic strategies that join somatic and sociological perspectives. In both school HPE and in PETE programmes more generally, when we do engage in critical pedagogies, it is usually rather strong in the sociological and rather weak in the somatic.

## A Preference for Certainty in an Uncertain World

A troubling reality underpinning the difficulty of providing a socially critical teacher education for HPE is that student teachers of HPE have been shown to have an aversion for the 'uncertain' knowledge of the social sciences (Macdonald & Brooker, 1999). Students schooled in anatomy, exercise physiology and biomechanics seek certainty, prefer facts and 'black or white' answers and are often uncomfortable with ambiguity and questions without simple answers. Since they must eventually work in schools with children and youth who are both biological and social beings, who live in both nature and culture simultaneously and for whom most pressing issues relate to the personal and the social, the science-based knowledge and their quest for certainty will often let them down.

For many student teachers, the rhetoric surrounding learning outcomes (in schools and universities) promises a ' . . . semblance of order, control, and certainty compared with the uncertainty and unpredictability to [sic] the world of teaching' (Smyth & Dow, 1998, p. 301). However, as Giddens (1991), Beck (1992), Bauman (2001) and many others argue, there is a crisis of legitimation both in terms of knowledge and the institutions of authority, and as a consequence, certainty is illusory in contemporary times. This has particular purchase for teacher education. While it is the case that the certainty of foundational knowledge that represents the disciplines, what Shulman (1986) called subject matter content knowledge, is increasingly challenged, there is even less certainty available in 'spaces' of curriculum content knowledge and pedagogical content knowledge. Accordingly, both the teacher educator and the student teacher alike must learn to live with uncertainty.

Kohli (1998) draws attention to the fact that the search for the 'clear and the distinct' which is underpinned by a notion of 'certainty' and 'perfect order' involves 'the separating out of the emotional, the sensuous, the imaginative' (p. 515). It involves a privileging of rationality as *the* way to emancipation. While the student teachers of HPE might privilege rationality as a result of their own experiences in coming to know the body through science, their orientation to life politics rather than emancipatory politics raises special challenges for teacher educators like myself who attempt to engage them in pedagogies that operate from a socially critical perspective. Zigmut Bauman's (2001, p. 125) words are apposite in regard to future HPE teachers:

> ... [i]f they expect to find a cohesive and coherent structure in the mangle of contingent events, they are in for costly errors and painful frustrations. If the habits acquired in the course of training prompt them to seek such cohesive and coherent structures and make their actions dependent on finding them – they are in real trouble.

## Thinking More Modestly

In response to some of these concerns, I found myself drawn to John Law's (1994) concept of a 'modest sociology'. Law is nervous of the 'the ordered society' but eager to understand the process of 'ordering modernity'. His modest sociology appeals to my nervousness with claims to certainty in the social world and to my reservations about some of the less modest, less self-disclosing accounts of social theory that have been appropriated in educational discourse. In my view, sustaining a partisan commitment to the social reconstructivist project while avoiding the folly of believing that we have *the* pedagogical solution is a considerable challenge. We need to be *modest* in our claims for what can be achieved in the critical classroom and gymnasium, and we should seek to develop forms of pedagogy that are more modest than certain.

The notion of a modest critical pedagogy is not intended to be a 'solution' to the criticisms levelled at critical pedagogy or a solution to the dilemmas of teacher education. It is more of an *orienting way of thinking* about what claims we can make in the name of teacher education pedagogies that might work for the social reconstructivist education project. Importantly, while there would be many forms of a modest critical pedagogy (just as there are critical pedago*gies*), they would share a certain circumspect disposition in their claims to know. They would not assume that there is a set of pedagogical procedures that, when found (discovered or invented), will lead to certainty with regard to the 'delivery' of certain outcomes (emancipatory or conservative).

A modest critical pedagogy would recognise the limits of rationality as a catalyst for change. The use of rational discourse to problematise taken-for-granted practices will be insufficient to change those practices unless there is a corresponding level of emotional commitment to change. We might need to take seriously the suggestion that there needs to be an emotional commitment to changing current practice lest the contingencies of traditional practice take charge to reproduce the existing reality.

## 'Truth Games' for HPE Teachers

According to Carlson (1998), in academic discourse, it is necessary to find something to say, to find a voice or rhetorical style in which to say or write it and to join in a conversation or 'truth game'. By truth game, he is referring to the Foucauldian notion of a 'discursive practice that establishes norms regarding who can speak, what they can speak about, and the form in which they speak' (p. 541). Significantly, different truth games produce different truths.

Carlson (1998, p. 543) takes us back to Plato's dialogues and the three rhetorical styles that produce different truths. They include:

- *Logos*; the analytic voice of critique associated with the truth games of science and philosophy
- *Thymos*; a voice of rage against injustice from the perspective and position of the disempowered, the disenfranchised and the marginalised
- *Mythos;* a personal voice of storytelling, cultural mythology, autobiography and literature

There is little doubt that *logos* is the privileged rhetorical style in the truth games of PETE and in the field of HMS. To understand some of background to this tension, it is useful to consider how students of the field of HMS learn to think about the body. In very fundamental ways, how HPE teachers think about health and physical education, and their developing identities as teachers, is integrally related to the ways in which they think about their bodies.

If we look at the courses that comprise the typical 4-year degree programme for the preparation of HPE teachers, we find that the 'disciplinary base' is human movement studies or exercise science. Within this disciplinary knowledge base, the most worthwhile (read essential) subject matter content knowledge is knowledge of the sub-disciplines of human movement, particularly those like anatomy, biomechanics and exercise physiology that focus on the body as a biological and mechanical 'thing'. Importantly, these foundation science disciplines are underpinned by a positivistic ideology and technicist ways of thinking (see McKay, Gore, & Kirk, 1990), and they are not conducive to the development of an appreciative understanding of the sociological concepts and the social model of health that underpin the new HPE KLA (Kirk, Macdonald, & Tinning, 1997).

Foucault informed us that knowledge *makes us its subject* (Gore, 1993), and the nature of the knowledge itself (see Pronger, 1995) has an influence on the type of person we become—on the identities we make offering a challenge to the dominant truth game of the body requires introducing students to understandings produced by different (alternative) truth games.

Encouragingly, there are now some physical education scholars who are engaging the work of social theory and the body (e.g. Armour, 1999; Evans, Davies & Wright, 2004; Garrette, 2004; Kirk, 1993; Oliver & Lalik, 2000). Issues concerning the social construction of the body, the place of physical education in disciplining the body, embodiment and identities are now on the agenda. Much of this new work is challenging to physical educators who were trained through the discourses of science in which the body as machine metaphor is dominant. But while social theorising about the body is exciting, challenging and at times provocative, it is not universally, or even largely, appreciated by HPE teachers who have embodied identities shaped by learning about the body in biological, technocratic ways.

There are also scholars, thinkers and writers from many different disciplines and backgrounds calling for new ways to think about the body, health, education and the world in general (e.g. Lupton, 1996; Wexler, 1995; Wright, 2000). As Kohli (1998, p. 518) observes '... a host of authors are [now] placing the body at the centre of their analyses of subjectivity, identity, and power', and for Caddick (1986, p. 76), '[w]e are our bodies and only in and only through them do we know ourselves and our relationships to others'.

However, the work of most, if not all, of these alternative thinkers will not appear on the reading list of most of the official HPE teacher education curriculum. Their ideas have little voice in the institutions that train future HPE teachers and human movement professionals:

> There is an interesting irony at work in the field of education at the beginning of the 21st century. As the education system continues to privilege science, rationality and the mind in the school curriculum, the body (as object, icon, pleasurable, consuming) has become a central concern in our society. The body (or more specifically the firm, slender body) is definitely 'in' and the field of HMS is creating and maintaining its place as central to the images, if not the reality, of healthy lifestyles as constructed around certain body management practices. (Tinning & Glasby, 2002)

A modest critical pedagogy would recognise, and try to work with/from, student (and teacher)-embodied subjectivities. It would not privilege *logos* (left-brain intellectualising), but would also use the rhetorical styles of *thymos* and *mythos* in seeking to develop emotional commitment in students to the socially critical project. It would recognise that emotional commitment is embodied. *Mythos* and *thymos* have greater potential to elicit emotional responses to, and connection with, the problematics of the cult of the body than the rational voice of *logos* (see Dowling, 2008).

# Conclusion

In this account, I am not suggesting we need to disconnect physical education from the HPE learning area and attempt return to some misty-eyed memory of PE in a previous time (like the 1960s). Nor am I suggesting that the socially critical liberal curriculum is an impossible task. In the final analysis, whether or not PETE can prepare teachers who have an emotional commitment to the principles underpinning the socially critical HPE curriculum and deliver on the objective of 'making' healthy, physically active, informed citizens will depend less on the sophistication of curriculum documents or explicit graduating standards and more on how prospective HPE teachers learn to *think* and *feel* about education, social justice, physical activity, bodies and health. In offering a modest critical pedagogy as a way of engaging and developing emotional commitment to the ideas and values of the socially critical project, I remain hopeful, but not confident.

# References

Armour, K. (1999). The case for a body-focus in education and physical education. *Sport, Education and Society, 4*(1), 5–17.
Bauman, Z. (2001). *The individualized society*. Cambridge, UK: Polity.
Beck, U. (1992). *Risk society: Towards a new modernity*. London: Sage.
Becker, H., Geer, B., Hughes, E., & Stauss, A. (1961). *Boys in white: Student culture in medical school*. Chicago: University of Chicago Press.
Biesta, G. (1998). Say you want a revolution… Suggestions for the impossible future of critical pedagogy. *Educational Theory, 48*(4), 499–510.
Brohm, J. M. (1978). *Sport, a prison of measured time: Essays*. London: Ink Links Ltd.
Brown, D. (1999). Complicity and reproduction in teaching physical education. *Sport, Education & Society, 4*(2), 143–160.
Buckingham, D. (Ed.). (1998). *Teaching popular culture: Beyond radical pedagogy*. London: University College London Press.
Caddick, A. (1986). Feminism and the body. *Arena, 78*, 60–90.
Carlson, D. (1998). Finding a voice, and losing our way? *Educational Theory, 48*(4), 541–554.
Crawford, R. (1980). Healthism and the medicalisation of everyday life. *International Journal of Health Services, 19*(3), 365–389.
Crowdes, M. (2000). Embodying sociological imagination: Pedagogical support for linking bodies to minds. *Teaching Sociology, 28*, 28–40.
Devis-Devis, J., & Sparkes, A. (1999). Burning the book: A biographical study of a pedagogically inspired identity crisis in physical education. *European Physical Education Review, 5*(2), 135–152.
Dewar, A. (1989). Recruitment in physical education teaching: Toward a critical approach. In T. Templin & P. Schempp (Eds.), *Socialization into physical education: Learning to teach* (pp. 39–58). Indianapolis, IN: Benchmark Press.
Dowling, F. (2008). Getting in touch with our feelings: The emotional geographies of gender relations in PETE. *Sport, Education & Society, 13*(2), 247–266.
Elliott, A. (2001). *Concepts of the self*. Oxford, UK: Polity.
Ellsworth, E. (1989). Why doesn't this feel empowering? Working through the repressive myths of critical pedagogy. *Harvard Educational Review, 59*(3), 297–324.
Ennis, C. (1994). Knowledge and beliefs underlying curricular expertise. *Quest, 46*(2), 164–175.
Evans, J., Davies, B., & Wright J., (Eds.). (2004). *Body Knowledge and Control. Studies in the Sociology of Education and Physical Culture*. London, Routledge.
Giddens, A. (1991). *Modernity and self-identity: Self and society in the late modern age*. Cambridge, UK: Polity Press.
Giddens, A. (1994). *Beyond left and right: The future of radical politics*. Cambridge, UK: Polity Press.
Glover, S., & Macdonald, D. (1997). Working with the health and physical education statement and profile in physical education teacher education: Case studies and implications. *ACHPER Healthy Lifestyles Journal, 44*(3), 21–26.
Goodson, I. (1992). Studying school subjects. *Curriculum Perspectives, 12*(1), 23–26.
Gore, J. (1990). Pedagogy as text in physical education teacher education: Beyond the preferred reading. In D. Kirk & R. Tinning (Eds.), *Physical education, curriculum and culture: Critical issues in the contemporary crisis* (pp. 101–138). Basingstoke, UK: The Falmer Press.

Gore, J. (1993). *The struggle for pedagogies: Critical and feminist discourses as regimes of truth.* New York: Routledge.

Gruneau, R. (1997). The politics and ideology of active living in historical perspective. In J. Curtis & S. Russell (Eds.), *Physical activity in human experience* (pp. 191–228). Champaign-Urbana, IL: Human Kinetics.

Gur-Ze'ev, I. (1998). Toward a non-repressive critical pedagogy. *Educational Theory, 48*(4), 463–486.

Hargreaves, J. (1986). *Sport, power and culture.* Cambridge, UK: Polity Press.

Hunter, L. (2004). Bourdieu and the social space of the PE class: Reproduction of doxa through practice. *Sport, Education & Society, 9*(2), 175–192.

Kenway, J. (1998). *Education in the age of uncertainty: An eagle's eye view, working paper.* Deakin Centre for Education & Change. Geelong: Deakin University.

Kenway, J., & Bullen, E. (2001). *Consuming children: Education-entertainment-advertising.* Buckingham, UK: Open University Press.

Kenworth-Teather, E. (1999). Introduction: Geographies of personal discovery. In E. Kenworth-Teather (Ed.), *Embodied geographies: Spaces, bodies and rites of passage* (pp. 1–27). London: Routledge.

Kirk, D. (1993). *The body, schooling and culture.* Geelong, Australia: Deakin University.

Kirk, D., & Colquhoun, D. (1989). Healthism and daily physical education. *British Journal of Sociology of Education, 10*(4), 417–434.

Kirk, D., Mcdonald, D., & Tinning, R. (1997). Physical education teacher education in Australia: Competing discourses and uncertain futures. *Curriculum Journal, 8*(2), 271–298.

Kohli, W. (1998). Critical education and embodied subjects: Making the poststructural turn. *Educational Theory, 48*(4), 511–519.

Lather, P. (1989). Staying dumb? Student resistance to liberatory curriculum. In P. Lather (Ed.), *Getting smart! Empowering approaches to research and pedagogy* (pp. 163–190). London: Routledge.

Lather, P. (1998). Critical pedagogy and its complicities: A praxis of stuck places. *Educational Theory, 48*(4), 487–497.

Law, J. (1994). *Organizing modernity.* Oxford, UK: Blackwell.

Lawson, H. A. (1984). Problem-setting for physical education and sport. *Quest, 36,* 48–60.

Luke, A. (2002). Curriculum, ethics, meta-narrative: Teaching and learning beyond the nation. *Curriculum Perspectives, 22*(1), 49–55.

Luke, C., & Gore, J. (Eds.). (1992). *Feminisms and critical pedagogy.* New York: Routledge.

Lupton, D. (1995). *The imperative of health: Public health and the regulated body.* London: Sage.

Lupton, D. (1996). *Food, the Body and the Self.* London, Sage.

Macdonald, D., & Brooker, R. (1999). Articulating a critical pedagogy in physical education teacher education. *Journal of Sport Pedagogy, 5*(1), 51–63.

Macdonald, D., Hunter, L., Carlson, T., & Penny, D. (2002). Teacher knowledge and the disjunction between school curricula and teacher education. *Asia-Pacific Journal of Teacher Education, 30*(3), 259–275.

Macdonald, D., & Kirk, D. (1996). Private lives, public lives: Surveillance, identity, and self in the work of beginning physical education teachers. *Sport, Education and Society, 1*(1), 59–76.

Macdonald, D., & Kirk, D. (1999). Pedagogy, the body and Christian identity. *Sport, Education and Society, 4*(2), 131–142.

McKay, J., Gore, J., & Kirk, D. (1990). Beyond the limits of technocratic physical education. *Quest, 42*(1), 52–75.

McLaren, P. (1998). Revolutionary pedagogy in post-revolutionary times: Rethinking the political economy of critical education. *Educational Theory, 48*(4), 431–462.

Oliver, K., & Lalik, R. (2000). *Bodily Knowledege.* New York, Peter Lang.

Petersen, A. (1997). Risk, governance and the new public health. In A. Petersen & R. Bunton (Eds.), *Foucault, health and medicine* (pp. 189–207). London: Routledge.

Petersen, A., & Lupton, D. (1996). *The new public health: Health and self in the age of risk.* Sydney, Australia: Allen & Unwin.

Pronger, B. (1995). Rendering the body: The implicit lessons of gross anatomy. *Quest, 47,* 427–446.

Pühse, U., & Gerber, M. (Eds.). (2006). *An international comparison on physical education: Concepts, problems and perspectives.* Oxford, UK: Meyer & Meyer Sport.

Queensland School Curriculum Council. (1999). *Health & physical education years 1 to 10 syllabus.* Brisbane, Australia: Education Queensland.

Shapiro, S. (2002). The life-world, body movements and new forms of emancipatory politics. In S. Shapiro & S. Shapiro (Eds.), *Body Movements: Pedagogy, politics and social change* (pp. 1–25). Cresskill, NJ: Hampton Press.

Shulman, L. S. (1986). Those who understand: Knowledge growth in teaching. *Educational Researcher, 15*(2), 4–14.

Smyth, J., & Dow, A. (1998). What's wrong with outcomes? Spotter planes, action plans and steerage of the educational workplace. *British Journal of Sociology of Education, 19*(3), 291–303.

Sparkes, A. (1999). Understanding physical education teachers: A focus on the lived body. In C. Hardy & M. Mawer (Eds.), *Learning and teaching in physical education* (pp. 171–186). London: Falmer Press.

Steinberg, S., & Kincheloe, J. (Eds.). (1997). *Kinderculture: The corporate construction of childhood.* Boulder, CO: Westview Press.

Templin, T., & Schempp, P. (1989). An introduction to socialization into physical education. In T. Templin & P. Schempp (Eds.), *Socialization into physical education: Learning to teach* (pp. 1–11). Indianapolis, IN: Benchmark Press.

Tinning, R. (1987). *Improving teaching in physical education.* Geelong, Australia: Deakin University.

Tinning, R. (1990). *Ideology and physical education: Opening Pandora's box.* Geelong, Australia: Deakin University.

Tinning, R. (1997). Performance and participation orienting discourses in the field of human movement: Implications for a socially critical physical education. In J.-M. Fernandez-Balboa (Ed.), *Critical aspects in human movement: Rethinking the profession in the postmodern era* (pp. 99–121). New York: SUNY Press.

Tinning, R. (2002). Towards a "modest" pedagogy: Reflections on the problematics of critical pedagogy. *Quest, 54*(3), 224–241.

Tinning, R. (2004). Rethinking the preparation of HPE teachers: Ruminations on knowledge, identity, and ways of thinking. *Asia Pacific Journal of Teacher Education, 32*(3), 241–253.

Tinning, R., & Glasby, T. (2002). Pedagogical work and the 'cult of the body': Considering the role of HPE in the context of the 'new public health'. *Sport, Education and Society, 7*(2), 109–119.

Wexler, P. (1992). *Becoming somebody: Toward a social psychology of school.* London: The Falmer Press.

Wexler, P. (1995). After postmodernism: A new age social theory in education. In R. Smith & P. Wexler (Eds.), *After postmodernism: Education, politics and identity* (pp. 56–81). London: The Falmer Press.

Wright, J. (2000). Bodies, meanings and movement: A comparison of the language of a physical education lesson and a Feldenkrais movement class. *Sport, Education and Society, 5*(1), 35–51.

# Chapter 17
# Reinvigorating Social Studies: A Desire for Powerful Learning

Robbie Johnston

## Introduction

Contemporary teacher education exists within a demanding policy landscape along with constructivist principles of teaching and learning. From this latter view, the learner is seen as an active participant in constructing an understanding of what it is to teach and the practical capacity to do so. In Australia, policy directives impact on what is possible in teacher education. Such policies act as structural constraints through the setting of standards for beginning teachers and the accreditation of courses of teacher education (Mayer, Reid, Santoro, & Singh, 2011), as well as through requirements to increase participation and social inclusion in higher education (Gale, 2011). Such directives emphasising content and tangible outcomes may constrain the professionalism of teacher educators and their attempts to build substantive courses based on constructivist principles.

Constructivist principles underpin the work of Doyle and Carter (2003) who promote the use of a narrative approach to teacher education, which breaks down the expert/novice separation and values the knowledge pre-service teachers (PSTs) bring to their learning. In this approach, PSTs bring personal stories as the starting point for their professional learning. According to this view, PSTs' prior experiences act as a springboard for learning and form a rich base for further exploration. Such approaches go beyond a deficit view of the learner—the background experiences and knowledge of the learner are starting points and a catalyst for learning. However, given the limitations of teacher education and changing demands—political and cultural—Luke, Luke, and Mayer (2000) recommend a radical revision of teacher

R. Johnston (✉)
School of Education, University of Tasmania, Launceston, TAS, Australia
e-mail: Robbie.Johnston@utas.edu.au

B. Down and J. Smyth (eds.), *Critical Voices in Teacher Education*, Explorations of Educational Purpose 22, DOI 10.1007/978-94-007-3974-1_17,
© Springer Science+Business Media Dordrecht 2012

education and a critical approach to curriculum. Given what they see as changing socio-cultural and political circumstances, these authors argue for new approaches for educating all within education—teachers and students alike:

> New tools are needed to prepare teachers and students as critically oriented knowledge 'workers' or knowledge designers, moving not just between cultures and media, but as well jumping the fences that we have helped create between the education in schools and the public education of everyday life in semiotic and information-based economies. (p. 10)

Others recommend a form of critical pedagogy—freeing up a sense of teacher and institutional control and creating the spaces for interaction (Lipponen & Kumpulainen, 2011). Kincheloe (1993) also promoted critical approaches for teachers along with teaching for social justice. However, with a backlash against constructivist and critical approaches (see Donnelly, 2006b, 2007; Vickers, 2010, pp. 321–323), teacher educators face challenges in using a critical pedagogy and in incorporating a critical approach to curriculum studies in their courses. Media debates are vociferous in their criticism of the critical approach, as is particularly evident in the many newspaper articles by Donnelly and criticisms of an integrated rather than discipline-based form of social studies (Donnelly, 2006a; Taylor, 2007).

Likewise, heated debate has surrounded recent national curriculum developments in Australia (see, e.g. Donnelly, 2006b, 2006c; Ferrari, 2010a, 2010b; Harrison, 2010; Henderson, 2010; Melleuish, 2009, 2010; Tomazin & Perkins, 2010; Tudball, 2010). With any curriculum developments, the situation is highly fluid and subject to heated public curriculum contests. There is evidence that the formulation of the Australian Curriculum is far from settled and these curriculum frameworks are continuing to evolve (Tudball). Notably, the area of school learning known very broadly by the term social studies is highly contested and characterised by complexity (see, e.g. Gilbert, 2011; Hill, 1994; Johnston, 1989; Vickers, 2010)—all the more so in light of public curriculum debates in Australia during the last decade. Changes in public policy exacerbate the inherent complexity of this area of learning—reflected in the variety of names used for it within the school curriculum. As Johnston indicated some time ago, recurring shifts in public policy arise from debates about the purposes of education according to interest groups within societal hierarchies.

## Balancing the Tensions: A Desire for Powerful Learning

As a teacher educator, with a desire to foster social studies curriculum and teaching and learning of some depth, I have conducted enquiry that evolved from action research in teacher education. Findings from this work have informed my practice in teacher education, all with a desire to move beyond a deficit view of the learner—in schooling and in higher education. In this chapter, I discuss catalysts that have shaped my work in developing an approach to the teaching of society and environment curriculum within teacher education that is based upon, and attempts to foster, a desire for powerful learning and a critical pedagogical approach to social studies curriculum. This view draws on the work of critical scholars (see, e.g. Apple & Beane, 2007; Hursh & Ross, 2000; Kincheloe, 2001; Ross, 1997). Thus, my view leans more to what Kennedy (2008) describes as a 'critical/radical approach' to curriculum than to an 'academic rationalist' one (p. 11). Notably, I have fostered a sense of student voice.

Accordingly, I have sought a way to acknowledge and value the experiences PSTs bring to their preparation as teachers and thus avoid bringing a deficit view of these learners to my own work in teacher education. I have explored a way for students to use these experiences as a springboard for a critical approach to their studies and their active participation in substantive discussions about the many issues facing them in their future roles as teachers. Through these wide-ranging conversations, PSTs work on developing a knowledge base along with pedagogical skills.

These aims stand in stark contrast with evidence of an expressed desire of some PSTs for definite answers from teacher educators about *what to do*, a trend that is evident in some teacher education research (see Johnston & Davis, 2008). In following sections of the chapter, I discuss research conducted with PSTs in Tasmania (Johnston, 2003). Findings from this research suggested that pre-service participants of the study mobilised hegemonic and dominant discourses evident in curriculum blueprints in use at the time. With this initial catalyst in mind, I then set out the rationale for a revised form of curriculum design in the teaching of society and environment curriculum in teacher education. This revised programme is further outlined and discussed, in relation to its goal of critical pedagogy, which Kress (2011) sees as a search for a 'more humane world' (p. 262) through fighting oppression in its various forms. In education, it seems that we must address not only tangible forms of oppression but also 'a quiet violence under the cover of hegemonic discourses and imagery distributed via popular media and social institutions (like schools)' (Kincheloe & Steinberg, 2004, cited in Kress, 2011, p. 262). As Kress implies, this 'quiet violence' emerges from 'power inequalities' (p. 262). In this chapter, I discuss what I see as a 'quiet violence' within society and environment curriculum and the ways I have attempted to address it. First of all, I outline the nature of social studies curricula and pedagogies.

In this chapter, I will use social studies as a broad overarching term for the various names attributed to this broad learning area. Although the names used for this area of learning imply particular curriculum perspectives and ways of organising the learning area, for the purposes of this paper, I will use this term interchangeably with society and environment, social and environmental studies and social studies and in conjunction with the related discipline area of history, geography and cultural studies. Other terms that have been in use in Australia at various times are social studies, Social Education, Human Society and its Environment, Studies of Society and Environment (SOSE), among others. In teacher education, the inherent tensions of the learning area add to the complexity teacher educators face in preparing PSTs to be proficient and knowing practitioners implementing a richly engaging social studies curriculum in schools. It would seem desirable for PSTs and all educators to understand and be proficient with many curriculum approaches, and particularly the meanings of critical ones.

## Social Studies: The Area of Learning

As with all curriculum, social studies is a construction (Brady & Kennedy, 1999; Gilbert, 1996, p. 9). Curriculum is shaped by choices (Kliebard, 1977, p. 260; Lovat & Smith, 1995, p. 24; Walker, 1992, p. 109) made within particular historical, social, cultural and political contexts. The learning area is further conceptualised, interpreted and negotiated by teachers, their students and their various communities. To add to these layers of curriculum construction and interpretation, the area of social studies is underpinned by the social sciences and humanities, both highly contested areas of enquiry and knowledge. It is not surprising therefore that social studies is subject to debate and a range of pedagogical problems, as a result of the tussles by different interest groups and societal concerns about this area of learning for children. The learning area continues to be the subject of controversy, conflict and uncertainty; as Johnston (1989) indicated, 'the old and new scholarly fields have made rival claims to representation in the school curriculum, as have the different schools of thought—positivist, relativist, functionalist and others—*within* the various humanities and social science fields' (p. 1).

Teachers work with reference to statutory curriculum blueprints, and, yet, the enacted curriculum is likely to be highly varied. However, there is evidence that the learning area in general lacks appeal for children, no matter whether the evidence comes from teaching and learning in history (Edwards & Flack, 2002), SOSE (Education Department of Western Australia [EDWA], 1994; Reynolds & Moroz, 1998) or the related area of civics and citizenship (Williamson & Thrush, 2001).

According to Gilbert (2011), changes to curriculum in Australia at the national level have been developed 'without systematic consideration of the overall learning needs of students and what kind of curriculum would most benefit them' (p. 5). Further, Kenway and Bullen (2005) argue that policymakers fail to consider the learner despite 'rapid cycles of policy change' (p. 33). Within the Australian Curriculum as it now stands (see Australian Curriculum, Assessment and Reporting Authority [ACARA], 2010, 2011, n.d.), society and environment curriculum focuses largely on the classical disciplines of history and geography. This move to an academic rationalist approach to curriculum is a radical swing away from curriculum approaches that prioritised the learner and attempted to engage students and promote learning (Vickers, 2010). A discipline-based approach is highly conservative and tends to be a pedagogical and curricular retreat to the past. According to Yates and Collins (2008, cited in Vickers, 2010), the worry is that such an approach acts as 'a socially discriminating force in upper secondary schooling' and thus is one of the constraints to 'full [student] retention' (p. 332). In the Australian state of Tasmania, from which I write this chapter, this matter of student retention resonates strongly; as with many regional and rural areas, the state performs relatively poorly when it comes to social indicators such as education.

With a resurgence of conservative curriculum developments in Australia, the tensions for teachers and teacher educators are all the more pressing when there is a desire to bring a critical edge to their work with students—either those in schools or in teacher education. As Vickers (2010) reminds readers, and as I indicated earlier in this chapter, media articles have directed a particularly vociferous and sustained attack against teachers with a 'social constructionist' view of curriculum, along with 'any curriculum based on critical pedagogy' (pp. 321–323). Hoepper (2011) sees critical pedagogy as being based on an emancipatory form of knowledge and a critical orientation to curriculum, both concerned with addressing disadvantage and oppression along with transformation to a more just society. Despite the intention of critical pedagogy to address disadvantage and, as Kress (2011) suggests, promote a 'more humane' society (p. 262), this form of teaching has met with resistance by students. Hoepper cites the work of several scholars in support of a warning to readers about taking up a critical stance to curriculum implementation through critical pedagogy. Further, with its focus on power and disadvantage, a critical stance is likely to open the way to controversial issues and debate. Yet, even when curriculum documents do incorporate critical thinking and perspectives, teachers and PSTs tend to sidestep these aspects of the curriculum—they avoid matters with the potential to raise controversy in their classrooms (Apple, 1990; Holden & Hicks, 2007; James, 2008; Levstik, 2000; Nelson, 1991).

Controversial issues are integral to the study of society and environment and its teaching, whether in schooling or teacher education (Gilbert, 2011; Hahn, 1991; Henderson, 2008), as is the concept of power. Some argue that discussion of controversial issues helps to enliven the learning area (Collins, 2010; Hahn, 1991; Taylor, 1998). There is also a view that 'social studies' is guilty of imposing views on students (Nelson, 1991, p. 335). As Reynolds and Moroz (1998, p. 50) argue, the learning area 'provides opportunities for teachers to peddle personal ideologies and critically unreflected political mythologies'. Thus, it seems that social studies may also be garnered for particular purposes and work against a desire to promote a 'more humane world' (Kress, 2011, p. 262).

## Pre-service Teachers' Curricular and Pedagogical Decisions

In this section, I discuss the longitudinal research I conducted in Tasmania with PSTs. Findings from the research point to the way that curriculum becomes interpreted in the matter of decision-making and planning for children's learning (see Johnston, 2007b). The research findings comprised the initial catalyst for my developing approach to teacher education in society and environment curriculum. In a later section of the chapter, I discuss the developing approaches that have emerged from the study I describe here.

The PhD research study (Johnston, 2003) evolved from an exploration of PSTs' choices of field sites for children's learning in Studies of Society and Environment (SOSE) (Australian Education Council, 1994a, 1994b) as well as Tasmanian interpretations of them (see, Department of Education and the Arts, 1995a, 1995b). The term, SOSE, was in use at the time of the research study and referred to nationally developed curriculum frameworks used as curriculum blueprints for what would once have been known as social studies. The PSTs selected the field sites for the purposes of a compulsory assessment task in a core unit of the 4-year undergraduate Bachelor of Education degree. As part of my ongoing investigation of the hidden and explicit curricula and pedagogies of fieldwork, PSTs were invited to reflect on their choices and to participate in a survey, as well as an interview in which they were asked about their fieldwork choices.

From my initial investigation of sites selected for children's learning, I explored several 'research questions about the teaching of SOSE in primary classrooms in Australia, both explicit and implicit, and in the frameworks provided by curriculum documents' (Johnston, 2007b, p. 352) and conducted a discourse analysis of the curriculum blueprints for SOSE that PSTs referred in their curriculum planning. As I have indicated previously (Johnston), the PST participants of the study took up three dominant discourses from the curriculum documents, namely, discourses of history, the immediate environment and the local community. Through these discourses, participants tended to perpetuate a hegemonic form of curriculum and a highly controlling pedagogy that worked against their desire to cater for children's learning. Findings indicated that the PST participants were selective in their use of these documents—they took up the dominant discourses, yet sidestepped aspects of critical thinking contained within them.

Despite the limitations I have indicated, the responses from participants reflect the depth of thought that went into site selection—there were many reference points for these decisions:

> I wouldn't want to look at colonial history or to glorify that. I remember that on a prac we went to a [historical house] and it was a fairly uncritical view. ... at the same time, I would want to make sure it was not glorified—or looking from one point of view.
>
> I don't know it really depends on your class. On the children. I guess you'd look at the economical side of it—you know the cost and also getting there.
>
> You see a lot of it depends on the children you're taking there and how well you know them and how well behaved they are ... and also how many parents are willing to go with you. So what is your ratio—adult to children ratio. All those have to be taken into consideration of where you go.
>
> So safety was probably my upper thought ... also keeping costs down.

Not surprisingly, matters of duty of care and safety loomed large in the field site choices. At the same time, participants seemed attuned to local tensions. They took their duty of care for their potential students seriously and conveyed a concern for the children they would one day teach. Despite these aspirations to implement a 'humane curriculum', participants restricted the opportunities for children's learning through limited access to a range of social realities. Overwhelmingly, participants constructed a curriculum that avoided difficult issues, controversy and difference; unwittingly, they fostered an anodyne, sanitised, hegemonic form of curriculum along with a controlling pedagogy. Findings suggested that the participants were acutely aware of much publicised tensions surrounding 'green politics' and forest industry debates in Tasmania. They sought to avoid sites and topics likely to raise controversy—matters of social justice, environmental issues, and creationist debates:

... but the only thing I was worried about there was because we were sort of tippy-toeing on ground as far as creation and those sorts of things... I don't know how we'd stand as far as bringing fossils and things into the classroom and how you'd sort of get around talking about those sorts of things yet.

... the central business district. I wouldn't have chosen that....because someone would have said you know my dad works here and somebody could have said 'oh my dad works for your dad!' ... I didn't want that to start occurring within the class. Domination type of thing already starting with the kids.

I guess the North Forest thing maybe seemed a little bit more daunting because of the issues that would come up are more current [than history] and maybe a little bit more— maybe confronting in the classroom which maybe I sort of felt a bit more scared about being able to manage. That you know disagreements that might come up in the classroom.

These statements suggest a thirst for learning about how to manage difference and varying points of view along with different demographic backgrounds and belief systems in the classroom. In talking about the kinds of sites they would not have selected, participants expressed concern about the kinds of sites appropriate for *children*. Places such as a church, cemetery and 'community institutions like a mental hospital' were excluded as being inappropriate for children to know about and visit; for example, in the words of one participant: ... *I didn't take up the option of doing the church. And their involvement in the community. And that was because I wasn't sure of whether or not the children could appreciate the aspects of social justice that particular institution was involved in.*

It seemed as if these decisions were based on a taken for granted Western construct of childhood as natural rather than socially constructed. Doyle and Carter (2003) point to the way that content is shaped in particular ways in the educational setting: 'to take any content into a classroom is to imbue it with social and pedagogical meaning' (p. 132). In this study, it seemed that a desire to address oppression led to a sanitised and hegemonic curriculum seen as appropriate for children.

Fieldwork pedagogies existed in a way that skewed children's opportunities for learning, not only about social differences and controversy but also in the field. The sites selected by the participants of the survey phase of the research were diverse; the 36 participants selected 31 different locations. However, these sites had many things in common and therefore limited opportunities for children's learning as well as that for the PSTs. Most of the sites—89% of them—were located in close vicinity of the three regional population centres in Tasmania and therefore overlooked small, rural centres. Unwittingly, through site selection, particular locations were ignored and the curriculum skewed in relation to urban sites. The choice of high status and publicly valued sites, in many cases associated with tourism locations, led to curricular bias. As I have indicated previously (Johnston, 2007b), 'participants justified their choice of well-known, named, highly visible, and bounded sites for implementing SOSE ... [in relation to] a range of discourses tending towards the culturally hegemonic' (p. 356), and as Kincheloe & Steinberg (2004, cited in Kress, 2011, p. 262) indicate, a 'quiet violence' can occur through the hegemonic discourses of schooling. Findings from this study indicated that, unwittingly, participants perpetuated this form of 'quiet violence' in drawing upon and mobilising three dominant discourses of SOSE, the curriculum blueprints in use at the time of the research.

Very briefly, the discourses skewed the curriculum and led to a controlling pedagogy. Through the discourse of community, participants mobilised a form of citizenship education that valued the local, along with an essentialised notion of community and community harmony. Through this discourse, participants mobilised a citizenship of compliance, obedience, cooperation and community responsibilities (Johnston, 2007a). Through this community discourse, sites with the potential to raise controversy were avoided; there seemed a neglect of 'the struggles that Apple (1990, p. 25) suggests are frequently a part of community life and yet overlooked in social studies education' (Johnston, 2007b, p. 357).

Through a discourse of history, participants perpetuated the valuing of history over other disciplines and areas of enquiry in the SOSE Statement—and earlier blueprints for the teaching of social studies (see Johnston, 2007b, p. 359). There was a focus on the distant past—Tasmania's so-called colonial history. Participants took up this discourse as a way to sidestep contentious issues. The analytic nature of historical enquiry and interpretation was avoided through a highly anodyne view of history.

Again in the discourse of the immediate environment, the experiences of some children were potentially marginalised. The local was seen as the most familiar environment for children and therefore appropriate for their learning. This discourse reflected a tabula rasa view of the learner—a view that was in tension with the way participants talked of their *own experiences* as children. There was evidence that PST participants had learned from these experiences in the field, whether in formal or informal contexts. The enquiry and experiential approach implemented in the teacher education course that was the basis of this research pointed to the need for teacher educators to discuss any blueprints *critically* with PSTs and to foster understanding of the potential impact of dominant and hegemonic curriculum discourses for the children they may teach (Johnston, 2007b). In addition, I have discussed the findings of this research with students as a catalyst for fostering a critical approach to teaching through fieldwork in society and environment curriculum.

## Building a Research/Teaching Nexus in Teacher Education

In addressing the kind of unwitting bias of teaching and learning in society and environment suggested by the findings of the research study discussed in the previous section, the contexts within which I had been working have defined what was possible. For example, with a small cohort of students in a postgraduate pre-service education course, I was able to discuss the research findings as preparation for the students' own fieldwork projects. With the small number of students (approximately 35), it was possible for small groups to plan and implement field experiences for their peers. These small groups were encouraged to consider the kinds of sites selected and together attempt to provide for learning at many different kinds of locations. Where students selected a museum, they were encouraged to consider the importance of incorporating a range of perspectives focusing not only on high status and well-known individuals and groups but also those marginalised in society and in curriculum. At other times, where students have been asked to implement community-based projects, they were encouraged to critique the notions of community evident in curriculum blueprints and to 'reflect on how such ideas [may be] represented in their own school-based projects' (Johnston & Davis, 2008, p. 353). In these various approaches, students were invited to engage in quite authentic situations where they brought their critique of the dominant discourses to their planning in society and environment curriculum or the closely related curriculum component of community-based learning.

While these attempts had much to recommend them and resulted in raising the bar on depth of thought in planning, there were tensions. Notably, as teacher educators implementing community-based approaches in teacher education, a colleague and I found that we needed to 'be willing to be challenged by students, to welcome debate and a certain degree of dissonance, including ... tensions that can emerge in student evaluations of unit curriculum and of teaching and learning' (Johnston & Davis, 2008, p. 358). These tensions arose as the approaches we were encouraging for our PSTs differed in some cases from the accepted practices in schools. However, in managing these tensions within our own teaching, we were able to model ways of incorporating controversy and tension within the learning context.

Both of the teacher education situations I have described so far involved face-to-face teaching with PSTs attending on-campus classes at the University of Ballarat where a colleague and I had trialled teaching through a form of narrative pedagogy.

As part of compulsory assessment, PSTs were required to write a narrative or snapshot of schooling and discuss the meaning of it in relation to literature incorporated in a second year unit. Students shared their narratives in class and discussed the themes they identified within them. In this way, the tutorials were closely linked with the assessment task. The unit fostered assessment *for* learning as well as *of* learning. Students drew upon their reading of key material recommended within the unit. In this way, the unit fostered a highly integrated approach for making meaning of situations observed in schooling.

With my appointment at the University of Tasmania, I was required to implement fully online and blended learning for a rapidly increasing PST cohort dispersed over many locations, within the state as well as nationally and internationally. This requirement acted as a catalyst for rethinking my pedagogical approach to society and environment curriculum. It seemed that narrative pedagogy would offer advantages for facilitating meaningful student discussions online and for encouraging students to see strong reasons to log on and participate. I therefore developed a fully online unit, based on a form of narrative pedagogy trialled initially in face-to-face classes at the University of Ballarat. Notably, the approach offered the opportunity for online students to shape the discussions—it was hoped that their participation would emerge out of the narratives they brought to the unit and from their reading of key literature recommended for it.

At the University of Tasmania, I received support from a team of experts in online teaching and learning and the unit evolved in discussion with them. A major consideration was to foster in-depth discussion and a constructivist approach to teacher education—to raise the bar on the expectation that students would log on to the discussion boards and be active participants. On the basis of this experience, the fully online approach was then adapted to suit a unit with face-to-face and online students. This new unit, a society and environment curriculum methods unit, Society and Environment (Introduction) (ESH260), is a second year compulsory unit of the Bachelor of Education (Early Childhood and Primary) degree courses at the University of Tasmania. In my planning, I wanted again to foster a critical curricular and pedagogical approach and to bring in a form of narrative pedagogy implemented previously. I will explain this approach in more detail in the next section.

## Social Studies Within Teacher Education

My aim in ESH260 is to implement critical pedagogy in teacher education as a way of contributing to a 'more humane world' (Kress, 2011, p. 262) but in a way that does not bring about a 'quiet violence' (Kincheloe & Steinberg, 2004, cited in Kress, 2011, p. 262) while doing so. I see narrative pedagogy as a way to foster a critical curricular and pedagogical stance that respects PSTs and values the experiences they bring to their learning.

In going back to my thesis (Johnston, 2003, pp. 163–164), and reflecting on some of the tensions that led to the discourse analysis of curriculum blueprints in use at the time, I am reminded that there was a tension between what participants remembered from their own fieldwork as children—either in schooling or *informal* fieldwork such as 'jaunts' taken with the family—compared with the expectations of them as teachers and as interpreted from curriculum blueprints. In my teaching when I have discussed this tension with PSTs, the atmosphere in the room has been palpable. I have found that PSTs seem to relate to this tension—they appear to have hopes for their work as teachers and feel a tension between these desires and the expectations of them by schooling, including as conveyed in curriculum blueprints.

In reflecting on the work of Doyle and Carter (2003) in relation to narrative pedagogy, I saw an opportunity for the *school experiences* of PSTs to be brought to their learning in relation to society and environment curriculum. The approach developed for the unit, Society and Environment (Introduction), is a form of autoethnography with research conducted by the PSTs as a means of promoting teaching for social justice (see Ayers, 2004). Further evidence for such an approach is highlighted in the work of Kincheloe and Steinberg (1998) who have argued a case for students as researchers.

If as some participants of the research I discussed earlier in the chapter indicated, the sites selected as fieldwork locations were chosen as familiar locations remembered from school fieldtrips, it seemed that bringing such memories as artefacts for reflection in teacher education would offer a rich catalyst for learning. It seemed these memories would act as a catalyst for reflecting on curriculum as a social construct, for comparing and contrasting pedagogical approaches as well as curriculum guidelines from varying contexts and timeframes, and reflecting on the way that the curriculum may have been received by these PSTs when *they* were children in school. Reflecting on fieldwork remembered may offer rich opportunities for depth of learning in relation to society and environment curriculum. In this way, PSTs would have an opportunity to reconsider evidence that children report dissatisfaction with the learning area of social studies (EDWA, 1994; Reynolds & Moroz, 1998).

I saw that the revised approach to teacher education may open discussions about society and environment curriculum in a way that went beyond the *intellectual* aspects of learning and tapped into a deeply expressed desire for their work as teachers. Yates (1992, cited in Hoepper, 2011) reminds us of the limits in 'intellectual critique' (p. 55) as a dimension of critical pedagogy. The approach can be heavy handed and a form of inculcation or, at its worst, indoctrination. It is the reason that Slater and Morgan (2000, p. 272), in relation to the teaching and learning of geography, recommend valuing the knowledge of the learner. I saw potential for a form of narrative pedagogy to be introduced in teacher education—to open the way for a critique of fieldwork pedagogies and society and environment curricula in a way that valued PSTs' prior experiences as quite legitimate for learning in relation to society and environment curriculum methods in teacher education.

As an introduction to this area of learning, I developed an assignment in which students would be asked to reflect on their learning through fieldwork as children in the early years or primary context. Students are asked to share their narratives in online discussion boards or in face-to-face classes. These narratives then become a base for reflection on fieldwork pedagogies and society and environment curricula more broadly. Students have an opportunity to critique their prior experiences, but with empathy and an ethical stance to all participants, whether in the previous learning context or in the current one in teacher education. The aim is not to castigate any actor or to negatively comment on teaching but to reflect on the approaches in use at the time (as remembered) and to examine them in terms of the possibilities for children's learning now and in the future.

The approach used for the assignment is a form of autoethnography and as such demands that the PSTs comply with ethical principles by maintaining the anonymity of all actors and places referred to in the narratives. PSTs are required to use pseudonyms in these snapshots of experience. They are encouraged to present the narratives in a balanced way and to bring balance to their analyses. The approach used for the assignment offers an opportunity to discuss sources of evidence and potential limitations of research such as that used in historical enquiry and interpretation of sources. In considering their own artefact of prior experiences from schooling, PSTs are encouraged to hypothetically consider how the same scenario may be considered by others who may have also been involved. Such ethical principles are an important aspect of the unit—teachers need to base their work with children on the same principles of respect for others, particularly with oral history and data gathering in places they may investigate for fieldwork. These data gathering approaches require teachers and students to follow ethical principles in any enquiry as part of the society and environment learning area and this assignment offers the opportunity to discuss such matters.

In analysing the narrative constructed as the basis for the assignment, the PSTs are encouraged to make links between the task and other forms of interpretation and analysis as they may do in historical enquiry. Links are made between this task and the content of the curriculum area. In this sense, the task is multilayered. Students are encouraged to seek out sources relevant to the narrative themes identified as the basis for discussion. This analysis is supported through discussion in tutorials, whether face-to-face or online. In discussions of these prior experiences, time is devoted to the tone used in critiquing narratives. Students are encouraged to bring a generous tone to their analysis—at the same time not stepping back from commenting on unwitting biases that may be perpetuated. This approach demands finely nuanced teaching and learning with the teacher education teaching team being willing to work with uncertainty and the material that PSTs bring to their studies. The narratives are analysed in relation to the substantive content of the introductory unit—namely, a focus on history, geography and civics and citizenship.

The approach used in preparation for this assessment task demands a flexible way of working with what students bring to the task. Sometimes, they find it difficult to remember any field trip or anything related strongly to learning of society and environment curriculum. As a teaching team, we work with students to identify— some snapshot that may be used as the basis of the assignment—we let students know there are lots of possibilities. They may draw on outdoor learning of any kind or even the lack of it—as with 'missed opportunities'. Students may reflect on a moment in their own schooling where they think that fieldwork may have enhanced their learning but was not included as a mode of teaching and learning. In this way, students may be drawn to the limitations of fieldwork and the opportunities offered in other pedagogical approaches. They may reflect on the possibilities for learning *if fieldwork had been incorporated*; they may reflect on the possibilities they see for teaching and learning a similar dimension of the curriculum through fieldwork. Perhaps the fieldwork they remember related to a different learning area—in that case, they may consider the potential for society and environment curriculum. They are invited to see many possibilities for their analysis, and these possibilities are discussed with students in tutorials, face-to-face or online. The two cohorts—face-to-face and online—also have the opportunity to share their views in discussion boards that are available to all students.

With large cohorts distributed over many locations, the opportunities for shared discussions and learning are expanded markedly; the online PSTs may be located anywhere in the world with online access, and the face-to-face cohorts are located on two campuses in Tasmania. Further, given the increasing mobility of the population from one place to another, it is usually the case that students bring background experiences from many different places to their learning. They also bring many different time frames to their analysis—students are mature age as well as recent school leavers. In combination, the opportunities for students to unpack their narratives in light of curriculum orientations are particularly rich.

The PSTs are encouraged to critically analyse the curriculum blueprints and field sites as they may have done in earlier iterations of teacher education courses I have developed. However, in this case, with the use of narrative pedagogy linked with prior experiences from their own schooling, a sense of student voice is welcomed into the curriculum in a way that was not in the pedagogical approach I used as the basis of the research discussed earlier in this chapter (see Johnston, 2007b). Potentially, the approach makes for a more democratic stance to curriculum and pedagogy. The inclusion of similar kinds of approaches for children's learning is modelled within teacher education and discussed with students.

## Conclusions and Further Planning

As is evident in the description of the unit, the PSTs are expected to bring a problem solving, enquiry-oriented and critical approach to their studies. The approach used in the unit makes demands on the students and staff and brings a discussion of the reasons for the approach to the fore. The implementation of the unit is yet to be researched in detail. However, students appear to respond positively, as indicated in official university student evaluations of teaching and learning (University of Tasmania [UoT], 2010a). Survey items, related to independence in learning and being encouraged to think, were rated particularly well. These evaluations give some hope that the aims of the unit to foster critique and depth of thinking were achieved, particularly as the evaluations were for a unit that was being offered for the first time.

The feedback is particularly pleasing, given that one of the learning outcomes stated that 'on completion of the unit, [students] should be able to critically appraise society and environment pedagogies and curricula' (UoT, 2010b, p. 3). Further corroboration of the data is required, and there is room for the unit to be further investigated *with students*, particularly through qualitative research so that the student voices may be heard.

This ongoing qualitative research is important to find out more about student views of the unit in terms of contributing to a 'more humane world', through their learning and developing knowledge of social justice, critical pedagogy and enquiry approaches, their stance towards these aspects as well as their lived experience of the unit. What evidence is there that students are attuned to social justice? In what ways has the unit fostered a sense of social justice in their eyes? Interestingly, this unit combines cohorts enrolled online as well as at two regional campuses. The unit was designed with each of these cohorts in mind and aimed to ensure equity for the learning of these different groups. Through the content of the society and environment curriculum unit, there are opportunities for the pre-service teachers no matter their form of enrolment to engage in critical discussions about dominant discourses of curriculum documents—and in society more broadly. Further research may be useful, however, to more fully inform the unit development. In addition, it seems important to more fully investigate the ways in which different groups of students engage with the unit and whether social justice aspirations extend to all pre-service teachers enrolled in ESH260.

This chapter has outlined an approach for bringing student voice and student *knowledge/s* to society and environment curriculum method studies in teacher education. There seems evidence for strengthening the ways in which the society and environment unit *listens* to students and challenges dominant discourses. In addition, there is a need to investigate lived experiences of social studies curriculum within teacher education for all students in this unit. Taking the courage to teach through student voice pointed to the possibilities for powerful learning in relation to social studies curriculum methods as well as for further teacher education research.

**Acknowledgements** With thanks to the Faculty of Education, University of Tasmania, and the School of Education, University of Ballarat, for the opportunity to develop the units discussed in this chapter. Thanks also to colleagues with whom I have worked at both institutions and to Sharon Fraser and Tony Dowden for their comment on earlier drafts.

# References

Apple, M. W. (1990). *Ideology and curriculum* (2nd ed.). New York: Routledge.

Apple, M., & Beane, J. (Eds.). (2007). *Democratic schools: Lessons in powerful learning*. Portsmouth, NH: Heinemann.

Australian Curriculum, Assessment and Reporting Authority [ACARA]. (2010, December). *The shape of the Australian curriculum* [Version 2.0]. Sydney, Australia: Author.

Australian Curriculum, Assessment and Reporting Authority [ACARA]. (2011). *Shape of the Australian curriculum: Geography*. Retrieved March 28, 2011, from http://www.acara.edu.au/verve/_resources/Shape_of_the_Australian_Curriculum_Geography.pdf

Australian Curriculum, Assessment and Reporting Authority [ACARA]. (n.d.). *The Australian curriculum: History (foundation to Year 10, Version 1.2)*. Retrieved March 28, 2011, from http://www.australiancurriculum.edu.au/History/Curriculum/F-10

Australian Education Council. (1994a). *A statement on studies of society and environment for Australian schools [SOSE Statement]*. Carlton, Australia: Curriculum Corporation.

Australian Education Council. (1994b). *Studies of society and environment: A curriculum profile for Australian schools [SOSE Profile]*. Melbourne, Australia: Curriculum Corporation.

Ayers, W. (2004). *Teaching the personal and political: Essays on hope and justice*. New York: Teachers College Press.

Brady, L., & Kennedy, K. (1999). *Constructing curriculum*. Sydney, Australia: Prentice Hall.

Collins, C. (2010). Thinking together about questions that matter in the SOSE classroom. *The Social Educator, 28*(3), 4–10.

Department of Education and the Arts. (1995a). *Studies of society and environment in Tasmanian schools K–8: Guidelines and support materials [SOSE Guidelines]*. Hobart, Australia: Author.

Department of Education and the Arts. (1995b). *Tasmanian studies of society and environment planning grid [SOSE Planning Grid]*. Hobart, Australia: Author.

Donnelly, K. (2006a, September 28). Geography has lost perspective. *The Australian*. Retrieved June 20, 2011, from http://www.theaustralian.com.au/news/opinion/kevin-donnelly-geography-has-lost-perspective/story-e6frg6zo-1111112277602

Donnelly, K. (2006b, October 20). The long march back to reason. *The Australian.* Retrieved June 20, 2011, from http://www.theaustralian.com.au/news/opinion/kevin-donnelly-the-long-march-back-to-reason/story-e6frg6zo-1111112387001

Donnelly, K. (2006c, November 28). Dumbed down and left out. *The Australian.* Retrieved June 20, 2011, from http://www.theaustralian.com.au/news/opinion/kevin-donnelly-dumbed-down-and-left-out/story-e6frg6zo-1111112593684

Donnelly, K. (2007, February 27). Ill-trained in the classroom. *The Australian.* Retrieved June 20, 2011, from http://www.theaustralian.com.au/news/opinion/kevin-donnelly-ill-trained-in-the-classroom/story-e6frg6zo-1111113062243

Doyle, W., & Carter, K. (2003). Narrative and learning to teach. *Journal of Curriculum Studies, 35*(2), 129–137.

Education Department of Western Australia. (1994). *Summary—Student achievement in studies of society and environment in Western Australian government schools* (Monitoring Standards in Education Achievement 1994). Perth, WA: Author.

Edwards, J., & Flack, J. (2002). *Question: Who was the rich, cool dude who came out on the First Fleet with his two greyhounds? Answer: you don't mean Joseph Banks do you?* A paper presented at the International Education Research Conference Brisbane December 1–5, 2002. Retrieved July 10, 2009, from http://www.aare.edu.au/02pap/edw02288.htm

Ferrari, J. (2010a, September 10). Teachers fear course neglect. *The Australian,* p. 2.

Ferrari, J. (2010b, October 9–10). History course 'cobbled together'. *The Weekend Australian Financial Review,* p. 1.

Gale, T. (2011). New capacities for student equity and widening participation in higher education [Editorial]. *Critical Studies in Education, 52*(2), 109–113.

Gilbert, R. (1996). Studies of society and environment as a field of learning. In R. Gilbert (Ed.), *Studying society and environment: A handbook for teachers* (pp. 5–19). South Melbourne, Australia: Macmillan.

Gilbert, R. (2011). Studies of society and environment in the Australian curriculum. In R. Glibert & B. Hoepper (Eds.), *Teaching society and environment* (4th ed., pp. 2–20). South Melbourne, Australia: Cengage.

Hahn, C. L. (1991). Controversial issues in social studies. In J. P. Shaver (Ed.), *Handbook of research on social studies teaching and learning* (pp. 210–221). New York: Macmillan.

Harrison, D. (2010, March 10). 'Black armband' view risks national curriculum. *The Age,* p. 2.

Henderson, D. (2008). Values, controversial issues and interfaith understanding. In C. Marsh (Ed.), *Studies of society and environment: Exploring the teaching possibilities* (5th ed., pp. 2–18). Frenchs Forest, Australia: Pearson Education Australia.

Henderson, D. (2010). Civics and citizenship in the national history curriculum: Conducting the same music by rehearsing an incomplete tune? *The Social Educator, 28*(1), 18–26.

Hill, B. V. (1994). *Teaching secondary social studies in a multicultural society.* Melbourne, Australia: Longman Cheshire.

Hoepper, B. (2011). Critical inquiry into society and environment: The big picture. In R. Glibert & B. Hoepper (Eds.), *Teaching society and environment* (4th ed., pp. 44–61). South Melbourne, Australia: Cengage.

Holden, C., & Hicks, D. (2007). Making global connections: The knowledge, understanding and motivation of trainee teachers. *Teaching and Teacher Education, 23,* 13–23.

Hursh, D., & Ross, E. W. (Eds.). (2000). *Democratic social education: Social studies and social change.* New York: Falmer Press.

James, J. H. (2008). Teachers as protectors: Making sense of pre-service teachers' resistance to interpretation in elementary history teaching. *Theory and Research in Social Education, 36*(3), 172–205.

Johnston, G. L. (1989). *Social studies: In search of a rationale.* Hawthorn, Australia: Australian Council for Educational Research.

Johnston, R. (2003). *On location/s: Seeking fieldwork sites for the study of society and environment within teacher education—An analysis of social constructs of place and space.* Unpublished PhD thesis, University of Tasmania, Australia.

Johnston, R. (2007a). Children and community: Looking beyond socialisation and the status quo. *New Community Quarterly [Theme: Community Development in Rural, Remote and Regional Areas], 5*(3), 45–49.

Johnston, R. (2007b). Dominant discourses and teacher education: Current curriculum or curriculum remembered. *Asia-Pacific Journal of Teacher Education, 35*(4), 351–365.

Johnston, R., & Davis, R. (2008). Negotiating the dilemmas of community-based learning in teacher education. *Teaching Education, 19*(4), 351–360.

Kennedy, K. (2008). Theoretical perspectives for understanding studies of society and environment. In C. Marsh (Ed.), *Studies of society and environment: Exploring the teaching possibilities* (5th ed., pp. 2–18). Frenchs Forest, Australia: Pearson Education Australia.

Kenway, J., & Bullen, E. (2005). Globalizing the young in the age of desire: Some educational policy issues. In M. W. Apple, J. Kenway, & M. Singh (Eds.), *Globalizing education: Policies, pedagogies, and politics* (pp. 31–43). New York: Peter Lang.

Kincheloe, J. (1993). *Toward a critical politics of teacher thinking: Mapping the postmodern*. Westport, CT: Bergin & Garvey.

Kincheloe, J. (2001). *Getting beyond the facts: Teaching social studies/social sciences in the twenty-first century*. New York: Peter Lang.

Kincheloe, J., & Steinberg, S. (Eds.). (1998). *Students as researchers: Creating classrooms that matter*. London: Falmer Press.

Kliebard, H. M. (1977). Curriculum theory: Give me a "for instance". *Curriculum Enquiry, 6*(4), 257–269.

Kress, T. M. (2011). Inside the 'thick wrapper' of critical pedagogy and research. *International Journal of Qualitative Studies in Education, 24*(3), 261–266.

Levstik, L. S. (2000). Articulating the silences: Teachers' and adolescents' conceptions of historical significance. In P. N. Stearns, P. Sexias, & S. Wineburg (Eds.), *Knowing teaching and learning history: National and international perspectives* (pp. 284–305). New York: New York University Press.

Lipponen, L., & Kumpulainen, K. (2011). Acting as accountable authors: Creating interactional spaces for agency. *Teaching and Teacher Education, 27*(5), 812–819.

Lovat, T. J., & Smith, D. L. (1995). *Curriculum: Action on reflection revisited* (3rd ed.). Wentworth Falls, Australia: Social Science Press.

Luke, A., Luke, C., & Mayer, D. (2000). Redesigning teacher education [Editorial]. *Teacher Education, 11*(1), 5–11.

Mayer, D., Reid, J., Santoro, N., & Singh, M. (2011). Quality teacher education: The challenges of developing professional knowledge, honing professional practice and managing teacher identities [Editorial]. *Asia-Pacific Journal of Teacher Education, 39*(2), 79–82.

Melleuish, G. (2009, September 1). Leave history alone. *The Australian*, p. 12.

Melleuish, G. (2010, March 3). The past is a dull place without human stories. *The Australian*, p. 12.

Nelson, J. L. (1991). Communities, local to national, as influences on social studies education. In J. P. Shaver (Ed.), *Handbook of research on social studies teaching and learning* (pp. 332–341). New York: Macmillan.

Reynolds, P., & Moroz, W. (1998). The society and environment curriculum framework for the new millennium: How prepared are primary teachers? *The Social Educator, 16*(2), 42–51.

Ross, E. W. (Ed.). (1997). *The social studies curriculum: Purposes, problems and possibilities*. New York: State University of New York.

Slater, F., & Morgan, J. (2000). "I haven't fully discovered it yet": Children experiencing environments. In M. Robertson & R. Gerber (Eds.), *The child's world: Triggers for learning* (pp. 258–275). Camberwell, Australia: ACER.

Taylor, P. (1998). *Redcoats and patriots: Reflective practice in drama and social studies*. Portsmouth, NH: Heinemann.

Taylor, T. (2007, May 7). Too many cooks spoil the SOSE. *The Age*, p. 16.

Tomazin, F., & Perkins, M. (2010, March 2). A sound beginning. *The Age*, p. 9.

Tudball, L. (2010, March 2). Curriculum's narrow focus leaves students bereft of big ideas. *The Age* [Comment and Debate], p. 11.

University of Tasmania. (2010a). *Student evaluation of teaching and learning: Statistics – Semester 2, 2010*. Hobart, Tasmania: Author. Retrieved from http://www.studentcentre.utas. edu.au/setl/statistics/setl_report_unit_sem2_2010.pdf

University of Tasmania. (2010b). *Unit outline: Society and environment (Introduction), ESH260*. Launceston, Australia: Author.

Vickers, M. (2010). Curriculum. In R. Connell, C. Campbell, M. Vickers, A. Welch, D. Foley, N. Bagnall, & D. Hayes (Eds.), *Education, change and society* (2nd ed., pp. 309–335). South Melbourne, Australia: Oxford University Press.

Walker, D. F. (1992). Methodological issues in curriculum research. In P. W. Jackson (Ed.), *Handbook of research on curriculum: A project of the American Educational Research Association* (pp. 98–118). New York: Macmillan.

Williamson, J., & Thrush, M. (2001). Tasmania. In M. Print, W. Moroz, & P. Reynolds (Eds.), *Discovering democracy in civics and citizenship education* (pp. 183–190). Katoomba, Australia: Social Science Press.

# Chapter 18
# Sustainability: Ambiguity and Aspiration in Teacher Education

Sandra Wooltorton

## Introduction: Predicaments and Possibilities

The second strategy of the Australian government's National Action Plan (NAP) for sustainability education is to reorient education systems to sustainability (Department of the Environment Water Heritage and the Arts [DEWHA], 2009). In this chapter, I put forward an activist-based socially critical viewpoint on the ambition to reorient education whilst uncovering a range of ambiguities, tensions and constraints which hinder meaningful change. I suggest that attention to these predicaments across curriculum, policy and accountability mechanisms will offer possibilities and hope. In this introductory section, I begin with the sustainability education NAP and provide a socioecological context before sketching out the issues to be addressed in the remainder of the chapter.

The UNESCO-driven agenda to reorient schools and universities towards sustainability, an agenda that is now more than 20 years old,[1] informs the NAP. It proposes a transformative approach to education, with the stated aim of 'achieving a culture of sustainability' in which teaching and learning for sustainability are reinforced by continuous improvement in the sustainability of campus management (DEWHA, 2009, p. 5). The NAP is part of Australia's contribution to the UN Decade of Education for Sustainable Development 2005–2014 (the Decade), and its intention is to reorient all education systems to sustainability through learning. In my view, the plan has much to offer. However, unfortunately, it is not clearly reflected in the new national curriculum for schools, revealing some philosophical

---

[1] The idea of the reorientation of education was first accepted in a UN context in 1977 at the Tbilisi Conference on Environmental Education (UNESCO, 1977). It was formalized in Rio de Janeiro through Agenda 21 Chapter 36 (United Nations Conference on Environment and Development, 1992).

S. Wooltorton (✉)
Education Programme, Edith Cowan University, Bunbury, Australia
e-mail: s.wooltorton@ecu.edu.au

B. Down and J. Smyth (eds.), *Critical Voices in Teacher Education*, Explorations of Educational Purpose 22, DOI 10.1007/978-94-007-3974-1_18,
© Springer Science+Business Media Dordrecht 2012

dissent between two key government departments being the Department of Sustainability, Environment, Water, Population and Communities; and the Department of Education, Employment and Workplace Relations. This reveals a structural polemic which manifests in many guises throughout sustainability education.

It is now generally acknowledged that the modernist ventures of economic growth and the domination of nature are fundamentally flawed (Orr, 2010, p. 75; UNESCO, 2002b). Distress signals such as the threat of cataclysmic climate change and massive species loss tell us that we need to transform the ways we live together and with nature on our precious planet. Unfortunately, education systems throughout the developed world have 'sustain[ed] unsustainability' (Sterling, 2001, p. 14) in the sense that the most highly educated countries which also have the highest per capita rates of consumption also have the highest ecological footprints (McKeown, 2002, p. 10). This calls into serious question what education is for and how it should function—at pre-primary, primary, secondary and tertiary levels.

To address these contexts, I make four main points in this chapter which are firstly that our system is underpinned by a structural tension which constrains progress towards sustainability. In essence, the system is regarded as a key to sustainability transformation whilst simultaneously preventing change. Paradoxically, on a daily basis, it reinforces unsustainable values and practices (Bowers, 1997; Sterling, 2001). The constraints work at the policy, curriculum and local levels of schools and universities.

My second point is that further to the structural issues in the system, the notion of sustainability itself has ambiguity at its core. Whilst this produces dilemmas, the lack of clarity itself can be a cause célèbre for attention and learning. Core issues include the question of what is being sustained and whether the solution involves technocratic or culturally derived agendas for change because whilst both purport to improve society, they each produce different visions of a sustainable future with disparate directions for action.

Thirdly, I suggest that our education system is biased against the development of active and informed citizens. There is increasing evidence that the current focus on literacy and numeracy causes the subversion of the idea of active and informed citizenship. I am saying that even though the priorities are equivocally distributed at the level of systemwide goals for education, by privileging literacy and numeracy in our teaching programmes, we are subverting citizenship and by extension sustainability—but we could easily do each of these well. Unfortunately, teacher education programmes are also being confined by the same political constraints.

Finally, I applaud the fact that sustainability education is now officially understood as being underpinned by transformative learning for social change (DEWHA, 2009, p. 9). Yet at present, as a culture, we neither have the know-how to be transformative nor do we know how and where to begin to work in different sustaining ways (Wooltorton, 2004, p. 2). Thus, in an individual and in a collective sense, we need to develop this practical knowledge. This objective will take time, resources, creativity, determination and strong commitment by policymakers and school communities, particularly in a context of systemic structural tension, ambiguity in the meaning of sustainability and the subversion of active citizenship.

## Structural Tensions and Constraints

In this section, I illustrate the structural tension as a double bind[2] which constrains progress towards sustainability reorientation in schools and universities whilst reinforcing the unsustainable values and practices that it professes to change (Bowers, 1997; Sterling, 2001). The history of this phenomenon is now well documented (e.g. see Smyth, 2001). In a nutshell, over the last 15 years or so, technical and utilitarian goals of education have increasingly been given priority in western countries, whilst social and democratic purposes have been subverted. This results from the right-wing agenda of an alliance of neoconservative and neoliberal forces using a market model for education together with slogans such as choice (Smyth, Angus, Down, & McIerney, 2009). Meanwhile, because of the minimization of the welfare state and the acceptance of user-pays principles, more of the cost for education, health and social well-being is reallocated back to individuals and families (Smyth et al., 2009).

Similarly, for over a decade, the case has been strongly argued that in the developed world, a deliberate mythology has been constructed in which teachers and schools are seen as the cause of economic failure. As part of the fiction, solutions that were generated include tighter accountability procedures such as performance management, hierarchical forms of discipline and national testing (Smyth, 2001). The connected belief is that schools would serve the economy more effectively once again when these remedies are applied (Smyth & Shacklock, 1998). Ten years after Smyth and Shacklock's critique, the National Assessment Program in Literacy and Numeracy (NAPLAN) was put into service to compare all Australian schools, students and systems and to monitor progress over time, underpinned by the speculation that there is a systemic link between economic prosperity and test scores (e.g. see Government of Western Australia [GWA], 2007, paragraph 1). Predictably, there is no intended link between future prosperity and citizenship, creativity, confidence, skills for sustainable living, interpersonal and social skills, curiosity and enquiry skills, problem solving, loyalty, capacity to care and be empathic, a sense of optimism, cultural competence, ability to envision and plan, knowledge of local geography, sustainability literacy or any other attribute required by employers of the present or the future.

As an example of the significance in terms of time and energy bestowed upon the testing, Western Australian state primary school teachers were asked to spend 50% of their teaching time addressing literacy and numeracy outcomes (GWA, 2007, p. 3), and this requirement has not yet been lifted. Sadly, the impact of spending so much school time on these two learning areas is seriously compromising the capacity of schools to organize and implement high-quality all-round educational programmes. Thus, whilst proponents argue that national testing

---

[2]By a double bind, I mean pressure from two sources such that a choice of one precludes or constrains the other.

is a cost-effective way of ensuring accountability in education, it is clear that the full cost of these procedures will not be known until environmental and social costs are acknowledged.

In this way, we can see how a double bind is the end result of the tension between a cultural agenda for school reform and a right-wing technocratic agenda of testing, hierarchical discipline and performance management. The cultural agenda is reflected in solutions such as culturally inclusive schooling, programmes to enhance social justice and democratic community participation, whole school sustainability projects, democratically oriented behavioural approaches, whole health programmes and active citizenship programmes to improve the local environment and community. Both the technocratic and the cultural agendas are expected to be implemented by the school. However, the technocratic overrides the cultural in a dualism of the kind described by Plumwood (1993) and Davison (2001). The apparatus for this is the logic of domination which results in the backgrounding of the culturally derived agenda of change, by the domination or foregrounding of a technocratically informed mindset that pervades our system.

The dualism is now played out through a technocratically informed regime underpinned by conformity to a rigid national curriculum which is surveilled by standardized Australia-wide testing of literacy and numeracy (NAPLAN) on the one hand. On the other hand is a culturally derived cross-curricular set of priorities and values of sustainability, Asia studies and indigenous studies. These do not yet have formal ACARA-endorsed syllabi[3] for implementation other than integration suggestions in the curriculum documents. Therefore, the requirements of the technocratic agenda simply overwhelm the cultural priorities by the overemphasis on the *My Schools* website[4] which was constructed to publish results of the competition between schools on the basis of literacy and numeracy scores (McGaw, n.d.). Thus, as a result of the demands created by this agenda, teachers simply do not have the time, resources or support to wholly follow through on a commitment to sustainability reorientation at school. In other words, they are stymied by the system which expects them to work in transformative, socially active ways.

## Sustainability as Process: Keeping Alive a Strong Vision

In this section, I offer a potted account of the development of the concept of sustainability since the early 1970s to present the political or strong view of it and illustrate the embedded ambiguities, tensions and paradoxes. The momentum was

---

[3]There is however an excellent 'Sustainability Curriculum Framework' produced by the Department of the Environment, Water, Heritage and the Arts (2010) that does not appear to be acknowledged by ACARA.

[4]www.myschool.edu.au.

set in motion about 40 years ago when it was acknowledged that environmental degradation is as much a social problem as it is a scientific one (Evans & Boyden, 1970; UNESCO, 1977), hence the emergence of environmental education as an interdisciplinary field of endeavour. Since then, a struggle for educators, writers and activists in the field has been to keep alive a strong vision of a liveable future. That is to say, foster a socially critical view that supports a cultural agenda of human flourishing and acknowledges the ecos as the ground of our way of life (Fien, 2001; Jucker, 2003; UNESCO, 2005). It is a picture of a culturally productive enterprise of envisioning and generating a socially just, ecologically healthy future as opposed to a narrow, technocratic enterprise based on prediction and technological solutions.

In the 1980s, concepts of sustainability and sustainable development[5] were widely deployed into the plethora of government, business and organizational policies, largely as a result of the World Commission on Environment and Development's report: 'Our Common Future' (Brundtland, 1987). The process involved discussions between parties with disparate worldviews (World Commission on Environment and Development, 1987, p. 8) which resulted in interpretations of sustainability that are value-laden and which serve particular economic, political or social interests. As a result, the intentions and rhetoric of the cultural and the technocratic discourses lead to very different processes and outcomes due to the differences in their organizing logic, even though the fundamental impetus of both is the ambition of humans to sustain the sources of our sustenance (Davison, 2001). This is the central ambiguity in the notion of sustainability.

The cultural discourse of sustainability is also referred to as the strong version[6] and features political and social justice, moral enrichment and enlivening artistic, ecological and spiritual practices, whereas the technocratic discourse features optimal, cost-effective, technological configurations. Thus, the technocratic discourse reduces our social and ecological reality to that of instrumentalism and uses the economy as the organizing principle (Davison, 2001), in effect delivering a consumerist[7] outlook which as a whole underpins the construction of our current ecological crises (Davison, 2001; Orr, 2002; Scott, 2002). Therefore, a socially critical action learning approach to sustainability transition is essential as it reveals: 'the economic, political, philosophical and epistemological roots of environmental issues and adequate examinations of social alternatives' (Jickling, 1992, p. 5).

---

[5]Due to the need for brevity, I have folded the terms sustainability and sustainable development together. These days, sustainability is usually the preference for general use due to the assertion that sustainable development is an oxymoron.

[6]Interestingly, a strong politically shaped version of sustainability is informed by the ethos of ecological democracy, which is often regarded as a theoretical framework for sustainability reorientation. Ecological democracy references its social critique to conceptions of ecological feminism, social democracy and deep ecology (Dryzek, 2005; Merchant, 2005).

[7]People of the early Australian suburban working classes probably saw themselves as producers— of food, clothing, meat, water, waste disposal and cottage industries, as they were quite self-reliant and independent. Thus, over time, a shift has occurred in how we see ourselves (Davison, 2006, p. 205).

Similarly, a spirit of enquiry into our daily routines is also necessary to diligently seek the deeply embedded contradictions between our espoused theories and our actions. This is because as academics we are, as Bowers (1997, p. 28) writes, still trapped by our language-embedded deepest assumptions about progress upon which the ecological crises are constructed. For example, in this chapter, I have produced a series of linked dualistic polemics to illustrate the context in which we attempt to change the status quo; however, my activities are still underpinned by the ideas of domination, competition, separation, atomism and rational thought—all of which underpin the technocratic discourse. That is, paradoxically, we are perpetrating the discourse and practices we are trying to change.

Keeping in mind the inherent tensions and contradictions, it is important to appreciate that both the cultural and the technocratic perspectives of sustainability are necessary in the task of creating a sustainable future; however, the central point is that one should not dominate the other (Dryzek, 1998; Schwarz & Thompson, 1990; Wooltorton, 2004). Further, good programmes will show the process for addressing ambiguities and their connected conundrums to avoid constraint in achievement of objectives. In fact, strong understandings of sustainability tend to comprise a process orientation derived from the inclusion of a political perspective, and this is now part of an international a definition of sustainability which is represented as a system of four interdependent[8] qualities:

- Biophysical systems which provide the life-support systems for all life, human and non-human
- Economic systems which provide a continuing means of livelihood (jobs and money) for people
- Social and cultural systems which provide ways for people to live together peacefully, equitably and with respect for human rights and dignity
- Political systems through which power is exercised fairly and democratically to make decisions about the way social and economic systems use the biophysical environment UNESCO (2002a, p. 8).

In essence, weak notions of sustainability avoid the political participative imperative whilst the strong versions embed a process focus which embeds learning opportunities. This is essential to collaboratively build knowledge, skills and cultural capital for living and working sustainably.

## Active and Informed Citizenship for Learning Sustainability

In this section, I point out that sustainability reorientation is increasingly being seen as a political rather than an economic activity (Orr, 2002, p. 108) essentially because the sociopolitical dimension enables an alternative organizing principle

---

[8]Unfortunately, one language-embedded dilemma with this definition is the separation of social justice from the ecological, which maintains the illusion that they are separate—once again reinforcing the logic of the neoliberal project (Bowers, 1997, 2005).

for sustainability transition. As I see it, this amounts to civil development through community-based democracy. Using this stance, the process for sustainability is one of human decision-making rather than one of a poorly self-regulating economy. That is, with politics as the organizing principle for sustainability, the central spheres of concern are problems of democracy and participation, facilitating participatory action learning and other forms of deliberative social learning.

With this in mind, a trap to be aware of is the possibility of becoming increasingly aloof from cultural and ecological embeddedness causing ungrounded change for its own sake (Bowers, 1997). Therefore, self- and collaborative reflection is an important element of any transition process (Hopkins, 2008) to be used, aiming for an empowerment that is strongly grounded in a sense of place and culture (Mortensen, 2000, pp. 15–23). Orr describes the impulse of sustainability as a design challenge unlike any other as it is about creating appropriate communities to fit their place with 'elegant frugality' (2002, p. 11). Education is central to this new ethic as we need to learn the practical knowledge, the know-how of sustainability. In social contexts, learning enables ongoing interpersonal support and the development of local community-based social capital—a culturally embedded active repository of knowledge, skills, experience, insights, wisdom and processes for change. Schools, colleges and universities have massive untapped potential in initiating, legitimating and authorizing this locally based social transition which requires a 'rejuvenation of civic culture' (Orr, 1992, p. 1).

The strong, socially critical perspectives on sustainability have important implications for organizing schools and universities as practical learning communities and as hubs for social change (Wooltorton, 2003). Orr draws particular attention to the correlation between environmental degradation and decay in the concept of citizenship, arguing that they are mutually reinforcing trends. Therefore, change is best enabled through an appropriate politic, an active, informed citizenry (Orr, 1992, p. 2) and a learning stance for acquiring practical, place-based knowledge of sustainability, a community literate in sustainability (Stibbe & Luna, 2009). Together with learning about the power of language to subvert or support intention through its embedded discourses, this approach forms the basis of an eco-justice pedagogy (Bowers, 2001, p. 259).

## Sustainability Transition in Australia: Anticipation and Constraint

In this section, my intent is to show how in Australia an increasing number of schools and universities host learning programmes underpinned by active citizenship; however, there are systemic constraints which prevent their flourishing. I begin with an outline of place-based education (Sobel, 2004) to explain that it facilitates local development of a community-based eco-justice pedagogy. Its rationale is: 'the realization that love—love of nature, love of one's neighbors and community—is a prime motivating factor in personal transformation, and the transformation of culture' (Sobel, 2004, p. ii). Thus, opportunities for sustainability literacy acquisition abound (Stibbe, 2009), enabling new ways of seeing and understanding ways people impact on place.

It is pleasing to see that as part of these place-based developments, playground harmony and social inclusion programmes are increasingly being seen as sustainability activities, as are global education and indigenous cultural programmes. The Australian Sustainable Schools Initiative (AuSSI)[9] in Western Australia encourages activities around the theme of 'increasing our social handprint, reducing our ecological footprint' (AuSSI WA, n.d.-a). Accordingly, plans to improve participation in school decision-making are included, particularly as this relates to questions of sustainability. As well as being officially encouraged (AuSSI WA, n.d.-b), participation in decision-making is currently embedded in Western Australia's Curriculum Framework (Curriculum Council, 1998, pp. 23–24; inside back cover; and pp. 261–262). Thus, in Western Australia, at the present time, state curriculum documents and AuSSI provide encouragement and guidance to teachers and school communities in their community-based sustainability transitions. Additionally, philanthropic organizations,[10] government departments and others—including an increasing number of corporations[11]—are moving into the role of supporting these transitions with finance and importantly the contribution of professional advice and skills.

It is important to note however that the development of a cultural base of sustainability practice in school and community takes time, patience, considerable dialogue and substantial effort and commitment by all parties. Every so often, there are conflicts—in some projects more than others. In my experience, these are often due to the not-yet fully developed skills and practical knowledge of working collaboratively. Whilst the resolution of these conflicts can provide the deepest learning opportunities, the point is that the acquisition of social capital for sustainability transition is complex and collaborative in nature because it builds upon multiple layers of engagement, critique, learning and change. This line of reasoning is often missed by policy writers and curriculum managers who relegate low priority in terms of time and resources to these active learning programmes. Thus, the goal of sustainability reorientation demands radically different ways of enacting schools and universities in relation to their communities and with regard to experiential-practical learning models, which first have to be learned through the provision of opportunities.

Unfortunately, the end result is that our education system is biased towards the development of successful learners (narrowly defined in terms of literacy and

---

[9]AuSSI is an Australian government programme of support for sustainability education that operates through joint funding with each state and territory.

[10]See, for example, HotRock (2011) and Alexander (2004).

[11]See, for example, Energy Challenge Project (n.d.). Corporate support is not without criticism due to the issues around the moral and sometimes explicit condition upon acceptance of funds to positively represent the corporation to the community.

numeracy outcomes) whilst allocating a lower priority to the development of active and informed citizens. This is even though the second goal of our national education system has three parts, as follows: 'All young Australians become successful learners, confident and creative individuals, and active and informed citizens' (Ministerial Council on Education Employment Training and Youth Affairs, 2008, pp. 8 and 9). I presume that bias is not the intention, but it is the outcome of a double bind in which the logic of domination subverts active and informed citizenship by privileging literacy and numeracy because it is seen as vital to economic prosperity. As described above, this is a deleterious outcome from the point of view of sustainability education, firstly because active and informed citizenship is key to a strong, socially critical view of sustainability and secondly because it is an important dynamic in the community space for experiential-practical learning of sustainability. The practical knowledge so formed is our know-how of sustainability transition.

Not surprisingly, the irony of the technocratic approach with a narrow focus on literacy and numeracy is that there have been a number of studies which show that the use of environment as an integrating context (EIC) for education produces increases in student learning and achievement across the curriculum including social studies, science, language arts and maths. Importantly, children also showed improvement in self-esteem, behaviour and higher-order cognitive skills (Sobel, 2004, pp. 25–32). These programmes also foster the development of a broader notion of intelligence which, it is argued, must be ecologically embedded because if a creature destroys its environment, collaboratively or individually, it displays insanity rather than intelligence (Bateson, 1972; Bowers, 1995, p. 129).

Overall, it seems that whilst the structures for sustainability reorientation are in place, for it to emerge in a more systemic, comprehensive way, a more expansive view of the role of education institutions and campuses will be necessary (Orr, 2010, p. 76). In my view, in Australia, this will need to involve public recognition of the systemic structural constraints that hinder transformation as well as acknowledgement, understanding and celebration of the ambiguities and tensions at the core of sustainability. At an even more basic level, it will also require a comprehension that learning—which takes time and effort—is the basis of sustainability transition.

## Learning Sustainability in Teacher Education: Issues and Reflections

In this section, I first briefly explain how the technocratic pressures on Australian schools in their sustainability reorientation efforts are also being applied to universities and are subsequently squeezing teacher education programmes. I illustrate this before summarizing progress in sustainability reorientation in Australian universities and teacher education courses.

Intentionally or otherwise, technocratic restrictions function to preserve an economic focus and give little consideration to consequent social justice or environmental impacts—in schools or universities. For instance, the impact of a structural double bind in universities caused by increased Commonwealth accountability mechanisms is that many academics must work extra hours to achieve their basic requirements. As a result, they often suffer a poor work/life balance, which makes personal practical learning of sustainability extremely difficult (Wooltorton, Palmer, & Steele, 2011). This quandary restricts the potential for cultivating new ways of thinking about and developing teacher education.

On top of this complication, Australian universities are increasingly regarded as narrow places for employment preparation, a stance which requires subservience to the workplace for skills and knowledge demanded by employers. Thus, in the case of Australian education departments, themselves now accountable to politicians rather than educators, the demand is likely to be for graduates to fill the mould of a teacher as shaped through systems of compliance, outcomes accountability and incentives. To guarantee this supply, teacher education courses must now comply with new registration requirements stipulating proportions of literacy and numeracy (Australian Institute for Teaching and School Leadership, 2011; Western Australian College of Teaching, 2009). This trend would appear to signal a very different role for teacher educators, a shift from having a proactive responsibility for socially critical knowledge creation to being deliverers of packages of material deemed by non-educators to be vocationally appropriate for pre-service teachers. In the USA, teacher education course registration has been in place for some years and receives considerable criticism for its trivializing of education, for its narrow, managerialist implementation strategies which demean the role of teacher educators and their institutions, for its political control which is located outside of academic scrutiny, for its cooptation of the concept of democracy into something resembling consumerism and for its role in authorizing testing which results in the aiding or emphasizing of stratification by class and race (Apple, 2005).

Consequently, in order to address the policy goal of reorientation to sustainability—and to ensure a place for our intellectual contribution—teacher educators will need to rethink the ways in which we nurture the development of a socially critical active citizenship in pre-service teachers. This is so that graduates can be confident of their capacity to create conditions for sustainability transition in schools. Thus, given what we know about the development of practical knowledge of sustainability, an overarching integrative focus on sustainability transition at the course level will be necessary. Therefore, in the context of ambiguity and tension around sustainability education in Australian schools and universities, it is testimony to the struggle embarked upon by academics that there are a range of sustainability education projects in many universities.

For instance, five universities in Queensland and four in NSW were involved in a programme to mainstream education for sustainability into pre-service teacher education (Ferreira, Ryan, Davis, Cavanagh, & Thomas, 2009). For this purpose, the Australian Research Institute in Education for Sustainability utilized a complex systems approach to holistic change in a university setting (Ferreira et al., 2009; Steele, 2010). At the same time, in a number of other universities, whole-of-university approaches to sustainability to link research, education and operational activities together are being developed to share information for knowledge building

(McMillan & Dyball, 2009). These include the development of a shared vision to encourage critical reflection through participation and dialogue. To support this and to address the issue of silos in university, collaborative interdisciplinary approaches to planning and teaching the curriculum are being implemented (Hammond, 2011; Paige, Lloyd, & Chartres, 2008; Sherren, 2006).

## Hope: Narratives of Local Transition

In this section, I exemplify the trend towards sustainability reorientation in universities by contributing a small case study written from an experiential perspective. I begin with the university-wide context of Edith Cowan University (ECU) before highlighting the early stages of sustainability transition in the Faculty of Regional Professional Studies (FRPS), as context for an overview of initiatives in the education programme. An account of an eco-justice pedagogy follows, and a short reflection on working against the grain is presented last. In that vein, I wish to explain that due to the requirement for brevity, I list projects without elucidating the struggles involved in setting up and maintaining them. This does a disservice to their organizers and paradoxically fulfils the technocratic demand for destoried, dehumanized results (Bowers, 1997). Therefore, I would like it understood that between the lines in the accounts below sit the political quandaries, ambiguities me (programme) and constraints which function at this university like every other.

At ECU, there are whole-of-university, top-down and bottom-up opportunities to reorient faculties, schools, programmes and operations to sustainability through substantial policy and more recently curriculum improvements (Edith Cowan University, 2005, 2007, 2010). Within this context, over the years, substantial progress has been made with a recently strengthened focus created by dedicated committees and workgroups. For example, in the FRPS, a range of projects are now in place including a whole faculty ongoing project based on conversations to develop a culture of social sustainability with the aim of informing teaching and learning transitions in each programme; festivals to celebrate and display sustainability education in local settings; business student projects in the community; an ongoing theory to practice project in nursing as well as a number of community engagement activities organized by the Nursing Programme; art exhibitions, poetry days and other public events organized by the Arts Programme; regular surfing events and other coastal science activities organized by the Surf Science Programme; the computing students conduct engagement-type projects for other programmes and organizations; and a wide range of community-based events are organized by the Social Work Programme. Key elements of FRPS projects include a practical learning focus, working collaboratively, interdisciplinarity, partnerships at the project and the whole-system level and community engagement.

In Education, a whole-programme plan to reorient teaching and learning to sustainability is being developed; a food garden has recently been installed to give teacher education a place-based focus and to link it with other Programmes including Social Work, and there are also two large ongoing community engagement projects, each comprising a wide range of multisector sustainability transition activities. In addition, a number of classroom-based innovations are in place including a programme called SEPH (social, emotional and physical health), cooperative learning and a range of extended practical learning projects focusing on active citizenship that students implement through collaborative enquiry-based assessments.

The active citizenship projects utilize an eco-justice pedagogy and commence on the first day of semester and conclude on the last. They require students to design and implement projects that will make an improvement to the social and/or ecological environment and which could later be modified for implementation in a school. Two parts to the assignment are submitted: the first is the proposal with literature review which is due in week four of semester, whilst the second is the social action approved by the lecturer through assessment of part one. Projects implemented by the students in the past have comprised the formation of student organizations to clean up rubbish from roads and beaches, implementing coast care activities, installation of bat boxes and possum lodges in appropriately selected trees, the construction of frog-scapes, the construction of a path for an outdoor eco-education centre, implementation of a number of vegetable and permaculture-type gardens at schools, and a range of social projects including organizing vegetables for a low-cost food service, as well as the design and implementation of a scented and kinaesthetic garden for a nursing home.

The active learning process is enriching as student work groups regularly present verbal progress reports to peers in tutorial groups, who listen and help to troubleshoot by identifying potential problems. They also make themselves available for mutual consultation about problems being experienced. In this way, students share each other's project implementation stories. The projects are intrinsically motivating as they are contributing to the betterment of their place. Further, as well as acquiring practical knowledge of sustainability, they actually make an improvement which is rewarding, empowering and memorable. Importantly, students usually need to persist with particular tasks until difficult problems are solved. In my case, the opportunity to work with pre-service teachers and academic staff who are committed to their work and to the social task of working for a better world is deeply appreciated.

Here, I offer a small reflection on the pragmatics of sustainability transition in a university. According to Smyth et al. (2009), an activist-based socially critical perspective is a courageous struggle for a more socially just world. In practice, for me it is one built upon a daily anthology of actions for a sustainable future—of linking people and narratives to facilitate transitions towards being grounded in place and culture. As in most other university contexts, this entails on the one hand complying with technocratic requirements whilst on the other hand regular transgression by acting to restore justice and equity. It also means respectfully toiling to change those routines which appear to serve no particular purpose other than to appease bureaucratic demands or serve the interests of authority.

## Conclusion: For a Sustainable Future, We Need Each Other

Within education contexts formed by teachers and academics who regularly transgress technocratic boundaries, sustainability transition is about collaboratively producing and then 'storying' a different future into being—by creating a positive, valid, reliable narrative to link our personal and community-based sustainability learning activities with our work as academics. That narrative needs to include functional ways to expose and address the logic of domination which operates through the paradoxes, tensions and constraints. It is an account of resistance, persistence and renewal; a story in which creation of a future worth living in is no longer a separate agenda in education—it is now *the* agenda (Sterling, 2002). There is no other valid narrative.

On the surface, it appears that schools and teacher education programmes in universities are well placed for implementation of the new National Action Plan for sustainability reorientation. That being said, systemic reorientation is a particularly complex task to undertake, especially where the central ambitions of sustainability education and of sustainability itself are ambivalent. These predicaments are un-doubtedly part of the matted underlying causation of unsustainable trends; however, the use of sociopolitical processes to investigate and address the core ambiguity of competing discourses is a cause célèbre for sustainability. The important questions are about the meaning and tensions in sustainability, the kind of future we want and the local pathways for the journey. It is precisely this ambiguity that suggests a rethink of the essential question: what are schools for? Is the role of the school to support the technocratic agenda that promotes economic goals above others? Or is it to support a culturally sustainable society intent on learning to reconnect to our place and each other? Our Federal government stipulates both, a stance that is dishonest as it is currently framed and that handicaps schools and universities in their efforts to reorient their operations and programmes (DEWHA, 2009; McGaw, n.d.).

Therefore, bringing sustainability reorientation into being is a messy, untidy, disordered process of change. It is inherently a generative transformative learning agenda that sits uncomfortably inside the constraints of a technocratic system upon which it is dependent for implementation. Importantly, it requires a comprehension that learning—which takes time and effort—is the basis of sustainability transition. So it is unfortunate that the practical knowledge acquisition made possible in projects based on active citizenship-type engagement is subverted and deprioritized in our system, which emphasizes skills identified as those narrowly associated with economic outcomes of schooling. Similar pressures are now being brought to bear on teacher education programmes in universities, as new Commonwealth regulations come into currency. Thus, in response, teacher education institutions will need to develop overarching linked sustainability programmes to enable the development of confidence in graduates to implement socially critical programmes for sustainability.

The logic of domination is inherent in technocracies designed for accountability rather than to bring forth a future worth living in, whilst the logic of sustainability holds the technocracy together with the eco-social sphere. Underneath the layers is the fundamental recognition that both discourses are required—we need each other—in a context of mutual respect. To enable sustainability reorientation to take hold and thrive, a pervading goodwill is necessary, an empowering spirit of contribution, cooperation and mutual care. This spirit, in the final analysis, is the essence of meaningful sustainability reorientation.

# References

Alexander, S. (2004). *The kitchen garden project*. Retrieved May 11, 2011, from http://www. kitchengardenfoundation.org.au/

Apple, M. (2005). Foreword. In D. Johnson, B. Johnson, S. Farenga, & D. Ness (Eds.), *Trivialising teacher education: The accreditation squeeze*. Oxford, UK: Rowman and Littlefield Publishers, Inc.

AuSSI WA. (n.d.-a). *Australian Sustainable Schools Initiative – WA*. Retrieved June 13, 2009, from http://www.det.wa.edu.au/curriculumsupport/sustainableschools/detcms/portal/

AuSSI WA. (n.d.-b). *A practical guide to the Australian Sustainable Schools Initiative WA*. Perth: Department of Education and Training.

Australian Institute for Teaching and School Leadership. (2011). *Accreditation of initial teacher education programs in Australia: Standards and procedures*. Retrieved April 26, 2011, from http://www.aitsl.edu.au/verve/_resources/Accreditation_of_initial_teacher_education.pdf

Bateson, G. (1972). *Steps to an ecology of mind: A revolutionary approach to man's understanding of himself*. New York: Ballantine Books.

Bowers, C. (1995). *Educating for an ecologically sustainable culture: Rethinking moral education, creativity, intelligence, and other modern orthodoxies*. Albany, NY: State University of New York Press.

Bowers, C. (1997). *The culture of denial: Why the environmental movement needs a strategy for reforming universities and public schools*. Albany, NY: State University of New York Press.

Bowers, C. (2001). Challenges in educating for ecologically sustainable communities. *Educational Philosophy and Theory, 33*(2), 257–265.

Bowers, C. (2005). Introduction. In C. Bowers & F. Apffel-Marglin (Eds.), *Rethinking Freire: Globalization and the environmental crisis* (pp. 1–10). London: Lawrence Erlbaum Associates.

Brundtland, H. (1987). *Our common future: Report of the world commission on environment and development*. Paris: United Nations.

Curriculum Council. (1998). *Curriculum framework*. Perth, Australia: Curriculum Council.

Davison, A. (2001). *Technology and the contested meanings of sustainability*. Albany, NY: State University of New York Press.

Davison, A. (2006). Stuck in a cul-de-sac? Suburban history and urban sustainability in Australia. *Urban Policy and Research, 24*(2), 201–216.

Department of the Environment Water Heritage and the Arts. (2009). *Living sustainably: The Australian government's national action plan for education for sustainability*. Canberra, Australia: Department of the Environment, Water, Heritage and the Arts.

Department of the Environment Water Heritage and the Arts. (2010). *Sustainability curriculum framework: A guide for curriculum developers and policy makers*. Retrieved May 11, 2011, from http://www.environment.gov.au/education/publications/curriculum-framework.html

Dryzek, J. (1998). Political and ecological communication. In J. Dryzak & D. Scholsberg (Eds.), *Debating the earth: The environmental politics reader*. Oxford, UK: Oxford University Press.

Dryzek, J. (2005). *The politics of the earth: Environmental discourses*. New York: Oxford University Press.

Edith Cowan University. (2005). *Edith Cowan University Environmental Declaration*. Perth: http://www.ecu.edu.au/fas/EcoECU/docs/Environmental_Declaration.pdf

Edith Cowan University. (2007). *Environment services: Big steps towards a smaller footprint.* Retrieved May 11, 2011, from http://www.ecu.edu.au/fas/EcoECU/index.php

Edith Cowan University. (2010). *ECU 2012 Undergraduate curriculum framework: Implementation resources package, Phase One 2 August 2010 to 1 March 2011.* Retrieved May 11, 2011, from http://secure.ecu.edu.au/Projects-and-initiatives/staffonly/ECU2012/ECU2012-Resources.pdf

Energy Challenge Project. (n.d.). *The energy challenge project.* Retrieved May 11, 2011, from http://www.energychallenge.org.au/

Evans, J., & Boyden, S. (1970, April 24–26). *Education and the environmental crisis.* Paper presented at the Conference of the Australian Academy of Science: Education and the environmental crises, Canberra, Australia.

Ferreira, J., Ryan, L., Davis, J., Cavanagh, M., & Thomas, J. (2009). *Mainstreaming sustainability into pre-service teacher education in Australia.* Prepared by the Australian Research Institute in Education for Sustainability, Canberra, Australia.

Fien, J. (2001). *Education for sustainability: Reorienting Australian schools for a sustainable future.* Canberra, Australia: Australian Conservation Foundation.

Government of Western Australia. (2007). *Western Australia's plan improve literacy and numeracy outcomes: Council of Australian governments, national reform agenda.* Retrieved June 19, 2009, from http://www.socialpolicy.dpc.wa.gov.au/documents/literacyNumeracy_20070409.pdf

Hammond, C. (2011). *Socially sustainable practice: Voices from within scholarly communities.* Unpublished Doctor of Philosophy, University of South Australia, Adelaide, Australia.

Hopkins, R. (2008). *The transition handbook: Creating local sustainable communities beyond oil dependency.* Totnes, UK: Green Books Ltd.

HotRock. (2011). *HotRock.* Retrieved May 11, 2011, from http://www.thehotrock.org.au/home/

Jickling, R. (1992). Why I don't want my children to be educated for sustainable development. *The Journal of Environmental Education, 24*(4), 5–8.

Jucker, R. (2003). UNESCO's teaching and learning for a sustainable future: A critical evaluation of underlying unsustainable progress myths. *The Trumpeter, 19*(2), 83–107.

McGaw, B. (n.d.). *A note from ACARA.* Retrieved May 11, 2011, from http://www.myschool.edu.au/

McKeown, R. (2002). *Education for sustainable development toolkit.* http://www.esdtoolkit.org

Mcmillan, J., & Dyball, R. (2009). Developing a whole-of-university approach to educating for sustainability: Linking curriculum, research and sustainable campus operations. *Journal of Education for Sustainable Development, 3,* 55–64.

Merchant, C. (2005). *Radical ecology: The search for a livable world.* New York/London: Routledge.

Ministerial Council on Education Employment Training and Youth Affairs. (2008). *Melbourne declaration on educational goals for young Australians.* Retrieved April 20, 2011, from http://www.curriculum.edu.au/verve/_resources/National_Declaration_on_the_Educational_Goals_for_Young_Australians.pdf

Mortensen, L. (2000). Global change education: Educational resources for sustainability. In K. Wheeler & A. Bijur (Eds.), *Education for a sustainable future: A paradigm of hope for the 21st century* (pp. 15–33). New York: Kluwer Academic/Plenum Publishers.

Orr, D. (1992). *Ecological literacy: Education and the transition to a postmodern world.* Albany, NY: State University of New York.

Orr, D. (2002). *The nature of design: Ecology, culture and human intention.* Oxford, UK: Oxford University Press.

Orr, D. (2010). What is higher education for now? In L. Starke & L. Mastny (Eds.), *State of the World, 2010: Transforming cultures from consumerism to sustainability: A WorldWatch Institute report on progress toward a sustainable society* (pp. 75–84). New York: W.W. Norton and Company.

Paige, K., Lloyd, D., & Chartres, M. (2008). Moving towards transdisciplinarity: An ecological focus for science and mathematics pre-service teacher education in the primary/middle years. *Asia-Pacific Journal of Teacher Education, 36*(1), 19–33.

Plumwood, V. (1993). *Feminism and the mastery of nature*. London: Routledge.

Schwarz, M., & Thompson, M. (1990). *Divided we stand: Redefining politics, technology and social choice*. Sydney, Australia: Harvester Wheatsheaf.

Scott, W. (2002). *Sustainability and learning: What role for the curriculum?* Bath, UK: University of Bath and Council for Environmental Education.

Sherren, K. (2006). Core issues: Reflections on sustainability in Australian university coursework programs. *International Journal of Sustainability in Higher Education, 7*(4), 400–413.

Smyth, J. (2001). *Critical politics of teachers' work: An Australian perspective*. New York: Peter Lang.

Smyth, J., & Shacklock, G. (1998). *Re-making teaching: Ideology, policy and practice*. London and New York: Routledge.

Smyth, J., Angus, L., Down, B., & McIerney, P. (2009). *Activist and socially critical school and community renewal*. Rotterdam, The Netherlands: Sense Publishers.

Sobel, D. (2004). *Place-based education: Connecting classrooms and communities*. Great Barrington, MA: Orion Society.

Steele, F. (2010). *Mainstreaming education for sustainability into pre-service teacher education in Australia: Enablers and constraints*. A report prepared by the Australian Research Institute in Education for Sustainability for the Australian Government Department of the Environment, Water, Heritage and the Arts, Canberra, Australia.

Sterling, S. (2001). *Sustainable education: Re-visioning learning and change*. Totnes, UK: Green Books.

Sterling, S. (2002). *Don't forget tomorrow*. Retrieved October 21, 2005, from wwflearning.co.uk

Stibbe, A. (Ed.). (2009). *The handbook of sustainability literacy: Skills for a changing world*. Totnes, UK: Green Books.

Stibbe, A., & Luna, H. (2009). Introduction. In A. Stibbe (Ed.), *The handbook of sustainability* (pp. 9–16). Totnes, UK: Green Books.

UNESCO. (1977). *Intergovernmental conference on environmental education: Final report*. Paper presented at the Intergovernmental Conference on Environmental Education, Tbilisi, Georgia

UNESCO. (2002a). *Education for sustainability. From Rio to Johannesburg: Lessons learnt from a decade of commitment*. Paper presented at the World Summit on Sustainable Development, Paris. Retrieved May 11, 2011, from http://www.mq.edu.au/sustainability/documents/e/EFS-FromRioToJohannessburg.pdf

UNESCO. (2002b). *Teaching and learning for a sustainable future: A multimedia teacher education program*. Retrieved May, 2006, from http://www.unesco.org/education/tlsf/

UNESCO. (2005). Reorienting existing education. In Curriculum Rationale: Reorienting education for a sustainable future. *Teaching and learning for a sustainable future: A multimedia teacher education program*. Retrieved July 28, 2008, from http://www.unesco.org/education/tlsf/index.htm

United Nations Conference on Environment and Development. (1992). *Earth summit: Agenda 21 – The United Nations program of actions from Rio*. Retrieved May 11, 2011, from http://www.un.org/esa/dsd/agenda21/index.shtml

Western Australian College of Teaching. (2009). *Initial teacher education programs: Accreditation processes and standards*. Retrieved May 11, 2011, from http://membership.wacot.wa.edu.au/INITIAL_TEACHER_EDUCATION_PROGRAMS-Accreditation_Process_and_StandardsOct09.pdf

Wooltorton, S. (2003). Education for sustainability: A background paper prepared for the State Sustainability Strategy. In *Hope for the future: The Western Australian state sustainability strategy*. Perth, Australia: Government of Western Australia.

Wooltorton, S. (2004). *School as community: Bridging the gap to sustainability*. Unpublished Doctor of Philosophy dissertation, Murdoch University, Perth, Australia.

Wooltorton, S., Palmer, M., & Steele, F. (2011). A process for transition to sustainability: Implementation. *Australian Journal of Environmental Education, 27*(1), 160–174.

World Commission on Environment and Development. (1987). *Our common future: Report of the World Commission on Environment and Development*. United Nations: http://conspect.nl/pdf/Our_Common_Future-Brundtland_Report_1987.pdf

# Chapter 19
# Afterword: We Can Enact Change

**Kenneth Tobin**

"Yes we can!" Who can forget the euphoria of Barack Obama's sweep into power in the 2008 presidential election in the United States? The promise of change at last was euphoric and a new age beckoned. However, 3 years later and 1 year before the next election, the political rhetoric and our lived reality is "No he didn't!" Whatever happened to the "we" in the enactment of the vision that carried Obama to the Presidency? Making the vision a reality was translated into an individual accomplishment. The futility of heroic individuals transforming society was never more apparent in the past few years, nor was it clearer that in the United States and possibly globally as well, individuals would be held responsible for the conditions of social life. The commonsense models for change and accountability are oversimplified and unworkable. In Obama's case, at least the "we" in "Yes we can" was truncated in enactment and lost in accountability.

For as long as I have been involved in education as a teacher and teacher educator, now approaching 50 years, the dominant ideology has embraced positivism (Kincheloe & Tobin, 2009). Elsewhere I have discussed ways in which tenets of positivism, related to neoliberalism, capitalism, and neoconservativism, have been globalized in ways that have maintained familiar approaches to teaching, learning, curriculum, and teacher education (Tobin, 2011). Of course, there are nuances to these claims. It is dangerous to overgeneralize based on patterns that recur and confirm evidence of reproduction without acknowledging that each moment of reproduction also is a moment of transformation. Wherever there is solid evidence for reproduction of practices in teaching, learning, and teacher education, there also will be evidence of transformation, contradictions that point to a necessity to nuance strong claims. Contradictions might represent resistance to tradition or alternatives considered to be improvements that also have the potential to replace

K. Tobin (✉)
Urban Education Program, Graduate Center, City University of New York, New York, NY, USA
e-mail: KTobin@gc.cuny.edu

B. Down and J. Smyth (eds.), *Critical Voices in Teacher Education*, Explorations
of Educational Purpose 22, DOI 10.1007/978-94-007-3974-1_19,
© Springer Science+Business Media Dordrecht 2012

mainstream practices. From a theoretical perspective, social life is complex, and when culture is enacted, it can be experienced as co-occurrent patterns that have thin coherence and contradictions to those patterns (Tobin, 2010). When researchers focus only on patterns as a basis for making assertions, the oversight can be highly significant. Contradictions to a pattern of coherence might be kernels for transforming a field. As contradictions occur, they are resources for action, and as such, they can be appropriated agentically or operate passively as seeds for the emergence of new streams of culture. Developing an understanding of ways in which social analysis can embrace nuance and complexity is a desirable feature of education and research in education. Having presented this caveat, I now venture into turbulent waters in an effort to identify, in a nuanced way, how many of the issues addressed in this volume edited by Barry Down and John Smyth have been manifest in my own experiences as a teacher, teacher educator, and scholar.

## Individual Models for Teaching, Learning, and Accountability

The ideology that appears to have pervaded everyday sensibilities about good teaching assumes that teachers establish control over students to create and sustain productive learning environments. Accordingly, most teacher education programs, including my initial teacher preparation program, had strong emphases on classroom management and use of effective techniques for controlling students. In teacher education programs, good learning is often equated with quiet classrooms, and conventional wisdom of senior educators suggests you can judge a good teacher by listening at the door. Effective classroom management is associated with teachers being able to manage student conduct and minimize noise. When I began to teach in 1964, school administrators counseled me that a good teacher's class had a working buzz that did not become louder if the teacher left the room (e.g., to get equipment from a storeroom). Quiet, serving as a proxy for effective control, was a barometer for effective teaching.

As is often the case with conventional wisdom, it was not deemed necessary to theorize the premise that effective teaching necessitated control over students. The assertion is coherent with other prevailing ideologies that are widely accepted without critique. For example, meritocracy assumes that students learn best when they compete on an equal footing with others (McNamee & Miller, 2004). Under this assumption, equity is regarded as having equal opportunity to compete, and learning is equated with effort. Students who make the effort learn and those who do not learn can do so by increasing effort. The emphasis is on individuals participating in ways that reflect traits such as motivation to learn. Models of accountability are built from assumptions associated with the quality of opportunities to participate and making appropriate levels of effort. Failure of individuals to succeed is frequently linked causally to the quality of teaching. When students fail, teachers are held accountable. This oversimplified model of accountability is often scaled up to the school level. Assumptions like these were prevalent in the early 1960s when I completed my teacher education and began to teach in Western Australia. Similar assumptions are very much alive today, not only in Australia but also in New York City where I am currently a professor of urban education.

What is it that sustains ideologies about teaching and learning that privilege the role of individuals over collectives and competition over collaboration? Joe Kincheloe and I argued that the vestiges of positivism saturated sensibilities and practices about education (Kincheloe & Tobin, 2009). Goals were set in terms of attaining identified canonical knowledges, such as science, and deficit perspectives underscored conceptual change approaches to teaching and learning. The mantra for teaching was to ascertain what individuals did not know and teach them accordingly—usually canonical representations, agreed to standards set by society. Differences were regarded through deficit lenses and were often represented as gaps between cultural majorities and cultural minority groups. Those whose average scores lagged behind were expected to work harder to attain specified benchmarks under stringent accountability measures designed to focus curricula on standards, provide appropriate practice, and measure achievement using standardized, high-stakes tests. The incentive to guarantee success is grounded in holding schools and teachers accountable and stipulating that high school graduation, for example, necessitates passing specific tests.

Chapter authors addressed ways in which teaching is increasingly deprofessionalized in a variety of ways. The ideology of capitalism provides an underpinning for rationales that view education and schools in terms of marketing mechanisms and their cost-effectiveness. It is a slippery slope that affords teachers being regarded as piecemeal workers who are interchangeable and a relative devaluation of relationships between teachers and students over time.

## Collaborative Approaches to Teaching and Teacher Education

In 1998, my research group initiated a program of learning to teach that was collective. I had come to the University of Pennsylvania and inherited a program that assumed learning to teach occurred best when student teachers (hereafter referred to as new teachers) were assigned to mentor teachers. The premises I found least useful were that effective teaching could reside in an individual and was independent of context. Questionable assumptions included mentor teachers being able to teach effectively across contexts, the transfer of knowledge from experts to novice being axiomatic, and improved teaching emerging from activities such as discussion about what happened and reflective writing. Although I was sure that pathways from texts about teaching to changed praxis could be worked out, I was concerned about ontological differences between talk about teaching and teaching as praxis. Highly significant to all these models was failure to acknowledge the cultural capital of new teachers. I was attracted to the possibilities of teachers from across the career ladder learning to teach from one another. Two teachers with relatively little formal teaching experience might learn to teach by teaching with one another in a coteaching arrangement. Similarly, it might be expected that learning from another is symmetrical even when an experienced teacher coteaches with a teacher with relatively little experience. It seemed just as likely that the senior teacher would learn from the new teacher as the new teacher would learn from the experienced teacher. I regarded effective teaching as collective and contingent on what happened in a class—needing to be adaptive to the unfolding situations as curricula were enacted.

There is a steady flight of teachers from inner-city to suburban schools where teachers are paid more and teach students who are more like them in terms of social class and lived experiences (Ingersoll & Perda, 2010). Furthermore, teachers who remain in inner-city schools seem to struggle for success, and most of them have to overcome significant obstacles that include misconduct from students, resistance to compliance, and shortage of material resources (Tobin, Seiler, & Walls, 1999). Rather than assigning new teachers to elite private schools in the inner-city or suburban schools, my stance reflects an axiology that new teachers can learn to teach while transforming urban education positively. As Director of Teacher Education, I was able to assign relatively large numbers of new teachers to small learning communities (SLCs)[1] within a small number of inner-city schools. For example, with the cooperation of school principals and the coordinators of SLCs, eight or nine new teachers were assigned for an academic year to a SLC that had seven full-time resident teachers and less than 600 students. The model we developed was to employ coteaching, involving two or three new teachers with one resident teacher. In this way, a minimum of two and occasionally as many as four teachers would coteach a particular class. This model applied not only as a way to enact initial teacher education but also to involve resident teachers in site-based professional development. The model could take advantage of the significant knowledge resources contributed by new teachers (Tobin & Roth, 2006).

The students benefited from having many teachers available to scaffold their learning, and the coteachers worked together to develop teaching roles that were complementary. Coteachers experienced a range of teaching strategies from which they learned by being in the same classroom with other teachers, thereby expanding possibilities for learning from other coteachers without conscious awareness or having a goal to learn particular teaching strategies. Just as some of what was learned unconsciously and without intent was beneficial to students and the teachers who had learned, some of what was learned also was deleterious to students and inconsistent with the values of the teacher who had learned the new teaching strategies (and was unaware of how she/he was teaching). Accordingly, we developed a reflective, dialogic activity in which the quality of teaching and learning would be reviewed with the goal of making improvements. The purpose of this activity, referred to as cogenerative dialogue (i.e., cogen), was to identify aspects of

---

[1] SLCs operated with a larger school as a school within a school. Each had its own coordinator, faculty, and students.

teaching and learning that worked well and other aspects that were deleterious and in need of change. Coteaching and cogen are complementary, collective activities that produce new forms of learning and transform teaching and learning practices. Identification of patterns and contradictions was a first step toward the creation of new roles to support productive learning environments. By sharing the amount and turns of talk, all participants in cogen had opportunities to contribute their ideas about preferred roles and the desired nature of learning environments. In addition, through the use of radical listening, each participant had an opportunity to learn from others. Since we selected the participants in cogen to be different from one another, the activity provided opportunities for all participants to produce new culture that could contribute to success, using differences as resources (agentically and passively). Important tenets of cogen were that participants respect difference, listen attentively, and learn from others to the extent possible, while making them aware of the possibilities inherent in personal standpoints. Cogenerated solutions to problems were outcomes of cogen along with acceptance of responsibility for enacting the curriculum in agreed to ways. Individual participants in cogen would understand their own perspectives on teaching and learning, the consensus view, and what was agreed to regarding roles to be enacted at the next class meeting.

Picking up on themes developed in the book, participants in cogen can speak about their experiences, challenge ideology, contest hegemony, unmask power, overcome alienation, issue liberation, reclaim reason, and practice democracy. An example addressed in the book is Islamophobia, which most recently arose globally after the events of September 11, 2001 when the World Trade Center was destroyed. Stereotyping associated with social categories such as Islamophobia is extremely harmful and has emerged as a primary cause for bullying and other forms of discrimination in education. Cogen can serve the purpose of raising awareness about the stigma of Islamophobia and similar social issues around which discrimination can emerge, for example, sexuality, cyber bullying, and race. Discussions about phenomena such as these are highly relevant and, like religion, are often treated with silence in education institutions and as sensations in the news media. As well as dialoguing about difficult topics pertaining to justice, participants in cogen propose new roles to overcome inequities and social violence. Cogen can improve the quality of social life in particular fields in and out of school and facilitate youth, teachers, and other stakeholders in education, developing relational power and roles associated with active citizenry in the fight against social injustice. Rather than being texts of despair, coteaching and cogen are transformative activities that can potentially educate teachers and students for collaborative strategies to improve the quality of teaching and learning.

Macrostructures such as the necessity to prepare students for high-stakes, statewide examinations together with policies that hold teachers accountable for students' performance are conducive to teachers being unable to teach in the way they believe they should. Teachers who believe that science learning is optimal when it is taught as inquiry, for example, might also believe that they will lose their job, unless students perform well on high-stakes tests. In such circumstances, it is understandable that teachers might set aside their preferences to teach using inquiry methods and instead adopt traditional methods in which they endeavor to establish control over students and teach to the test. Students found such curricula boring, having little relevance to their lives. This scenario, which can catalyze frustrations for the teacher and students, differs greatly from the relational approach presented by Smyth, which focuses on students' interests and life experiences. The vision for curriculum described by Smyth emphasizes the importance of youth having relational power and being afforded relational trust. In our work, cogen has the potential to emphasize relational constructs such as these. However, it is imperative that policies associated with traditional fare are repealed so that teachers and students can enjoy and find satisfaction in their learning as well as experience the relevance of what they have learned.

Deprofessionalization is pervasive within teaching due to hegemonic structures that support economic rationalism as an underpinning for schooling. Throughout the book, evidence is provided that the rationale for evaluating schools is associated with managerialism, competition, standards, markets, and measurement. Decisions enacted by policymakers employ rhetoric such as failing schools and teachers, and it is apparent that a technical and managerial approach has diminished the autonomy of teachers. Authors in the book argue that critical practitioners who employ reflective engagement and critique can question conventional wisdom and challenge dominant views of authority. In our own work, we have found it useful to employ radical listening as a technique to allow participants to "walk in someone else's shoes." The essence of radical listening is to listen attentively to a speaker making sure that engagement focuses on a hermeneutic activity of understanding what the speaker is saying rather than opposing what the speaker is saying. Initially, radical listening is hermeneutic, and as understanding expands, the listener begins to apply what has been learned in thought experiments to test the efficacy of what is proposed. Only when the viability of a perspective has been fully tested should alternative possibilities be explored. The central purpose of radical listening is to build an understanding of others' perspectives and test their viability. After this has been accomplished, it is acceptable to compare the possibilities of those perspectives with the potential of personal perspectives and preferences. Radical listening is a tenet of cogen, which appeals as an activity that is potentially transformative, while being educative for all participants.

What is very clear from the chapters in the book is the centrality of teachers collaborating to produce solidarity while respecting one another's differences. If education is to be transformative, it seems clear that the collaboration should not just occur among teachers but should also involve students. That is, students and teachers collaborate and show solidarity around the goal of creating and sustaining productive learning environments. Teachers and students can be regarded as partners in education and value difference, regarding it as a resource to support their learning. In order to learn from one another, there needs to be a relational space where it is safe to talk about possibilities and test the efficacy of different ideas. In this afterword, I have presented three such spaces, each being complementary to the other, coteaching, cogen, and buddy groups (Tobin & Llena, 2011). The central part of collaborative approaches appears to be regarding difference as a resource for learning and identity.

## Emotions and Teaching

Teaching and learning involve emotions in a variety of ways, including emotions expressed in the moment and emotional climates that reflect ways in which emotions can saturate social artifacts over time and space. Accordingly, schools, classrooms, and teachers can be imbued with the emotions produced during inter-action rituals, for example (Tobin, Ritchie, Hudson, Oakley, & Mergard, in press). Similarly, emotions are valenced, positive and negative, and aggregate over time to build emotional energy, which structures activities and imbues social artifacts with an emotional character that is reproduced when the participants encounter similar structures in the future (Collins, 2004). It is most important to realize that emotions are produced continuously as part of cultural production and their pervasive presence structures teaching and learning. Accordingly, relational bonds between participants in a lesson are mediated by in the moment emotions, emotional energy, and emotional climate. Smyth describes how auditing practices produce undesirable emotions in teachers, including fear, loathing, hatred, and emotions associated with guilt and moral contamination—such as feeling dirty, implicated, and complicit. Trends such as these are unhealthy for teachers and students. Research shows a relationship between poor health and negative emotions such as continuous anger and sadness (Philippot, Chapelle, & Blairy 2002). Accordingly, negative emotions held by teachers can be deleterious to their health, and the students they teach can rapidly reproduce similar emotions, thereby catalyzing pathways to poor health (Goleman, 2006).

In our research, negative emotions were consistently revealed as teachers did their work while confronting continuous contradictions. For example, in a study of teacher identity, a chemistry teacher was assigned to teach life sciences without consultation even though he was not certified to teach life sciences. Also, midyear he was reassigned from teaching his life science class to teach another that contained a majority of special education students. The teacher felt punished and what he was required to do, teaching a class containing such a high percentage of special education students, contravened school district policy because there was no qualified special educator to coteach with the science teacher, as is required by law (Tobin & Llena, in press). Lack of respect and trust produces environments in which negative emotions such as anger and sadness are produced and these emotions might correlate with physical manifestations such as stress, illness, and absence from school. Quite possibly, the pervasiveness of negative emotions across time and space is associated with high levels of absence on the part of students and teachers in urban schools (Tobin & Llena).

# Equity and Social Justice

Differences are manifest in social categories that have been studied in education and social sciences for many years, including religion, race, class, gender, ethnicity, and disability. There is a priority to examine identities in different fields and ways in which they vary at the intersection of social categories such as those listed above and a continuous quest for social justice and improved lifestyles. An important goal for educators and teacher educators is for all participants in education to be able to identify and overcome structural inequalities associated with equity and social categories in different fields within and outside of education. Autonomy and agency are important constructs that should be examined across an individual/collective dialectic.[2] In fact, the ways in which educators think about social life might be extended to include multilectic relationships in which numerous social categories presuppose the presence of one another, are constituents of the whole, and are recursively interrelated (Fellner, 2011).

Social justice has been regarded as a central aspect of social life, especially as it pertains to education. However, the theoretical underpinnings of social justice might be examined from the perspective of critical theory to include constructs such as autonomy, agency, and active citizenry. In our research, we adopt a set of authenticity criteria that include and expand on those initially described by Guba and Lincoln (1989). Relevant to this conversation is tactical authenticity, which we refer to as social justice. The idea is that researchers must do more than identify inequities in social justice, they should help those individuals and groups of individuals who are unable to really help themselves to overcome disadvantage. Tactical authenticity applies to material as well as symbolic resources and is often addressed effectively in cogen where all stakeholders have a voice in decision-making, self-development, and self-expression.

Two thrusts related to social justice appeal as desirable. The first is to involve all participants as researchers of their own practices and accomplishments. If this is to be accomplished successfully, then teachers and students as well as school leaders and administrators should engage in learning to do research. For example, all participants could learn social theory to highlight inequities in relation to social categories such as gender, ethnicity, native language, and religious affiliation. In order to identify and understand inequities and their distribution in social space, it might be advantageous to learn how to record and save digital files and analyze the audio and video components using readily available software. The development of skills such as these not only provides tools for analyzing social life but also prepares participants for different roles in social life, including employment. When analyses have been undertaken, for example, in classrooms, cogen can be organized as an activity within the regular curriculum so that all students have opportunities to identify and discuss what they have learned from the research.

---

[2]A dialectical relationship regards specified entities as constituting a whole, being recursively related, and each presupposing the presence of the other.

A second thrust involves collective/collaborative participation in coteaching, cogen, and what we refer to as buddy systems. Reynaldo Llena developed the buddy system to ensure that disadvantaged students created peer networks to support one another academically. Small groups of three to five students worked together in class, throughout the school, and out of school to ensure that each person in a buddy group came to school, arrived in class on time, did homework and submitted it, participated in class activities, and understood the subject matter as it was being taught. A buddy group is a social network consisting of peers who undertake activities such as peer teaching, with the active agreement of their teacher. The idea to create buddy groups arose and was developed in cogen and was an outstanding success within the school in which it was created. There were anomalies, however, when the teacher reverted to traditional methods of teaching and admonished students from a buddy group for practices such as "speaking when I am speaking" (Tobin & Llena, in press). Despite these contradictions, the quality of education was enhanced by buddy group participation and collective agency was expanded. An individual/collective relationship is assumed to be important in all educational activities. It is important that all participants in education learn to effectively collaborate with others, understand and strive for collective motives as well as individual goals. It is potentially illuminating to rethink classrooms in terms of a dialectical relationship between competition and collaboration.

Teacher education programs can emphasize the necessity for teachers to be socially responsive and active agents in social change, especially when it comes to catalyzing equity, overcoming deficit perspectives identified to exist in the social worlds that are part of the curriculum, and engage in critically reflexive practices. Teaching can be represented as intellectual and transformative work, and all teachers can learn to be autonomous and agentic, using theories and technological tools to afford analyses of practices as a component of professional practice. Teacher educators have a responsibility to project teaching as a profession and ensure that teachers have the professional attributes to engage in forms of conduct that extend far beyond the conventional wisdom possessed by those who have not engaged in teacher education. It is time to address the paradox that everyday folks represent themselves as experts on teaching based on spending a large proportion of their lives in classrooms as learners. In much the same way that society does not present itself as expert on building bridges and designing cities, everyday folks should have an image of teaching in which teachers are regarded as highly professional, having forms of competence associated with admired forms of scholarship.

## What Are the Next Steps?

The edited volume by Down and Smyth makes it clear that there is a high priority for the transformation of teacher education and teaching. In this afterword, I have indicated that the need for reform was present and strong 50 years ago. A question that needs to be considered is "Why haven't many desired recommendations for reform been adopted in the past five decades?" One possibility is that calls for reform that are analogous and to those described in this book are associated with scholars who are educators and social scientists. Scholars in education and teacher education do not have the status of scholars in fields that are awarded a Nobel Prize, for example. Accordingly, their voices carry little weight when it comes to policy formulation. In this afterword, I have identified several candidate ideologies that are high priorities for change. For example, at the present time, everyday common sense supports the idea that those with the responsibility should be held accountable for what happens. This ideology is connected to individualism, which is axiomatic in most walks of life in the United States especially. Even though Western countries like Australia and the United Kingdom are more socially inclined in a political sense, when it comes to accountability, there is an alignment with individualism. Competition in an open marketplace is regarded as an important criterion for learning. Accordingly, teachers are encouraged to adopt practices to allow students to compete with one another to enhance learning. When his model is accepted, equity is considered to be the opportunity to participate rather than a right to share products of activity. Adherence to these "principles" supports particular forms of teaching that emphasize students being involved and teaching practices being used to keep everybody involved.

There are many forces that fragment educators and prevent them from creating an alliance to support the kinds of changes that are desperately needed to support learning in schools and other institutions that seek to educate the public. These forces incorporate the very same ideologies of individual accountability and equity framed in terms of the right to compete in an open marketplace. For example, university faculty are accountable for their scholarly productivity, and important activities such as promotion, tenure, and salary increases are tied to peer review of productivity. An important criterion for many faculty is being able to obtain external financial support for research. Faculty compete with one another for funding and have to meet the criteria associated with requests for proposals. Unfortunately, many requests for proposals are grounded in paradigms for research that orientate toward scientistic models for the social sciences. To successfully compete for funds necessitates that projects are aligned with assumptions underlying "request for proposals." This is an enormous social force that distorts the nature of research/scholarship in the social sciences and tends to support maintenance of the status quo as far as setting standards is concerned, designing high-stakes tests to assess those standards, formulating accountability measures to ensure that the standards are taught and learned, and aligning schools with "society's standards." Designing research that aligns with standards and insisting that policy and reform efforts also align with them maintain symmetry. As is evident in the stability of many facets of education, alignments that are insisted upon, based on the logic of common sense, are almost impossible to resist. This may be why in 50 years time another volume such as this might be written, calling for reforms that carry a familiar refrain.

There is no one-size-fits-all formula to underwrite successful revolution. As I write, there is an effort within New York City to resist the capitalistic excesses of the upper class, who have pillaged the economic system to become richer, creating an economic crisis that has swept the world into deep recession. As countries fall under the weight of crippling debt, entrepreneurs are ready to move in to procure resources that have value, thereby situating them to become increasingly wealthy when the inevitable economic recovery occurs. Dissatisfied with the neoliberal principles that have produced such circumstances, every day thousands of people gather in Wall Street, Manhattan. The movement is slowly spreading to other cities in the United States and even around the world, but law enforcement agencies and governments who are eager to sustain the status quo closely monitor activities. If necessary, lethal force will be used to ensure that the capitalistic ideologies are supported and the marketplaces remain open for those with wealth to participate (Harvey, 2005). Of course, there is a possibility that "rising up" of the working classes will succeed—however, it is a remote possibility. Is there something similar that could happen such that educators would come together in a critical mass to take actions that aligned with sensibilities about the reform of education policies and practices? It seems apparent that more needs to be done under the banner of active citizenry, such that stakeholders in education come together for the purpose of being leaders in formulating policies and practices. It is timely to ask where education scholars would assemble to catalyze global action for reform of teaching and teacher education. Are there parallels with the Arab Spring? Could social media be used to coordinate activities to overthrow the hegemony of teaching and associated policies and practices in teacher education? Is it possible for coordinated actions to arise from general feelings of dissatisfaction in much the same way those recent movements began? People assembled and the threads of reform emerged from social gatherings. Perhaps the reform of teaching and teacher education is an activity waiting to be launched!

# References

Collins, R. (2004). *Interaction ritual chains*. Princeton, NJ: Princeton University Press.

Fellner, G. (2011). *Don't quantify my students! A multilectical approach to pedagogy and the teaching of language arts*. Unpublished doctoral dissertation, The City University of New York, New York.

Goleman, D. (2006). *Emotional intelligence*, The 10th Anniversary edn. New York: Bantam Dell.

Guba, E., & Lincoln, Y. S. (1989). *Fourth generation evaluation*. Newbury Park, CA: Sage Publications.

Harvey, D. (2005). *A brief history of neoliberalism*. Oxford, UK: Oxford University Press.

Ingersoll, R. M., & Perda, D. (2010). Is the supply of mathematics and science teachers sufficient? *American Educational Research Journal, 47*, 563–594.

Kincheloe, J. L., & Tobin, K. (2009). The much exaggerated death of positivism. *Cultural Studies of Science Education, 4*, 513–528.

McNamee, S. J., & Miller, R. K., Jr. (2004). *The meritocracy myth*. Lanham, MD: Rowman & Littlefield.

Philippot, P., Chapelle, G., & Blairy, S. (2002). Respiratory feedback in the generation of emotion. *Cognition and Emotion, 16*, 605–627.

Tobin, K. (2010). La colaboración para transformar y reproducir la didáctica de las ciencias. *Enseñanza de las Ciencias, 28*, 301–313.

Tobin, K. (2011). Global reproduction and transformation of science education. *Cultural Studies of Science Education, 6*, 127–142.

Tobin, K., & Llena, R. (2011). Producing and maintaining culturally adaptive teaching and learning of science in urban schools. In C. Murphy & K. Scantlebury (Eds.), *Coteaching in international contexts: Research and practice* (pp. 79–104). Dordrecht, the Netherlands: Springer.

Tobin, K., & Llena, R. (in press). Colliding identities, emotional roller coasters, and contradictions of urban science education. In M. Varelas (Ed.), *Identity construction and science education research: Learning, teaching, and being in multiple contexts* (pp. XXX–XXX). Dordrecht, The Netherlands: Sense Publishers.

Tobin, K., Ritchie, S. R., Hudson, P., Oakley, J., & Mergard, V. (in press). Relationships between emotional climate and the fluency of classroom interactions. *Learning Environments Research*.

Tobin, K., & Roth, W.-M. (2006). *Teaching to Learn: A view from the field*. Rotterdam, the Netherlands: Sense Publishers.

Tobin, K., Seiler, G., & Walls, E. (1999). Reproduction of social class in the teaching and learning of science in urban high schools. *Research in Science Education, 29*, 171–187.

# About the Editors

**Barry Down** is the City of Rockingham Chair in Education at Murdoch University, Western Australia. His research interests include teacher education, policy ethnography and critical pedagogy. He has a particular interest in marginalized students, social justice, vocational education and training and popular culture. Barry teaches courses in the fields of social studies education, education policy and teachers' work and connectionist pedagogy. His recent books are *Critically Engaged Learning: Connecting to Young Lives* and *Activist and Socially Critical School and Community Renewal: Social Justice in Exploitative Times* (co-authored with John Smyth, Lawrence Angus and Peter McInerney) and *'Hanging in With Kids' in Tough Times: Engagement in Contexts of Educational Disadvantage in the Relational School* (co-authored with John Smyth and Peter McInerney). Barry's current research focuses on the impact of global capitalism on the youth labour market, education and training.

**John Smyth** is Research Professor of Education, School of Education, University of Ballarat, Australia. He is the leader of the multidisciplinary research theme *Addressing Disadvantage and Inequality in Education and Health*. He is an Emeritus Professor, Flinders University of South Australia, a former Senior Fulbright Research Scholar and recipient of the *Palmer O. Johnson* and *Interpretive Scholarship* Awards from the American Educational Research Association. In 2011, he was elected a Fellow of the Academy of the Social Sciences in Australia. He has published 20 books and many articles on his research interests in social justice, educational sociology and policy ethnography. His recent works include: (with Down & McInerney) *'Hanging in with Kids in Tough Times: Engagement in Contexts of Educational Disadvantage in the Relational School'* (New York: Peter Lang); (with McInerney) *From Silent Witnesses to Active Agents: Student Voice in Re-engagement with Learning* (New York: Peter Lang); and *Critical Pedagogy for Social Justice* (London & New York: Continuum).

B. Down and J. Smyth (eds.), *Critical Voices in Teacher Education*, Explorations of Educational Purpose 22, DOI 10.1007/978-94-007-3974-1,
© Springer Science+Business Media Dordrecht 2012

# About the Contributors

**Lawrence Angus** is Professor of Education at the University of Ballarat, where he was Head of the School of Education for the past 9 years. Having stepped down from that position in mid-2011, he is now pursuing his interests in critical ethnographies of educational institutions and contexts, the dynamics of policy adaptation and contestation and the relationship between education and social justice. These interests have recently come together in books coauthored with John Smyth, Barry Down and Peter McInerney (*Critically Engaged Learning: Connecting to Young Lives*, Peter Lang, 2008; and *Activist and Socially Critical School and Community Renewal: Social Justice in Exploitative Times*, Sense Publishers, 2009).

**Nado Aveling** is a Senior Lecturer in Education at Murdoch University, with responsibilities for teaching undergraduate and graduate units in social justice studies. Her research is grounded within a critical, postcolonial/feminist framework, and while broadly focusing on anti-discriminatory education, her most recent research falls within an action research tradition and explores the ways in which educators can work with their students to deconstruct the normativity of 'whiteness'.

**Lisa J. Cary** is a senior lecturer in the School of Education at Murdoch University. She has worked in educational contexts in Australia, Canada and the USA for over 25 years. Her experience and qualifications have led to the analysis of curriculum at the local, national and international level and she has a strong international reputation as a curriculum scholar and educational researcher. In particular, her research approaches the study of curriculum, from development to critical analysis. This move provides a significant contribution to the field of Curriculum Studies by deconstructing central notions of schooling. This focuses on revealing the way social constructions of worthwhile knowledge and good teaching (for example) are inextricably linked to issues of social justice and equitable access to learning opportunities. Lisa's work brings together theory and practice in educational research by making the ethical move towards the study of discourses that frame our knowing and the way we know Others as an ethical move towards social justice. (Others is capitalized in this summary to emphasize the way power excludes certain

B. Down and J. Smyth (eds.), *Critical Voices in Teacher Education*, Explorations of Educational Purpose 22, DOI 10.1007/978-94-007-3974-1, © Springer Science+Business Media Dordrecht 2012

individuals in social institutions, such as education.) Lisa has published in a number of journals, including *Qualitative Studies in Education* and *Theory and Research in Education and Qualitative Inquiry*. Her book, *Curriculum Spaces: Discourse, Postmodern Theory and Educational Research,* was published in 2007. She is also the editor of the *The Social Educator*.

**Wendy Cumming-Potvin** is a Senior Lecturer in the School of Education at Murdoch University, Western Australia. With a strong interest in new literacies, social justice and communities, she specializes in a sociocultural approach to researching teaching and learning. As a member of an Australian Teaching and Learning Council research team, Wendy is investigating social justice and engineering education. Wendy recently prepared a special issue about mentoring in diverse communities as an invited co-editor for the *McGill Journal of Education* (Montreal, Canada). Her forthcoming publications include 'They Didn't Have *Out There* Gay Parents—They Just Looked Like *Normal* Regular Parents': Investigating Teachers' Approaches to Addressing Same-Sex Parenting and Non-normative Sexuality in the Elementary Classroom (Martino & Cumming-Potvin, in press, Curriculum Inquiry).

**Cal Durrant** is an Associate Professor of English Literacy at the Australian Catholic University ACU (NSW) and the Commissioning Editor for AATE (The Australian Association for the Teaching of English). He has taught, researched and published in the areas of English curriculum, literacy, technology and media education for over 25 years, and his most recent publication is a co-edited text with Karen Starr based on the 2008 Australian Government's Summer School for Teachers of English called: 'English for a New Millennium: Leading Change' (2009, Wakefield Press). Together with Andy Goodwin (Reading University) and Louann Reid (Colorado State University), he is co-editing a text for the International Federation for the Teaching of English called 'English in a Globalised World: International Perspectives on the Teaching of English' to be published in 2012 by Routledge.

**Marilyn Frankenstein** is a Professor at the College of Public and Community Service (CPCS), one of the six colleges at the University of Massachusetts/Boston. The focus of her work at CPCS is convincing people that quantitative reasoning is vital to understanding and acting to create a more just world, and that all of us can understand and reason quantitatively. She teaches courses in Quantitative Reasoning, Understanding Arguments and Media Literacy. She has written about the curricula she develops for her CPCS classes, covering such topics as the mathematics of political knowledge (i.e. how mathematics can deepen our understanding of the institutional structures of our society) and the politics of mathematical knowledge (i.e. how seemingly neutral mathematical descriptions of our world often conceal political choices/struggles). In addition to numerous articles and book chapters, she has written a text, *Relearning Mathematics*, which teaches quantitative reasoning in an interdisciplinary context, as part of the knowledge we collectively need to create a more just world. She has spoken about this work at CPCS internationally, including in South Africa, Mozambique, Brazil,

Denmark, Japan, Australia, New Zealand, England, Canada and across the USA. She is also co-editor, along with Rutgers University Professor Arthur B. Powell, of *Ethnomathematics: Challenging Eurocentrism in Mathematics Education.* Her current work focuses more on the quantitative aspects of media and economic literacy, and a project for community education about tax policy that will involve community discussions about philosophical issues connected to the public sphere and lots of culture jamming.

**Robbie Johnston** is a Senior Lecturer in Education (Rural and Regional) at the University of Tasmania. Her research is built upon a strong research/teaching nexus and a particular interest in education and participation in rural/regional contexts. Her PhD research investigated society and environment curriculum in teacher education. Recent projects have focused on community and place attachments as well as student participation and rurality. Robbie's teaching encompasses sociology of education and society and environment curriculum methods. From 2008 to 2010, she was Editor of *The Social Educator*, the journal of the Social Educators' Association of Australia (SEAA), and is currently on the Editorial Committee for this journal.

**Libby Lee-Hammond** is an Associate Professor in the School of Education at Murdoch University. Her research interests are focused in the early years of education and care. She has obtained Australian Research Council funding for two large projects investigating children's use of digital media in the early years of education and has more recently completed a federally funded project investigating issues around transition to school for young Aboriginal children. She is co-author of *Rethinking Learning in Early Childhood* (2008) with Yelland, O'Rourke and Harrison. Libby is a staunch advocate for children's right to play and connect with the natural environment in order to experience the joy of childhood.

**Wayne Martino** is Professor of Education in the Faculty of Education at The University of Western Ontario, Canada. His research interests are in the field of gender equity, masculinities and anti-oppressive education. His books include: *What About the Boys?* (with Bob Meyenn, Open University Press), *Boys' Stuff: Boys Talking About What Matters* (with Pallotta-Chiarolli, Allen & Unwin), *So What's a Boy? Addressing Issues of Masculinity and Schooling* (with Maria Pallotta-Chiarolli, Open University Press), *'Being Normal is the Only Way to Be': Adolescent Perspectives on Gender and School* (with Maria Pallotta-Chiarolli, University of New South Wales Press) and *Gendered Outcasts and Sexual Outlaws: Sexual Oppression and Gender Hierarchies in Queer Men's Lives* (with Christopher Kendall, Haworth Press). His most recent books include: *Boys and Schooling: Beyond Structural Reform* (with Bob Lingard & Martin Mills, Palgrave) and *The problem with Boys' Education: Beyond the Backlash* (with Michael Kehler & Marcus Weaver-Hightower, Routledge). His latest book (with Goli Rezai-Rashti) is entitled: *Gender, Race and the Politics of Role Modelling: The Influence of Male Teachers* (Routledge). Currently he is working on a sole-authored book, entitled *Masculinities in Education: A Critical Investigation* (Dordrecht, the Netherlands).

**Peter McInerney** is a Research Associate at the University of Ballarat. His research interests span the areas of policy sociology, school reform for social justice and critical ethnography. He is the author of *Making Hope Practical: School Reform for Social Justice (2004)* and joint author of several books including: '*Hanging in With Kids in Tough Times': Engagement in Contexts of Educational Disadvantage in the Relational School* (Smyth, Down, & McInerney, 2010), *Activist and Socially Critical School and Community Renewal: Social Justice in Exploitative Times* (Smyth, Angus, Down, & McInerney, 2009), *Critically Engaged Learning: Connecting to Young Lives* (Smyth, Angus, Down, & McInerney, 2008) and *Teachers in the Middle: Reclaiming the Wasteland of the Adolescent Years of Schooling* (Smyth & McInerney, 2006). He is currently involved in ARC-funded projects which have a focus on school retention, student engagement and community renewal.

**Jane Pearce** is a Senior Lecturer in Education at Murdoch University, where she teaches undergraduate and postgraduate students in the areas of critical pedagogy, literacy learning and research methodology. Jane's formative teaching experiences were as a high school teacher and adult literacy tutor in northern England. There, she began to recognize how schooling practices can work to marginalize and exclude particular groups of students. It is this understanding that now fundamentally shapes her work as a teacher educator. She is the author of *Identity and Pedagogy: Critical Reflections on University Teaching* (2008) and co-author (with Christopher Crouch) of *Doing Research in Design* (2012).

**Shirley Steinberg** is the Director and Chair of The Werklund Foundation Centre for Youth Leadership in Education, and Professor of Youth Studies at the University of Calgary. She is the author and editor of over 35 books in critical literacy, critical pedagogy, urban and youth culture and cultural studies. Her most recent books include: *Kinderculture: The Corporate Construction of Childhood* (2011); *Teaching Against Islamophobia* (2011); *19 Urban Questions: Teaching in the City* (2010); *Christotainment: Selling Jesus Through Popular Culture* (2009); *Diversity and Multiculturalism: A Reader* (2009); *Media Literacy: A Reader* (2007); the award-winning *Contemporary Youth Culture: An International Encyclopedia*; and *The Miseducation of the West: How Schools and Media Distort Our Understanding of the Islam World* (with Joe L. Kincheloe) (2004). She is currently finishing two books: *Writing and Publishing* (Fall 2011) and *The Bricolage and Qualitative Research* (Fall 2011) and *The Critical Qualitative Research Reader* (with Gaile Canella) (Spring 2012). A regular contributor to CBC Radio One, CTV, The Toronto Globe and Mail, The Montreal Gazette, and Canadian Press, she is an internationally known speaker and teacher. She is also the founding editor of *Taboo: The Journal of Culture and Education*, and the managing editor of *The International Journal of Critical Pedagogy*. The organizer of The Critical Pedagogical Congress, she is committed to a global community of transformative educators and community workers engaged in radical love, social justice and the situating of power within social and cultural contexts.

**Richard Tinning** is Professor of pedagogy and physical education in the School of Human Movement Studies at the University of Queensland, and professor of physical education in the School of Critical Studies in Education at the University of Auckland, New Zealand. Richard has long-standing interests in school PE, teacher education, critical pedagogy and pedagogy for human movement. His latest books are *Pedagogy and Human Movement: Theory, Practice, Research* (Routledge, 2010) and (co-edited with Karen Sirna) *Education, Social Justice and the Legacy of Deakin University: Reflections of the Deakin Diaspora* (Sense, 2011).

**Kenneth Tobin** is Presidential Professor of Urban Education at the Graduate Center of the City University of New York. Prior to becoming a university science educator in Australia in 1974, Tobin taught high school physics, chemistry, biology general science and mathematics for 10 years. He began a programme of research in 1973 that continues to the present day—teaching and learning of science and learning to teach science. In the USA, Tobin has had professorial appointments at Florida State University, the University of Pennsylvania and the Graduate Center. As well as research being undertaken in the Bronx of New York City, Tobin is involved in collaborative research in Brisbane, Australia; Sao Paulo, Brazil; and Kaohsiung, Taiwan. His current research involves multilevel studies of the relationships between emotions and physiological factors associated with the wellness of teachers and students. In his career, Tobin has published 22 books, 203 refereed journal articles and 115 book chapters. With Barry Fraser and Campbell McRobbie, he is co-editor of the second edition of the *International Handbook of Research in Science Education* to be published in 2012 by Springer. Tobin is the founding co-editor of *Cultural Studies of Science Education*.

**Sandra Wooltorton** is Associate Professor of Education at Edith Cowan University's Bunbury Campus, where she teaches undergraduate and graduate students in social science education, indigenous education and a range of pedagogy units. Her background is in cultural studies, geography and education, and she taught in the Kimberley, Pilbara and Northern Territory before becoming a teacher educator. She is an active member of the Australian Association for Environmental Education, is on the editorial board of the *Australian Journal of Environmental Education* and is the author of a number of articles and chapters on sustainability education, ecological literacy and place-based learning. Sandra leads several sustainability education projects in Edith Cowan University and in her local community, is currently writing a cultural geography of her local estuary and is also involved with an ARC-funded project investigating sustainable environmental management in small businesses.

**Peter Wright** is a Senior Lecturer in Arts Education and Research Methods at Murdoch University in Perth, Western Australia. He works across the Arts with a commitment to personal, social and cultural inquiry, agency, education and expression, health and well-being. His research interests include teaching, learning and healing in, through, and with the arts; artistically based approaches to research; creativity and socially engaged arts; drama education; applied theatre;

transformational learning; teacher development in the arts; and playback theatre. Central to this work is an interest in social justice, social pedagogy and social inclusion, and the way they are mediated in and through the arts. Peter is a member of the International Arts Education Research Network (Australia Council for the Arts/UNESCO) and the UNESCO LEA (Links to Education and Art) International Network of Experts in Arts Education. Recently, Peter acted as an editor for a special themed issue of *Forum Qualitative Sozialforschung/Forum: Qualitative Social Research* on Performative Social Science, a reviewer for *Qualitative Inquiry in Education, Issues in Educational Research*, the *McGill Journal of Education*, the e-journal of *UNESCO Observatory: Multi-Disciplinary Research in the Arts* and the *Journal of Arts and Communities.*

# Author Index

B. Down and J. Smyth (eds.), *Critical Voices in Teacher Education*, Explorations
of Educational Purpose 22, DOI 10.1007/978-94-007-3974-1,
© Springer Science+Business Media Dordrecht 2012

# Subject Index

B. Down and J. Smyth (eds.), *Critical Voices in Teacher Education*, Explorations
of Educational Purpose 22, DOI 10.1007/978-94-007-3974-1,
© Springer Science+Business Media Dordrecht 2012